☀ INSIGHT GUIDES

aRGEnTina

Discovery CHANNEL

APA PUBLICATIONS   L
Part of the Langenscheidt Publishing Group

INSIGHT GUIDE
ARGENTINA

ABOUT THIS BOOK

Editorial
Project Editor
Huw Hennessy
Editorial Director
Brian Bell

Distribution
UK & Ireland
GeoCenter International Ltd
The Viables Centre, Harrow Way
Basingstoke, Hants RG22 4BJ
Fax: (44) 1256 817988

United States
Langenscheidt Publishers, Inc.
36-36 33rd Street, 4th Floor
Long Island City , New York 11106
Fax: 1 (718) 784 0640

Canada
Thomas Allen & Son Ltd
390 Steelcase Road East
Markham, Ontario L3R 1G2
Fax: (1) 905 475 6747

Australia
Universal Publishers
1 Waterloo Road
Macquarie Park, NSW 2113
Fax: (61) 2 9888 9074

New Zealand
Hema Maps New Zealand Ltd (HNZ)
Unit D, 24 Ra ORA Drive
East Tamaki, Auckland
Fax: (64) 9 273 6479

Worldwide
Apa Publications GmbH & Co.
Verlag KG (Singapore branch)
38 Joo Koon Road, Singapore 628990
Tel: (65) 6865 1600. Fax: (65) 6861 6438

Printing
Insight Print Services (Pte) Ltd
38 Joo Koon Road, Singapore 628990
Tel: (65) 6865 1600. Fax: (65) 6861 6438

©2005 Apa Publications GmbH & Co.
Verlag KG (Singapore branch)
All Rights Reserved
First Edition 1988, Fourth Edition 1999
Updated 2004, Reprinted 2005
Revised 2005

CONTACTING THE EDITORS
We would appreciate it if readers
would alert us to errors or out-
dated information by writing to:
**Insight Guides, P.O. Box 7910,
London SE1 1WE, England.
Fax: (44) 20 7403 0290.
insight@apaguide.co.uk**

www.insightguides.com

This guidebook combines the
interests and enthusiasms of
two of the world's best known
information providers: Insight
Guides, whose titles have set
the standard for visual travel
guides since 1970, and Discovery Channel, the world's premier
source of nonfiction television
programming.

The editors of Insight Guides
provide both practical advice
and general understand-
ing about a destina-
tion's history, culture,
institutions and peo-
ple. Discovery Chan-
nel and its Web site,
www.discovery.com, help millions of
viewers explore their world from the
comfort of their home and also en-
courage them to explore it firsthand.

Argentina, a colorful addition
to the Insight series, has become a democracy confidently
outgrowing its military past.
Beyond the tango clubs of
Buenos Aires, this vast South
American republic also offers a
stunning range of
dramatic landscapes,
with a growing tourist
demand for "white-
knuckle" adventure
sports and for eco-
tourism activities.

How to use this book

The book is carefully structured to convey an understanding of Argentina and its culture and to guide readers through its sights and attractions:

◆ The **Features** section, with a yellow color bar, covers the country's history and culture in lively essays written by specialists.

◆ The **Places** section, with a blue bar, provides full details of all the sights and areas worth seeing. The chief places of interest are coordinated by number with specially drawn maps.

◆ The **Travel Tips** section, with an orange bar, at the back of the book, offers a convenient point of reference on practical aspects of the country. Information may be located quickly using the index printed on the back cover flap, which also serves as a handy bookmark.

The contributors

This new edition was supervised by **Huw Hennessy**, building on material written in the previous edition by writers **Deirdre Ball, Elena Decima, Philip Benson, Tony Perrottet, Federico Kirbus** and **Parry Jones**. The history articles were revised and updated by **Nick Caistor**, who is the Latin America Editor at the BBC World Service. The majority of the Places section was updated by **Jill Hedges**, with information on Tierra del Fuego supplied by **Caroline Mouzo**, who lives in Ushuaia. **Fiona Anderson**, a writer who lived for six years in Bariloche, updated the Patagonia chapter and also wrote new features on The National Identity, Food and Wine, and Outdoor Adventure.

Latin dance expert **Shannon Shiell** updated the Tango article and also wrote about other music and dance in Argentina. Natural history writer **David Burnie** revised the feature on Wild Argentina, as well as writing the color feature on Patagonian wildlife.

Many of the photographs were taken by **Eduardo Gil**, with others by **Volkmar Janicke** and **Mireille Vautier**. The book was indexed by **Isobel McLean** and proofread by **Sylvia Suddes**. **Jane Egginton** updated the latest version of this book.

Map Legend

——–·–	International Boundary
– – – –	Province Boundary
⊖	Border Crossing
–·–·–	National Park/Reserve
– – – –	Ferry Route
Ⓜ	Metro
✈ ✈	Airport: International/Regional
🚌	Bus Station
Ⓟ	Parking
❶	Tourist Information
✉	Post Office
† ⳾	Church/Ruins
†	Monastery
☾	Mosque
✡	Synagogue
⌂ ⌂	Castle/Ruins
∴	Archeological Site
∩	Cave
⎮	Statue/Monument
★	Place of Interest

The main places of interest in the Places section are coordinated by number with a full-color map (e.g. ❶), and a symbol at the top of every right-hand page tells you where to find the map.

INSIGHT GUIDE
argentina

CONTENTS

Maps

Introduction

History

Features

The multicolored façades of
El Caminito, Buenos Aires

Travel Tips

Places

BIENVENIDOS

*Argentina, South America's second-largest country, is just
beginning to realize the appeal of its vast open spaces*

Some of Argentina's characteristics are world-famous, while
its other charms have gone unheralded. Everyone knows it is
the home of the tango, but less well-known is the fact that the
highest peak in the Americas, Aconcagua, lies on its western border; Argentine beef is world-renowned, but few have heard about
the rare glacial formations of the Lake District; and while the
name Tierra del Fuego is familiar to most, not many know that
Ushuaia, on its lower shore, is the southernmost town in the world.
Ushuaia is also the main port for wildlife cruises through the
Straits of Magellan and as far afield as Antarctica.

In recent years, Argentina also made the headlines when the
country's financial and economic system crashed. Its well-to-do
middle classes joined the ranks of the unemployed, and hunger
and poverty increased dramatically. There was violence on the
streets, and tragic loss of life. However, this anger and frustration
has never been aimed at foreign travelers, who always receive a
warm welcome.

Beyond Buenos Aires, rough-riding *gauchos* (cowboys), the
wide open spaces of Patagonia and the pampas, Argentina will
astonish the visitor with fine wines, jungle waterfalls, colonial
cities, and penguin colonies. You can create a vacation here with
activities as diverse as horseback trekking in the Andes and gambling in a seaside casino.

While certain attractions in Argentina have long been appreciated by select groups, such as climbers and ornithologists, the
country has gone virtually undiscovered by the traveling world at
large. Argentina is enough off the beaten track that you can be on
a resort beach surrounded only by locals, and it is possible, on a
lucky day, to have a national park all to yourself.

As visitors go about enjoying the refinements of Buenos Aires
or the natural beauties of the interior, they should make a point of
meeting Argentines along the way. An afternoon spent chatting
with a bunch of spirited *porteños* (residents of Buenos Aires) in a
café, or talking horses with a seasoned *gaucho* in Patagonia, will
help first-time visitors to appreciate the Argentines' fascinating
culture, of which they are justifiably proud. ❑

PRECEDING PAGES: the Perito Moreno Glacier, southern Patagonia; riding up to the
south face of Aconcagua; art for sale in La Boca, Buenos Aires; the hard-working
face of a *gaucho*.
LEFT: a *gaucho* in the making.

FROM JUNGLES TO GLACIERS

Its enormous latitude span gives Argentina a dramatically varied landscape, from windswept southern steppe to the subtropical north

Argentina is a land of many riches, but silver is not one of them. This is something that the early Spanish explorers did not know when they gave the country its name (*argentum* is the Latin name for silver). The precious ore was discovered in great quantities to the north, in Bolivia and Peru, but no matter – the name stuck here.

Present-day Argentina is an enormous country, the eighth largest in the world and the second largest (in population and area) in South America, after Brazil. It is made up of 23 provinces, one of which includes part of Tierra del Fuego, several South Atlantic islands and a 49-degree wedge of Antarctica which ends at the South Pole. However, the Antarctic sector overlaps with claims by Chile and Great Britain, and the South Atlantic islands in question (Falklands/Malvinas) are currently under British control.

Disputed territories aside, Argentina covers an area of nearly 2.8 million sq. km (1.1 million sq. miles). The islands and Antarctic land together cover an additional 1.2 million sq. km (480,000 sq. miles). The country is 3,500 km (2,170 miles) long and 1,400 km (868 miles) across at its widest point.

As one might expect, a country covering this much terrain has a great diversity of topography and climate. While most of Argentina lies within the temperate zone of the Southern Hemisphere, the climate ranges from tropical in the north to subantarctic in the south. In general, Argentina's climate is moderated by the proximity of the oceans on either side of the continental landmass, and the towering barrier of the Andes to the west also plays an important part. This diversity of environments has endowed Argentina with a broad spectrum of plant and animal life.

PRECEDING PAGES: sunset over Mt. Aconcagua, South America's highest peak (6,980 meters/23,034 ft).
LEFT: husband and wife in the Northwest.
RIGHT: the high-flying Andean condor.

The country can be divided roughly into six geographical zones: the fertile central pampas, marshy Mesopotamia in the northeast, the forested Chaco region of the central north, the high plateau of the northwest, the mountainous desert of the west, and the windy steppe of Patagonia. Within these areas you can find

everything from steamy subtropical jungles to the lofty continental ice cap, and just about any kind of environmental feature in between.

Grassy heartland

The pampas are, perhaps, the terrain that Argentina is best known for. These fertile alluvial plains were the home of the legendary *gaucho* (cowboy), and today they are the base for a large percentage of the nation's economic wealth.

These grasslands cover much of central Argentina, stretching south, west, and north in a radius of 970 km (600 miles) from the city of Buenos Aires. Argentines boast of the richness of the pampean earth – some saying the topsoil reaches a depth of 2 meters (6 ft), others say the soil reaches 5 meters (16 ft).

The pampas has two subdivisions: the humid pampa *(pampa húmeda)* and the dry pampa *(pampa seca)*. The humid pampa lies in the easterly portion of the country, mostly in the province of Buenos Aires. This wetter area supports much of the nation's agriculture; grains, primarily wheat and soya, are grown here. The humid pampa is also the heart of the cattle industry. The grass-feeding of cattle gives Argentine beef its celebrated flavor. The pampas' development took a large leap with the British building of a railroad system and the importing of British cattle breeds.

Virtually all of the *pampa húmeda* has been carved up and cultivated. Many of Argentina's landowners have their *estancias* here, properties which often run to hundreds of thousands of hectares. The dry pampa lies further to the west, where the Andes help bring about a less humid environment.

Sierras and rivers

The smoothness of the pampas is broken up at several points by low-lying sierras. The major ranges are the Sierra de Tandil and the

A BARREN LAND

There is little vegetation that is native to the pampas. In some areas there is a fine grass that grows low, while in other places there are tall, coarse grasses mixed with low scrub. The only tree that grew here as a native, the ombú, is not even really a tree; it's a weed. Although it grows to a substantial size, its moist fibers are useless as fuel for burning. Historically, its most useful function was to provide shade for tired gauchos as they rested beneath its branches to sip their mate tea. Over the years, many non-indigenous plants have been brought in. Tall rows of trees serving as windbreaks are everywhere and break the monotony of the landscape.

Sierra de la Ventana in the east, and several parallel ranges in the central provinces of Córdoba and San Luis.

The Río de la Plata (River Plate) basin has as its tributaries more than six major rivers, among them the Paraná, the Uruguay, and the Paraguay. It drains a huge area of South America, including eastern Bolivia, most of Paraguay and Uruguay, and a large part of southern Brazil.

The Río de la Plata basin finds its outlet in the Río de la Plata estuary, the mouth of which lies just northwest of Buenos Aires. The delta area of the river is laced with countless small waterways which have created a unique marshy ecosystem. The major port of Buenos Aires was developed along the marshy banks of the estuary, but constant dredging is needed to keep the channels free from silt deposits.

Subtropical forests

The isolated northeast area of Argentina is referred to as Mesopotamia, as most of it lies between the Paraná and Uruguay rivers. The whole area is crosscut by rivers and streams, and much of the land is marshy and low, receiving a lot of rainfall.

The southern sector, with its swamps and low, rolling hills, has an economy supported by sheep-farming, horse-breeding, and cattle- raising. This is one of the major wool-producing areas of the country.

Toward the north, the climate becomes subtropical and very humid. The economy here is based on agriculture, with the principal crops being a form of tea, *yerba mate (see page 92)* and various types of fruit. Enormous tracts of virgin forest have been lost to a lumber business that has become increasingly important to the Argentine economy.

Toward the northern tip of Misiones province in the northeast, a plateau of sandstone and basalt rises from the lowlands. The landscape here is characterized by a rough relief combined with fast-running rivers. Straddling the northern border with Brazil are the magnificent Iguazú Falls *(see page 235)*, which have more than 275 separate cascades, falling more than 60 meters (200 ft) through the lush subtropical forest.

The hunting ground

North-central Argentina is called the Chaco. It is the southern sector of the Gran Chaco, which extends into Bolivia, Paraguay, and Brazil, and which borders on the north with Brazil's Mato Grosso region. In the local dialect, *chaco* means "hunting ground," and across this wide, empty region there are many animals that would justify the name.

The area is covered by flat jungle plains, marshland, and palm groves in the east, and

> ### THE TREE OF LIFE
> One of the Chaco's main economic activities is the harvesting of the *quebracho* tree, which has a resin used in the tanning of leather. Fine leathers are a major by-product of the cattle industry in Argentina.

by drier savanna to the west; and the climate ranges from the tropical to the subtropical. The Chaco lies within the Río de la Plata river basin, and although it is dry throughout most of the year, the torrential summer rains cause extensive flooding.

Forests in this area contain high-quality hardwoods, and lumbering is a major industry. Most of the cleared areas of the forest are used for cattle-ranching, but cotton and other crops, such as sunflowers and maize, are also planted.

High desert and mountains

Going west from the Chaco, you reach the plateau region of the northwest, where the bordering Andes create an arid or semi-arid environment over much of the terrain. Here the elevation rises steadily until it reaches the *altiplano* (high plateau) on Argentina's northern border with Bolivia. Along this stretch, the Andes are divided into two parallel *cordilleras* (ranges), the Salta-Jujeña to the west and the Sierra Sub-andinas to the east.

The Puna is a dry cold desert that stretches over the Andes, north from the province of Catamarca toward Bolivia and covers part of

LEFT: Lago Argentino, Santa Cruz province.
RIGHT: toco toucan, from the subtropical northeast.

northern Chile as well. Here the population, largely of *mestizo* (Amerindian-Hispanic) stock, raises goats, sheep, and llamas.

Further to the east, the barometer swings dramatically once more as the climate across much of the provinces of Tucumán, Salta, and Jujuy becomes mountain tropical, with mild winters. Along with cattle-ranching, there are vineyards, olive and citrus groves, and tobacco and sugar cane plantations. Vegetable farms lie in the valleys and piedmonts.

WEALTH OF A NATION

The Cuyo area is blessed with mineral wealth. Copper, lead, and uranium are mined, and oil discovered here and in Patagonia has made Argentina nearly self-sufficient in that vital resource.

eroded, and merely dotted with scrub vegetation. Rivers nourished by the melting snows of the Andes cut through the desert. It is these same rivers which, with the help of an extensive irrigation system, allow for large-scale agriculture in the region. The Cuyo is the heart of Argentina's wine country; the arid climate, sandy soil, and year-round sunshine provide the ideal conditions for viticulture (*see page 93*). Citrus fruits are also grown here.

Open steppe

South of the Río Colorado, covering more than a quarter of Argentina, is Patagonia, where a series of dry plateaux drop from the Andes toward the rugged cliffs of the Atlantic coast.

The Patagonian Andes are lower than those to the north, and are scattered with lakes, meadows, and glaciers. Many of the slopes are forested. The central steppes are battered by sharp winds, and toward the south these winds become nearly constant. The terrain has been eroded by these winds as well as by rivers and glaciers.

In the low, wide river valleys of northern Patagonia, fruit and vegetable farming is made possible with irrigation. Toward the south, the rivers run through deep, flat-bottomed canyons. But although there is rainfall throughout most of the year, the climate is cold and doesn't lend itself to successful vegetation. The plains are covered by grasses, shrubs, and a few hardy trees. The harshness of the land means that sheep-raising is the major economic activity.

To the south, between the Strait of Magellan and the Beagle Channel, lies Tierra del Fuego. The climate here is subantarctic, and although that sounds rather intimidating, it could be worse, given the latitude. The nearness of the Atlantic and the Pacific waters helps to moderate the temperatures somewhat, and some parts of the island are quite green, also providing grazing for sheep. ❑

Grapes and citrus fruit

The central western section of Argentina, comprising the provinces of San Juan, Mendoza, and San Luis, is known as the Cuyo. The Andes here become a single towering range, with many peaks reaching over 6,600 meters (21,780 ft). West of Mendoza lies Aconcagua, at 6,980 meters (23,030 ft) the highest peak in the Western Hemisphere. Just south of Aconcagua is the Uspallata Pass (a former Inca road), which at its highest point of 3,800 meters (12,540 ft), crosses into Chile.

Fingers of desert extend eastward from the glacial mountains and down into the plains. A great deal of the land here is dry and wind-

LEFT: giant *cardon* cactuses of the Northwest.
RIGHT: Cerro Torres in Parque Nacional Los Glaciares, southern Patagonia.

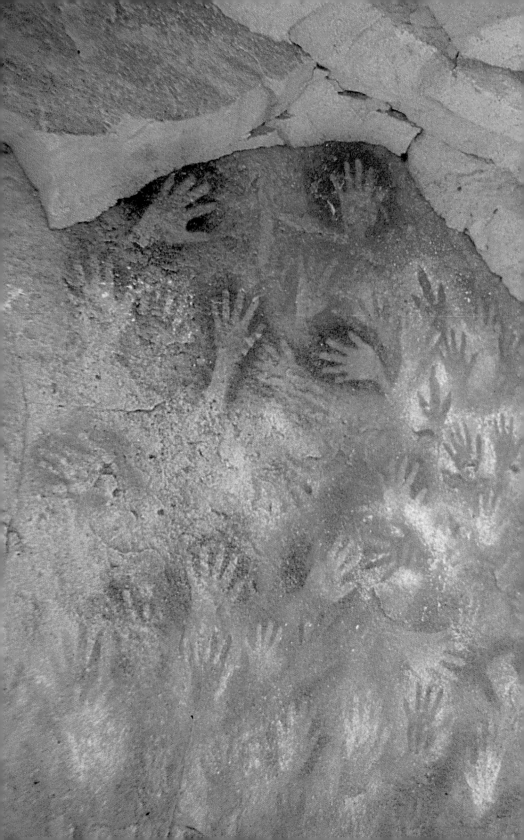

Decisive Dates

PRE-COLUMBIAN PERIOD: 10,000 BC–AD 1480

c. 10,000 BC Nomadic tribes reach Argentina from the north, settle in Andes and along the coast.

500 BC–AD 600 Ceramic cultures emerge in Jujuy and San Juan. Tafi culture flourishes in present-day Tucumán, in the northwest.

600–1480 Growth of urban centers in the northwest and west; development of skills in fine metalwork.

1480 The Incas conquer northwestern Argentina, building roads and fortresses and forming trade links.

THE SPANISH EMPIRE: 1516–1809

1516 Spaniard Juan Díaz de Solis discovers Río de la Plata (River of Silver) and claims it for Spain.

1536 Pedro de Mendoza founds the settlement of Nuestra Señora de Santa María del Buen Aire (Buenos Aires). It is wiped out by disease and attacks from local indigenous tribes.

1551 Santiago del Estero, in the foothills of the Andes, is founded by colonists from Peru. It is the oldest permanent Spanish settlement in Argentina.

1580 Buenos Aires is founded a second time by the conquistador Juan de Garay.

1594 Decree by King of Spain that no trade should go through Buenos Aires, but instead has to leave South America via Lima, Peru.

1776 Buenos Aires is made capital of fourth Spanish viceroyalty in Americas, covering the present-day Argentina, Uruguay, Paraguay, and Bolivia.

1806–07 British troops invade and occupy Buenos Aires, but are twice expelled.

THE INDEPENDENT REPUBLIC: 1810–1900

1810 With Spain occupied by Napoleon's troops, an independent junta of government is named in Buenos Aires. May 25 celebrated as the day of declaration of independence from Spain.

1816 Argentine Congress formally declares itself a state on July 9.

1817 Argentine independence hero José de San Martín leads Argentine troops across Andes mountains to fight Spanish loyalists in Chile. Battles of Chacabuco and Maipú.

1820 Battles break out between the *caudillos* (landowners) representing interior provinces and forces of Buenos Aires for dominance of newly emerging state.

1826–27 Bernardo Rivadavia is elected president and curbs the power of the Catholic church.

1829–52 Argentina is dominated by the *caudillo* Juan Manuel de Rosas, who gradually assumes dictatorial powers, and rules continuously from 1835–52.

1852 Rosas' army is defeated by Urquiza. Rosas flees to England, where he dies in exile in 1877.

1853 Argentina's constitution is adopted on May 1. Buenos Aires province is separated from the rest of the country; Paraná is the national capital until 1861.

1862 The capital is moved back to Buenos Aires.

1864–69 Argentina joins Uruguay and Brazil to fight against Paraguay in the War of the Triple Alliance.

1869 The total population of Argentina is around 1.8 million with 178,000 living in Buenos Aires.

1879 The "War of the Desert" – General Julio A. Roca defeats remaining indigenous tribes and pushes back southern frontiers. Roca elected president.

1890 Radical Party (Radical Civic Union) is formed.

1898 General Roca's second term in office.

INTO THE TWENTIETH CENTURY: 1900–45

1910 First century of independence is celebrated. Argentina is one of the richest nations in the world.

1916–30 Radical Party comes to power. Hipólito Irigoyen is president from 1916–22 and 1928–30.

1930 Military step into politics for the first time in 20th century, under General Jose F. Uríburu.

1932 General Agustín P. Justo is elected president, representing the military-conservative alliance.

1943 Government is overthrown by the military GOU (Group of United Officers), one of whom is Colonel Juan Domingo Perón.

PERONISM AND AFTER: 1945–82

1945 Juan Perón, now Minister of War, is arrested in October after the formation of the General Confederation of Labor (CGT), then released after huge rally.

1946 Perón, now married to Eva Duarte (Evita), is elected Argentine president on February 24.

1949 Peronista Party is formed.

1951 Perón is re-elected with 67 percent of vote. A year later Evita dies from cancer.

1955 Protests from Catholic church and unrest among armed forces leads to coup. Perón flees into exile.

1958 Arturo Frondizi (Radical Party) becomes president.

1962–63 Military government returns to power.

1963–66 Government of moderate Arturo Illía, but unions and electorate are still dominated by Peronism.

1966 Armed forces intervene again; General Juan Carlos Onganía is made president.

1970 Growing labor and political unrest leads military to oust Onganía. General Alejandro Lanusse eventually comes to power, and announces presidential elections for March 1973. Perón declares intention of returning to Argentina.

1973 Peronists win elections, with Héctor Cámpora as candidate. Violence breaks out among opposing left- and right-wing factions within Peronism.

1974 Perón takes over as president. Isabel, Perón's third wife, is made vice-president amid social tension and violence. Perón dies on July 1; Isabel is declared president of an increasingly divided nation.

1976 Military junta overthrows Isabel Perón on March 24. "Process of National Reorganization" begun under leadership of General Jorge Videla, the army commander-in-chief. "Dirty war" is launched to suppress opposition. Between 9,000 and 30,000 Argentines are abducted, tortured and killed by security forces.

1980–81 General Videla steps down and is replaced by General Viola, but is removed by General Galtieri.

1982 General Galtieri sends troops to occupy the Falklands Islands/Malvinas, claimed by Argentina since independence from Spain. Argentina surrenders with the loss of 600 soldiers.

ARGENTINE DEMOCRACY: POST-1983

1983 In the wake of defeat in the South Atlantic, military government collapses. Radical Party candidate Raúl Alfonsín is elected president on December 10.

1985 Report on disappearances during military dic-

tatorship is published: *Nunca Más* documents almost 9,000 cases of people secretly abducted.

1985–87 Trial and conviction of military junta leaders held responsible for disappearances.

1986 Argentina wins its second World Cup, in Mexico.

1989 Unable to control inflation or offer coherent economic policy, Radical Party loses election. Peronist candidate Carlos Saúl Menem is elected president.

1991 The *peso* is pegged to the US dollar. Economic stability is restored for the first time in three decades.

1992 Restoration of diplomatic relations with Great Britain for the first time since 1982.

1993 National constitution is changed to allow re-election of president.

1995 President Menem is re-elected.

1999 Fernando de la Rúa wins election.

2000 Vice-president Carlos 'Chacho' Alvarez resigns when de la Rúa refuses to investigate allegations of government corruption.

2001 President de la Rúa resigns after protests at rising poverty in which 27 protesters are killed. Argentina has four presidents in a fortnight.

2002 Peronist Duhalde is appointed interim president.

2003 Three unofficial Peronist candidates stand in first-round of presidential elections. Former president Carlos Menem receives most votes, but withdraws before second round in favour of Nestor Kirchner.

2003 May 25, Nestor Kirchner, governor of Santa Cruz province, takes office as president. ❑

PRECEDING PAGES: the prehistoric Cueva de las Manos, in Santa Cruz Province.

LEFT: early depiction of Patagonian Amerindians.

RIGHT: President Carlos Menem meets Prince Andrew in Falklands/Malvinas War commemoration in 1998.

PRE-COLUMBIAN PERIOD

Though less well documented than their counterparts elsewhere in South America,
Argentina's early inhabitants were self-sufficient peoples with basic artistic skills

Argentina and Chile were the last areas into which recently evolved humans moved in their quest for new lands and new food resources. Looking far beyond and north from Argentina, the story began many years ago and many miles away, when the first group of Asians entered the North American continent. It is a theory accepted by most archeologists that the early Americans arrived via the Bering Strait in one of the many Ice Ages, at a time when the oceans of the world were a great deal lower than at present. The Bering Strait became a perfect land bridge between America and Asia. If we accept the early archeological dates of the Yukon Valley in Alaska, placing the first waves of immigrants at 29,000–24,000 BC, it is possible that the early Americans reached the southern tip of South America by 10,000 BC. The Los Toldos site in southern Buenos Aires province seems to corroborate this theory.

The movement of people and the settlement of groups throughout the Americas were seriously hampered by the Ice Age, with its many advances and retreats of ice. Movement through North America was extremely difficult when two huge ice sheets covered most of the continent. Although the effects of the Ice Age in South America are not yet completely understood, it is thought that advances and retreats of the ice characterized the Pleistocene Epoch in the Southern as in the Northern Hemisphere.

Different climate

The last advance of the ice sheet in South America occurred between 9,000 and 8,000 BC, provoking different effects from those in North America. No ice sheets covered the pampas of Argentina or the jungles of Brazil. The principal manifestation was that the Andes, the great chain of mountains that forms the spine of South America, had more ice covering it then than it does today.

LEFT: petroglyph, thought to depict the devil, from Talampaya, La Rioja province.
RIGHT: pre-Columbian ceramic figure, from Córdoba.

The environment was also different, since many more lakes existed than is the case today, and the sea level was lower, rendering many areas, now under water, very tempting campsites. The Atlantic side of the continent, which today has a large and not very deep submarine platform, was very likely much wider, extending outward from today's pampas and Patagonia to form a still larger plain. The rainfall pattern was also different during the Pleistocene Epoch, and areas such as now-arid Patagonia were then covered with grass.

For many thousands of years the natives of this area developed separately from the inhabitants of other continental land masses. And, it seems, they had relatively little contact with the great civilizations of the Central Andes.

When the first Spaniards finally entered Argentina during the 16th century *(see page 37)* they did not find the great cities and pyramids of Meso-America or a splendid empire such as the one the Peruvian Incas had built in only 100 years; they found a country sparsely populated from the northwestern Puna to the tip of Tierra del Fuego. Nor was this population homogeneous in its cultural development.

Forts and farming

What is now Argentina's northwest was definitely the most culturally developed area. Throughout the centuries this area received the influences that diffused from Bolivia (during the peak of the Tiahuanaco empire) and Peru (especially during the expansion of the Inca empire, which incorporated northwestern Argentina within its great realm).

(mostly consisting of copper and bronze pieces), and stone sculptures have been found, relics of the different groups living in the area. Tribes and confederations of tribes were the units of political organization.

The Central Mountains and the region around Santiago del Estero were less developed. Small villages existed in this region, in some cases with semi-subterranean houses. Although agriculture was practiced, hunting and gathering still played an important role. Ceramics were made but were rather crude, and little to no metal was worked in the area. Many of the metal pieces were imported from the northwest.

The early 16th century found the natives of the northwest living in architecturally simple stone houses, in towns with populations that might have reached 3,000 people in some cases, making this area the most densely inhabited.

Many of the towns were walled, located on hilltops for defense purposes, and had their own ceremonial buildings. Intensive agriculture and irrigation were practiced everywhere and domestic animals, mostly camelids such as the llama and alpaca, were widely used for transportation, wool, and meat.

Most of the arts had reached a high level of development by the 16th century; good ceramics, woodcarvings, excellent metalworking

Fish and nomads

Life in the northeastern region of Argentina had many of the characteristics of that in the Central Mountains, except that the presence of two major rivers, the Paraná and the Uruguay, added a new dimension in the region's economies: fishing. Although pottery was known, metallurgy seems to have been absent. Unfortunately, to date this is one of the less archeologically studied areas of the country.

The region which encompasses the southern half of the country from Santa Fe and Córdoba to the southernmost islands, had little or no permanent architecture. Many of the groups here were nomadic and erected temporary settlements with simple houses of branches or hides. Almost no agriculture was practiced, with hunting (both on land and at sea) and gathering playing important roles. Pottery was either not known or, when practiced, very crude. Metalworking was unknown until the migration of Araucanian tribes from Chile. Most of the tools were of stone or bone and, in both mediums, they reached a highly developed technology. In Patagonia it is estimated that some of these roaming bands had up to 150 members.

Hunter-gatherers

Although there are many archeological sites throughout Argentina, the dating of many of them has still not been satisfactorily settled, and only a few can be ascribed to the end of the Pleistocene and beginning of the Holocene Epoch, about 10,000 to 9,000 BC.

Many archeologists call the earliest-known cultural tradition the "hunting tradition" or the "hunting and gathering tradition." As the names suggest, these early groups roamed the country, living from the hunting of big game and the collection of plants, seeds, and fruits. Many of the animals hunted and eaten are now extinct. The early sites occupied are often either rock shelters or caves.

The Los Toldos caves have walls and ceilings covered with paintings, mostly of hands, done in what is called "negative technique" (the hand is placed on the wall and the paint applied around it). Because some of the stone artifacts from the early levels have paint remains, it is thought that the cave paintings also correspond to the early levels, that is circa 9,000 BC.

Stone points

The hunting tradition survived for several thousand years, even until European contact in some areas. These manifestations appear in the different regions in the form of archeological sites which have certain common characteristics: the absence of ceramics and metal, no clear sign of the practice of agriculture (although by 2,500 BC, some milling stones are present in some of the places), and the presence of stone and bone tools and objects for personal decoration.

LEFT: finely worked ancient stone tools.
RIGHT: carved obelisk from the Parque de los Menhires, Tucumán province.

Both the stone and bone tools exhibit change through time. One of the most useful tools for gauging change is the stone point, as its development reflects technological advances, functional changes, specialization in hunting, and discovery of new and better raw materials.

Sea hunters

Development was uneven throughout the country and certain areas within the Patagonia and Tierra del Fuego zones never moved beyond the hunting tradition stage. The Tunel site, on the Beagle Channel, on the southern coast of Tierra del Fuego, testifies to that. After a first

CAVES OF KNOWLEDGE

Bones and other items found in caves have yielded much information about Argentina's early history.

The Fells and Pailli Aike caves, located on the southern tip of the continent, contain horse, guanaco (llama family), and ground sloth bones, together with those of humans. In Southern Chile, the Eberhardt Cave has remains of the Mylodon (giant sloth) and Onohippidon (early horse). The Los Toldos site, in Santa Cruz, is a group of caves containing horse bones. All these sites have stone tools; some of them have bone tools and Eberhardt has worked hides. The sites represent a pattern of seasonal nomadic occupation that followed the food resources.

occupation, oriented on guanaco (a relative of the llama) hunting, the inhabitants gradually converted to a sea-oriented economy.

For 6,000 years – until their full contact with the Europeans in the late 1800s – their economy and way of life remained mostly within a sea-based hunting and gathering pattern, complemented by guanaco hunting and seed and fruit collection. The lack of revolutionary changes does not reflect primitiveness or cultural backwardness but a successful and, with time, comfortable adaptation to the local environment by people who knew the resources and exploited them.

Agriculture arrives

In other areas the hunting tradition gave way eventually to agriculture. The transformation was from a pattern of collecting fruits, seeds, and leaves when and where they could be found (nomadism being a consequence of this regime) to an organized pattern of planting, tending, and collecting the fruits within a more restricted area, usually under sedentary patterns of settlement.

Within the New World, Mexico and the Andean area were the centers of domestication of wild plants. The vegetables and fruits that with time became the main staples of all the pre-Columbian societies and later of the European settlements – maize, potatoes, squash, beans, peppers – appear in either Meso-America or the Andean area by approximately 5,000 BC.

Ceramics and standing stones

The advent of agriculture is often closely followed by the development of ceramic skills. It is possible that the harvesting of crops and the new phenomenon of surplus food was an incentive for the making of containers which could hold and store seeds and fruits. Although pottery appeared in the New World during the 4th millennium BC, it is not seen in Argentina's archeological record until circa 500 BC.

This period of transition between hunting and collecting patterns and sedentary agriculture is called either incipient agriculture or Early Ceramic (when ceramic is present). The Ceramic Period is usually subdivided into Early, Intermediate, and Late, according to the different styles that succeeded each other in different areas. Most ceramic cultures occurred in the northern half of what is now Argentina.

To the Early Ceramic Period, which extended from about 500 BC to AD 600, belong several cultures which occupied an arch extending from the center of Jujuy to the eastern part of San Juan. One of the early complexes is the Tafí culture of Tucumán, which is noted for its stone sculptures. Some of these beautiful carved monoliths (some of which reach 3 meters/10 ft in height) have stylized human faces.

The people of the area lived in settlements formed by groups of houses arranged around a patio. Their diet included *quinoa* (an Andean cereal), potatoes, and possibly maize, and they practiced llama herding. Mounds have been found, which were used either for burials or as platforms for special structures.

Another extraordinary example of excellent stone sculpture is found at the site of the Alamito culture, on the Tucumán–Catamarca border. The statues here (both of women and men) reached an unusual level of development, with an almost abstract style both powerful and expressive.

In contrast to these stone-oriented cultures there is Condorhuasi, a culture in which ceramic art reached levels of expression not known in any other groups. Strange figures, often with both animal and human characteristics, are shown sitting and crawling, usually with globular bodies and legs, painted in a variety of white and red, cream and red, or black and red combinations.

Defensible settlements

The Middle Ceramic Period, dating from AD 650 to 850, witnessed the development and continuation of the advances made by preceding cultures, the existence of full agricultural communities living in permanent settlements, and the herding of llama and alpaca.

Architecture was still not impressive–at times just clay walls, probably with straw or wood roofs. Ceramic art continued to be developed, but stone work declined. Metalworking was by then highly developed, with the making of bronze and copper axes, needles, tweezers, bracelets, and disks with complicated designs. The distinct differences in the quantity of artifacts found in the graves is a clear indication that by now social stratification existed. The lack of monumental works or clear examples of organized labor points to a still simple political organization. The Aguada complex (mostly from Catamarca and La Rioja) is a good representative of this period.

The Late Ceramic Period, AD 850–1480, witnessed some changes. Settlements became larger, some in defensible locations, and thick walls made of round stones are found in many sites. Roads, cemeteries, irrigation works, and what were probably ceremonial centers gradually began to appear.

The ceramic urn (used for the burial of children) is one of the markers of the period. These vessels (40–60 cm/16–24 inches in height) often have painted human faces showing what could be tear marks. Other markers for this period are beautiful metal disks or breastplates lavishly decorated with human head and snake motifs.

Inca invasion

Finally, in AD 1480, the invading forces of the Incas arrived, led by Topa Inca. This period saw the peak expansion of the vast Inca empire, as they conquered what was to become the northwest region of Argentina. Remains of Inca roads, *tambos* (places of rest, supply, and storage), and *pucarás* (forts) can be found in the region. The Incas introduced their well-formed styles and artistic values and many of the pieces of this period are little more than local reproductions of original Inca pieces.

LEFT: stone face of unknown significance, from the Parque de los Menhires, Tucumán province.
RIGHT: the ruins of Quilmes. Tucumán province.

Dawning civilization

On their arrival, the Spaniards found a mosaic of cultural developments in Argentina ranging from groups which were still practicing a hunting and gathering mode of subsistence to others that were beginning to move to the threshold of civilization.

The story of the area's uneven cultural development goes back to about 10,600 BC and still has not been completely revealed. However, the continuing work of archeologists is slowly but surely filling the gaps in our understanding of the prehistory of what we now know as Argentina. ❏

CAVE DECORATIONS

Examples of cave and rock art are found all over Argentina, but it is in Patagonia that it has been most closely studied. Within this area several styles have been recognized. The painted hands style is present in many caves. Done with the negative technique, the depictions are mostly of adult left hands. An excellent example is found at the Cave of the Painted Hands in Santa Cruz. Another style is the naturalist or scenes style, depicting dancing ceremonies and the hunting of guanacos. Along the upper Pinturas River in Santa Cruz several such paintings can be found on gully walls. Footprint paintings and the geometric design style complete the range of motifs.

MER
DE
Tropicque du Capricorne
SUD, ou
PACI:
MER
FICQUE.
DE
CHILI.
MER
LANIC

ARTIE

DU
PE
Los
Char
CAS.
ROU

CHA
PA

Tama
Tobares
Mathagua
seis
Titanes
Taguamaicu

Moconos
Xaquelles
Xacoues
Guararapos

Paraguaes
Guebecuses
P.da de la Candelaria
Surucusi
Bascherepe
Payembo
M. S. Fernande

CO.

Atacama
Deserum

P
Tonoco
tetes

TU

CU
G

Carcaraes
Diaguitas
MAN.
Iuries

TRAPALANDA
Reg.

Vall. Fertil

Chi
cu

TERRE MA=

GELLA.
Bahia sin for

Costa de
Sierra
Puerte de los Leo
Cabe Redonde
Ancon de Sardinia
I. Regum
C. de Matos
Camarones
C. Pequeno
C. de S. Jorge
Port Desire
I. de los Leones
I. de S. Dionisio
B. de S. Iulian
Morro de S. Ynes
C. de las Barreras
I. de los Leones
I. de las Arenas
R. Gallegos
C. de los Virgines
Ins Sebaldt de
Werde

Lacus del
Desaguadero

NIC

Pata

QUE

gons.

Entrada de S. Sebastian
Pta de Synas

TERRE DE
FEU ou ISLES MAGEL

FROM CONQUEST TO INDEPENDENCE

The Spanish invasion brought civilization and increased population to Argentina, but by the 19th century the people were keen to break free from their distant rulers

The history of Argentina has been written in blood, from the earliest colonial days until recently. There have been periods of democratic rule in the past, but the tradition of representative government does not run deep in the people of this vast South American nation.

Admirable achievements and depressing low-points have marked the development of the Argentine nation as it has struggled to liberate itself first from a distant master and then from the cruel and selfish local potentates, the *caudillos*.

Heroic actions such as San Martín's crossing of the Andes, and the liberation of workers from a status similar to serfdom have often, unfortunately, been overshadowed by an ultra-nationalistic conceit that borders on hubris and has proved time and again to be self-defeating. The conflict between Buenos Aires and the interior, which persists to this day, has also been an obstacle in the development of the nation.

The first explorers

From a European perspective, the first half of the 16th century was a period of intense exploration on behalf of the Portuguese and Spanish crowns. Not quite 10 years after Columbus's first voyage to the New World, Amerigo Vespucci was probing the eastern shores of South America. Today, many credit him with the discovery of the Río de la Plata, although standard Argentine accounts cite Juan de Solís as the first European to sail these waters.

Solís reached the Río de la Plata estuary in 1516 and named the river Mar Dulce or Sweet Sea. Not long after, while Solís was leading a small party ashore, he was killed by Charrúa tribesmen, along with all but one of the sailors accompanying him. After killing the Spaniards, the natives proceeded to eat them in full view of the rest of the crew still on board ship.

In 1520, Ferdinand Magellan, on his voyage to the Pacific, was the next explorer to reach what is now Argentina. Then came Sebastian Cabot. Sailing under the Spanish flag, and drawn by rumors of a mountain of silver, he was the next to venture into the Río de la Plata region in 1526. He reached modern-day Paraguay,where the Guaraní Amerindians gave him some metal trin-

kets. Thus inspired, Cabot named the muddy stretch of water, the "River of Silver."

The Spanish nobleman Pedro de Mendoza led a large expedition to the area, also drawn by reports of great wealth in the region. On February 3, 1536, he founded Santa María de los Buenos Aires. The natives were at first helpful, but then they turned furiously against the Spaniards. As one of Mendoza's soldiers wrote: "The indians attacked our city of Buenos Aires with great force… There were around 23,000 of them… While some of them were attacking us, others were shooting burning arrows at our houses…" The natives finally retreated under the fire of Spanish artillery.

PRECEDING PAGES: 17th-century map of Argentina.
LEFT: a satirical view of the conflicts between the Spanish conquistadors and the Amerindians.
RIGHT: mural of the resettlement of Buenos Aires.

Mendoza and his men never did locate any great mineral wealth and left Buenos Aires for the more hospitable Asunción in Paraguay.

A second group of Spaniards, this time approaching overland from Chile, Peru, and Upper Peru (today's Bolivia), was more successful in founding lasting settlements. The northwest towns of Santiago del Estero, Catamarca, Mendoza, Tucumán, Córdoba, Salta, La Rioja, and Jujuy were all founded in the second half of the 16th century, with Santiago del Estero being Argentina's oldest outpost (founded in 1551).

For all of the following century and most of the 18th, the northwest was the center of most

activity in Argentina. This was mostly due to protectionism on the part of the King of Spain, who in 1554 prohibited traffic on the Río de la Plata. Manufactured goods from Spain and enslaved Africans were shipped in a South American triangular trade via Panama and then Peru. The king's ruling was of great benefit to the Spanish colonial cities of Lima and Mexico City but kept the Río de la Plata estuary isolated and commercially backward.

Northwest and central supremacy

While Argentina was part of the Peruvian viceroyalty until 1776, two areas of the colony became important centers. Tucumán developed

into a successful agricultural region, supplying wheat, corn, cotton, tobacco, and livestock to neighboring Upper Peru. Somewhat later, Córdoba attained status as a center of learning, with the establishment of the Jesuit university in 1613.

Córdoba also prospered economically, owing to its central location and fertile lands. By contrast, Buenos Aires, which had been refounded in 1580, was a small town that relied on smuggling for its income. Because all manufactured goods had to come the long route from Spain via Panama, their prices were very high, and this led to the cheaper contraband traffic.

Shift from west to east

The decline of the Andean mining industries, coupled with growing calls for direct transatlantic trade, finally persuaded the Spanish Crown to establish the new viceroyalty of Río de la Plata, with its administrative center at Buenos Aires.

With a new viceroyalty, which included Uruguay, Paraguay, and parts of Upper Peru and the Argentine, Spain hoped to exert greater control over a region which was growing in importance. Buenos Aires experienced an explosion in population, increasing its numbers from 2,200 in 1726 to more than 33,000 by 1778. Upwards of a quarter of this rapidly growing population was Afro-Argentine and still held in bondage. Many others were of mixed Amerindian and Spanish parentage, a consequence of the Spanish men suffering a paucity of Spanish women in the viceroyalty.

Another important appearance in the demographic picture was the *gaucho*, which came with the large ranches in the latter half of the 18th century. The *gaucho* represented a culture very different from that of the perfumed and groomed inhabitants of Buenos Aires.

The growing importance of the viceroyalty of the Río de la Plata did not go unnoticed in Europe. The Franco-Hispanic alliance during the Napoleonic Wars (1804–15) resulted in a loosening of Argentina's ties with the motherland when Spain's fleet was destroyed by the British Royal Navy. The Spanish colonies in Latin America were open for English attention.

The British invasion

In 1806, and again the following year, the British invaded Buenos Aires. During the first invasion, the inept Spanish viceroy fled to Montevideo, across the Río de la Plata, taking with him many of his troops. The retaking of the city was left to Santiago de Liniers, who organized the remaining Spanish troops and the local inhabitants. The British were quickly routed but were to return soon afterwards.

After seizing Montevideo, the British tried to recapture Buenos Aires with an army of 10,000. They were met by Liniers and his men, and by women pelting them with roof tiles and pouring boiling oil on them from above. The English commander of the expedition promptly evacuated his troops.

Beyond the immediate consequences of

DEATH ON THE STREETS

When the British invaded Buenos Aires in 1807, the city's streets were turned into what they later called "pathways of death."

dent-minded local élite. Thoughts of developing a booming economy without the strictures and regulations of a distant Crown began to enter the minds of the *criollos*.

Independence steps

Napoleon Bonaparte's invasion of Spain in 1808 provided the final push for a rupture in relations; a *cabildo abierto* (open town council) in Buenos Aires deposed the Spanish viceroy and created a revolutionary junta to rule in his stead.

Bernardino Rivadavia, Manuel Belgrano, and

repelling the invaders, a number of important effects stemmed from the confrontations with the British. Pride in the colony was a natural outcome of having defeated a large and well-trained army with a mostly local militia. Also, tensions arose between the *criollos* (Argentine-born colonists) and the Spanish troops, who realized they could not be of any assistance in their present position to their native Crown far away in the troubled Iberian Peninsula.

The creation of a rudimentary provisional government also helped to foster an indepen-

Mariano Moreno were three *criollo* intellectuals, inspired by European liberal thought, who channelled their energies toward the creation of a new nation based on a re-ordering of colonial society. Naturally enough, the old order – rich merchants, *estancieros* (large landowners), members of the clergy and, indeed, the whole colonial administration – was violently opposed to any tampering with its status in the country.

A house divided

This lack of unity made the realization of an independent nation much more of a tortured process than the *criollo* intellectuals could have imagined. Indeed, a civil war was in the making

LEFT: rampant Spaniards on the hunt in 1586.
ABOVE: the first British invasion, 1806.

following what the Argentines call the May Revolution. On May 25, 1810, an autonomous government was set up in Buenos Aires. This date is still celebrated in Argentina as the birthday of independence, although a formal declaration was not made until 1816.

These early years were not easy; the people of the viceroyalty were split along political, class, and regional lines, setting a Buenos Aires élite against the loyalists from the interior provinces. The *Unitarios* (Unitarians) were intent on having a strong central government, to be based entirely in offices in the capital, Buenos Aires. Meanwhile, the *Federales* (Federalists) campaigned for a loose confederation of autonomous provinces.

A confusing series of juntas, triumvirates, and assemblies rose and fell, as one group would have the upper hand for a brief period only to lose the advantage to another. The eight original jurisdictions of the viceroyalty dwindled to three, and these then fragmented into seven provinces.

A congress was called to maintain whatever unity was left. On July 9, 1816, the congress at Tucumán formally declared independence under the blue and white banner of the United Provinces of South America.

Enter José de San Martín

The task of ridding the continent of Spanish armies remained. José de San Martín was to execute one of the boldest moves of the South American wars of liberation. Gathering a large army, San Martín crossed the icy Andes at Mendoza in 21 days and met and defeated a Spanish army at Chacabuco in Chile (1817). He again engaged the Spaniards, this time at Maipú (1818), where he ended the Spanish menace to Chile once and for all.

San Martín then amassed a fleet of mostly English and American ships to convoy his army the 2,400 km (1,500 miles) to Lima. The Spanish army evacuated the city without fighting, wishing to keep their forces intact. It was at this time, in 1822, that San Martín met the other great liberator of South America, Simón Bolívar, at Guayaquil. What was discussed at this meeting is not known and has kept historians speculating ever since. The upshot, though, was San Martín's retirement from battle, leaving the remaining honors to be garnered by Bolívar.

From obscurity to sainthood

San Martín was posthumously elevated to a position of sainthood by the Argentines. Today, every town in Argentina has a street named after him and every classroom a portrait of the general crossing the Andes on a gallant white horse. However, it was a different story when he returned to Buenos Aires in 1823 from his campaigns on behalf of Argentina. He received no acknowledgment for the services he had rendered his country. Soon afterwards San Martín left for France, where he was to die in obscurity. ❑

A CHARISMATIC LEADER

Basil Hall, a contemporary of José de San Martín's, described him thus: "There was little, at first sight, in his appearance to engage attention; but when he rose up and began to speak, his great superiority over every other person… was sufficiently apparent… a tall, erect, well-proportioned, handsome man, with a large aquiline nose, thick black hair, and immense bushy whiskers… his complexion is deep olive, and his eye, which is large, prominent and piercing, jet black; his whole appearance being highly military… The contest in Peru, he said, was a war of new and liberal principles against prejudice, bigotry and tyranny."

LEFT: the formal declaration of independence on July 9, 1816, in Tucumán.

The case of the Afro-Argentines

Argentina's greatest puzzle is the vanished Afro-Argentines. Historians throughout the years have offered diverse explanations. Ordinary citizens are ready with stories that range from the plausible to the ludicrous.

Argentines of African heritage existed in large numbers – comprising 30 percent of the Buenos Aires population for almost 40 years (1778–1815). Slaves were first brought to Argentina in the 16th century by their Spanish owners. Due to the peculiar trading arrangements with the Spanish Crown, most slaves were imported to Buenos Aires via Panama and Peru and then overland from Chile, thereby greatly increasing their price. Others were brought in illegally, directly to Buenos Aires or from Brazil.

Argentine slaves were generally domestic servants but also filled the growing need for artisans in the labor-short colony. While the degree of their labor differed greatly from that of plantation workers in Brazil and the United States, they suffered similarly. Families were torn apart, gruesome punishments awaited runaways, and blacks' status in society was kept low, even after emancipation.

In the post-independence era, the move to free slaves was fitful at best. While the majority of slaves had gained their liberty by 1827 (through military service, the largesse of friendly masters, or by purchasing their own freedom), some remained in bondage until 1861. One early 1800s law stipulated that the children of slaves would be free upon birth, though their mothers would remain slaves. However, it was not unusual for slaveowners to spirit their pregnant slaves to Uruguay, where slavery was still legal, and then bring both mother and child back to Argentina as slaves.

The North American professor George Reid Andrews has done much research to uncover the fate of the blacks in his important work, *The Afro-Argentines of Buenos Aires, 1800–1900*. He offers no definitive conclusions, but he has explored in depth some of the more likely theories.

Reid Andrews researches four strong possibilities. A great percentage of Afro-Argentine males served in the army, organized into their own battalions. Many of them might have perished in the incessant warfare during and after independence. Miscegenation, or the mixing of races, is an explanation that many ascribe to. This might also seem sensible given the degree to which the black community was swamped by the hundreds of thousands of European immigrants who reached Argentina after the mid-1800s. The great yellow fever epidemic of 1871 and the general ill health and horrendous living conditions of the blacks is also cited as a possible factor. Finally, Reid Andrews explores the decline of the slave trade (outlawed in 1813) and its impact on a community that would not have its numbers refreshed with new shipments of human chattel.

Census figures for the city of Buenos Aires from 1836 to 1887 point to a steep decline in the numbers and percentages of blacks, from a figure of 14,906 or 26 percent of the total population to 8,005 or 1.8 percent.

The contributions blacks made to Argentine society have, for the most part, been written out of the records. After the early 19th century, Afro-Argentines to all intents and purposes disappeared or were intentionally made to vanish. One must sift through prints and photographs of the late 1800s to discover that this group, although in decline, remained a part of the greater community. In these representations we might see blacks working as *gauchos* or as street vendors or artisans in Buenos Aires. ❑

RIGHT: an Afro-Argentine street vendor, a common sight in mid-19th century Buenos Aires.

JIJOTE

EL JUICIO

Lit. J. Ribas y Hⁿᵒ

A VISITOR'S VIEW

Travelers in the 18th and 19th centuries painted a colorful
picture of Argentina as a country where wild-west violence was a part of daily life

Today's traveler to Argentina follows in the wake of a tremendously diverse group of characters which has probed and prodded the country for its secrets, climbed every mountain, witnessed the major events in its history, and invariably compared the customs and mores of its people, so similar yet so different from themselves.

While Magellan and Darwin are the most familiar names, a surprising number of others have felt compelled to publish their travel diaries. Perhaps these visitors were encouraged to share their experiences because many in Europe and the United States were curious to know what it was really like in the distant reaches of Patagonia and Tierra del Fuego.

The reader of travel literature, especially of the 18th- and 19th-century vintage, discovers many of the wonders of Argentina that no longer exist. These fabulous tales do need to be approached somewhat cautiously because many of the travelers neither spoke the language nor necessarily understood the events unfolding before them. Nonetheless, these accounts provide the color and flavor that is sometimes missing from published scientific diaries.

As one might expect, the early traveler faced a broad spectrum of perils that, in the case of Argentina, included robbery, Amerindian attacks, diseases such as yellow fever and syphilis, lack of adequate food and shelter, and often painful modes of transportation.

The dangers, though, seemed to be far outweighed by the joys the voyager experienced. Unexpected hospitality in the most out-of-the-way places, chance encounters along the road, the sight of Tehuelche natives and *gauchos* displaying their equestrian skills, and the exhilaration of visiting places few had seen before were some of the high points the foreigner might come across.

PRECEDING PAGES: a caricature of Argentine political life, 1893, from the magazine *Don Quijote.*
LEFT: morning *mate* in an upper-class salon.
RIGHT: 19th-century watercolor of a colonial church.

The city of good air

The 19th-century traveler would often commence his or her itinerary in Buenos Aires. Charles Darwin, in 1833, described the city as "large and I should think one of the most regular in the world. Every street is at right angles to the one it crosses, and the parallel ones being equidistant,

the houses are collected into solid squares of equal dimensions, which are called *quadras*."

Writing 10 years after Darwin, Colonel J. Anthony King commented that: "The market place of Buenos Ayres [*sic*] is… the center of all public rejoicings, public executions, and popular gatherings. It is in the market place that Rosas hung up the bodies of many of his victims, sometimes decorating them… with ribbons of the Unitarian color [blue], and attaching to the corpses labels, on which were inscribed the revolting words, 'Beef with the hide'."

J.P. and W.P. Robertson wrote a series of letters from South America which they published in 1843. What first impressed them were the methods of transportation in the city. "Nothing strikes one more on a first arrival in Buenos Aires than the carts and carters. The former are vehicles with large wooden axles, and most enormous wheels, so high that the spokes are about 8 feet [2 meters] in diameter, towering above both horses and driver; he rides one of these animals… The first sight you have of these clumsy vehicles is on your landing. They drive off like so many bathing-machines to your hotel, a dozen carters, just like a dozen porters here, struggling… for the preference in carrying ashore passengers and their luggage."

By the turn of the 20th century, Buenos Aires had become the noisiest and brashest city in Latin America, as wealth poured into the country and chilled beef was exported to Europe.

Thomas Turner, who lived in Argentina from 1885 to 1890, was greatly amused by some of his compatriots who brought to the capital their preconceptions, expecting to find a wild and uncivilized place. They arrived "so thoroughly imbued with these silly notions that the outfits they have brought with them would have been better suited to the necessities of the Australian bush or the Canadian backwoods than to the requirements of the life they were likely to

experience in Argentina. Where they should have brought dress suits and dancing shoes, they came provided with a whole defensive arsenal and a supply of coarse apparel."

Perils of the unknown

Dangers on the road were certainly plentiful for both traveler and native alike. Francis Bond Head, an English mining engineer who spent two tempestuous years, 1825–26, in the Argentine outback, and whose book *Rough Notes Taken During Some Rapid Journeys Across the Pampas and Among the Andes* is one of the best travelogues on Latin America, was well prepared for the violence he knew he would face.

Head wrote that, "In crossing the pampas it is absolutely necessary to be armed, as there are many robbers or *saltadors*, particularly in the desolate province of Santa Fe. The object of these people is of course money, and I therefore always rode so badly dressed, and so well armed that although I once passed through them with no one but a child as a postilion, they thought it not worth their while to attack me. I always carried two brace of detonating pistols in a belt, and a short detonating double-barreled

A HAZARDOUS LAND

Darwin described the trials of the terrain. "Changing horses for the last time, we again began wading through the mud. My animal fell, and I was well soused in black mire – a very disagreeable accident."

ride so quick, and the country is so uninhabited, that it is impossible to gain any information."

A woman traveling alone faced another sort of problem. The American Katherine S. Drier described what she had to contend with in Buenos Aires in 1918. "Before leaving for Buenos Aires everybody in New York told me that the Plaza Hotel was the only hotel in Buenos Aires, and that of course I would make it my headquarters during my sojourn there. But my information had been given me by men, and

gun in my hand. I made it a rule never to be an instant without my arms, and to cock both barrels of my gun whenever I met any *gauchos*."

Head, aptly named "Galloping Head", describes the dangers Amerindians posed. "A person riding can use no precaution, but must just run the gauntlet, and take his chance, which, if calculated, is a good one. If he fall in with them, he may be tortured and killed, but it is very improbable that he should happen to find them on the road; however, they are so cunning, and

LEFT: *boleadora*-wielding Amerindians on the pampas.
ABOVE: indigenous settlement on the Sierra de la Ventana pampas.

neither they nor I expected to find that the Plaza did not take women unaccompanied by their husbands or supposed husbands. Not even sisters accompanied by their brothers, or wives whose husbands have to travel, or widows, are made welcome. Much less respectable maiden ladies!"

Tehuelche and Puelche

The native Americans were of constant interest to the traveler of the 1800s, although by the 1870s they were becoming rarer as the campaigns to conclude the "Indian problem" reached their peak. One intrepid individual, the Jesuit Thomas Falkner, spent almost 20 years living among the Puelche and Tehuelche tribes of southern Argentina, from the 1730s until the religious order was expelled from the country. His account published as *A Description of Patagonia*, was used as a guide by Charles Darwin a century later.

Meeting an Amerindian could be a highpoint of a journey, as Lady Florence Dixie related in her *Across Patagonia* (1881). "We had not gone far when we saw a rider coming slowly towards us, and in a few minutes we found ourselves in the presence of a real Patagonia Indian. We reined in our horses when he got close to us, to have a good look at him, and he doing the same, for a few minutes we stared at him to our

hearts' content, receiving in return as minute and careful a scrutiny from him."

One of Galloping Head's fondest wishes was to be able to spend time with the native South American. "His profession is war, his food simple, and his body is in that state of health and vigor that he can rise naked from the plain on which he has slept, and proudly look upon his image which the white frost has marked out upon the grass without inconvenience. What can we 'men in buckram' say to this?"

Country life

The *gauchos* (Argentine cowboys) were often perceived as being as wild as the Amerindians, and just as interesting. Additionally, the *gauchos* and others living in the countryside were noted for their hospitality. Colonel King writes that, "whether in health or sickness, the traveler is always welcome to their houses and boards, and they would as soon as think of charging for a cup of water, as for a meal of victual or a night's lodging."

Darwin, too, was greatly struck by their manners. "The *gauchos*, or countrymen, are very superior to those who reside in the towns. The *gaucho* is invariably most obliging, polite, and hospitable. I did not meet with even one instance of rudeness or inhospitality." And once, when Darwin inquired whether there was enough food for him to have a meal, he was told, "We have meat for the dogs in our country, and therefore do not grudge it to a Christian."

But traveling in the countryside was generally not a very comfortable affair. Galloping Head presents a none too appealing description of his night's accommodations. "We arrived an hour after sunset – fortified post – scrambling in the dark for the kitchen – cook unwilling – *correo* (the courier) gave us his dinner – huts of wild-looking people – three women and girls almost naked – our hut – old man immovable – Maria or Mariquita's figure – little mongrel boy – three or four other persons. Roof supported in the center by crooked poles – holes in roof and walls – walls of mud, cracked and rent… Floor, the earth – eight hungry peons, by moonlight standing with their knives in their hands over a sheep they were going to kill."

In the country, far from doctors and hospitals, the people often relied on an assortment of folk medicine. Darwin was appalled at the remedies:

"One of the least nasty is to kill and cut open two puppies and bind them on each side of a broken limb. Little hairless dogs are in great request to sleep at the feet of invalids."

Travelers were impressed by the skills *gauchos* showed as they worked their horses, threw *bolas* to fell cassowaries – the South American ostrich – or lassoed cattle. Darwin witnessed such a sight: "I was amused by the dexterity with which a *gaucho* forced a... horse to swim a river. He stripped off his clothes, and jumping on its back rode

ARMS AT THE READY

Darwin wrote that, "A traveler has no protection besides his firearms, and the constant habit of carrying them is the main check to a more frequent occurrence of robbery."

Earth and sky

The size of the country and the rough paths made the traveler's trip through Argentina a very long one indeed. E. E. Vidal, another early 19th-century traveler, quotes the unnamed author of *Letters from Paraguay,* who describes his trip from Buenos Aires to Mendoza, at the foot of the Andes, as taking 22 days in a large cart drawn by oxen. "We set off every afternoon about two, and sometimes three hours before sunset, and did not halt till about an hour after sunrise."

into the river till it was out of its depth; then slipping off over the crupper, he caught hold of the tail, and as often as the horse turned around, the man frightened it back by splashing water in its face. As soon as the horse touched bottom on the other side, the man pulled himself on, and was firmly seated, bridle in hand, before the horse gained the bank. A naked man on a naked horse is a fine spectacle; I had no idea how well the two animals suited each other. The tail of a horse is a very useful appendage."

LEFT: mural of indigenous tribesmen from Ushuaia, Tierra del Fuego.
ABOVE: Darwin's research vessel, the HMS *Beagle.*

Having a sufficient supply of water was one of the obstacles the writer faced in his journey. "We were obliged to halt in a spot, where even the grass seemed to have been burned to the very roots, and nothing was presented to the eye but barrenness and desolation...We had but one small jar of water left, our thirst seemed to increase every moment."

Nature intervened as a thunderstorm struck the camp. "'Look at the oxen; they smell water.' We all... turned to the poor panting animals, and saw them stretch their heads to the west, and snuff the air, as if they would be certain of obtaining drink could they but raise themselves into the atmosphere. At that moment not a cloud was to be seen, nor a breath of air felt; but in a few minutes the cattle began to move about as if… possessed by some invisible spirit, snuffing the air with most violent eagerness, and gathering closer… to each other; and before we could form any rational conjecture as to what could occasion their simultaneous motion, the most tremendous storm of thunder, lightning, and rain I ever witnessed in my life came on. The rain fell in perpendicular streams, as if all the fountains of heaven had suddenly broken loose."

Many travelers commented on the seemingly endless flat pampas. W. J. Holland, an American scientist on an expedition to Argentina in 1912,

described the scene from his train compartment. "I have crossed the prairies of Minnesota and the Dakotas, of Kansas and Nebraska, of Manitoba and Alberta; I have traveled over the steppes of Russia; but in none of them have I seen such absolutely level lands as those which lie between Rosario and Irigoyen. The horizon is that of the ocean; an upturned clod attracts attention; a hut looks like a house; a tree looms up like a hill."

Food and politics

The customs of the Argentines, whether of city folk, *gauchos*, or Amerindians, have always been cause for comment. Thomas Turner, describing one well-known and wealthy family at supper in the 1880s had this to say: "Of the domestic habits of the Argentines, their manners at table, *en famille*, it is impossible to give an attractive description. Their manners at table are ultra-Bohemian. They read the papers, shout vehemently at each other, sprawl their limbs under and over the table, half swallow their knives, spit with true Yankee freedom on the carpeted floor, gesticulate and bend across the table in the heat of argument, smoke cigarettes between the courses, and even while a course of which some of them do not partake is serving – a soothing habit which stimulates expectoration and provokes discussion – use the same knife and fork for every course – fish, entree, or joint, in a word, the studied deportment of the street is, in the house, exchanged for the coarse manners of the tap-room."

Turner was also shocked at the way politics dominated discussions, something that still is prevalent. "Although forbidden subjects are discussed by both sexes with zest and freedom, the staple topic of conversation is politics. Everybody talks politics… Even children talk politics, and discuss the merits of this, that or other statesmen with parrot-like freedom of opinion and soundness of judgment."

Whether positive or critical, the wanderers and explorers have passed on the country's lore, which might otherwise have been lost to us. Their tales are sometimes unintentionally amusing to today's reader but they are almost always fascinating and illuminating. ❏

SUPERIORITY COMPLEX

Many of the travelers' accounts are tinged with racism and the deep-seated assumption that the writers' own cultures were nearly always superior to that of the Argentines. Comments abound such as "Most of the corruption which exists in public life is due to the participation of foreigners therein; Italians chiefly" or, "I was becoming accustomed to the polite airs of this town that prints literature mad with Yankeephobia to snarl and bite all over SA against North America whose Monroe Doctrine, money, mentality and morality have been Argentina's help in the past and is her only hope in the future."

LEFT: a *pulpería* – multi-purpose saloon, general store, and community social center on the pampas.
RIGHT: a 19th-century gentleman farmer.

CAUDILLOS, TYRANTS, AND DEMAGOGUES

For most of the past two centuries Argentina has suffered under the political ambitions and misguided economic policies of dictators and military rulers

The years from independence to the commencement of the dictatorship of Juan Manuel de Rosas in 1829 were difficult for the United Provinces of the Río de la Plata (the earlier and grander name of the United Provinces of South America was dropped when the original grouping broke up). Bernardino Rivadavia, a man of great vision, valiantly but vainly attempted to shape the country's future.

Rivadavia was interested in establishing a constitution for the nation, forming a strong central government, dividing up the land into more equitable shares, and attracting immigrants to settle in the United Provinces. His plans were quickly sidetracked, however, by both *caudillos* in the interior, who were none too anxious to surrender any of their power, and by the draining Cisplatine War (1825–28) with Brazil over the status of Uruguay. When Rivadavia resigned from the presidency of the United Provinces in 1827 and went into exile, there remained little to show for his years of effort.

Caudillo and tyrant

Juan Manuel de Rosas, who ruled much of Argentina as his personal domain for more than 20 years, must be one of the most intriguing, if blood-thirsty figures in Latin American history. In his quest for power, Rosas forged a coalition of *gauchos*, wealthy landowners and others who represented the Federalist cause, a combination that proved formidable for many years.

Although born in Buenos Aires in 1793, Rosas was a product of the open pampas. It was here on his family's *estancia* that he learned to ride, fight, and toss the *boleadoras* (three stones attached to connected thongs, used to bring livestock down by tangling around their legs). Rosas became as skilled in these pursuits as any of the *gauchos* with whom he kept company, gaining their respect and later their support.

LEFT: a colorful portrayal of the emerging new nation.
RIGHT: the tyrant Juan Manuel de Rosas.

Rosas became wealthy in his own right at an early age. By his mid-twenties, he owned thousands of acres of land and was a successful businessman, having helped to establish one of the first meat-salting plants in his province. He

chose well when he married María de la Encarnación Escurra, the daughter of another rich family. She would later prove quite invaluable to Rosas' ascent to power, loyally plotting and organizing in a subtle and effective way on her husband's behalf.

To stem the rising tide of anarchy that followed the exile of Rivadavia, Rosas was asked to become the governor of the province of Buenos Aires in 1829. Rosas, a powerful *caudillo* and experienced military man, seemed the perfect individual to restore order and stability.

The problem with the Federalists was that there was little unity among the various factions. Those in the provinces demanded autonomy and an equal footing with Buenos Aires, while those espousing the Federalist cause in Argentina's major city were not willing to surrender their premier position. As governor with extraordinary powers, Rosas signed in 1831 the Federal Pact which tied together the provinces of Buenos Aires, Entre Ríos, Santa Fe, and Corrientes.

The opposition to Rosas, the Unitarian League, was dealt a severe blow when its leader, José María Paz, was unhorsed by a Federalist soldier wielding *boleadoras*. Paz was jailed by Rosas. By 1832, the Unitarians had suffered a number of reverses on the battlefield and, for the moment, did not pose a deep threat to the Federalists.

When Rosas' first term as governor ended in 1832, he refused to accept another stint in office because the council of provincial representatives was unwilling to allow him to maintain his virtually unlimited authority.

Darwin and Rosas

In the midst of this struggle, Rosas did not absent himself from combat. He took command of the campaign against the native Argentine tribes in the south, and earned himself even more dubious glory by wiping out thousands.

During this Desert Campaign of 1833–34 the British naturalist Charles Darwin was entertained by Rosas. Of his meeting, Darwin wrote: "General Rosas is a man of extraordinary character; he has at present a most predominant influence in this country and may probably end up by being its ruler… He is moreover a perfect *gaucho*: his feats of horsemanship are very notorious. He will fall from a doorway upon an unbroken colt, as it rushes out of the Corral, and will defy the worst efforts of the animal. He wears the *gaucho* dress and is said to have called upon Lord Ponsonby in it, saying at the time he thought the costume of the country the proper and therefore the most respectful dress. By these means he obtained an unbounded popularity in the Camp, and in consequence despotic power… In conversation he is enthusiastic, sensible and very grave. His gravity is carried to a high pitch."

While Rosas was campaigning in the south, his wife waged a "dirty war" to have her husband reinstated as governor of Buenos Aires, forming the *Sociedad Popular Restauradora* and its terror-wing, the *mazorca*. Doña Encarnación effectively hampered the efforts to rule of the three governors who followed Rosas.

The junta finally acquiesced to Rosas' demands and he assumed his post as Restorer of the Laws and governor in a regal ceremony on April 13, 1835. The red color of the Federalists became a distinguishing factor. Women wore scarlet dresses and men red badges that proclaimed "Federation or Death". Decorating in blue, the color of the "savage Unitarians", could be cause enough for imprisonment or execution.

Climate of fear

While Rosas did not create the brutal methods of repression that so characterized his regime, he did give a certain order and system to them in making himself supreme dictator. Generally

THE KILLING GAME

Under Juan Manuel de Rosas, horrific methods of silencing opponents became institutionalized.

The favored manner of despatching them was throat-cutting, reflecting the tradition of the *gauchos*. W. H. Hudson, naturalist and chronicler of the pampas, wrote that the Argentines "loved to kill a man not with a bullet but in a manner to make them know and feel that they were really and truly killing."

Another method employed was lancing: two executioners standing on either side of the prisoner would plunge lances into the body. Castration and tongue extraction were other acceptable means of torture.

speaking, Rosas' victims were not massacred wholesale but rather executed on an individual basis. Long lists of suspected Unitarians and the property they possessed were drawn up by Rosas' effective spy network, the police, the military, and justices of the peace. The actual numbers of those who perished remains unclear, but estimates range in the thousands. Whatever the number, Rosas created and maintained a climate of fear for more than 20 years.

With Rosas at the helm, Argentina did not prosper. He meddled in the affairs of neighboring Uruguay, expending resources, but he was never able to conquer its capital, Montevideo.

In response to the atmosphere of terror and lack of freedom, Argentines organized in secret, and some in exile, to overthrow Rosas. These intellectuals, whose ranks included such luminaries as Bartolomé Mitre, Juan Bautista Alberdi, and Domingo Faustino Sarmiento, provided the rhetoric which galvanized the opposition.

A quick end

Justo José de Urquiza, a *caudillo* who had long supported Rosas, turned against the Restorer and organized an army that soon included thousands of volunteers, and even many Uruguayans and Brazilians. On February 3 1852, Urquiza's

Extreme xenophobia on Rosas' part also kept the country from attracting much-needed immigrants and foreign capital. During two periods, the first from 1838 to 1840 when French troops occupied a customs house on the Río de la Plata, and then during the 1845–47 Anglo-French blockade of the river, the finances of Buenos Aires suffered severely. Rosas' treatment of European nationals, his extreme paranoia, and the inevitable consequences did nothing to help the growth of the nation.

LEFT: a Rosas soldier in Federalist colors.
ABOVE: Amerindians captured during the Desert Campaign.

army engaged Rosas' demoralized and rebellion-weary troops at Caseros, near Buenos Aires. "The battle" as Mitre later wrote, "was won before it was fought." A new age in Argentina's history had begun, with Urquiza intent on consolidating the nation as one unit and not a collection of semi-independent provinces; progress in all areas came quickly.

State foundations

The period from Rosas' downfall to 1880 was a time of organizing the nation-state and establishing the institutions required to run it. The major conflict of this period was an old one: the status of Buenos Aires in relation to the interior.

This issue was finally settled in 1880 by federalizing the city and making it something like the District of Columbia in the United States.

Urquiza's first task was to draw up a constitution for Argentina. A constitutional convention was held in the city of Santa Fe and this meeting produced a document modeled on the Constitution of the United States. Among its provisos were the establishment of a bicameral legislature, an executive chosen by an electoral college, and an independent judiciary.

The Argentine constitution was accepted by the convention on May 1, 1853. Not surprisingly, Urquiza was chosen as the first president.

to Mitre, he found himself distracted by the Paraguayan War (1865–70) in which it took five years of bloody fighting for the triple alliance of Brazil, Uruguay, and Argentina to subdue the Paraguayan dictator Francisco Solano López.

Mitre was succeeded by Domingo Faustino Sarmiento whose role in promoting education in Argentina has taken on mythic proportions. It was during Sarmiento's administration (1868–74) that Argentina's progress soared. Hundreds of thousands of immigrants poured into the city of Buenos Aires, railroads were built, and the use of barbed-wire fencing spread, controlling the open range. Sarmiento continually stressed the

During his tenure, he established a national bank, built schools, and improved transportation in the republic. But the role of Buenos Aires was still uncertain. There were, in fact, two Argentinas, one in wealthy Buenos Aires and the other in the interior with its capital at Paraná. A congress met in Buenos Aires in 1862 and decided that Buenos Aires would become the capital of both the republic and the province.

A succession of presidents

Bartolomé Mitre, an historian and former governor of the province of Buenos Aires, became the next president. Although the task of creating a national infrastructure was of great importance

need to push for a removal of the "barbaric" elements within Argentine society, namely the *caudillos* and the *gauchos*. He believed that groups such as these had kept Argentina from advancing at a faster rate.

Following Sarmiento came President Nicolás Avellaneda, whose inauguration in October 1874 almost didn't happen. Mitre, fearing a decline in Buenos Aires' prestige at the hands of such non-*porteños* (residents of Buenos Aires) as Sarmiento, Avellaneda, and Julio Roca, led a revolt against the government. It took three months to crush this rebellion.

As Avellaneda's minister of war, Roca headed a series of expeditions against the natives of Patagonia in the infamous Conquest of the Desert which was concluded by 1879. Many thousands of square miles were opened up for settlement and exploration after this war of genocidal proportions.

Golden age

The most profound changes lay the foundation for Argentina's golden age, which would last until World War I. New methods for chilling and then freezing meat, innovations in shipping, and the construction of rail networks all made possible intensive ranching and farming. The amount of cultivated land multiplied 15 times from 1872

number of growing towns (Rosario, Santa Fe, Bahía Blanca), but the majority settled in the capital, Buenos Aires.

There was a corresponding growth in the intellectual field, as well. Newspapers were founded, political parties sprang up, books were published, and a world-class opera house, the Teatro Colón, opened in Buenos Aires.

This is not to say that all was well in Argentina. Politics remained closed to most Argentines; a few had taken it upon themselves to run the country. The middle class, supporting the new political party, the Radical Civic Union, pressed for entry into what had been a government run by a

to 1895, and cereal exports exploded between 1870 and 1900. Behind this accelerated economic growth lay the increased demand for foodstuffs created by the British factory system.

The new meat and cereals economy required workers, and by the 1890s Argentina was receiving thousands of immigrants – mostly Italian and Spanish. The population grew from 1.8 million in 1869 to more than 4 million by 1895. With land already in the hands of the great *estancieros*, immigrants settled in a small

small group of conservative families. Workers also became politicized and were attracted to the Socialist Party and the anarchists. Strikes hit Argentina at the turn of the 20th century and labor unrest grew. The workers found themselves expendable as the country struggled to pay back international loans and as imports began to exceed exports.

The effects of World War I

The war in Europe stimulated the Argentine economy in two ways. First, the belligerents' need for agricultural products skyrocketed; and second, the paralysis of European trade in manufactured goods encouraged local production.

LEFT: the masses turn out for Loyalty Day, 1946.
ABOVE: Perón and Evita soak up their supporters' adulation from the balcony of the Casa Rosada.

Impoverished urban artisans began to fill domestic demand as imports fell by 50 percent. This industrial boom revealed weaknesses in the Argentine economy – dependence on imported raw materials, lack of energy resource development, and a capital goods sector – that would stand out during the Great Depression, when the nation once more relied on local production.

One of the worst periods of governmental repression occurred in 1919. In what was called the *Semana Trágica* (Tragic Week), troops

WORKERS UNITE

The *descamisados* that supported Perón were the working-classes, literally meaning "the shirtless ones" or the poor workers.

Ramón Castillo, who reversed his predecessor's campaign to cleanse the political system of corruption. It was this man's blatant dishonesty that triggered the military's coup d'état in 1943. The real significance of the intervention this time around cannot be underestimated for it was during this regime that Juan Domingo Perón emerged to lead the nation.

A demagogue's demagogue

Perón's background certainly indicated no pro-labor tendencies. He attended a military col-

opened fire on strikers and many lives were lost. The Radical Civic Union governed Argentina from 1916 until 1930. Hipólito Yrigoyen served as president for all but six of those years.

With the coming of the Great Depression, the military swept Yrigoyen from office. With this move, a new element entered modern Argentina's political body. The pattern was to be followed all too frequently over the next half-century.

The Radicals staged a comeback with the ascension of Roberto Ortiz in the fraudulent elections of 1937. Ironically, Ortiz then set about restoring voter confidence by annulling the corrupt elections that followed. Ortiz died in office and was succeeded by Vice-President

lege and rose through the ranks as a career officer. While stationed in Italy in 1939 as a military observer, he was impressed by the nationalism of the fascists. He also thought the state's intervention in Italy's economy to be logical. On his return to Argentina, Perón involved himself deeply in the secret military organization, the GOU (*Grupo Obra de Unificación* or Unification Task Force), which was composed of young agitators bent on remodeling Argentina's political system along the lines of those in Germany and Italy.

The GOU overthrew Castillo on June 4, 1943. Perón was given the post of Secretary of the Labor and Social Welfare Ministry from which he was to build his power base. His labor reforms – job security, child labor laws, and pensions among them – were immensely popular with the working class. Furthermore, Perón tied union and non-union members together through the national welfare system, a move that assured him control over and allegiance from most workers.

The military became uneasy with Perón's growing power and arrested him. This led to a series of demonstrations, capped by a gigantic display in the Plaza de Mayo by the *descamisados* ("the shirtless ones"). Perón's consort, Eva Duarte, and labor leaders were behind these actions, rallying support for the imprisoned Perón. Within weeks he was free. He would soon marry Eva to legitimize their relationship in the eyes of the voters and the church. Perón sensed correctly that his moment on the national stage had arrived. In the presidential elections of 1946, Perón won with a majority of 54 percent. The clumsy US intervention in these elections, operating through its ambassador to Buenos Aires, ironically contributed to electing the man described by Washington as a "fascist."

In the years immediately following World War II, Argentina was wealthy and seemed to be a nation on the move. The country possessed a healthy surplus in its treasury, workers' salaries increased, and industrialization proceeded apace. Although storm clouds were gathering on the economic horizon, nobody seemed to notice: this was a golden age when every family could eat steak twice a day, and Perón was re-elected in 1951 with a massive 67 percent majority.

Severe droughts and a decrease in international prices of grain led to a 50 percent increase in Argentina's trade deficit. Eva Perón's death shortly after her husband's second inauguration left him without one of his most successful organizers and contributed to the malaise of the nation. Perón seemed to lose his willpower and left many decisions to his increasingly radical acolytes. Also, his affair with a 13-year-old did not sit well with more traditional Argentines.

Middle-class revolt

A triumvirate of middle-class forces gathered to push Perón from office in 1955. Students resented the total Peronist control over their institutions, and the church hierarchy felt threatened by Perón's secular views regarding education, divorce, and prostitution. The armed forces, having been removed from the center of attention, were convinced that they would see their power diminished. A church-sponsored demonstration drew 100,000 to the center of Buenos Aires, and was soon followed by the rebellious airforce's bombing of the Casa Rosada and the Plaza de Mayo. The army struck back against the dissident airforce while Peronist mobs burned churches.

Events were rolling out of control as the navy then rebelled, joined by some army units in the

interior. Perón spared his country enormous bloodshed by not making good his promise to arm the workers and instead fleeing to Paraguay.

Economically, Peronism left a contradictory heritage that was only dismantled under President Menem in the 1990s. Under strong protection from imports, local manufacturing grew but remained inefficient, costly, uncompetitive, and unable to provide sustained growth. At the same time, continued dependence on imported raw materials and capital goods, vulnerability to agricultural price cycles, and the burden of a state sector which was designed to provide high levels of employment and social welfare led to a series of balance of payment crises, beginning in the

LEFT: the revolution of September 6, 1930, in which General Uríburu ousted President Hipólito Yrigoyen.
RIGHT: President Onganía (left) and General Lanusse.

late 1950s. The interregnum that followed, before Perón's triumphant return, lasted 18 years.

During this period, Argentina would suffer nine leaders, none of whom succeeded in taming the economic demons that tormented the country's health.

Leaders come and go

It would be difficult to describe these years in a positive light. The military constantly meddled in politics, overthrowing presidents and installing generals when it was felt that politicians were not guiding the country correctly.

Perón's influence continued to be felt although

he was in exile. No group, not the military nor the other political parties such as the UCRP (People's Radical Civic Union) and the UCRI (Intransigent Radical Civic Union), could totally ignore the strongman or his workers' party.

Arturo Frondizi was the first president to be freely elected after Perón, in February 1958, and his tenure was marked by a state of siege, an economic downturn, and some 35 coup attempts.

What brought Frondizi down was his decision to allow Peronists to participate in the congressional elections of 1962. Frondizi's attempts to accommodate the Peronists disturbed the Argentine military; they ordered him to annul the election results and when he

refused to declare all Peronist wins illegal, the army stepped in.

Arturo Illia did not fare much better when he won the presidential elections in 1963. Although the economy was stronger than under Frondizi's administration, inflation remained oppressively high. Illia's minority government stood little chance of survival; the military was apprehensive over the president's inability to hold back the increasingly popular Peronist party, then called the Popular Union.

The next in line to try his hand at governing Argentina was General Juan Carlos Onganía, leader of the 1966 coup against Illia. Onganía ushered in a repressive era: political parties were banned; Congress was dissolved; and demonstrations were outlawed. The economy reached new lows. Foreign ownership hit 59 percent in 1969, as workers' income slumped.

The *Cordobazo* (Córdoba coup) of 1969 precipitated Onganía's departure from government. Argentina's second-largest city was the focus of anti-government activity among a new alliance of students, workers, and businessmen, all of whom had been badly hurt by Onganía's policies. Córdoba became a war zone, as soldiers battled with demonstrators. Over 100 were killed or wounded in the street-fighting.

Onganía was ousted by General Lanusse and other military representatives. An obscure general assumed the presidency, lasting only nine months in office before Lanusse himself took charge and prepared the nation for a return to civilian elections, which were to be held in 1973.

Continued repression by the military spawned a number of guerrilla groups in Argentina, chief among them the Montoneros and the People's Revolutionary Army (ERP). Torture and murder by Lanusse led to a new cycle of violence in which both sides were engaged. More than 2,000 political prisoners languished in jail, reflecting the broad subversion laws Lanusse decreed.

In this climate, the presidential election of 1973 took place. Perón chose Héctor Cámpora to run as his proxy as the head of the Peronist Justicialist Party. On a platform of national reconstruction, Cámpora won just less than half the vote. It was time for Perón to end his exile.

Round two for Perón

Perón's return to Argentina did not have auspicious beginnings. Two million were on hand at the international airport to greet the aging man they thought could restore order to the economy and dignity to the working classes. Riots among different groups of demonstrators and security police at the airport turned into pitched battles that left hundreds dead.

Cámpora resigned from office and in the new presidential elections Perón won with ease. Following past form, his wife, Isabel, was given political power, as vice-president. Perón's initial efforts at reconciliation appeared to work but again the economy began to unravel and with it the unity that Perón had achieved.

The sudden death of Juan Domingo Perón on July 1, 1974 brought Isabel to the supreme

Reportedly, under Lopéz Rega's influence, Isabel even took to employing astrological divination as a means to determine national policy.

Isabel Perón's inability to come to grips with Argentina's chronic economic problems, and her failure to curb rising terrorism, led the military to intervene yet again. In a move that was widely expected and hoped for, they removed the last Perón from the Casa Rosada on March 24, 1976.

The Proceso

Although the military had never proved itself any more able to solve the nation's problems, there seemed to be a different attitude with

position in the land, but her administration was an unmitigated disaster. She was no Evita and she had little to offer Argentina except her husband's name. Her government was marked by ultra-conservatism, corruption, and repression.

Additionally, Isabel came to rely for advice on one of Argentina's most bizarre and sinister figures, the ex-police corporal José López Rega. This Rasputin-like character wielded great power and founded the infamous right-wing terrorist group, the Alianza Argentina Anticomunista.

LEFT: Perón's third wife, Isabel.
ABOVE: the Mothers of the Plaza de Mayo demonstrating over the "dirty war" of the 1970s.

PERÓN STILL AT LARGE

Although Juan Domingo Perón served as president for only 11 years, his shadow remains over Argentina. Even since his death in 1974, the man and his ideology have remained strongly influential. He elicits the most powerful and polarized of responses from the citizenry: complete adoration or utter revulsion. In his name, governments have fallen, terrorist acts have been committed, and workers organized. His greatest achievement was to harness the energy of the Argentine laborer. Through the workers Perón established a political party that is still a force to be reckoned with, and which abandoned its pro-labor stance only recently.

this band of uniformed men steering the nation. Each of the four successive juntas made a point of co-ordinating efforts among the various branches of the armed forces. The first junta tried to lend legitimacy to its leadership by amending the constitution. This amendment, the Statute for the National Reorganization Process, called for the junta to shoulder responsibility of executive and legislative functions of the state. The period of military rule from 1977–83 has come to be known as the *Proceso*.

General Videla was chosen as the first president and he attacked the problem of left-

wing guerrilla action through a campaign dubbed the "dirty war". The military had set about "cleansing" Argentine society of any left-wing influence, whether real or imagined, by eliminating union leaders, intellectuals, and student radicals – even executing a group of high school students who had staged a protest against rising bus fares. The whole campaign was conducted secretly, abductions often occurring at night. It was in this "dirty war" that the military lost all claims to represent the civilized and often touted European standard of conduct which Argentines believe they uphold.

Attempts by university professors and students to gain greater control over their institutions were regarded as subversive, and so the universities were gutted. The heavy hand of censorship of the media also fell across the country.

International condemnation, the pleas of human rights groups, and the efforts of the mothers of the disappeared – the *Madres de la Plaza de Mayo* who have marched every Thursday since the late 1970s *(see page 153)* – did not alleviate state-sponsored terrorism.

Videla was succeeded by General Viola who was then forced from office and replaced by General Galtieri. In economic matters, the military fared no better than it had in politics. The foreign debt soared to $45 billion while the inflation rate went from bad to worse, unemployment increased, and the peso was constantly devalued. It was in this climate that General Galtieri and his junta chose to try something new.

The Malvinas conflict

It was ironic that the Argentine military, having won its dirty war against its own people, was forced from power, through waging – and losing – a conventional conflict. Galtieri hoped to divert public attention from the growing domestic crisis through the traditional method of turning their eyes to foreign matters, in this case the British-occupied Malvinas (Falkland) Islands.

The ensuing South Atlantic War was brief but bloody, beginning on April 2, 1982 with the Argentine invasion of the islands and ending with their surrender at Port Stanley on June 14.

The disputed archipelago appeared the perfect target for Galtieri: the tiny and sparsely populated islands lay more than 13,000 km (8,000 miles) from Great Britain. However, Galtieri and the other military commanders did not consider the possibility that Britain would

THE DISAPPEARED

It was while General Videla held office that the majority of the *desaparecidos* (disappeared) vanished. Anyone who was suspected of anti-government activity, as broadly defined by the military, could be made to disappear.

Nuns, priests, schoolchildren, and whole families were kidnapped, raped, tortured, and then murdered by a nefarious coalition of the military, police, and right-wing death squads acting in the dubious name of Christianity and democracy. Estimates of the numbers of *desaparecidos* range from 10,000 to 40,000 people, of whom only the tiniest fraction had actually been involved in any kind of real terrorist activities.

actually fight to retain its claims to the islands.

This major miscalculation was one of many that the Argentine junta was to make during the following weeks. Technically, tactically and politically, Argentina's rulers blundered badly. The conscripted army was ill-prepared for battle against trained professionals and did not put up much of a fight, while the navy stayed in port after a British submarine sank the cruiser *General Belgrano* on May 2. Only the heroic efforts of the Argentine air force salvaged some military honor for the country.

Although, initially, most Argentines were enthusiastic in their support of the military's

the rate rocketed to 433 percent in 1983. Additionally, the junta was under increased pressure to lift the siege on democracy and hold elections for a civilian government; massive demonstrations at the Plaza de Mayo helped to force the government to honor its promises.

End of military power

The military, knowing its days in power were numbered, sought to protect itself from anticipated criminal prosecution for human rights abuses by issuing its own study, *The Final Document of the Military Junta on the War Against Subversion and Terrorism.* This white

adventurism, their euphoria soon collapsed. The people began to realize that their government had consistently fabricated stories of success in the field and that rather than having achieved a glorious repossession of islands, which all Argentines feel are theirs, the country was made to suffer a humiliating blow.

General Galtieri resigned three days after the Argentine surrender and was replaced a week later by the retired general, Reynaldo Bignone. Bignone's attempts to curb inflation failed as

LEFT: a pro-democracy rally of the 1980s.
ABOVE: the Mothers of the Plaza de Mayo campaigning for their "disappeared" loved ones.

paper praised the efforts of the armed forces in combating and defeating terrorism and denied any involvement by the administration in the barbaric actions undertaken during the "dirty war". As an extra protection, the government proclaimed a general amnesty for all those involved in the "extralegal" efforts to crush the opposition.

The election campaign of 1983 was full of surprises. Many analysts expected a Peronist return to power or possibly a coalition government. A majority of voters, however, selected Raúl Alfonsín and his Radical Party to lead the nation out of repression. Alfonsín was sworn in as president on December 10, one day after the military junta dissolved itself. ❑

Evita

Although María Eva Duarte de Perón, known throughout the world as Evita, lived in the limelight only briefly, her impact on Argentine politics was enormous and continues today, more than five decades after her death. Her memory is zealously protected. The 1996 film of the stage musical *Evita*, starring Madonna, provoked outrage among many Argentinians, who felt the sacrilegious popstar was sullying the name of their heroine.

Evita was venerated by the Argentine working class, mocked by the *grandes dames* of Buenos

Aires society, and misunderstood by the military establishment. Through all of this, she came to symbolize a wealthy Argentina, full of pride and with great expectations following World War II.

Her meteoric rise from her beginnings as a poor villager in the backwaters of the interior to a status as one of the most intriguing, engaging, and powerful figures in a male-dominated culture is a tale worth retelling because it is so extraordinary.

Evita was born in the squalid village of Los Toldos in 1919, one of five illegitimate children her mother bore to Juan Duarte. After her father's death, the family moved to the northwestern provincial town of Junín, under the patronage of another of her mother's benefactors.

It was in Junín that Evita, at the age of 14, became determined to be an actress. In the company of a young tango singer, she ran off to Buenos Aires, the cultural mecca of Latin America, where she faced almost insurmountable odds in landing jobs in the theater. Her opportunities took a dramatic leap forward when a rich manufacturer fell for her and provided her with her own radio show. Shortly thereafter, Evita's voice became a regular feature on the airwaves of Radio Argentina and Radio El Mundo.

Evita's energy was boundless; her work pace became frenetic and she made powerful friends. Her lack of acting talent and sophistication did not seem to hinder her ability to attract important people to her cause. Among her admirers were the president of Argentina and, more importantly, the Minister of Communications, Colonel Imbert, who controlled all radio stations in the country.

Evita met Colonel Juan Domingo Perón, the reputed power behind the new military government, at a fund-raising event for victims of the devastating 1944 San Juan earthquake. She left the event on the widowed colonel's arm.

Despite being exactly half Perón's 48 years, Evita assisted his rise to power in ways that were beyond the imagination of even the most astute politicians. When Perón became Minister of Labor and Welfare, Evita convinced him that his real power base should be the previously ignored masses of laborers living in the horrible *villas miserias* (slums) that still ring the capital city.

A stream of pronouncements issued forth from the ministry instituting minimum wages, better living conditions, salary increases, and protection from employers. The working class, for the first time, began to see some of the profits of its labor. Additionally, and most brilliantly, Perón won the support of the giant Confederación General del Trabajo (CGT or General Confederation of Labor), which embraced many of the trade unions. In the process, however, recalcitrant labor leaders were picked up by the police and sent to prisons in Patagonia.

It was not long before Evita called Perón's constituency to his aid. An army coup was on the point of success when Evita called in all her chips. Upwards of 200,000 *descamisados* – the shirtless ones – entered the capital city and demanded that Perón be their president. The colonel accepted the mandate of the Argentine people.

Evita, now married to Perón, cemented her ties with the workers by establishing the Social Aid Foundation. Through this charity, scores of hospitals and hundreds of schools were built, nurses trained, and money dispensed to the poor. Evita also formed the first women's political party, the Perónista Feminist Party.

Although a cult was developing around her personality, she always told the people in her countless speeches that all credit should go to her husband and that she would gladly sacrifice her life for him, as they should sacrifice theirs. Perhaps Evita's finest hour came with her long tour of Europe, during which she met Franco, the dictator of Spain, Pope Pius XII, and the Italian and French foreign ministers. She dazzled postwar Europe with her jewels and elegant gowns. Her rags-to-riches story

work schedule. During her last speech, on May Day, her husband had to hold her up as she spoke to the *descamisados*. Evita's death on July 26, 1952 brought the whole of Argentina to a standstill. Her body was embalmed, and at her wake thousands paid their last respects.

Death brought no respite however, and in 1955, Evita's corpse disappeared, stolen by the military after they had deposed Juan Perón. It was carried to Germany and then Italy, where it was interred for 16 years under another name. After negotiations, it was returned to her husband in Spain. Evita's long odyssey came to an end when Juan Perón died in Argentina in 1974. Her coffin was brought from

was told and retold in the press, and she was even on the cover of *Time* magazine.

On the negative side, Evita would brook no criticism of her husband. Newspapers were closed, careers destroyed, and opponents jailed on trumped-up charges. She could be extremely vindictive, never forgetting an insult, even if it lay years in the past. Family and friends were placed in positions well above their levels of competence.

The people's heroine was dying by 1952, a victim of uterine cancer, but she kept up her intense

LEFT: Evita at her dazzling peak
ABOVE: a personal portrait of the Peróns with their pet poodles.

Spain and lay in state next to that of the one she had said she would die for.

Even though efforts to have her canonized in Rome have been met with polite refusal, Evita still holds near-saint status in Argentina. Graffiti proclaiming *¡Evita Vive!* (Evita lives!) can be seen everywhere. At the Duarte family crypt in the Recoleta Cemetery of Buenos Aires *(see page 177),* devotees still leave flowers and written tributes.

Her epitaph, famously paraphrased in the Andrew Lloyd Webber–Tim Rice rock opera *Evita* and in Alan Parker's subsequent film of the musical, reads: "Don't cry for me Argentina, I remain quite near to you." It still rings true, several decades after her premature death. ❑

THE MODERN DEMOCRACY

As Argentina fervently embraced free-market capitalism, inflation was defeated and the future seemed bright. Then everything went horribly wrong

For many Argentines, the collapse of the military government in 1983 marked the end of a cycle of armed forces interference in political life which had begun in 1930. There was great enthusiasm for civilian rule, which brought new freedom in the press, in literature, and in general discussions. Many thousands of Argentines who had fled military rule to live in exile returned, helping to add to the sense of a fresh start in political and social life.

This was combined with an attempt to explain and come to terms with what had happened during the military dictatorship. In 1987 the Radical Party and its president, Raul Alfonsin, set up a commission to report on the political violence and its victims. The result was *Nunca Mas* (Never Again) which detailed how the military dictatorship had kidnapped, tortured, and killed at least 9,000 Argentines whom they had regarded as "subversive." The evidence gathered helped lead to the public trial of the leaders of the military juntas, and the historic decision to condemn five of them to imprisonment for crimes against humanity.

The civilian government's determination to prosecute the military leaders caused great unease among the armed forces. There were several military uprisings against Alfonsin, which were put down only thanks to popular support for him, and the oyalty of the new military commanders. In response to this pressure, President Alfonsin brought in two laws, one which limited responsibility for the "disappeared" to the military high command, and the other which declared the time for prosecutions for human rights abuses to have a definite end.

Inflation and debt

Another legacy from the military dictatorship which President Alfonsin found hard to cope with was its economic mismanagement. The

juntas had borrowed money internationally to fund huge projects and to balance their budgets. Now inflation and debt, combined with the Radical Party's lack of experience in government, undermined President Alfonsin's popularity. To try to remedy matters, a new currency, the *austral*, was introduced, but within months infla-

tion of several hundred percent wiped out many people's savings, and restricted the government's ability to plan coherently.

This was the situation in 1989, when Argentines were called on to vote for a second time in their newly restored democracy. By now, many of the voters thought that the Radical Party had failed in their attempt to bring prosperity and good government to Argentina. So they turned once more to the Peronists, and voted for Carlos Saul Menem. The flamboyant Mr. Menem was the governor of a small interior province, who had been imprisoned by the military dictatorship, and seemed to represent traditional Peronist economic and social values: support

---

PRECEDING PAGES: a political meeting outside Buenos Aires' Cathedral in the historic Plaza de Mayo.
LEFT: Congreso Nacional, the political think-tank.
RIGHT: Peronist demonstrators, drumming up support.

for working people and national industry, and an "anti-imperialist" stance in foreign affairs.

The end of the Alfonsin administration was a sorry affair. During the period between Mr. Menem's election and the official handover, the Argentine economy collapsed to such an extent that there were serious outbreaks of social unrest.

It soon became clear that Menemism was very different from traditional Peronism. From the start of his administration, Menem followed the recipes for success suggested by the International Monetary Fund. He began to sell off much of Argentine industry, from the nationalized oil concern, to the telephones and the railways. He

United Kingdom – although the question of sovereignty over the Falkland Islands remained unresolved. Argentina left the non-aligned movement, and declared that its interests were the same as those of the developed Western world. At the same time, the president declared an amnesty for the military personnel and the guerrillas who had been involved in the political violence of the 1970s, thus attempting to draw a line on this tragic episode in the country's history.

The early 1990s were boom years for Argentina. Buenos Aires once again rivalled the cities of Europe and North America not only for the choice of goods in the huge new shopping

removed all tariff protection for Argentine industry, allowing cheaper foreign imports to start to flood Argentina. But his boldest and most controversial move was to pass a law which put the Argentine peso on a par with the US dollar. This was intended to solve all of Argentina's chronic inflation problems. The value of the Argentine currency was guaranteed by government reserves, which were boosted by strong exports and the revenues from privatization.

Prosperous interlude

President Menem attempted to change Argentina's relations with the rest of the world. Great efforts were made to heal the rift with the

malls, and its glitzy restaurants and elegant cafés but also in the quality and range of its films, plays and books. Many of the middle class looked down on President Menem, with his love of fast cars and his taste for the celebrity lifestyle (memorably characterized as "pizza with champagne") but they enjoyed being consumers of the newly available goods, they traveled abroad again, and for the first time in many years rediscovered a pride in being Argentine.

This sense of satisfaction helped Menem easily to win a second period in office in 1995. But problems soon began to mount. The fact that the Argentine peso was the same value as the US dollar made the country's exports over-priced compared to that of its regional rivals. The imported goods that middle-class Argentines enjoyed so much were also very costly, making it hard for the government to balance the books. Many thousands of Argentines had been put out of work by the sell-off of state concerns, and could find no other employment. All this put a great strain on social security and pension provisions, which also made it hard for the central government to achieve stability.

> **CHANGE OF FACE**
>
> Soon after his election as president, Menem's picturesque long hair and sideburns were shortened to acceptable First World lengths and his Third World *ponchos* were left for special visits to the interior.

tization had ended up in the politicians' pockets.

The discontent led to the creation of an anti-Peronist alliance of parties, inlcuding the Radical Party and the FREPASO (Front for a Country of Solidarity). This alliance was triumphant in the 1999 presidential elections, while the Peronists were divided in internal wrangling between supporters of President Menem and the candidate who eventually stood, Eduardo Duhalde, governor of the province of Buenos Aires.

The new president was Fernando De la Rua,

Scandals and discontent

There was an increasing feeling that the Menem administration was mired in corruption. The press began to reveal all kinds of scandals, from the discovery that one of the congressmen voting for the government was a distant relative of the elected representative, brought in to support the Peronists, to accusations that the president and other high-ranking officials had been involved in multi-million dollar illegal arms sales. A lot of the money earned through priva-

LEFT: President Nestor Kirchner with wife Cristina – a federal senator.
ABOVE: a spirited display of support by *Menemistas*.

and once again there was optimism that things might change. In the event, Mr. De la Rua and his allies failed to grasp the opportunity. His biggest mistake was to continue with the policy of parity between the Argentine peso and the US dollar. He also failed to create new employment opportunities, while Argentina increasingly struggled to keep up with its debt repayments.

Calamity

The crisis came to a head in December 2001. Exasperated unemployed workers and government employees who had not been paid in many months, joined with Peronist trade unionists in violent street protests. As many as 30 people are thought to have died in the demonstrations, and the situation was so unstable that President De la Rua resigned, fleeing the presidential palace in a helicopter to avoid the angry crowds.

At the end of 2001, Argentina had four presidents in two weeks. Eventually it was the head of Congress, Eduardo Duhalde, who was appointed interim president and had sufficient authority to calm the situation. His government declared it would not meet the payments due on foreign debt, and to try to re-activate exports and reduce debts, he ended the peso-dollar parity. This led to a huge devaluation, with the peso soon having only one third of its previous international value.

Controversially, to avoid the complete collapse of the economy, the government froze all the dollar deposits that Argentines had in their local banks, and the middle classes joined the demonstrations.

The emergency measures brought some financial stability but did not solve the underlying problems. The years of unemployment and under-investment had led to unprecedented poverty and economic hardship and Argentines were shocked to see pictures of children dying of malnutrition. Many turned against all politicians: "Que se vayan todos" (Get rid of them all) was the rallying cry at the continuing street protests.

Many ordinary Argentines began looking for alternatives to the corrupt rule by career politicians. There was a huge growth in popular assemblies – local residents getting together in parks or street corners to press for solutions to their problems. Dozens of the factories that had been forced to close were re-opened as co-operatives by workers who had been laid off. Because of the lack of cash, centers for bartering goods instead of buying them mushroomed.

After many delays, it was decided to hold new presidential elections in April 2003, with a second round of voting if necessary in mid-May. Despite the effervescence of new political ideas at street-level, the choice for the Argentine voters was much the same as before.

The Peronists were so divided that they could not agree on a single candidate, so that three men who claimed to represent the movement stood separately. Such was the disgust with Mr. De La Rua that the official Radical Party stood little chance, while several independent candidates lacked the resources to pose any real challenge. In the end, the contest in April 2003 was between former president Carlos Menem, who was seeking a third term in office, and the governor of the remote Patagonian province of Santa Cruz, Nestor Kirchner.

In the first round, Menem won the most votes, with his promise of a return to the "golden days" of his earlier presidencies. He was followed by Mr. Kirchner, which meant that the two men had to face each other in a runoff vote. In the event, Menem realized that his percentage of the vote was not going to increase sufficiently to give him any chance of winning; he pulled out of the second round, leaving Kirchner as president-elect, although he had only polled a little over 20 percent of the total vote in the first round.

Rebuilding confidence

Nestor Kirchner was sworn into office on 25 May 2003. He faces a daunting challenge in restoring Argentina's economic fortunes and trying to reduce the poverty now affecting almost half of all Argentines. But perhaps his biggest challenge is to restore the country's belief that after 20 years of civilian rule, democracy means something more than voting for politicians from the same old parties which few Argentines trust or respect. ❑

LEFT: bleak news from the currency exchange market.
RIGHT: brightening up a quiet corner of Buenos Aires.

A PEOPLE OF PASSION

The country's large and varied immigrant populations
make for a colorful and disparate national identity and cultural life

Visit Bariloche in July and the Fiesta de las Colectividades ("Community Festival") will give you a taste of the different immigrant groups that make up Argentina. Spaniards, Italians, Germans, Swiss, Russians, Austrians, Slovaks, Danes, and Norwegians are there, amongst others, taking out and dusting off an often dormant sense of national identity, keeping alive the dance and song of a former life and entering a bustling mêlée around colorful stalls that sell typical food from pizzas to blinis. It's a vibrant celebration, with a characteristic indifference to time. And it's a curious revelation when friends who are indubitably Argentine unearth their cultural roots.

The original inhabitants of Argentina were divided into many distinct tribes, but their numbers were few. The first European settlers, in the 16th century, were almost all Spanish, as were those arriving over the next 300 years. A minority population of *mestizos* (mixed Amerindian and Hispanic stock) developed early. A large number of enslaved Africans were brought in during the 17th and 18th centuries, and *mulatos* (mixed black and Hispanic stock) and Amerindian/black Afro-American were added.

Yet the 19th century saw severe changes in this ethnic make-up of Argentina. Through a concerted effort, the vast majority of the Amerindian population was wiped out by the Argentine army. They freed the land for European settlers, though some say Patagonia is cursed because of the brutal manner of its liberation. After the abolition of slavery, the black population also faded from view *(see page 41).*

A new frontier

At the end of the 19th century and turn of the 20th century, there was another wave of immigration across the Atlantic from Europe.

Between 1857 and 1939, more than 3½ million laborers were added to the population. The majority by far were from just two countries: Spain and Italy. But many fled here from other parts of war-torn Europe too. And not only Europe. A look at the list of approved names which governs what you can call your child is a

guide to the many different nationalities represented, including Syrians and Armenians – not least ex-President Carlos Menem, who is of Syrian stock. Argentina was seen as a land of opportunity. Cynics argue it still is and always will be, thanks to an indefinable yet fatal flaw which thwarts all efforts to realize that potential.

By 1914, the population of Argentina was about 30 percent foreign-born, and in some of the larger cities, the foreigners outnumbered the so-called natives. These new hands were put to work filling positions in the expanding agricultural industry, in cattle-raising and processing, and in the developing economies of the big cities.

PRECEDING PAGES: religious pilgrimage in the Northwest; Easter week procession in Jujuy province.
LEFT: lost in thought.
RIGHT: Russian immigrants in the 1930s.

Patagonia's Welsh

The Welsh, who left their native valleys to pursue such opportunity, must have had their doubts when the first arrivals in the 1860s walked for days across Patagonia's barren wastes in search of fresh water, until they reached the River Chubut.

The initial co-operation of the indigenous peoples and their own tenacity eventually yielded a string of prosperous settlements along the Chubut valley and so with legitimate pride the Welsh cling to their national identity more fiercely than most. One of these Welsh towns, Gaiman, brings over someone from Wales each year to preserve and protect the native culture, and the annual *Eisteddfod* is as much a feature of life here as in Wales itself.

More English than the English

One community which, since the 1980s at least, has kept a low profile at the Fiesta de las Colectividades is the Anglo-Argentine population. The first British settlers came to administer the building of the country's infrastructure, and their services helped to make Argentina one of the world's 10 richest countries by the beginning of the 20th century. To a large extent, it was British capital which built the Argentine railroad and banking systems in the 19th century. British money also helped develop the cattle industry, with modern methods of refrigeration, packaging, and transportation. Some Englishmen bought huge tracts of land in the south to raise sheep and, for a time, southern Patagonia seemed an extension of the British empire.

The 1982 war over the Malvinas (Falkland) Islands was inevitably a tense time for Anglo-Argentines. Some left, but for most loyalty to Argentina triumphed. Argentines remain convinced of the legitimacy of their claim to the islands: even in the most remote and unlikely places stand large signs proclaiming "*Las Malvinas son Argentinas.*"

Yet, for the most part, they are too aware of the generals' dubious motives in invading the islands, and too glad of the demise of military rule that the defeat brought about, to harbor any lingering animosity *(see page 53)*. Meanwhile, as with many immigrants, the Anglo-Argentines' recollections of home are frozen in the past. There is a slightly archaic refinement, a quaint trust in "things British" which would, no doubt, be jolted by a brush with today's multicultural Britain.

British schools such as St. Andrew's and St. George's continue to thrive in Argentina, as does the British hospital. Polo and cricket continue to be played at weekends on the manicured lawns of the exclusive Hurlingham club outside Buenos Aires. Rugby and football are other British imports, as evidenced by the English names of many of the leading soccer clubs – River Plate and Racing, for example.

The British heritage, however, is fading as new generations feel that American Business

NATIVE SURVIVORS

Argentina has a huge immigrant population, each one maintaining parts of its culture. Indigenous populations survive in pockets, and while some native languages continue and traditional crafts enjoy a revival of interest, few tribes practice traditional lifestyles in more than a ceremonial sense. Quechua is still spoken in the Northwest, where the Colla are the largest group. Chiriguan, Choroti, Wichi, Mocovi, and Toba are spoken in the Chaco; the Chiriguan are the principal tribe of Mesopotamia. The Araucano-Mapuches and the Tehuelche were the major groups in Patagonia and the pampas, but very, if any few pure-blooded descendants survive today.

English is more useful than the Queen's English, and pervasive cable TV reinforces the point. The trend now is to send children to US colleges rather than to more traditional English boarding schools.

Economic migrants

The presence of Chileans, Bolivians, and Peruvians reflects the oscillating economic fortunes of Argentina and its neighbors.

The Argentines' relationship with Chile is a somewhat uncomfortable one. In January 1982, the two countries teetered on the brink of war, in a long-standing territorial dispute over

The national identity

The Argentine nature is a bundle of paradoxes which resists stereotyping. All too common is the picture of an angst-ridden people in search of a national identity. This does no justice to the vibrancy and color of Argentine society, the kaleidoscope of animated and opinionated personalities, a tendency toward extremes, a curious coexistence of vigor and indolence.

For a start, there is the contrast between urban and rural life, all the more sharply drawn in a nation where suburbia scarcely exists. Of a total population of 37 million, some 11 million live in Buenos Aires.

islands in the Beagle Channel. The proposed conflict was averted only through the intervention of the Pope. Many Chileans have spilled over the Andes in search of work, although the Argentine economic crisis has reversed this trend. While free-spirited Argentines tend to mock their rather earnest neighbors, there is a wistful envy of the benefits that Chile's more liberal economic policy has brought. Despite the disparaging remarks, Argentines are all too ready to sample the bargains over the border.

The *porteño*, as the resident of Buenos Aires is known, thrives on the pace and bustle of life in the capital. Walk along Florida, Buenos Aires' busiest shopping street, and the sleek sophistication is palpable, further accentuated by the inherent stylishness of the people. Fashion icons may sneer at the dilatory response of taste here, but the Argentines don't need anyone to tell them how to look good, and sleek shopping malls continue to open in the capital.

Outside the capital, dress is generally more relaxed, though stylish nonetheless. Designer jeans are more commonplace than suits. Ties for men are not *de rigueur*.

LEFT:. Araucanian woman. **ABOVE:** ephemeral masterpiece on a San Telmo sidewalk.

City talk

In the coffee houses of Buenos Aires one thing is clear. The Argentines love to talk. People are articulate and lucid, confident in expressing their opinions. All matters, small or large, are worthy of a comment. The most routine of meetings can erupt in animated discussion. Teenagers are rarely reticent. The problem is not getting people to talk, but rather to listen, with a rich and expressive vocabulary of gestures jostling with words for attention.

> ### LED BY THE STARS
>
> The increasing number of foreign stars such as Sylvester Stallone and Jane Fonda who have bought land in Patagonia has given locals a renewed interest in their land.

Soccer and politics are among the topics most likely to ignite conversation. Soccer is the big national sport, and team allegiances are strong. At a fairly early age most Argentines decide where those allegiances lie.

The political renaissance of the Alfonsín years, immediately following military rule, gradually slipped into disenchantment with politics and politicians during the Menem years. Menem's major achievement was reining in hyperinflation, and maintaining parity between the US dollar and the peso, albeit at a cost of severe recession – the economy shrank by 4.4 percent back in 1995. However, he betrayed the Peronist ticket on which he was elected by privatizing state-owned companies shortly after he came to power, and did nothing to challenge the corruption which dogs the country's political and judicial systems, not to mention business. The economic crisis and rampant corruption which his successors have failed to resolve have further undermined faith in the political system, and political parties and disillusionment is widespread.

"In the camp"

Out on the *estancias*, or "in the camp" as the Anglo-Argentines say, it's a different story. The archetypal male is taciturn, especially in mixed company. He will still hold firm his opinions, often tinged with a wry melancholy, but he will waste fewer words on them.

Here the forum for discussion is not the coffee house but a *mate (see page 92)*. The thirst-quenching qualities of this home-brewed tea are of secondary importance to its social role. Passing the *mate* around is a decorous ritual. Traditionally the water is heated in a crude tin or kettle over an open fire, brewed in a small gourd, and sipped through a perforated metal straw called a *bombilla*. It's a convivial part of life, and not only in the camp.

So too is the *asado* (barbecue), where Argentines indulge their passion for meat to the full. Barbecues are usually communal affairs where everyone will be expected to put away about half a kilo (one pound) of meat. Salads are served nowadays as a concession to health fads, but real men stick to meat and dry bread washed down by beer and then a *mate*.

It's a way of life which exercises an inimitable appeal. Some young professionals abandon the city's stresses for the quieter life of the smaller towns in the south.

Chivalry and chauvinism

Nowhere more than at an *asado* is Argentine conservatism and chauvinism apparent. Preparing the *asado* is a male preserve involving a certain way of positioning and timing of the meat to ensure it is cooked to perfection. Men stand around the fire cutting hunks of meat from the carcass with showy *asado* knives, while women sit at a rustic table and chat together. When all have eaten their fill the men continue their discussions over a *mate*, while the women depart to wash the dishes.

Nonetheless, Argentine family life has undergone a striking metamorphosis. Women now comprise nearly half of the workforce; 40 percent of Argentine households are supported by female breadwinners; and 50 percent of students at university are women. Argentina was the first country in Latin America to introduce quotas for women in elective congressional posts. As a result, women now hold 25 percent of seats compared to 6 percent in 1991, and Brazil, Bolivia, Venezuela, Peru, and Ecuador have followed this radical lead. While the statistics demonstrate that there are changes, certain attitudes die hard.

KISS ON THE CHEEK

In familial, social, and even formal situations there is rarely any agonized uncertainty about the right greeting. People just kiss.

The extended family

Yet although old-fashioned chauvinism and its counterpart chivalry still exist, the overwhelming flavor of society, especially among the young, is of freedom and informality. This is in part a reaction, some say, to the years of military repression. Its also a reflection of the strength of the extended family.

Young people usually live at home until they get married, and even then may only move a few blocks away. Students do not often move out when they enter university, as they frequently attend schools in their home towns. The generation gap is far less apparent than in some countries. Young and old are used to each other's company, sharing news and ideas comfortably in contexts like family *asados*. Cousins are often best friends. The cool and studied indifference of adolescence exists, of course. But the overall impression is of people visibly enjoying life.

When a child reaches school-leaving age, most parents will put considerable effort into planning and preparing the class celebration. It's a milestone, a shared occasion among families and classmates, and just one telling demonstration of how much the Argentines know about the art of celebration. Nightlife, for example, is vigorous. Many discotheques don't even get going until the early hours, and the music doesn't finish until daybreak.

Group mentality

Among young people, there is a keen sense of the individual, and yet there is also a very strong feeling of group identity. Children will pass through school with virtually the same classmates throughout. Usually all will share their birthday celebrations together. All will take part in a week-long school trip to mark the end of their primary and secondary schooling and, by the time they emerge, the common bond of shared experience is enough to cement relationships for a lifetime. Besides,

the Argentines are by nature gregarious. Find an idyllic quiet picnic spot and, if a car should happen to pass, the occupants are as likely to join you as search for their own patch of solitude. Or witness the streets of Bariloche or Carlos Paz, popular destinations of these *Viajes de Egresados* (school-leaving trips), when students move in packs singing and chanting, crowding into group photographs, all sporting matching hats or jackets.

Tactile behavior in Argentina is the norm. Not just a polite social peck, but touching, kissing, hugging, and linking arms, all with an easy, uninhibited warmth which no one in the country will misconstrue.

LEFT: the tradition of drinking *mate* is still kept up by the younger generation.
RIGHT: a child of the Northwest.

Taking their time

The relaxed social approach also applies to time frames. If it doesn't get done today it will surely get done tomorrow – the infamous Spanish "*mañana*". When waiting for an Argentine to keep an appointment, whether for a cup of coffee or a business meeting, allowance should be made for benign tardiness. It's a way of life. Beware of being asked to wait "*un momentito,*" literally a little moment – which might be considerably more; or of being assured that something is about to

RED TAPE MAZE

Excessive bureaucracy is a part of daily life – buying a car or obtaining a passport involves an inordinate amount of paperwork.

does the President have to be a Catholic. About 90 percent of the Argentine population is Catholic, but less than 20 percent are practicing. Strict faith no longer seems to have a firm grip on the national psyche and only periodic observances remain, like catechism and first communion.

However, it was only in 2002 that the government managed to pass a law to allow family-planning advice and free birth control. Until then the move was resisted strongly by Catholic groups in a

happen "*ya,*" or right away, which is similarly elastic. If you ask the mechanic when your car will be ready, the answer is usually "*última hora*" – closing time, whenever that might be.

This is partly due to a different work ethic. Here people are always ready to sacrifice a little efficiency for the sake of making work more enjoyable with a chat, a *mate*, and a few *facturas* (pastries).

Church and bureaucracy

The church is still a pervasive, if nominal influence. Constitutional reforms in 1994 continue to guarantee religious freedom, but Catholicism is no longer the state religion, nor

country where abortion is still illegal and an imprisonable offense.

Argentina is a country which operates on a low level of trust. It may be because a chancer *(vivo)* who gets away with something is more likely to evoke grudging admiration here than moral indignation. As a result, bureaucracy has had to build in elaborate and often cumbersome systems of verification and security to reduce the scope for dishonesty. The public sector often lacks the resources to implement modern systems and is frequently unwieldy and inefficient. Obtaining a simple document may involve trips to the bank, the post office, and the police station, all in pursuit of the appropriate array of rubber stamps and validated papers. To open a business in Argentina demands 12 separate bureaucratic procedures and takes over three months. A paper chase which would drive many other nationalities wild is met with resigned acceptance by the otherwise volatile Argentines.

More than 80 percent of Argentines do not have faith in the legal system and do not use it, according to a national newspaper survey. Corruption has always been rife in the country but has increased owing to its economic woes.

OLD WIVES' REMEDIES

Anyone suffering from a stomach complaint, *empacho*, may be cured by a deft pull of the skin covering the lower vertebrae – *tirando el cuero*. It seems to work, whatever the logic.

Health matters

Visiting the doctor also requires this patience in abundance. Even children rise to the occasion, waiting passively, with neither toys nor books to distract them. But health matters are ready fuel for conversation. People exchange news of their ailments with remarkable openness. Virtual strangers will pat a pregnant woman's stomach as they make inquiries and pass judgment on the likely sex of the impending arrival.

Sophisticated medical care is available in Buenos Aires, less so in the provinces. There is also a growing interest in alternative medicines, and many traditional remedies are held dear.

Psychology, too, is something of a national hobby. A school may not have a photocopier or even stationery, but it will certainly have an educational psychologist. The study and practice of psychology was suppressed during the years of the Proceso (military rule from 1977-83). Military authorities viewed the field as subversive, and books on the subject were removed from public and private shelves. University departments were cut or closed down.

Living with the past

Ironically, repression in the Proceso era, together with the dirty war's legacy of harrowing memories, has contributed to the resurgence of interest in psychology. While the government's policy has been to draw a line under the past and move forward, with an early amnesty for many military offenders of the period, public pressure has challenged this approach.

LEFT: a game of two generations.
RIGHT: a butcher takes a breather.

Mothers of the "disappeared" still rally in the Plaza de Mayo each Thursday. Their white headscarves are neatly embroidered in blue with the names of their lost children *(see page 153)*. Long years of faithful campaigning have met with success that at times is bitter-sweet. Grandparents have been united with grandchildren they never knew – children taken from pregnant women for adoption by childless couples in the militia while their natural mothers were then killed. Some of these children,

brought up in loving homes, have been, and are being, torn apart by the truth. Can they reject the only home they have ever known, and now accept these grandparents whom they never knew, who are often from such different backgrounds, and the other side of the political divide? For some of the grandparents, meeting with their grandchildren for the first time may be the fulfillment of a dream, but for many has become a turmoil of disappointment and despair.

Argentina is still searching for a satisfactory way to unravel the long-term consequences of the Proceso. Beneath the exuberance of Argentine society, there is still disquiet about the nation's clouded history. ❑

THE TANGO

*Out of the immigrants' melting pot that is Argentina, tango was born,
working its way out from the brothels and into the rest of society*

Argentina has, in reality, two national anthems: one is its formal ceremonial hymn, and the other, *Mi Buenos Aires Querido* (My Beloved Buenos Aires), is a tango. This, the country's most authentic form of popular music, has made Argentina famous throughout the world.

Most of the legendary clubs and music halls that gave birth to the tango exist only in lyrics and in the memories of old-timers who recall dancing its intricate steps during its pre-World War II golden era.

However, the tango is in the midst of a revival. The international success of neo-*tanguero* Astor Piazzolla, the appearance of dance classes for young and old in Buenos Aires and all over the world, as well as the launch of the International Tango Festival in Buenos Aires in 1999 are all signs that tango's special magic is being rediscovered around the globe.

But what are the origins of this sensual and melancholy music, so intimately identified with Argentina and its nerve center and capital, Buenos Aires? The story begins just as the 19th century was ending.

At this time, the whole Río de la Plata region, in Uruguay as in Argentina, began to receive great waves of European immigrants, along with thousands of returning *criollos*, the discharged veterans of the 50-year-long civil wars that followed independence from Spain. Most of these settled in and around the growing ports of Buenos Aires and Montevideo.

The mixture of Italian, Spanish, East European, and Jewish newcomers mingled with the local population, itself a combination of Hispanics, blacks, and indigenous Americans. Each of these groups had its own musical heritage.

In the rough-and-tumble world of the predominantly male immigrants, war-weary ex-soldiers, and working poor, the pulsing rhythm known as the *candombe* that arrived

with African slaves mixed with the haunting melodies of Andalusia and Southern Italy and the locally popular *milongas* (traditional *gaucho* songs). Sometime during the 1880s, all these cultural elements fused to give rise to something completely new – the tango.

Music of the night

Exactly when and exactly where is both a mystery and a hotly disputed controversy. The most important gathering place for the working classes in this period was the brothel. Located in the semi-rural areas of Buenos Aires around Retiro (now the site of the northern train terminals) and Palermo, and in the port areas of La Boca and 25 de Mayo Street, as well as around Plaza Lavalle, brothels were the epoch's cultural melting pots.

In the parlors, as customers awaited their turns, musicians played and sang suggestive and often obscene lyrics that gave the tango its early fame for ribaldry. Because of the context,

---

LEFT: bringing a touch of style to the streets.
RIGHT: a tango duo in La Boca port district.

only fragments of the earliest tango lyrics survived, and their authors remain anonymous or known only by colorful nicknames. It wasn't until 1896 that pianist Rosendo Mendizabal, put his name to *El Enterriano,* making it the first signed tango.

But the men who spent their nights listening to tangos in the brothels lived by day in the over-crowded tenements that were concentrated in the older, southern areas of Buenos Aires. Inevitably, the tango began to spill out into the patios, there

TANGO FOR TOURISTS

A number of clubs located in San Telmo feature tango music and professional dancers who provide tourists with the variety of tango flavors which made the dance a successful exotic export.

that most special of all tango instruments, the bandoneon, a close relative of the accordion.

In the 20th century's first decade, Buenos Aires, and with it the tango, underwent a transformation. The agro-export economy brought closer contacts with Europe, and wealthy Argentines, after visiting the clubs and cafés of Europe, looked for similar entertainments at home. A number of the old bawdy clubs and brothels responded to the new demand and elegant cabarets appeared.

to be played by the local organ grinders, and to become part of other popular cultural forms, such as the much-attended theatricals known as *sainetes.*

A new audience

By the turn of the 20th century, the tango had increased its audience to include all but the still disapproving upper classes.

During these early years, the configuration of a tango orchestra varied greatly. As many of the musicians were poor, they relied on whatever instruments could be hired, as they could be rented quite cheaply. Guitars, violins, flutes, and the less transportable piano were joined by

Carlos Gardel

Another source of change was the arrival of the recording industry. By 1913 a limited number of local recordings were being made, and in 1917 Victor Records captured the young voice of Carlos Gardel singing *Mi Noche Triste (My Sad Night).* It was the end of one era and the beginning of another.

Carlos Gardel became tango's first international superstar. This career shows the most important developments of the genre in its golden era. Despite the debate among aficionados, it seems likely that Gardel was born in France (Toulouse) sometime around 1891. What transformed Gardel into a star and the tango into music with a far wider appeal, were recordings, radio, and cinema. Gardel went to France in 1929 and made films at Joinville, and in 1934 he signed a contract with Paramount in Hollywood, where he made five films.

By the time of his death in a plane crash in Colombia in 1935, Gardel had become the personification of the tango. When his body was brought to Buenos Aires, thousands gathered to say goodbye to the *"pibe de Abasto"* (kid from Abasto), the neighborhood around the old

MUSIC MAKERS

Edmund Rivera, one of the great tango singers of all time, said: "When all is said and done, the tango is no more than a reflection of our daily reality."

followers suffered political defeats, but also because of the onslaught of new forms of music, mainly rock, and because the great names of tango were fading away.

Tango renaissance

Tango is now enjoying a welcome revival worldwide, partly through mixing with mainstream Latin American styles. One unusual arrangement was *Tango, Salsa y Arrabal*, produced by Colombian salsa band La Sabrosura. Twenty-five different countries participated in the Internationl Tango Fes-

Central Market. In 1984 the local subway stop was renamed in honor of Gardel.

Highs and lows

The tango's ebbs and flows in popularity were always tied to politics and the broader social condition of Argentina. In the late 1930s it dipped, only to hit a new peak under the Peronist governments of 1945 and 1955, when, with heightened nationalism and increased wages, new clubs and dance halls boomed. In the late 1950s, the tango had entered a crisis, partly because its keenest

---

LEFT: painted plaque recalls a well-known melody.
ABOVE: it takes two – and a lot of passion.

tival in Buenos Aires in 2003, when for the first time it held a dance tournament.

Neo-*tanguero* Astor Piazzolla continued to dominate the contemporary scene until his death in 1992. Several highly successful innovative musicals have been performed. *Forever Tango*, the Broadway hit of Luis Bravo, has been touring the globe since 1990, along with other shows such as *Tango Argentino* and *Tango Pasión*.

Films, such as Sally Potter's *The Tango Lesson* (1997) and Spanish director Carlos Saura's *Tango* (1998), which explored the history and evolution of the dance itself have enjoyed runaway success. The latter was nominated for an Oscar. ❏

FOOD AND WINE

Argentine cuisine may not be the world's finest, but no visitor should miss its homegrown beef, washed down with a glass of local red wine

Argentine cuisine is neither sophisticated nor elaborate; one of the surprising aspects of the food compared with that of most of South America is its blandness. To call something spicy is tantamount to calling it inedible. Argentine conservatism is entrenched in the kitchen. But here the quality of the meat is unquestionable. It may not always be tender, but it is tasty. Adornment is adulteration.

A meat-eating nation

Beef is the Argentine's pleasure and joy, and there is a fierce pride in the quality of the meat. The best way of eating out here is to go native; often there is no choice. *Parrillas* or grills are ubiquitous and opting for a *parrillada mixta* (mixed grill) is an opportunity to try out the full range of the cow's anatomy without deference to personal scruples. The meal will usually begin with *chorizo* (spicy sausage), *morcilla* (blood sausage), or an *empanada* (meat pasty), before the real meat is served.

Cuts of meat aren't always comparable with those elsewhere, but some that are well worth trying are the *bife de lomo* (fillet steak), or *bife de chorizo* (rump steak) – distinct from the spicy sausage mentioned above. For all the pride in their meat, the Argentines are not above eating offal: *riñones* (kidneys), *mollejas* (sweetbreads), *hígado* (liver), and *chinchulines* (the lower intestine, truly delicious when well crisped) are all eaten with relish.

Chicken is frequently included, but pork is rather despised. A *parrillada mixte* will usually comfortably serve two Argentines or four to five uninitiated tourists

Eating alfresco

Ideally, food in Argentina should all be tasted in context. The quintessential Argentine experience is the *asado*, or outdoor barbecue. At weekends you will see people leaving the

LEFT: fresh beef at La Cabaña, Buenos Aires.
RIGHT: a quiet neighborhood cafe in San Telmo.

butcher with enough bags of meat to serve most cholesterol-conscious adults elsewhere in the world for the best part of a month.

Salads are rudimentary, but the preparation of the meat is elevated to an art form. Cuts of meat and sausages are spread over *parrillas* the size of bed frames. Whole lambs are staked and

cooked slowly by adjusting their distance from the coals. Everyone eats their fill with appreciation and enthusiasm. *Chimichurri*, a delicious sauce of parsley, garlic, chili, and lemon, is used as a marinade and a condiment.

Filling up with snacks

An Argentine favorite is *milanesas* and fries. *Milanesas* are the same as German *wiener schnitzel*, and are a staple of Argentine cuisine; sometimes they come topped with cheese and tomatoes *(napolitana)*. The Italian influence is nowhere more apparent than in the food. Pizza and pasta of a high standard can be found everywhere and, until recently, were Argentina's only convenience food. *Empanadas* are another specialty which might fall into this category. These small pastries, which come fried or baked, are usually filled with either meat, chicken, or ham and cheese. *Humita*, a corn-based filling, is also sometimes used not just in *empanadas* but also in corn husk parcels, prepared particularly around Easter.

Polenta is commonplace in the home, usually served with *tuco* or sauce, and so too *ravioles* which are bought fresh in boxes. *Noquis* – small potato dumplings (similar to Italian *gnocchi*) – are another regular feature of the diet.

Locro is a popular cheap and cheerful stew.

The essential ingredients are butter beans, haricot beans, sweetcorn, butternut squash, and *chorizo*. Scraps of meat will be thrown in to the pot as well. It is filling and nutritious, but immensely variable in quality.

Sweet fancies

There are plenty of sweet things to offset the bitter taste of *mate*. *Dulce de leche* is at the heart of most of these. Literally "milk sweet," it is made by boiling up milk, sugar, and vanilla until it reaches a sticky caramel-like consistency. It can be eaten as a spread on bread – any supermarket will have an impres-

sive array of brands. It is also invariably the filling for cakes, and in restaurants is offered on its own as a dessert.

Another type of conserve is made from the deep purple berries yielded by the calafate bush in Patagonia. Legend has it that those who eat the calafate will return to Patagonia.

One of the simple pleasures of Argentine life are the *facturas*, which can be found in any *panadería* or bakery. These are small pastries such as *caras sucias*, literally "dirty faces," encrusted with brown sugar; *vigilantes*; or *media lunas*, which are usually sweet and rather doughy croissants. Others are topped with conserve, *dulce de leche*, chocolate, or ricotta cheese. *Facturas* are bought by the dozen and consumed as a snack at any time of the day from breakfast onwards.

Also popular to share at social gatherings are *masitas*, an infinite variety of tiny fancy confections. The bakery will make up trays of these delicacies by weight. *Churros*, Spanish-style fingers of deep-fried dough filled with *dulce de leche* and sprinkled with sugar are another delight, especially with hot chocolate. *Alfajores* are cookies filled with all manner of tasty sweet stuff and often coated in chocolate.

But the ultimate Argentine confection is *mil hojas* in which layers of fine pastry are glued together with *dulce de leche* and then smothered in meringue. Even the Argentines eat this in only small quantities

World-class wines

Argentina is the world's fourth-largest wine producer behind Italy, France, and Spain, and ahead of Germany. The country's wine, like neighboring Chile's, is a reasonably priced export. The devaluation of the peso at the end of 2001 increased its competitiveness, and it enjoyed rising international sales.

A French group invested US$50 million to build seven new vineyards in the country, a clear indication that Argentine wines are earning widespread respect. The first bottles hit the shelves in July 2003.

Almost 90 percent of Argentina's wine is produced in the Andean provinces of Mendoza and San Juan, with Río Negro, Salta, and La Rioja producing the rest. Fine wines represent less than 10 percent of production, with jug (table) wine, regional wine, and a few special wines such as sherries, ports, and vermouths making up the larger balance.

Although domestic consumption has declined in recent years, it is still high. Wine has been made in Argentina since the time of the European conquest but only in the past 80 years has winemaking become an organized activity with wine reaching accepted quality standards.

Only four or five wineries can claim more than a century of uninterrupted production, and just one boasts over 160 years of continuous winemaking (Gonzalez Videla, founded

in 1840). Some 2,000 wineries now exist, although only a handful make fine wine, and even fewer estates bottle or sell their own brand names.

The wine industry here was traditionally based on European grape varieties. However, Argentine producers have now turned to their own specialty grapes.

Argentina has historically been a red wine country, and in the opinion of many international experts the reds are still superior to the whites, with the odd exception. The most popular and expensive reds are those made entirely from the Cabernet Sauvignon grape,

but more recently the extraordinary qualities of the Malbec have been discovered. Vintages from 1999 to 2002 have been the best seen in the country.

White wines are largely Chardonnay and Chenin, with some good Rieslings coming along. A distinguished wine among the Argentine whites is produced principally in the northernmost province of Salta, where the Torrontes grape is grown. It's of Spanish origin and yet develops its full potential, according to connoisseurs, only in the high Andean valley of Cafayate, to the west of Salta.

Wine tours of the country are proving increasingly popular with international tourists. ❏

LEFT: the "national" dish of steak and red wine.
RIGHT: waiter at La Biela, one of Buenos Aires' most famous traditional cafes.

ORPHANS OF THE PAMPAS

Gauchos, once free-spirited individuals who lived off the land, have been tamed and, through land privatization, driven to near extinction

The *gaucho* stands as one of the best-known cultural symbols of Argentina. This rough, tough, free-riding horseman of the pampas, a proud cousin of the North American cowboy, is maintained in Argentine culture as the perfect embodiment of *argentinidad*, the very essence of the national character. He has been elevated to the level of myth, celebrated in both song and prose, and well endowed with the virtues of strength, bravery, and honor.

However, as with all elements of national history, the *gaucho* and his culture continue to be hotly debated topics among the Argentines.

Some say the *gaucho* disappeared as an identifiable social character in the late 19th century. Others will argue that, although his world has undergone radical changes in the past few centuries, the *gaucho* still survives in Argentina. However, while there are still people scattered throughout the country who call themselves *gauchos*, their lives bear a limited resemblance to those of their forebears.

Pampean orphans

Gaucho life had its beginnings on the pampas, the vast grasslands of the east-central Southern Cone sometime in the 18th century. As to the origin of the name *gaucho*, there are many theories which trace the word to everything from Arabic and Basque, to French and Portuguese. The most likely answer is that the word has joint roots in the indigenous dialects of Quechua and Araucanian, a derivation of their word for orphan. It is not hard to imagine how a word meaning orphan evolved into a term for these solitary figures, neither loved nor ruled by anyone.

The first *gauchos* were mostly *mestizos*, of mixed Spanish and native American stock. As with the North American cowboy, some also had varied amounts of African blood, a legacy of Argentina's slave trade.

PRECEDING PAGES: a *gaucho* displays his wealth.
LEFT: *gauchos* from Salta with their stiff leather *guardamontes* (saddle-guards).
RIGHT: *gaucho* from Estancia la Esocondida, Santa Fe.

Hides and tallow

Cattle and horses that had escaped from early Spanish settlements in the 16th century had, over the centuries, proliferated into enormous free-roaming herds, and it was this wild, unclaimed abundance that was the basis for the development of the *gaucho* subculture. The

horses were first caught and tamed, and then used to capture the cattle.

Beef at that time did not have any great commercial value; there was more meat than the tiny population of Argentina could consume, and methods to export it had not yet been developed. This surplus led to waste on a grand scale; any excess meat was simply thrown away.

The primary value of the cattle was in the hides and tallow they provided, which were non-perishable exportable items. The first *gauchos* made their living by selling these in exchange for tobacco, rum, and *mate*; *gauchos* were said to be so addicted to this stimulating tea that they would rather have gone without their beef. Their existence was fairly humble, with few needs. Most did not possess much beyond a horse, a saddle, a poncho, and a knife. The work was not terribly rigorous, and early travelers' accounts of the *gauchos* portray them as savage vagabonds who spent much of their free time drinking and gambling.

This combination of activities often led to a third favorite pastime: the knife fight. The violent lifestyle of the *gaucho* was looked upon with horror and disdain by city folk, but the animosity was mutual. The *gauchos* had nothing but scorn for what they saw as the fettered and refined ways of the city dwellers.

Skilled horsemanship

The primary reputation of the *gaucho*, however, was that of a horseman, and this was well deserved. It was said that when a *gaucho* was without his horse he was without legs.

Almost all his daily chores, from bathing to hunting were conducted from atop his steed. The first *gauchos* hunted with lassoes and *boleadoras*, both of which were borrowed from the indigenous peoples. *Boleadoras* consisted of three stones or metal balls attached to the ends of connected thongs. Thrown with phenomenal accuracy by the *gauchos*, this weapon would trip the legs of the fleeing prey.

FEARLESS COMPETITORS

Hair-raising competitions were commonplace, as *gauchos* took great pride in displaying their impressive equestrian skills. A good illustration of how these competitions were born of the necessity to develop skills in everyday survival is the practice of *pialar*. In this challenge, a man would ride through a gauntlet of his lasso-wielding comrades, who would try to trip up the feet of his mount. The object of the exercise was for the unseated man to land on his feet with reins firmly in hand. This kind of control was often necessary on the open plain, where hidden animal burrows presented a constant danger underfoot.

Charles Darwin, in his descriptions of Argentine life in the 1830s, has an amusing account of his own attempt to throw the *boleadoras*. He ended up catching nothing more than himself, as one thong caught on a bush, and the other wound around his horse's legs. As one might imagine, this ineptitude was the source of much chiding and laughter from the attendant *gauchos*.

The great emphasis placed on equestrian skills led to competition. Strength, speed, and courage were highly prized, and the chance to demonstrate these came often.

In one event, the *sortija*, a horseman would ride full tilt with a lance in his hand to catch a tiny ring dangling from a crossbar. Another test, the *maroma*, would call for a man to drop from a corral gate as a herd of wild horses was driven out beneath him. Tremendous strength was needed to land on a horse's bare back, bring it under control, and return with it to the gate.

But as outsiders bent on enforcing order in the countryside sought to control the lives and activities of the *gauchos*, these competitions came under increasing restrictions. Soon organized and contained rodeos became the forum for the showing off of skills.

> ## DISPLACED PEOPLE
>
> With the privatization of land and cattle, when *gauchos* got into trouble in one area, they simply rode on to another, and little by little, they were found further from the settled areas.

them under authoritarian control and to put them at the service of the new landowners.

It was not only the land which came under private ownership, but the cattle and horses that were found on them as well, making them inaccessible to the free riders. The *gauchos* were suddenly put in the position of being both trespassers and cattle thieves. This made their situation similar to that of the remaining tribes of plains Amerindians. The already shaky reputations of the *gauchos* grew worse.

Ranch-hands

Profound change came to the *gauchos*' way of life as increasing portions of the pampas came under private ownership. Beginning in the late 18th century, large land grants were made to powerful men from Buenos Aires, often as a form of political patronage.

The *gauchos*, with their anarchistic and highly independent ways, were seen as a hindrance to the development of the land. Increasing restrictions were put on their lives, in order to bring

LEFT: early *gaucho*, with distinctive toe-held stirrups.
ABOVE: round-up in Corrientes province, where the *gauchos* are renowned for working barefoot.

New order

With such an obvious conflict of interests, there had to be a resolution, and it was, predictably enough, in favor of the landowners. The open prairie lands were fenced off, and the disenfranchized *gauchos* were put to work at the service of the *estancieros*. Their skills were employed to round up, brand, and maintain the herds. Wages were pitifully low.

However, the *gauchos* maintained their pride. They refused to do any unmounted labor, which was seen as the ultimate degradation. Everyday chores such as the digging of ditches, mending of fences, and planting of trees were reserved for the immigrants who were arriving in increasing numbers from Europe. As the opportunities for exports to the European markets opened up, an ever-increasing amount of land was turned over to agriculture. The stubborn *gaucho* work ethic ensured that the business of planting and harvesting was all done by the immigrants.

Yet when barbed-wire fencing was put up, fewer hands were needed to maintain the herds. Combined with the increase in agriculture, this led to even harder times for the *gauchos*.

Through the 19th century a whole new order came to rest on the pampas; the *gaucho* had ceased to be his own man. His new status as a

LIFE FOR *LAS CHINAS*

The family life of the *gaucho* was never a very settled one. Supposedly, the women of their early camps were captives from raids on nearby settlements. This primitive theft was perhaps one of the practices that made the *gauchos* so unpopular with city folk. But even when women later moved voluntarily out onto the pampas, the domestic arrangements were somewhat informal, with common-law marriages being the norm. These *chinas* (from the Spanish for servant or mistress), were rarely welcome on the *estancias* where the *gauchos* worked. The few that were allowed were employed as maids, wet nurses, laundresses, and cooks.

hired ranch-hand did not sit well with the *gaucho*'s rebellious spirit. But the forces working against him were strong. The landowners had powerful friends in the capital, and the politicians saw the ordering of the countryside as a major priority. Argentina was beginning to take its place among the developing nations, and the traditional life of the *gaucho* could only be seen as a hindrance to that course.

Informal armies

However, while the *gaucho* ceased to present an independent threat, he still had a role to play in the new social structure of the rural areas, and soon new bonds of loyalty were formed between the worker and his master.

Powerful *caudillos* were gaining control over large parts of the interior, backed up by their *gauchos*, who served as irregular troops in private armies. This formation of regional powers was in direct contradiction to the goals of centralized government.

Gauchos were also, at various times, put to work in the defense of the central government. These skilled horsemen were first used in the armies that routed the British invasion forces in 1806 and 1807, and by all accounts, their services were invaluable.

Gaucho squadrons were next employed in the war of independence from Spain, and again they displayed great valor. The last time that the *gauchos* fought as an organized force in the nation's army was during the Desert Campaign of the 1880s *(see pages 56–7)*.

Years of civil warfare followed Argentina's independence from Spain, and it was only when the Unitarians, led by Justo José de Urquiza, gained the upper hand, in the mid-19th century, that the powerful Federalist bands were finally brought under control.

Stylish dressers

Although *gaucho* clothing was originally designed simply for comfort and practicality, the men of the pampas were born dandies, and their traditional outfits were always worn with a certain amount of flair.

The *chiripá*, a loose diaper-like cloth draped between the legs, was very suitable for riding. It was often worn with long, fringed leggings. These were later replaced by *bombachas*, pleated pants with buttoned ankles that fitted inside their boots.

Although store-bought boots with soles became popular with *gauchos* in later years, the first boots were homemade, fashioned from a single piece of hide, slipped from the leg of a horse. Often the toe was left open. This had a practical function, as the early stirrups were nothing more than a knot in a hanging leather thong. The rider would grasp the knot between his first and second toes. Over time, this caused the toes to be permanently curled under, and gave the *gaucho* an awkward gait, in addition to the permanent bowlegged stance characteristic of the professional rider.

> ## UNDER THREAT
> Low wages and poor living conditions have continued to drive *gauchos* into other pursuits. And in recent years, many have drifted to the cities rather than return to the hard outdoor life.

Around his waist the *gaucho* wore a *faja*, a woolen sash, and a *rastra*, a stiff leather belt adorned with coins. This leather belt provided support for the back during the long hours in the saddle. At the *gaucho*'s back, between these two belts, was tucked the *facón*, a *gaucho*'s most prized possession after his horse. This knife was used throughout the day for skinning, castrating, eating, and self-defense.

The outfit was completed with a kerchief, a hat, a set of spurs, and a vest, for more formal occasions. Over all this, a *gaucho* wore his poncho, which also served as a blanket at night and a shield during a knife fight.

The *gaucho* saddle was a layered set of pads, braces, and molded leather, on top of which sat a sheepskin that made the long rides more comfortable. In the region of the pampas where high thistles grew, a set of stiff, flared leather guards called *guardamontes* were used to protect the legs. The *rebenque*, a heavy, braided fine leather crop, was always carried in the riding *gaucho*'s hand.

LEFT: a *gaucho* showing off his horseback skills, in a *sortija* competition.
ABOVE: a *gaucho's* grip is put to the test.

Martín Fierro

Just as the traditional *gaucho* way of life was fading in reality, it was being preserved in art. Poetry and music had always been popular with the *gauchos*, and the poet was usually a revered figure within the community.

The songs, stories, and poems of the *gauchesco* tradition, many of them composed in colorful dialect, often deal with the themes of love and nostalgia, but many of them are highly political in nature.

A masterpiece of Argentine literature is a two-part epic poem, *El Gaucho Martín Fierro*. Written by José Hernandez, and published in the 1870s, the work is a defense of the proud, independent ways of the *gaucho*, and a diatribe against the forces that conspired to bring him down, from greedy landowners to corrupt policemen and conscription officials.

Ironically, such works served to elevate the stature of the *gaucho* in the minds of the public, but not enough and not in time to save him. The free-riding *gaucho* passed into

the realm of myth, a folk hero who was the object of sentimentality and patriotic pride in a nation searching for cultural emblems.

Gauchos, paisanos and peones

Although the historical line places the demise of the *gaucho* in the late 19th century, there is much that remains of the culture in Argentina today. While the reduction of labor needs in the countryside forced many *gauchos* into the cities, many remained on the *estancias* to work under the new established order.

Wherever cattle- and sheep-ranching is done in Argentina, you will find ranch hands working at the rough chores of herding and branding.

> **GAUCHO-SPOTTING**
>
> Today, in small towns it is possible to stop for a drink in the *boliche* or *pulpería* (local bars), where *gauchos* gather for a gambling session after a hard day's work.

Most are settled with a regular wage, but there are still itinerants who provide services such as fence mending and sheep shearing.

While many of these men call themselves *gauchos*, the job of a ranch-hand has taken on different names in the different regions of Argentina. Some are called *paisanos*, others are called *peones*. These cowboys are still found on the *estancias* of the pampas but they are being pushed into reaches further and further from Buenos Aires.

As with the original *gauchos*, many of these men are *mestizos*. Generally those in the northeast are of Guaraní stock, while the Araucanians work on the ranches of Patagonia deep in the south. However, over the years there has been a mixing of blood, with everything from Basque to Italian to that of the North American cowboys who came to work here in the 19th century.

Despite the regional differences in nomenclature, dress, and bloodlines, these men share one tradition that makes them all *gauchos* in spirit, that of excellent horsemanship. A *gaucho*'s pride is still his horse, and, as before, he usually does not own much beyond his mount besides his saddle, his poncho, and his knife.

The rodeo

Visitors can be rewarded for a little exploration along the back roads of Argentina, for that is where you can still find the *gauchos* at work. On a visit to an *estancia*, you might perhaps see a *domador* breaking horses, or men riding at breakneck speed with lassoes flying.

One of the biggest treats is to see a rodeo. Some of these are large organized events, with an accompanying fiesta of eating, dancing, and singing. Bowlegged men gather at these celebrations, dressed up in hats, *bombachas*, and kerchiefs, with their *chinas* by their sides.

With some investigation and a little luck, it is possible to find more informal rodeos in the villages of the outback, where the *gauchos* will come from miles to compete in rough tests of skill and bravery. Amid flying dust and spirited whooping you will see *gauchos* barrel racing and lassoing cattle with as much panache and pride as their ancestors ever had. ❏

LEFT AND RIGHT: *gauchitos* and *gauchos* in the distinctive ponchos of the Northwest.

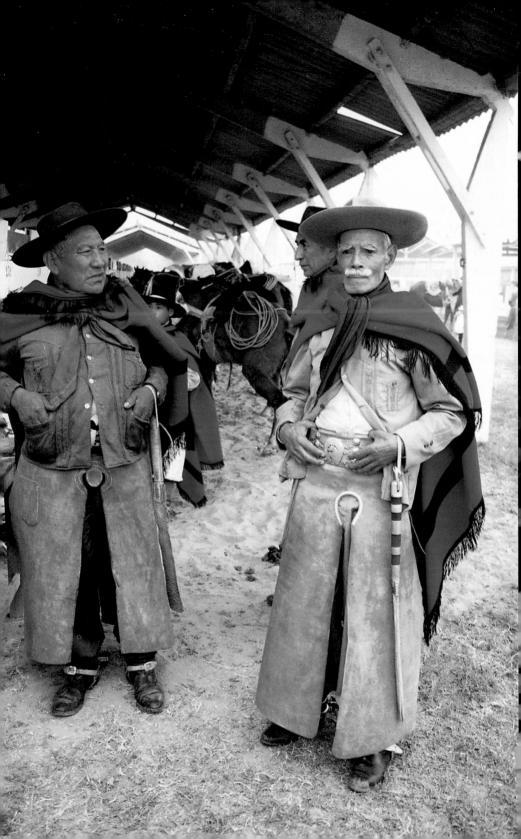

A DAY IN THE COUNTRY – *GAUCHO*-STYLE

Argentina grew rich on its agricultural output, and a visit to a traditional ranch provides an insight into the gaucho's *livelihood*

One of the options for a day trip out of the city is a visit to an *estancia* (ranch), many of which receive either day visitors or weekend guests, although most are also still active in their traditional livestock and agricultural work. There are a number of these establishments, particularly within a couple of hours' drive of Buenos Aires. Most were founded early in the 20th century and follow a similar layout: a tree-lined entry and main residential area (the trees forming a wind break in the flat and often bare pampas), with a large main house in traditional *criollo* or imitation English or Italian style, surrounded by gardens and lawns.

WORKING UP AN APPETITE

Although agricultural methods have obviously changed since the 1920s heyday of the *estancias*, it is still possible to see traditional methods demonstrated for visitors. For those who can spare only one day for the outing, most *estancias* offer transport, and a traditional *asado* lunch composed of *empanadas*, grilled meat, sausage, and sweetbreads, usually accompanied by red wine. Thereafter, most offer a *gaucho* display of horsemanship and roping in the best rodeo style; in many cases, it is also possible to go horse riding or take a ride in a sulky (open carriage). *Estancias* near the coast or one of Buenos Aires' many lakes may also provide fishing, and all offer fresh air, blue sky, green grass, and a glimpse of the endless pampas.

◁ *GAUCHO* **GAMES**
Many *estancias* will put on traditional horseback contests, giving the *gauchos* the chance to show off their riding skills.

▷ **A NEW INCOME**
Many *estancias* have been forced to open their doors to visitors in order to pay the bills, and tourism often becomes their main source of income.

△ **IVY-COVERED** *ESTANCIA*
San Antonio de Areco has a number of beautiful old *estancias*, such as the typical ivy-covered Los Patricios.

△ **LAS SANSAS, SALTA**
Traditional *estancias* can still be found, such as El Bordo de Las Lanzas in Salta province, with its cozy and elegant sitting room.

▽ **LA ESCONDIDA**
A parade of *gauchos* dressed to kill in their best clothes; and fine horses, also showing off their best tack and adornments.

GAUCHOS OF ARGENTINA

Argentine *gauchos* have always been proud of the tools of their trade, and these have become a highly decorative part of their wardrobe.

The traditional *gaucho* knife *(facón)*, used for butchering and skinning, as well as eating and many other functions, is often ornately decorated with a carved silver handle. Their spurs may also be made of silver and – like their wide belts with ornamental silver buckles – are designed to stand out as well as to serve a practical purpose. The wide crops are made of braided leather with a loop at the end to make a sharp cracking noise.

The *boleadoras*, a set of three balls linked by rope, are used to capture and bring down livestock; the throwing of *boleadoras* was an indigenous art learned by the *gaucho*, and is a highly skilled task which requires infinite practice.

Also essential is the traditional *mate* gourd and *bombilla*, used to drink the tea-like *mate*, though now-adays these are often made of ornately carved silver or alpaca.

◁ **ESTANCIA LA CINACINA**
Another San Antonio de Areco *estancia* specializes in tourist activities such as group barbecues and a musical show in the former barn.

▷ **MARTIN FIERRO BOOK**
José Hernández's epic poem *Martín Fierro*, tells of the life and struggles of a hero epitomizing the 19th-century *gaucho* and his betrayal.

WILD ARGENTINA

From the humid subtropics to the windswept Patagonian steppe, Argentina's diverse landscapes contain a dazzling array of exotic plants and animals

If Argentina could be stretched out over Europe, with its northwest corner positioned over London, the country's easternmost point would lie roughly over Budapest. Its southernmost tip, Tierra del Fuego, would be roughly over Timbuktu in Mali, about a third of the way down the African continent.

Given this immense geographical spread, it is not surprising that Argentina has such a great diversity of plant and animal life. But biologically, size alone isn't everything. The country's varied terrain – from the flat pampas in the east to the Andes in the west – ensures that the country has a wide variety of different wildlife habitats. The great climatic variation between north and south, and between lowlands and mountains, accentuates these differences, creating the right conditions for species as diverse as penguins and parrots, or cacti and alpine flowers.

Local species

For a long period in the Earth's distant history, South America was an island continent. During this time, families of species evolved that are found nowhere else. When the present land bridge formed between North and South America, several million years ago, this isolation was brought to an end. But even today, its effects can still be seen. Many of Argentina's mammals and birds are "homegrown" South American specialties: first encounters with them always leave a lasting impression.

Compared to many countries, Argentina's population, which numbers about 37 million, is small and mainly urban, and its impact on wildlife has been patchy. The pampas has been transformed by farming, but in less fertile parts of the country it is still possible to find places where signs of human impact are few and far between. But with improved communications and a drive for increased production, this is steadily changing.

PRECEDING PAGES: a female elephant seal.
LEFT: a battle-scarred male elephant seal.
RIGHT: Magellanic penguins at Punta Tombo, near the Península Valdés in Patagonia.

Competition and survival

Argentina extends from the tropics to the sub-antarctic. It includes the highest point in the Americas – Aconcagua, at 6,900 meters (22,800 ft) above sea level – and also one of the lowest, the Salinas Depression on the Península Valdés, which is about 55 meters (180 ft) below sea

level. The country has both very dry areas and very wet ones, but it lacks the extreme winter temperatures found in most continental climates. This is due to the fact that, in the south at least, the sea is never far away, and it checks the worst of the winter cold.

Much of Argentina is either completely open, or only lightly wooded. This kind of terrain makes watching wildlife easy – if anything moves, you have a good chance of spotting it. This is particularly true in the vast expanses of Patagonia, and in Argentina's share of the Andean *altiplano*. Some animals – such as Patagonian foxes – can be remarkably unfussed by the presence of humans, and will trot across dirt roads in broad daylight, giving cars a quick glance before moving on. Magellanic penguins, which are a highlight of any visit to Argentina, are even less concerned. They usually ignore people, until someone ventures within pecking distance of their nests.

But after a long history of being hunted, other animals are more elusive. Despite being up to 1.5 meters (5 ft) tall, rheas – Argentina's equivalent of ostriches – can disappear among shrubs and bushes in less time than it takes to focus a pair of binoculars.

PICK AND CHOOSE

In such a vast country, it is easy to be over-ambitious in planning to see wildlife. In general, it's better to stay longer at fewer places than cram too much into one visit.

his book *Far Away and Long Ago* – has struggled in the face of these changes. Many of the birds mentioned by Hudson are still to be seen, but mammals have coped less well to the alterations produced by over a century of intense farming, and many of them are now scarce.

In this largely agricultural landscape, sporadic wooded areas and lakes act as magnets for wildlife. So does marshy ground, particularly where it backs onto the coast. Despite its notoriously hazardous traffic, Ruta 2, from

Guanacos (relatives of the llama) also move off briskly at the first hint of disturbance, although at some parks and reserves, such as Cabo Dos Bahías in Patagonia, they are both so plentiful that they are almost impossible to miss.

In search of the pristine pampas

Buenos Aires province, which lies at the heart of the pampas, is the obvious stepping-off point for a visit to Argentina. These huge, flat grasslands, where the soil is very fertile, have been almost completely fenced in, and most are either ploughed or grazed. The original wildlife of this area – described so evocatively by the writer W. H. Hudson (1841-1922) in

FAR AWAY AND LONG AGO

In an age of rapid communications, it can be hard to imagine what life was like for the earliest European settlers on the pampas. One way to find out is to read *Far Away and Long Ago*, written by the novelist and naturalist William Henry Hudson. Hudson was born near Buenos Aires in 1841, and grew up on a sheep farm. In his book, Hudson describes what often sounds like an idyllic childhood, with a vast natural playground full of wildlife at his doorstep, waiting to be explored. Hudson actually wrote the book in his seventies, when he was living in England, but his reminiscences of pampas life proved to be a lasting bestseller.

Buenos Aires to Mar del Plata, crosses this kind of country in its first 200 km (125 miles) outside the capital. Away from the main road, the region's lakes, rivers, and canals attract many different fish-eating birds, including herons and snowy-white great egrets.

Perhaps the most representative pampas left today, largely because of the absence of ploughing, is the area surrounding General Lavalle and south to Madariaga. Between Lavalle and San Clemente there is a wildlife sanctuary, man-

once common throughout the pampas. They can weigh up to 9 kg (20 lbs), and their night-time calls are loud, varied, and unnerving. The viscachas at El Palmar are unusually tame, but campers here must be tidy, as the animals may steal anything that is left out at night and cart it quickly off to their dens.

Forests of the north

In northern Argentina, the climate becomes progressively warmer and more humid, with enough rain to allow forest

aged by Fundación Vida Silvestre Argentina, where the last surviving pampas deer can be seen in the wild.

Northwards from Buenos Aires, El Palmar National Park in Entre Rios province gives a flavor of a different kind of habitat, where the open pampas is replaced by palm-studded savannah. The park preserves only a few square kilometers of the palm-and-grassland landscape, but its wildlife makes the trip well worthwhile. Among its inhabitants are viscachas, nocturnal burrowing rodents that were

LEFT: flamingos along the Patagonian coast.
ABOVE: a group of alert vicuñas.

to replace the open pampas. At its furthest north, Argentina only just nudges into the tropics, but even so, some of its forested regions have a distinctly tropical feel. In the far northwest, Calilegua National Park preserves an area of cloud forest that flanks the Andes, while in the northeast, Iguazú National Park contains the nearest that Argentina comes to lowland rainforest.

Calilegua lies on the eastern slopes of the Andes, between 600 and 4,500 meters (2,000–15,000 ft). Visits are only practicable during the dry season (June to October or November) as the roads are frequently washed out the rest of the year. The road through the park rises steeply, crossing through a series of vegetation zones in rapid succession. The lowest is the chaco vegetation, with its drunken or bottle trees (*Chorizia*), known locally as *palos borrachos*. This zone also has jacarandas and tabebuias – trees that often burst into bloom while they are still leafless, toward the end of the dry season. Their spectacular lilac, yellow, or pink flowers are an impressive sight, attracting pollenating insects from afar. Higher up, the journey continues through a jungle dominated by

tipa trees (*Tipuaria*) and into the cloud forest of coniferous podocarp trees (*Podocarpus*) and moisture-loving alders (*Alnus*).

The forest's animal life also changes with altitude, although many of the larger predators range throughout the park. Wildcats, including jaguars, pumas (cougars), ocelots, and jaguarundi all live here, although it takes skill and luck to spot them. They prey on deer, tapirs, peccaries, agoutis, and even capuchin monkeys, as well as many local birds.

Subtropical east

In the east, the Iguazú Falls are a highlight for any visitor to Argentina, but once the thrill of

> **MARSHLAND DELIGHTS**
>
> The Iberá Marshes are hard to get to and are virtually impenetrable. On the edges of the marsh, however, waterbirds of many kinds provide a great spectacle.

watching the water has worn off, the surrounding forest has much to offer: some 2,000 species of flowering plants, nearly the same number of butterflies and moths, 100 species of mammals including the elusive jaguar, and nearly 400 kinds of birds including hummingbirds and toucans. However, like Calilegua, this kind of habitat is notorious for hiding its inhabitants. Seeing its richness requires time and patience.

Elsewhere in Misiones province, Argentina's subtropical east, the future of the region's native hardwood forests looks uncertain. Many stretches have been felled, and the trees replaced by crops that give a more immediate yield, or in some cases by grazing land. Some areas are planted with pines for the paper pulp industry: although these are technically still "forested," their value for wildlife is low.

The Gran Chaco

The Gran Chaco is a vast low-lying region that straddles northern Argentina, as well as parts of Bolivia and Paraguay. The climate here becomes drier from east to west, splitting the Chaco into two merging parts. The Dry Chaco, in the west, is likely to appeal only to the most adventurous of travelers. Its wildlife is hugely diverse – reputedly including some exceptionally large snakes – but even for reptile-lovers, getting about in this region is a daunting task. The country is covered with dense thorn thickets crossed by very few roads, and there are no amenities for visitors.

The Wet Chaco to the east is easier to visit. Although it has undergone some major clearance for agriculture in the past 25 years, it still contains some beautiful tracts of woodland interspersed with marshes, and is rich in wildlife. Traveling west from Corrientes or Resistencia, Route 16 is worth exploring at least as far as Chaco National Park.

The wet season in the summer (from December to March) is best avoided, for the heat is intense and the roads become impassable. Between April and November, conditions are more congenial, making it a good time to visit the national park. Here there are howler monkeys and many other mammals, but the main attraction for most visitors is the park's bird life, which includes guans, chachalacas, whistling herons, jabirú storks, jacanas, and ducks galore.

From Corrientes, both east and south, there are some very rich woodlands interspersed with wide open grasslands and enormous marshes. Ruta 12 is paved in both directions, but the tougher earth roads which run northeast-southwest between the paved stretches, through places such as Mburucuyá and San Luis del Palmar, generally get into far more interesting wildlife habitats (*see page 232*).

In Corrientes, in the region of the headwaters of the Iberá complex, where grass seas stretch from horizon to horizon, visitors sometimes

fascinating wildlife, spread over a dizzying range of altitudes.

To avoid mountain sickness, or *soroche*, it's best to take the climb into the Andes slowly, and an ideal way to do it is to travel up the Quebrada de Humahuaca in Jujuy (*see page 261*). The journey begins in lush subtropical farmland, and ends in the thin and stunningly clear air of the *altiplano*, more than 3,000 meters (10,000 ft) up. In this part of the Andes, water is often in short supply, and plants and animals have to cope with drought as well as intense sunlight by day and often chilling cold at night.

catch a glimpse of the rare maned wolf. More closely related to foxes than to wolves, this slender member of the dog family has very long legs, making it look almost as if it is on stilts. Marsh deer also survive here – albeit in small numbers – and on larger *estancias* that are run with conservation in mind the endangered pampa deer can also be seen.

The Andean Northwest

The provinces of Jujuy, Salta, and Tucumán have a mixture of extraordinary scenery and

LEFT: the chimango caracara, a widely seen hawk.
ABOVE: sea lions at the Península Valdés.

THE ARGENTINIAN OSTRICH

For the original inhabitants of the Argentinian pampas, the rhea – or *ñandú* – was an important source of food, and of skin and feathers for clothing. Rheas were traditionally hunted with a *bolas* – a collection of stones tied together with rope, which was thrown at the birds' necks or legs. During his extensive journeys in South America, the English naturalist Charles Darwin established that there are actually two species of these ostrich-like birds. The common rhea lives in the pampas, while the smaller species – known as the long-billed or Darwin's rhea – makes its home in Patagonia and in the foothills of the Andes.

One animal – the vicuña – is quite at home in these conditions. Despite its dainty appearance, this smallest wild relative of the llama can survive at over 5,000 meters (16,400 ft), and it can run effortlessly in mountain air that leaves visitors gasping for breath. For a grazing animal, its hearing is not particularly good, but its large Bambi-like eyes give it superb long vision, allowing it to spot any kind of movement from a great distance.

The road up the *quebrada* gorge eventually leads to the dusty town of Abra Pampa, where the level landscape is ringed by distant mountains. At this altitude, the climate is too harsh for trees to thrive, but there is no shortage of wildlife. The region's woodpeckers and owls are particularly interesting, because they have had to adapt to a habitat without any cover. The owls dig burrows, while the woodpeckers peck nest-holes into earth banks – both can often be seen in action from the road.

To the northwest of Abra Pampa, a vast natural bowl cradles Laguna de los Pozuelos, a protected lakeland reserve and home to thousands of flamingos (*see page 262*). Three species live here, together with a host of waterbirds, including puna teal, avocets, and giant, and horned and Andean coots. At Lagu-

nillas, on the western side of Pozuelos, there is a lake some distance from the road, giving a closer look at these birds.

Dinosaur country

Roughly 800 km (500 miles) south of the Abra Pampa region is an equally spectacular part of the Argentinian Andes that sees far fewer visitors from abroad. In this stark landscape, erosion has carved out bizarre formations in sediments laid down millions of years ago. At Talampaya National Park in La Rioja province, deep-red cliffs flank a precipitous gorge – ideal country for the condors that soar overhead. In neighboring San Juan, the Ischigualasto Reserve

HOME AND AWAY

Ask anyone where marsupial mammals come from, and the chances are that they will answer Australia. But, surprisingly, pouched mammals first evolved in the Americas. From here they reached Australia by spreading out across Gondwanaland, an ancient southern supercontinent. Marsupials still live in the Americas today, with several species in Argentina. Your chances of seeing any are very small, but if you are walking in wooded country after dark, look out for red eyes: the chances are that they belong to a mouse opposum. Another marsupial is the yapok, a large, semi-aquatic animal, which lives in and near rivers in the semi-tropical northeast.

contains a moonscape of eroded clay with rocky pillars and cliffs (*see pages 281 and 283*).

Country like this has yielded a treasure trove of fossil animals over many decades. Discoveries at Ischigualasto have included Herrerasaurus, an early meat-eating dinosaur that lived over 200 million years ago, and many other reptiles alive at that time. Further east on the pampas, Argentinian palaeontologists have unearthed fossils of what may be the largest flying bird ever to have existed. Named *Argentavis magnificens*, it had a wingspan of about 7.5 meters (25 ft), and measured over 3 meters (10 ft) from beak to tail. Like today's condors, this gigantic creature probably flew by soaring, a technique that works well in open, sunny landscapes that generate currents of rising air.

LAKE WITH A VIEW

The lakes fed by the Campo de Hielo glaciers are good places for visitors to catch a glimpse of waterfowl – including the region's famous black-necked swans.

Trees and ice

The Patagonian Andes, which stretch from Neuquén, through Río Negro, to Chubut and Santa Cruz, are one of the main playgrounds of Argentina, and also a stronghold of many of the country's native plants and animals. Among the animals visitors can expect to see are condors, geese, and parakeets, while native plants include southern beeches (*Nothofagus*), an attractive broadleaved tree that is covered with small scallop-edged leaves.

Southern beeches are a living legacy of South America's very distant past. At one time, South America formed part of Gondwanaland, a southern supercontinent that also included Antarctica and Australasia. The southern beech family evolved when Gondwanaland was still intact, but its member species became separated as Gondwanaland broke up, and the continents drifted apart. This explains the remarkable distribution of southern beeches today: as well as growing in South America, they also grow in Australia, New Zealand, and New Guinea – thousands of miles away on the other side of the Pacific.

Unlike the mountains further north, the icy Patagonian Andes have a distinctly temperate feel. Rainfall increases toward the Chilean border, creating a landscape that contrasts vividly with the dry plains to the west.

The Patagonian Andes is home to large flocks of upland geese in grassy valleys, ashy-headed geese in clearings in woods near lake shores and rivers, and noisy buff-necked ibises nearly everywhere. The woods also contain rich and colorful flocks of austral parakeets and hummingbirds called greenbacked firecrowns. Both seem out of place in such surroundings, but they have successfully adapted to the region's cool conditions.

One of the most spectacular birds in the Patagonian Andes is the Magellanic woodpecker, the giant of its family. The male sports a bright scarlet head with a small crest, while his all-black mate has a very long and floppy crest that curls forward.

This region is also the home of the torrent duck, which, as its name implies, is only seen in white-water rivers and streams. Torrent ducks dive and swim close to furious rapids as nonchalantly as if they were in a pond.

For many visitors, the highlight of a trip to this region is a chance to see Argentina's glaciers, which spill down from the Campo de Hielo – Patagonia's southern ice cap, out of

LEFT: the solitary puma ranges from the tropics down to the southernmost tip of the continent.
RIGHT: a Patagonian fox sits for a portrait.

view on the crest of the Andes. Some of the most spectacular glaciers are contained within Los Glaciares National Park, near to El Calafate (*see page 316*).

Tierra del Fuego

When Charles Darwin sailed up the Beagle Channel in 1832, Tierra del Fuego was almost unknown to the outside world. Since then, European settlers have done much to transform the ecology of this remote and stormy region. Sheep and rabbits arrived in the 19th century, and beavers and muskrat were introduced in the 1940s, creating havoc in the island's wood-

might also come across kelp geese, as well as flightless steamer ducks. These remarkable birds are a local specialty, and they get their name from the dramatic paddlewheel-like spray they generate as they chase or escape from their rivals.

Where they are still intact, Tierra del Fuego's southern beech forests have a sombre and otherworldly feel. The winds this far south can be fierce and unrelenting, and growth is a slow business, with bleached branches showing where trees have lost their battle against the elements. But despite the hostile conditions, these forests are far from lifeless: austral parakeets fly among the trees, and condors often soar overhead.

lands by felling trees and damming streams.

More recently, unrestrained development has turned Tierra del Fuego's southernmost town, Ushuaia, into a sprawling eyesore, complete with the most southerly traffic jams in the world.

Despite this, Tierra del Fuego is a fascinating destination for anyone interested in wildlife. The Beagle Channel is as beautiful as it was in Darwin's day, and its cormorants, sea lions, and fur seals can be seen at close quarters by taking a boat trip from Ushuaia (*see page 364*). The Channel also has small colonies of Magellanic penguins, together with the occasional gentoo, a larger species with a bright red beak.

Take a boat trip, and there's a good chance you

The desert coast

Turning northward once more, the journey back to Buenos Aires crosses hundreds of miles of Patagonian steppe – a vast windswept plateau that rises gently from east to west. In this part of South America, the Andes intercept most of the moisture carried by the prevailing westerly winds, creating a rain-shadow in their lee. As a result, Patagonia is unusually dry for somewhere so far south – the inland city of Sarmiento, for example, receives just 13 cm (5 inches) of rain a year.

The continental shelf east of Argentina is bathed by a nutrient-rich current flowing up from the south, and so inevitably attracts prodigious numbers of marine mammals, as well as seabirds. At one time many of these were ruthlessly hunted, but today the whales, seals and penguins breed here largely unmolested.

In Chubut province, two reserves – Punta Tombo and Cabo Dos Bahías – are home to hundreds of thousands of Magellanic penguins during the summer breeding season. Further north, the Península Valdés is famous for its sightings of whales and seals. There is something to see on the coast through-

months of March and May, as they lie in wait for young sea lions that venture innocently beyond the beach.

Moving inland

Away from the starkly beautiful coast the Península Valdés's protected status benefits land animals as well. This is a very good place to see guanacos and rheas, and also maras – long-legged rodents that look something like a cross between a hare and a small deer. The peninsula also teems with the well-

---

WILDLIFE EXCURSIONS

A range of overland safaris and whale-watching boat trips around the World Heritage Site, Península Valdés, are available, most of which are organized in nearby Puerto Madryn (*see page 364*).

out the year, with southern sea lions hauling out to breed between January and March, migrating southern right whales arriving in June, and elephant seals which begin breeding from September. By December they have given birth, and the adults can be seen lazing on the shingle, flicking flipper-loads of shells all over their bodies to help dislodge their moulting fur.

In the shallows, a spectacular presence are the marauding orcas (killer whales), which create a threatening atmosphere between the

known tinamous, dumpy ground-feeding birds that can often be seen on the side of the road. Despite their squat shape, biologists conclude that tinamous are probably more closely related to ostriches and rheas than to the game birds they resemble.

Heading north along the South Atlantic coast, the Patagonian plateau blends gradually with the pampas, and leads back to Buenos Aires. After the vast space and solitude of the far south of the country, the bustling crowds and hectic traffic can come as a shock. Nevertheless, even here you can be assured that the varied wildlife of Argentina is never far away. ❑

LEFT: the mara, or Patagonian cavy.
ABOVE: the maned wolf.

OUTDOOR ADVENTURE

The vast landscape of Argentina provides plenty of opportunity to enjoy the great outdoors, in either strenuous or leisurely activity

Those looking for adventure and excitement in Argentina need not look beyond a bus ride in Buenos Aires. But, if you do wish to go farther afield, the opportunities are as immense as the country is vast.

One of the difficulties in tasting all that is on offer is the sheer distance that separates one place from another. Features which would be well-trodden tourist destinations in Europe often attract little attention, simply because they are literally hundreds of miles from anywhere, so that only the more intrepid traveler has the time to seek them out.

From the lush rainforests of Misiones to windswept Tierra del Fuego, there is varied and abundant wilderness to experience and explore. Too many places to mention have the potential for outdoor pursuits.

For the truly adventurous, the absence of commercial development on any significant scale in large tracts of Argentina is just an added attraction. There are, however, a string of developed and developing centers in the Andean foothills and also on the Atlantic Coast, which offer a rich variety of adventure activities.

Climb and climb again

The Andes mountains, which run the length of Argentina's western border with Chile, have long attracted climbers from around the world. One of the main centers for climbing is in the province of Mendoza, about 1,300 km (800 miles) west of Buenos Aires, where the highest peak in the Western Hemisphere – Aconcagua (6,962 meters/22,841 ft) – is found. Scores of expeditions have scaled Aconcagua since Matias Zurbriggen of Switzerland first conquered it in 1897.

There are 10 recognized routes up the mountain, the northern approach being the most popular. It is possible to reach the top without any technical climbing expertise, although a guide and appropriate acclimatization for the altitude are essential.

A somber warning for those less prepared is the small cemetery at the foot of Aconcagua in Puente del Inca, the burial place of a number of climbers who have lost their lives in the attempt.

The main center for trekking and climbing in this area is Villa Los Penitentes en route from Mendoza to the frontier. The Tupangato peak – a volcano reaching 6,650 meters (21,000 ft) – is also difficult, and can be reached only by riding mules part of the way. Less demanding peaks in the Andes include Catedral, Cuerno, Tolosa, Cúpula, Almacenes, and Pan de Azúcar, all between 5,300 meters/17,390 ft and 5,700 meters/18,700 ft.

One popular range is the Cordón de Plata, just 80 km (50 miles) from the city of Mendoza. Here you can find fairly easy climbing. Such peaks as El Plata (6,300 meters/21,000 ft), Negro, Pico Bonito, Nevado Exelsior,

---

PRECEDING PAGES: a tent with a view.
LEFT: climbers dwarfed by the sheer granite face of Monte Fitz Roy, in southern Patagonia.
RIGHT: proud conqueror of the feisty *dorado*.

Rincón, and finally Vallecitos, ranging from 5,000 meters/16,500 ft to 6,300 meters/21,000 ft, attract large numbers of hikers and climbers every year, both local and foreign.

For those without a head for heights, the whole area to the west of Mendoza also offers plenty of scope for mountain-biking, trekking on foot or horseback across the Andes, and photographic safaris in off-road vehicles.

There are five key rivers in the area on which rafting is offered; the Mendoza, Tunuyán,

ADVENTURE TOURS

There are local tour operators and organizations who specialize in many of the activities described here. See the Travel Tips section, pages 362–4, for more details.

important center for a whole range of outdoor pursuits, from mountaineering to paragliding. It lies at the heart of Argentina's lake district, otherwise known as the "Switzerland of South America". The Club Andino in Bariloche is a good place to find out just what's on offer and to book up mountain lodges or *refugios*. The club can also arrange guides, who lead climbing and hiking expeditions. Most readily accessible are Cerro Otto for paragliding or the granite pinnacles of Cerro Catedral for climbers.

Diamante, Atuél, and Grande. Kayaking and canoeing are also available, together with windsurfing, diving, water-skiing, and sailing.

South of Mendoza

Malargüe, to the south of Mendoza, is a much smaller center but with particular attractions. The nearby Cueva de las Brujas is the most important cave network in the country. And the Cueva del Tigre is also close at hand. Southeast of Malargüe lies Lago Llancanelo, a superb location for bird-watching, with pink flamingos and black-necked swans among the species found there.

Farther south, Bariloche, some 1,700 km (1,050 miles) from Buenos Aires, is another

Tronador and Bariloche

A couple of hours' drive away lies the region's largest peak by far. Tronador, at 3,500 meters (11,500 ft), is 1,500 meters (5,000 ft) higher than any of the surrounding mountains. Its name, meaning the thunderer, derives from the rumbling of its glaciers. There is a hostel in Pampa Linda at the foot of Tronador and a number of *refugios* for trekkers in the area. Although these tend to be crowded in December and January, the tourist trade in Bariloche is sharply seasonal, and outside these months (apart from the skiing months of July and August) is generally a much quieter time. It's an ideal area for horseback riding, with the option of crossing over to Chile.

One of the particular attractions of Bariloche is the sheer variety of vegetation within a radius of just 30 km (19 miles), by virtue of its position in the rain shadow of the Andes. Trek west and you soon enter temperate rainforest with dense thickets of bamboo and often impenetrable vegetation. Trek east and you find the magnificent sculptured landscape of the Valle Encantada, for example, and beyond it the vastness of the Patagonian desert.

There is rafting on the relatively gentle Limay, which flows into Lago Nahuel Huapi, or on the Río Manso, whose name – "gentle" – belies the tougher challenge that its waters

ilarity. Lanín offers a classic ascent for experienced climbers. To the south, the national parks of Lago Puelo and, nearer Esquel, Los Alerces, are beautiful areas for trekking and camping.

Santa Cruz province

El Calafate is the gateway to the Parque Nacional Los Glaciares, in Santa Cruz province. This is the main base for exploring the area, and in particular for visiting the Perito Moreno glacier, 80 km (50 miles) away at the far end of Lago Argentino. Trekking on the glacier is possible, both as a short trip and as part of a longer expedition taking in the Frias

offer. Nahuel Huapi lake is part of the National Park of the same name. Although the temperature of the waters and the treacherous winds which whisk down the arms of the lake have tended to discourage commercial development of water sports, plenty of opportunities do exist for windsurfing, scuba diving, canoeing, and sailing.

To the north of Nahuel Huapi is the Parque Nacional Lanín, named after the volcano which is the same height as Mount Fuji (3776 meters/ 12,389 ft) and to which it bears a striking sim-

glacier as well and the ascent of Cerro Cervantes, over a period of two or three days.

The options for trekking in the area seem limitless. It is also ideal terrain for mountain bikes and four-track vehicles, both of which can be hired locally. Various *estancias* in the region offer horseback riding and trekking.

Some 230 km (140 miles) from Calafate – about four hours' journey – lie the spectacular Monte Fitz Roy (3,440 meters/11,000 ft) and Cerro Torre. Professional climbers regard Fitz Roy and the surrounding peaks as among the most difficult in the world to climb. It was scaled for the first time in 1952 by Lionel Terray and Guido Magnóne. Cerro Torre (3,128

LEFT: paraskiing *(pato)* at Las Leñas.
ABOVE: cyclists take a break in Bariloche.

meters/9,500 ft) and its neighbors are right on the fringe of the Patagonian ice cap, and as the westernmost peaks of the Fitz Roy chain they receive the full force of winds blowing in from the Pacific. The Italian Cesare Maestri and Austrian Tony Egger are credited with the conquest of the mountain in 1959, although Egger died in the descent, and there were serious doubts about the veracity of Maestri's claims.

Those keen to explore the area more fully would do better to stay in the developing settlement of El Chaltén, where there is a hostel and basic supplies. Although it lacks many of the tourist facilities of Calafate, it obviously

gives much readier access to the mountains. Buses leave Calafate for El Chaltén early in the morning, giving an ideal opportunity to see rheas and guanaco en route.

Take to the slopes

Skiing and snowboarding have grown steadily in popularity, and facilities are being constantly upgraded. The two main centers are Bariloche, with its purpose-built resort of Cerro Catedral, and the newer Las Leñas (1,200 km/750 miles from Buenos Aires) in the province of Mendoza. Although the snowfall is notoriously unpredictable, the best season for snow is generally from June to October.

Bariloche is South America's biggest skiing resort, with more than 30 chair-lifts and ski-tows. There is a small ski-run at Cerro Otto on the outskirts of the town, and it's also possible to do cross-country skiing in this area. Villa La Angostura on the other side of Lago Nahuel Huapi has limited facilities. To the north, San Martín de los Andes is a more picturesque and exclusive ski center, and correspondingly more expensive, although neither is cheap. Esquel, to the south, has limited skiing facilities, too, at La Hoya. Built in 1983, Las Leñas has excellent slopes although less diverse attractions than other centers.

Anglers' idyll

Argentina is criss-crossed by rivers and lakes (both natural and artificial) and includes more than 4,000 km (2,500 miles) of coastline along the Atlantic Ocean. Those features make it a fisherman's paradise, and species such as eel, catfish, trout, salmon, sea-bass, shark, swordfish, sole, shad, and dorado are plentiful.

Year-round fishing is available at Argentina's coastal resorts, many of which are between 300–500 km (180–300 miles) from Buenos Aires. Mar del Plata is a prime fishing spot, as are the nearby resorts at Laguna Brava, where the local authorities regularly stock the waters and boats can be rented.

Quequén Grande, on the banks of the Río Necochea, is noted for its excellent trout fishing. Salmon and trout are also plentiful in the inland rivers and lakes to the south of Buenos Aires in the provinces of Neuquén and Río Negro. However, these regions are under the jurisdiction of the National Parks Board and a fishing license is required.

THE TIP OF THE WORLD

Ushuaia is the world's southernmost town and the obvious center for exploring Tierra del Fuego. Various *estancias* near the town offer accommodation and opportunities for riding, hiking, and participating in the day-to-day work of the ranch.

Much of Tierra del Fuego's swampy or forested terrain is more readily accessible on foot or on horseback rather than by vehicle. From Ushuaia itself there are daily boat trips to the outlying islands to see cormorants and sea lions. It is also possible, although not always easy, to charter yachts to Cape Horn or to see spectacular glaciers along the coast.

As well as being a ski resort, the attractive town of Bariloche on the shores of Lago Nahuel Huapi is also one of the best locations for trout fishing, and trout as heavy as 16 kg (36 lbs) are known to have been caught here. Some *estancias* in the surrounding area have lodges to cater for tourists and regularly draw dedicated fishermen from the United States to fish the superb rivers and lakes of the region. Carefully controlled hunting is allowed, too, subject to license.

In San Martín de los Andes, north of Bariloche, there are fly-fishing outfits that provide a comprehensive service, including lodging and equipment as well as skilled guides.

For those prepared to travel to the extreme south, Río Grande is the center for trout fishing on Tierra del Fuego. The winds are fierce but the size of the trout due reward. The Argentine Fishing Association (Asociación Argentina de Pesca) in Buenos Aires has more information (tel: 5411-4313 4279).

Swing into action

Golf is another sport which has benefitted from the wide open spaces and the even climate of Argentina. The World Golf Championship was held in Buenos Aires in 2000 and there are numerous golf clubs all over the country, including the prestigious Jockey Club course in Buenos Aires, the picturesque Mar del Plata course on the Atlantic coast, and the course at the spectacular Hotel Llao-Llao near Bariloche.

The wind in your sails

Argentina has some of the most ideal sailing conditions in the world: gentle climate, strong winds, and an abundance of lakes, rivers, and reservoirs. This potential is often still underdeveloped commercially in outlying regions.

However, there are yacht clubs along the banks of the fabled Río de la Plata, where the public can hire sailboats, sailboards, and yachts. There are also several rowing clubs clustered around the pleasant delta region of Tigre, on the outskirts of Buenos Aires.

A wild world

One of Argentina's key attractions is its wildlife (*see pages 109–117*), with the World

Heritage Site of Península Valdés renowned for its wildlife watching.

The Golfo Nuevo and the Golfo San José are important breeding grounds for the southern right whale, which can be observed even from the shore between September and mid-December. It is also possible to go by boat to observe the whales at close quarters. At the northernmost point of the peninsula killer whales are regularly seen, and at various spots around the shores one can see penguins, seals and elephant seals. Inland there are guanaco, maras and rheas, particularly around the Salina Grande, the lowest point on the continent.

Puerto Madryn is the main tourist center, about 100 km (60 miles) from the peninsula, offering scuba diving, mountain-biking and trekking. On Valdés itself, Puerto Pirámide lacks the facilities of its larger neighbor (accommodation is limited), but if camping by the shore you have ready access to the rugged coastline and can be woken by the sound of whales.

There are isolated attractions along the coast to the south of Puerto Madryn, such as the Punta Loma Fauna Reserve and Punta Tombo. Visiting these may involve traveling along stretches of dirt road, although the effort is worthwhile. ❏

LEFT: canoeing on a lonely lake in northern Patagonia.
RIGHT: windsurfing on the open sea.

SPECTATOR SPORTS

*The Argentine love of sport is clearly demonstrated by the stars now flooding
the international soccer fields, tennis courts, and polo grounds*

It should be an average enough day in Buenos Aires, yet the streets are strangely deserted. The banks are empty, the restaurants are quiet, and an eerie silence has settled over the entire city. The only people in sight are huddled around portable radios or television sets, their attention tightly focused on the latest news.

The outbreak of war? Some national disaster? No, this scenario occurs every time Argentina's national soccer team takes to the field, ample evidence of the sport's hold on the country. Every match commands the nation's rapt attention, and victories are cause for unrivaled celebration.

When Argentina won the 1986 World Cup tournament in Mexico, the highest honor in soccer, several hundreds of thousands of fans flooded the streets of Buenos Aires, Córdoba, Rosario, La Plata, and beyond. Makeshift parades materialized out of nowhere, thousands of cars jammed the avenues and side streets, and the nation found itself swathed in blue and white.

The world championship was the second for Argentina, having also captured the cup in 1978. But that tournament, hastily staged in Argentina by the ruling military government that had come to power not long before, fostered little of the pride and enthusiasm seen in 1986. The 1978 World Cup was perceived by many as a simple exercise in public relations designed to avert the world's eyes from Argentina's soaring inflation, mounting national debt, and human rights violations. The national team has had more recent successes, reaching the final in 1990 and the quarter-final in 1998.

Soccer history

Soccer was introduced to Argentina in the 1860s by British sailors who passed the time in port playing "pick-up" games before the curious local onlookers. The large British community in Buenos Aires finally organized the game officially in 1891, and the balls, goal posts, and nets imported from Europe were checked through customs as "some silly things for the mad English".

But by the turn of the 20th century, Argentina had established its own soccer league. The Quilmes Athletic Club was formed in 1897, making it the country's oldest soccer team. Rosario Central (1899), River Plate (1901), Independiente (1904), and Boca Juniors (1905) quickly followed suit.

Argentina's national team also progressed rapidly, as proven by its performance in the inaugural World Cup held in Uruguay in 1930. Although still amateur and lightly regarded, Argentina defeated strong teams such as France and Chile en route to a place in the finals, before losing to Uruguay, 4–2.

Soccer became a professional sport in Argentina in 1931, and the league games began to draw large, vociferous crowds. River Plate and Boca Juniors, which emerged from the middle-class Belgrano neighborhood and the working class. Italian Boca district in Buenos Aires *(see page 163–5)*, quickly became the two most popular teams in Argentina. Even today, around 50 percent of the nation's soccer fans support one of these two clubs. Such unbridled support is not necessarily a good thing – Argentine soccer has been increasingly troubled in recent years by crowd violence at its league matches, especially when rival fans such as River Plate and Boca Juniors meet.

Each club has its fanatical supporters, a group of hardcore and often violent fans called the "*Barra Brava.*" As a result, many of the country's stadiums – including Boca's La Bombonera, are complete with moats, fences, and barbed wire designed to keep fans off the field and rival factions apart. But these measures have not stopped the violence. Critics blame soccer club presidents for giving their *Barra Bravas* free tickets, paying for their journeys to away games, sponsoring their trips to World Cups, and even admitting them to board meetings.

Nineteen teams compete annually in the Argentina First Division, playing a total of 36 matches between September and June. In addition, many of the top clubs compete in international tournaments such as the World Club Cup and the Libertadores Cup.

Argentines, like most South Americans, seem to have a special skill for soccer. Diego Maradona was a national hero long before he gained international prominence at the 1986 World Cup. When Maradona threatened to leave his club, Boca Juniors, for Europe in 1982, the government unsuccessfully tried to intervene by declaring him to be part of the "national patrimony."

Polo prowess

Of course, soccer is not the only sport in Argentina. Blessed with a climate that allows for a wide variety of sports year round, the country is also known for its polo, rugby, horse- and auto-racing, and tennis.

One of the first things many visitors ask is where can they see polo being played. Although it did not originate in Argentina, polo has evolved into an integral part of the national sporting heritage. Many of the world's best players and teams have come from this country. In addition, Argentina has top-flight breeding programs for ponies.

As with soccer, polo was introduced to Argen-

tina by the English in the mid-19th century. The inherent riding skill of the Argentines, as proved by the *gauchos*, and the abundance of space, helped ensure that the sport flourished. At present, there are over 6,000 polo players registered in the country.

Polo tournaments are held all over Argentina throughout the year, but the bulk are played in spring and autumn. The top teams compete each November in the Argentine Open championship in the picturesque polo fields of Palermo, in central Buenos Aires, a competition which began in 1893. There is no distinction between amateur and professional polo in Argentina. But

STAR TURN IN SOCCER FORTUNES

As the leading all-time star of the country's greatest spectator sport, Diego Maradona is the Carlos Gardel of the Argentine sports scene. He still commands the support of most Argentine soccer fans, despite his suspensions by FIFA for drug abuse while playing for the Naples team in Italy and for the Argentine national side in the 1994 World Cup in the US.

After two failed attempts at coaching second-line clubs in Argentina, Maradona returned to his first love, Boca Juniors, to play as center forward. But further drug tests and his unreliability forced him into retirement and he now lives in Cuba.

PRECEDING PAGES: a pukka game of polo.
LEFT: *pato*, now played with a leather ball.
RIGHT: a River Plate soccer match.

many of the top players are regularly hired by foreign teams for huge sums. The favorite team in an international tournament is often the one with the most Argentine players, and there is big demand overseas for Argentine-trained polo ponies.

Passion for *pato*

The game of *pato* has been described by some observers as basketball on horseback, and it is one of the few sports indigenous to Argentina. The earliest references to the game can be

> ### PONIES IN DEMAND
>
> Specially trained by *petiseros* (trainers) at an *estancia* where polo is played, the short, stocky Argentine polo ponies are prized for their speed, strength, and ability to work with their riders.

was that the rider in possession of the *pato* had to keep it extended in his right hand, thus offering it to any opponent who caught up with him. Such skirmishes inevitably resulted in a fierce tug-of-war, and the unfortunate riders pulled from their saddles were often trampled to death. The government banned *pato* in 1822, but a group of ardent supporters revived the game in 1937. They drew up a new set of rules, refined the sport, and established a *pato* federation in 1938. Today, the game is

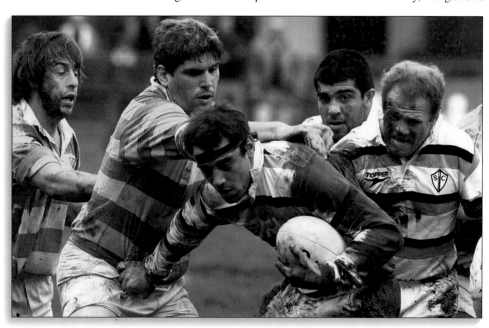

dated back as far as 1610, but the game was probably played by the native inhabitants long before that time.

Pato is Spanish for "duck," and the unfortunate duck certainly got the worst of it in the game's formative stages. A duck was placed inside a leather basket with handles, the possession of which was then contested by two teams of horsemen – often farm-workers or indigenous people – who attempted to grab the basket and return it to their *estancia*.

Any number of riders could participate in the game, and anything from lassoing an opponent to cutting free his saddle was permissible in pursuit of the prize. The sole rule of the sport

played by teams of four riders, with a basket (like the type used in basketball) at each end of a regulation field.

The original duck has been replaced by a more acceptable leather ball with handles, and points are scored by passing the ball through the basket. This sport has steadily grown in popularity and is now as socially acceptable as polo. The annual national open championship is held in mid-December in Palermo, Buenos Aires.

Other equestrian sports

In a country where horses are plentiful and breeding is big business, horse-racing and showjumping are also popular. There are racetracks in most Argentine towns and plenty of opportunities for off-track betting, although the government oversees the official odds. The big races are held in Buenos Aires, often at the Jockey Club in the San Isidro suburb.

Horse shows are staged at numerous clubs in Buenos Aires and other major cities, taking place almost weekly from March to December. There is a fine tradition in this sport – as there is for dressage – and only the regular exportation of top horses has kept Argentina from gaining international stature.

Boom-time for tennis

Tennis has been played in Argentina since the 19th century, but it has always been a game largely for the middle and upper classes – until now. Fueled by the meteoric rise of Guillermo Vilas, an energetic and talented player who gained international prominence on the world's courts in the 1970s, tennis has since experienced an unprecedented boom.

The driven, dashing Vilas won the Masters in 1974 and the US Open in 1977, and soon became known as an international playboy. Linked romantically with such women as Princess Caroline of Monaco and countless Hollywood starlets, Vilas emerged as a national hero at a time when Argentina had no other.

Virtually overnight, every young Argentine dreamed of being a professional tennis player. The number of players skyrocketed, as did the sales of racquets, balls, and shoes. Courts sprang up all over the suburbs of Buenos Aires – both municipal and privately owned – and Argentine players flooded the professional circuit.

One of the finest of that boom was Gabriela Sabatini, the teenage sensation who emerged as one of the top women's players of the mid-1980s. Dubbed "Gorgeous Gabby" by the international press, Sabatini played her way into the top 10 rankings in 1986, quickly rising to the third seed. Sabatini retired from professional tennis in 1996. Although no other Argentine players have yet equaled the accomplishments of Vilas and Sabatini, the sport remains popular in Argentina, and the Buenos Aires River Plate Stadium was enlarged in 2003 to hold 10,000 spectators, in time for the Davis Cup.

LEFT: rugby has become one of Argentina's most popular spectator sports.
RIGHT: at Palermo's racetrack in Buenos Aires.

Rugby on the up and up

As with soccer and polo, rugby was introduced to Argentina by the British. But the sport inexplicably failed to catch on until the mid-1960s. That was when the Pumas, Argentina's national rugby team, rose to prominence with a string of international successes. Like tennis, the sport experienced a rapid growth of interest and a massive infusion of young talent.

Today, Argentine rugby ranks among the best in the world. Virtually every province has its own federation, and international matches draw more than 50,000 fans, compared with the mere 15,000 who showed up in the 1960s.

Cricket catches on

It may come as a surprise to many to learn that cricket is played in Argentina. Yet another British import, it remained the property of that close-knit community for much of the 20th century. The North v South series goes back to 1891 at Palermo Gardens, Buenos Aires, the home of the Buenos Aires Cricket Club. This was the golden age of local cricket.

The quality of Argentine cricket declined after World War II and a some of the famous clubs gave up the sport. However, Argentines have recently taken an interest in the game and the country has produced a number of top-notch players. ❑

PLACES

*A detailed guide to the whole of Argentina, with principal
sites clearly cross-referenced by number to the maps*

Argentina's landscapes are some of the most stunning in the
world. From the thundering waterfalls of Iguazu to Tierra del
Fuego with its soaring glaciers, the country's geographical
features delight. Roam the windswept grasslands of the pampas, ski
in sophisticated resorts arond Bariloche, or taste wine from the vineyards of Preton Mendoza. Then there's the sophisticated city of
Buenos Aires with its rich cultural life, tree-lined boulevards, and
bohemian coffee houses. Visiting Argentina takes planning, for it is
a huge country and destinations often lie far apart. Getting from the
deserts of the northwest to the coastal wildlife of Patagonia requires
organization and time. Fortunately, Argentina has a solid infrastructure geared for tourism. Comfortable hotels are available in all popular spots, and in even the most remote reaches there are usually at
least camp grounds. Planes and buses run on convenient schedules
and cars can be rented. In some areas, one might even prefer to get
around on foot or horseback. An Aerolíneas Argentinas air pass
enables one to cover the larger distances at reduced rates.

In the following chapters the country has been divided up into territories that one is likely to see as a whole: Buenos Aires, the vacation coast, the central sierras, the northeast, the northwest, the western
wine country of the Cayo, Patagonia, and Tierra del Fuego. How
much of an adventure you make of it is up to you.

Be mindful of the conditions dictated by the time of year when
you visit. During the regional high season, reservations may be hard
to come by; winter rains may make a park inaccessible; wildlife you
will see in a particular spot depends on migration patterns. These
chapters will help you decide whether you'd like to be sunbathing on
the beaches of Mar del Plata in January, gliding down the ski slopes
of the Andes in August, or eating a *bife de chorizo* in Buenos Aires
any time of the year. ❑

PRECEDING PAGES: the Ftizroy range in Santa Cruz province; a *gaucho* surveys his
fertile land; Recoleta Cemetery, Buenos Aires.
LEFT: the prickly landscape of the northwest.

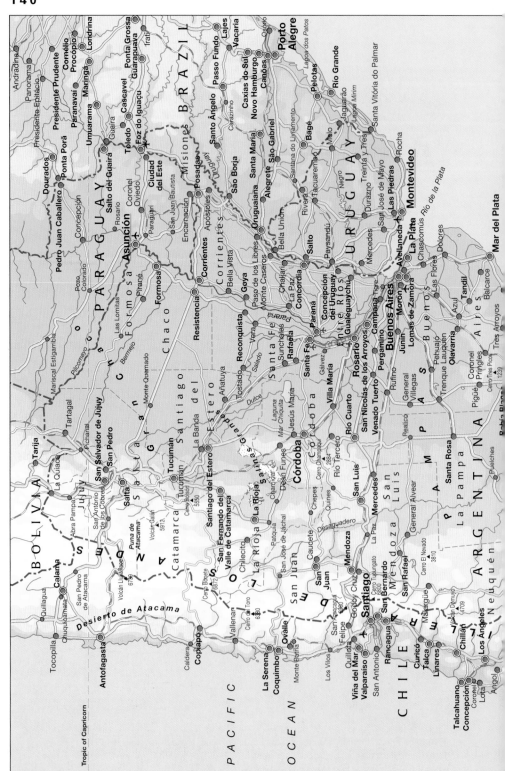

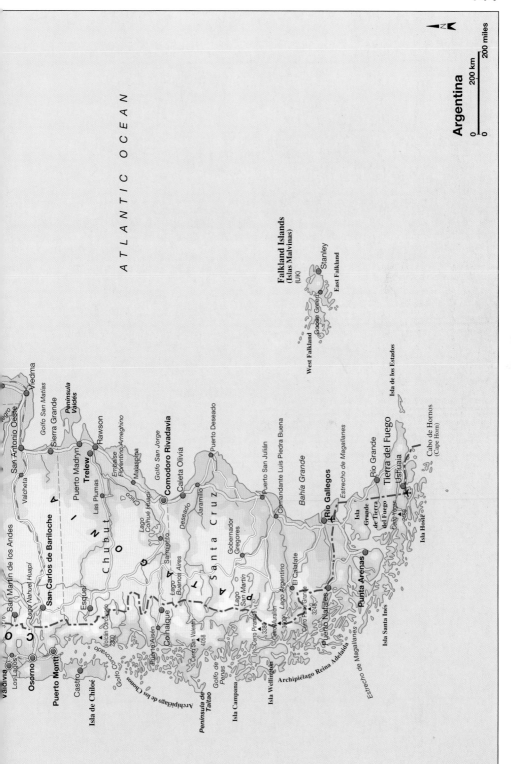

Argentina

0   200 km
0   200 miles

ATLANTIC OCEAN

Falkland Islands
(Islas Malvinas)
(UK)

West Falkland
Goose Green
Stanley
East Falkland

Isla de los Estados

Cabo de Hornos
(Cape Horn)

Viedma
Golfo San Matías
Península Valdés
San Antonio Oeste
Valcheta
Sierra Grande
Puerto Madryn
Trelew
Rawson
Las Plumas
Embalse Florentino Ameghino
Majaspha
Chico
Golfo San Jorge
Comodoro Rivadavia
Caleta Olivia
Puerto Deseado
Lago Colhué Huapi
Sarmiento
Deseado
Jaramillo
Puerto San Julián
San Martín de los Andes
San Carlos de Bariloche
Lago Nahuel Huapi
Los Lagos
Valdivia
Osorno
Puerto Montt
Castro
Isla de Chiloé
Esquel
Volcán Corcovado 2290
Golfo Corcovado
Puerto Aisén
Coihaique
Cerro San Valentín 4058
Lago Buenos Aires
Chubut
Santa Cruz
Gobernador Gregores
Comandante Luis Piedra Buena
Bahía Grande
Lago San Martín
Lago Argentino
El Chaltén
El Calafate
Cerro Fitzroy 3406
Cerro Chaltén 3375
Lago Viedma
Cerro Murallón 3600
Cerro Pirámide 3389
Puerto Natales
Punta Arenas
Río Gallegos
Estrecho de Magallanes
Río Grande
Tierra del Fuego
Ushuaia
Isla Grande de Tierra del Fuego
Cerro Vigía 2438
Isla Hoste
Isla Santa Inés
Estrecho de Magallanes
Archipiélago Reina Adelaida
Isla Campana
Isla Wellington
Golfo de Penas
Península de Taitao
Archipiélago de los Chonos
Negro

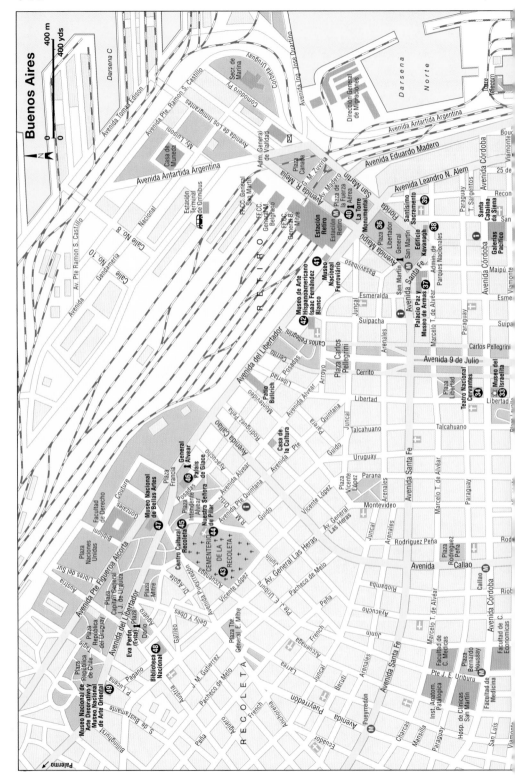

Buenos Aires

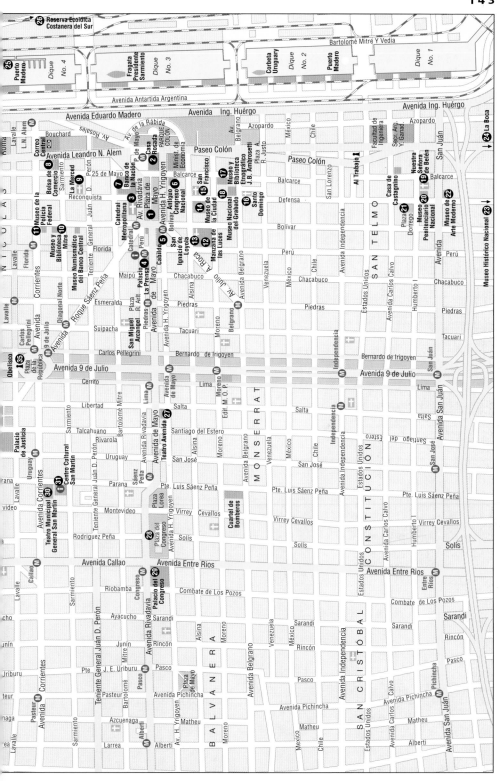

BUENOS AIRES

Arguably the most cosmopolitan city in all South America,
Argentina's historic capital has breathtaking energy, spacious
grandeur, and self-confident style

Map on pages 142–3

Despite grand boulevards and hefty, ostentatious architecture, this is a city of villages, or more correctly *barrios* (districts) – 47 of them. It has been famously described as the Paris of South America, or as travel writer Paul Theroux put it, a "most civilized anthill." Despite the current political and economic woes, it is still exuberant, stylish, and full of great pretense and hot gossip.

For visitors, the easternmost section of the city along the bank of the Río de la Plata (River Plate) will be the main area of interest. Hotels, museums, government buildings, shopping, and entertainments are located here in the districts of Palermo, Recoleta, Retiro, San Nicolás, Monserrat, San Telmo, and La Boca.

The country's economic woes have attracted foreign investors and many new shops and restaurants have opened over the past few years. The Puerto Madero opened in 1994 with exclusive eateries and apartments, and developments continue. Palermo Viejo is the latest area to have been dramatically revitalised and now boasts cultural centers, designer shops, and chic restaurants.

PRECEDING PAGES: early morning along Avenida 9 de Julio. **LEFT:** on guard duty at the Casa Rosada. **BELOW:** street tango in San Telmo.

Buenos Aires, for all its enormity, is a very easy city to get around. Streets run on a logical grid pattern with regular numbering. The bus system is extensive and efficient. Taxi fares are currently ridiculously low. But the nicest way to get around Buenos Aires is to walk. This is how you stumble upon the parks and interesting holes in the wall. The terrain is very flat, so it is easy on the walker. In fact, the largest altitude variation comes at the drainage runs at the intersections. But as you go, just be aware that pedestrians aren't accorded too many rights. Good luck, or as the locals say – *Suerte!*

Founding and settlement

Historians still dispute the date of Buenos Aires' founding and the identity of its founder. What is certain is that in 1516, Juan de Solís disembarked here in his search for a western route to the East. Buenos Aires lies at the mouth of one of the world's largest rivers, which Solís named Mar Dulce (Sweet Sea). The western banks lead onto the pampas: flat, treeless land, with extraordinarily rich black top-soil, ideal for agricultural planting. Solís also gave the river another name, the Lion's Sea, because of its brown tone and its vastness. This estuary later acquired the name Río de la Plata *(see page 37)*.

Pedro de Mendoza was the next European to arrive. In 1536, under Spanish royal auspices, he established the first settlement (some say in what is today Parque Lezama). He encountered the fertile pampas, as well as its inhabitants: hostile indigenous tribes.

After five years of continual attacks, the group moved upriver to Asunción, Paraguay. Mendoza left two important legacies: the city's name, Nuestra

The Argentine poet
and writer Jorge Luis
Borges called Buenos
Aires "a city of
nostalgia ... it seems
to me a tale that
Buenos Aires ever
began; I consider it
as eternal as water
and air."

Señora de Santa María del Buen Aire, and hundreds of horses and cows that were to multiply and later become the foundation of the Argentine economy.

Finally, in 1586, Juan de Garay, a *mestizo* (of Spanish and indigenous blood) from Asunción, Paraguay, returned with 70 men and established a permanent settlement. A fortress was built facing the river, and the town square, Plaza de Mayo, was marked off to the west. At the far end of the plaza they built the Cabildo (the town council) and on the northern corner, a small chapel. Although new buildings have been constructed on the ruins, the plaza maintains this basic structure and is still the center of the city's official activities.

Buenos Aires was the last major city in Latin America to be founded. Not only was it geographically cut off from more developed trade routes, but, under Spanish law, the use of its ports for European imports and export of precious metals from Potosí and Lima was prohibited. Logically, the English, Portuguese, and French took advantage of the lack of Spanish presence on the Río de la Plata, and illegal trade flourished. The settlement was able to survive in large part due to this contraband.

Manufactured goods were exchanged for silver brought from northern mining centers, and for cow hides and tallow. Construction materials also began to be imported, since the pampas had neither trees nor stones. Homes were originally built of adobe and straw.

Faced with competition in the region from other European nations, in 1776 Spain declared what is now Argentina, Uruguay, Bolivia, Paraguay, and the northern section of Chile a viceroyalty. Buenos Aires was made the site of the central government. With its new judicial, financial, and military role, the city burgeoned as a regional power. Functionaries, lawyers, priests, military personnel, artisans, and slaves soon arrived, and the small village began its transformation into a major cosmopolitan city. In Latin America, only Lima and Mexico City exceeded the economic development at the time.

The *porteños* were accustomed to a certain economic and political independence from Spain. When, alone, they were able to repel two British invasions in 1806 and 1807, pride in the city's military prowess, and what later was to be called nationalism, ran high.

Independence and development

In 1810 the city's residents took advantage of Spain's preoccupation with Napoleon, and won more autonomy for themselves. However, it was not until 1816 that independence was declared for the whole country.

In the subsequent decades, the government of Buenos Aires was consumed with the struggle for control over the rest of the country. The Federalists, represented by Juan Manuel Rosas, the governor of Buenos Aires from 1829 to 1852, believed each province should maintain considerable power and independence. The Unitarians, who came to power when General Urquiza overthrew Rosas, sought the dominance of Buenos Aires over the rest of the country. The tension between residents of the interior and the *porteños* still exists.

Finally, in 1880, the dispute was resolved in a small

BELOW: booming trade in a 19th-century dockside warehouse.

Map
on pages
142–3

street battle, and the city became a federal district, rather than simply the capital of the province of Buenos Aires. This was also to be a decade of intense change for the city. Under President Julio Roca, the mayor of the city looked to Europe and especially Paris as a model for change in Buenos Aires. Hundreds of buildings were constructed in imitation of the latest Parisian styles. New neighborhoods were created for the wealthy by filling in huge sections of the river, particularly in the northern parts of the city, where Retiro, Recoleta, and Palermo lie.

Boom and slump

It was also in the 1880s that mass immigration from Europe began, principally from Italy and Spain although also from Germany, Poland, and Britain, as well as Lebanon and Syria, and later Russia. By 1910, the city's population had risen to 1,300,000. Public services such as the tramway, running water, schools, and police protection were well under way. The city's literature, opera, theater, and other arts were spreading around the world. Suddenly, Buenos Aires was the Paris of Latin America for upper-class European and North American tourists.

In the past 20 years or so, the city has lost out to other major cosmopolitan cities. The results of political and economic instability can be seen in the old cars, buildings in disrepair, and lack of construction. Where buildings have sprung up, there is little regard for maintaining the beauty of the old city, and virtually no urban planning for a new city. At the same time, there has been very little attempt to restore some of the city's oldest and most typical buildings, although in San Telmo, Buenos Aires' original center, many of its crumbling colonial buildings have been converted into loft-style apartments.

Turkish immigrant with hookah pipe.

BELOW: soaking up the sun in one of the city's parks.

Colonial detail on Calle Florida.

The incongruous architecture of some areas of Buenos Aires may disappoint those who had imagined a picturesque European city. But it's the real city; a city in crisis, a city whose future is undefined, and a city that reflects the special character of its residents.

Getting your bearings

To understand Buenos Aires, you have to venture beyond the downtown area. Walk the daytime streets of residential areas, ride buses, sit in cafés, and, above all, talk – and listen – to the people. Their conflicting and emotional feelings about the city and the whole country are contagious.

Buenos Aires is not only enormous in relation to the population of the rest of Argentina, but is also one of the largest cities in Latin America. The Federal District occupies 200 sq. km (77 sq. miles) and the entire metropolitan area spans over 2,915 sq. km (1,121 sq. miles). Approximately 12 million people, or one third of the country's population, live in the city and surrounding areas. Three million reside within the Federal District.

Buenos Aires is marked to the north and east by the Río de la Plata and, on a clear day, you can see all the way across the mud-colored river to the Uruguayan coast. To the south, the city limit is marked by the Riachuelo, a shallow channel constructed to permit entrance to the major ports.

The city's landscape is varied. There are wide boulevards and narrow cobblestone streets. The downtown area boasts chic boutique windows, outdoor cafés, simple but elegant restaurants, and grand old cinemas and theaters. In residential districts, ornamental old apartment buildings, with French doors that open onto plant-filled balconies, stand side by side with modern buildings up to 20

BELOW: life reflects art.
RIGHT: a mural of the colonial past.

stories high, most with sliding glass doors that open onto balconies. Sycamore and *tipuana* trees line the streets, providing shade for little boys playing soccer. There are innumerable parks and plazas, where you may opt to go jogging, or simply sit quietly and watch the old men playing *truco* (a card game) or chess in the summer.

Map on pages 142–3

A city of barrios

There are 47 *barrios* (districts) in Buenos Aires, each with its own special history and character. With few exceptions, the neighborhoods have a Roman grid structure around a central plaza with a church. Most *barrios* also have a main street for commerce, with a two-story shopping mall, as well as a butcher, baker, and vegetable and fruit stand. A sports club, a movie theater, a pizzeria, and an ice-cream parlor also form part of the typical *barrio*.

The social atmosphere in these neighborhoods is much warmer than in the busy downtown area, where pedestrians, as in most big cities, are on the run and will barely stop to give the time of day. In a *barrio*, a lost tourist will be rescued by helpful and curious residents.

To grow up in a *barrio* is to acquire a special allegiance to it; soccer teams from each club compete in national competitions that create passionate rivalries among many of the districts.

In order to get a sense of Buenos Aires' layout, it is useful to simplify and talk about major blocks of the city. From Plaza de Mayo, two diagonal avenues extend to the northwest and southwest (avenidas Roque Sáenz Peña and Julio A. Roca). The central track between the two is the most populated area of the city. To the south is the oldest part of the city, including San Telmo and La

BELOW: taking time out from the daily grind.

Boca, where many working-class and some middle-class people live. To the
north are the *barrios* of Retiro, Recoleta, and Palermo, where the wealthy moved
when yellow fever hit the southern district in the 1870s. A fourth zone lies to the
west. With the opening of two railway lines – the Once line that runs along
Rivadavia, and the Retiro line that runs northwest along the river – new *barrios*
such as Palermo Viejo began to spring up.

The center of Buenos Aires

The center is truly the city's "downtown", and while most *porteños* live in outer
barrios, everyone comes here, either to work, to eat, or to find entertainment.
Residential *barrios* have their own mini-commercial areas, so that except to
visit friends, many *porteños* never cross the city; they simply head downtown.

As in every big city, there are many hurried, well-dressed business people in the
center of Buenos Aires, but there are also Argentines here enjoying the bookstores,
the movies, the theater, the café conversations on every imaginable topic, the
plazas, the shopping, and the political and cultural street life. Some streets, like
Florida, Corrientes, and Lavalle, are for strolling, and are filled with leisurely visitors come to walk, watch, and be watched. A two-hour walk around the center
starting at the Plaza de Mayo provides a quick introduction to the government
buildings as well as the commercial, financial, and entertainment districts.

Plaza politics

BELOW: El Cabildo,
historic heart of
the independence
movement.

Buenos Aires began with the **Plaza de Mayo ❶**, today a strikingly beautiful
square with its tall palm trees, elaborate flower gardens, and central monument,
set off by the surrounding colonial buildings. The plaza has been and still is the

pulsating center of the country. Since its founding in 1580, as the Plaza del Fuerte (fortress), many important historical events have been celebrated or protested against here.

The most eye-catching structure in the plaza is unquestionably the **Casa Rosada**, the seat of the executive branch of the government, which has recently been renovated. Flanking it are the Banco de la Nación, the Catedral Metropolitana, the Palacio Municipal (city hall), and the Cabildo (town council).

The Casa Rosada was originally a fortress overlooking what is now the **Plaza Colón**, but was at that time the river's edge. When attacks by the indigenous inhabitants subsided, the plaza became Plaza del Mercado, a market place and social center. The name and role of the plaza changed again with the British invasions of 1806 and 1807, when it became the Plaza de la Victoria. Finally, following the declaration of independence, the plaza assumed its present name, in honor of the month of May in 1810 when the city broke away from Spain.

The date also marks the first mass rally in the plaza, on this occasion to celebrate independence. Subsequently, Argentines have poured into the plaza to protest and celebrate most of the nation's important events. Political parties, governments (de facto and constitutional), and even trade unions and the church call people into the plaza to demonstrate a symbolic power.

Map on pages 142–3

The Plaza de Mayo has a central pyramid that was built on the first centennial of the city's independence. Among other purposes, it serves as the centerpiece for the weekly rounds of the Madres de la Plaza de Mayo.

Historic demonstrations

Salient events in the history of the Plaza de Mayo include the October 17, 1945 workers' demonstration, organized by the General Confederation of Labor to protest the brief detention of then vice-president Juan Perón. Ten years later, the airforce bombed the plaza while hundreds of thousands of Perón's supporters were rallying to defend his administration from the impending military coup. In 1982, Argentines flooded the plaza to applaud General Galtieri's invasion of the Malvinas/Falkland Islands. A few months later, they were back again, threatening to kill the military ruler for having lied about their chances of defeating the British. In 1987, the plaza was jammed with 800,000 *porteños* demonstrating against a military rebellion, and again at the end of 1989, protesting President Menem's pardon of convicted generals.

But the most famous rallies have been those of the *Madres de la Plaza de Mayo* – the mothers of the many people who disappeared during the "dirty war" *(see page 62)*. The Mothers still demonstrate every Thursday afternoon, demanding information on their missing children's whereabouts, and calling for the punishment of those responsible.

During the last years of the military regime, young people accompanying the Mothers would taunt the menacing army and police units with chants of, "Cowards, this plaza belongs to the Mothers." The white headscarves the Mothers traditionally wear at all the demonstrations have been painted around the base of the pyramid, marking their weekly route. Another group protesting against the crimes comitted by the dictatorship is *Hijos*. Formed in 1995 by children of the disappeared, it aims to make those responsible for the deaths of their parents accountable.

BELOW: Santa enjoying Christmas in the sunshine.

Young porteño *facing up to a guard at the Casa Rosada.*

The Pink House

Leaders of the nation traditionally address the masses from the balconies of the **Casa Rosada** ❷, an architecturally imbalanced building constructed on the foundations of earlier structures in 1894. Sixteen years earlier, President Sarmiento had chosen the site for the new government house. There are several explanations for why he had it painted pink, the most credible of which is that it was the only alternative to white in those days. The special tone was actually achieved by mixing beef fat, blood, and lime. Some insist that Sarmiento chose pink to distinguish the building from the White House. Still others say that pink was selected as a compromise between two feuding parties whose colors were white and red.

The **Museo de la Casa Rosada** (open weekdays except Wed 11am–6pm and Sun 2–6pm, with guided tours 11am and 4pm; Sun 3.30pm and 4.30pm; free) is a small gallery that contains antiques and objects identified with the lives of different national heroes. The entrance is on Avenida Yrigoyen. The Grenadiers Regiment guards the Casa Rosada and the president. This elite army unit was created during the independence wars by General San Martín, and its soldiers wear the same blue and red uniforms that distinguished them in those times. Between 6 and 7pm each day, they lower the national flag in front of the Casa Rosada. On national holidays the Grenadiers often parade on horseback, and they accompany the president on his public appearances.

BELOW: Casa Rosada, the presidential palace.

Church and state

The **Catedral Metropolitana** ❸ (open daily except Sat pm and Sun am. Guided tours in Spanish Mon–Fri 11.30am) is the next historic building on the plaza and

the seat of Buenos Aires' archbishopric. The cathedral's presence in this highly political plaza is appropriate. The Catholic church has always been a pillar of Argentine society, and since the city's founding, the church has shared the Plaza de Mayo. In a mural at the northern end of Avenida 9 de Julio, two symbols are used to illustrate the founding of the city: a priest and a spade, the latter representing the military.

Map on pages 142–3

The cathedral was erected over the course of several decades and was completed in 1827. It was built, like the Cabildo and the Casa Rosada, upon the foundations of earlier versions. There are 12 severe neo-classical pillars at its front that are said to represent the 12 apostles. The carved triangle above reputedly portrays the meeting of Joseph and his father Jacob. This section is generally considered to be the work of architects. Yet a theory persists among some that it was created by a prisoner, who was then set free as a reward for its beauty.

Inside are five naves housing important art relics. The oil paintings on the walls are attributed to Flemish painter, Sir Peter Paul Rubens (1577–1640). There are also beautiful wood engravings by the Portuguese Manuel Coyto de Couto.

On the steps of the cathedral on Flag Day (Día de la Bandera).

For Argentines, the most important aspect of the cathedral is the tomb of General José de San Martín, liberator of Argentina, Chile, Peru, Bolivia, and Uruguay. San Martín, who died during his self-imposed exile in France, is one of the few national heroes to be revered by Argentines of all political persuasions.

The first eye-catching building on Avenida de Mayo on the way from Plaza de Mayo is the **Palacio La Prensa** ❹, until recently housing Argentina's oldest and most conservative national newspaper. It is located opposite the Cabildo and adjacent to the Palacio Municipal, an ornamental old building with an enor-

BELOW: grandiose sculpture on the Avenida del Libertador.

mous pentagonal clock in its tower. The La Prensa building, which now houses the Casa de la Cultura of the city of Buenos Aires, is French-style in architecture, unlike most of the Spanish-style Avenida de Mayo, and the ground floor is worth a look for its stained glass, decoration, and wood work.

Across the Avenida de Mayo, and on the western end of the Plaza de Mayo, is the **Cabildo** (town council) ❺, a key historic building and perhaps the greatest patriotic attraction in Argentina. School children are brought here and told how their forebears planned the nation's independence.

The town council has been on this site since around the time of the city's founding in 1580, although the present building was constructed in 1751. Originally, it spanned the length of the plaza with five great arches on each side. In 1880, when Avenida de Mayo was built, part of the building was demolished. And once again, in 1932, the Cabildo was further reduced, this time to its current size, with two arches on either side of the central balconies.

The Cabildo also houses an historic museum, the **Museo del Cabildo** (open Tues–Fri 12.30–7pm and Sun 3–7pm), exhibiting furniture and relics from the colonial period. Behind the museum is a pleasant patio, which features a simple outdoor snack bar and on Thursday and Friday afternoons you will find a small arts and crafts fair. Continuing around the plaza, on the southeastern corner is the **Antiguo Congreso Nacional** ❻ (open for guided tours Thur 3–5pm; library open Mon–Fri 1–7pm), the former House of Congress, built in 1864. It served as the seat of government until 1906 and since 1971 it has been used by the National Academy of History as a conference center, with a history library.

BELOW: balancing the national diet of beef.

La City

The main banking area of Buenos Aires, known as "La City", extends four blocks north from the Plaza de Mayo to Corrientes along the parallel streets in between, and west for three blocks as far as pedestrianized Florida. Here you can find the major national as well as international banks.

Opposite the Antiguo Congreso Nacional, at the northeastern corner of Plaza de Mayo, is the **Banco de la Nación** ❼. The old Teatro Colón was on this site before it reopened on Lavalle Plaza in 1908. The imposing marble and stone bank was inaugurated in 1888. On the first floor of the Banco de la Nación is the **Museo Numismático** (open Feb–Dec Mon–Fri 10am–3pm), whose entrance is at Bartolomé Mitre 362. Apart from a large collection of coins, notes and medals, the museum has a private research library and offers tours of the bank itself, available by prior appointment.

Nearby, at San Martín 216, the **Banco Central** (open Tues–Thur 10am–2pm) also has a currency museum. With some 14,000 exhibits it claims to be the biggest of its kind in the Americas.

The **Bolsa de Comercio** ❽ (Stock Exchange) (open Mon–Fri 10am–5pm) is located three blocks from the Plaza de Mayo, at 25 de Mayo between Sarmiento and Corrientes. The building was inaugurated in 1919, and its features such as its wood and metal work, the cupola, and the internal staircase are worth a look. Also within this area are the **Basílica de la Merced ❾**, at Reconquista and Perón, an 18th-century church and convent with lovely gardens and a restaurant in the patio offering one of the few peaceful oases in central Buenos Aires.

There has been a church on the site since 1712, and there was a convent there from 1600 to 1823. At San Martín 336, between Sarmiento and Corrientes, is the **Museo y Biblioteca Mitre ❿** (open Mon–Fri 1–6.30pm), which includes oil paintings, the personal effects of President Mitre, important historical and map libraries, as well as a currency museum. In front, at San Martín 322 is the **Museo de la Policía Federal ⓫** (open Tues–Fri 2–6pm) containing exhibits charting the history of a police force whose actions have not always provoked widespread admiration.

The southern quarter

The expansion of Buenos Aires in the 17th century first occurred toward the south, making the southern quarter one of the city's oldest residential areas.

There are three areas of interest to most tourists: La Manzana de las Luces ("The Enlightenment Block"), one block south of the Plaza de Mayo; San Telmo, historically a fascinating *barrio* and today inhabited by artists and antique dealers; and La Boca, at the southeastern tip of the city, which is famous for the pastel-colored tin houses where dock workers used to live, and for the raucous restaurants where tourists come for a lively evening's entertainment.

La Manzana de las Luces ⓬ refers to a block of buildings that were constructed by the Jesuits in the early 18th century. The church of San Ignacio, the old Jesuit school, and underground tunnels are bordered by calles Bolívar, Alsina, Peru and Moreno.

Map on pages 142–3

TIP

The Feria de las Artes, on the Plazoleta de los Franciscanos, at the corner of Alsina and Defensa, is a weekly market offering a good selection of art and crafts (Fridays from 10am–5pm).

BELOW: many *porteños* employ professional dog walkers.

The interior of the
Farmacia la Estrella,
whose shelving
is crafted from
Italian walnut.

BELOW:
tango and the
news in San Telmo.

The area was originally granted to the Jesuits at the end of the 17th century. In 1767, the Spanish Crown withdrew the gift, in light of what was perceived as the group's increasing power. In fact, of principal concern in this case, as with Jesuit missions throughout the world during this period, were the egalitarian principles practiced by the priests within their social organizations. Today, La Manzana de las Luces serves as a cultural center, but tours of its historical past are available for a small fee (open Sat and Sun 3.30pm and 5pm).

Despite the repression against the Jesuit order, many of the churches still stand, the oldest of which is **San Ignacio de Loyola** ⓭ (open during Mass, Mon–Fri 7pm), at the corner of Alsina and Bolívar 225. This impressive baroque church, which is also the oldest of all the remaining six colonial churches in Buenos Aires, was founded in 1675 and completed in 1735.

Walking south on Defensa from the Plaza de Mayo, one finds the **Farmacia la Estrella**, a 19th-century drugstore with marvelous metaphorical murals on the ceiling and walls portraying disease and medicine.

On the second floor of the same building is the **Museo de la Ciudad** ⓮ (open Mon–Fri 11.30am–7pm, Sun 3–7pm). The small museum features rotating exhibitions of aspects of the city's past and present, including architectural photo studies, and curios, such as old postcards of the city.

On Defensa and Alsina is the **Basílica de San Francisco** ⓯ and the **Capilla de San Roque**. The main church, finished in 1754, is the headquarters of the Franciscan Order. Parts of the neo-classical building were rebuilt at the end of the 19th century, in imitation of the German baroque styles in vogue at the time. The chapel was built in 1762.

San Francisco was severely damaged in 1955, as were a dozen other churches,

when angry Peronist mobs attacked and set fire to the historic structure. The violence was a response to the Catholic church's opposition to the Peronist government, and its support for the impending military coup.

Santo Domingo ⑯, located at Belgrano and Defensa, is another important church that was partially burned in 1955, including the destruction of much of the principal altar. This former convent contains the mausoleum of independence hero General Manuel Belgrano. The basilica (correctly known as Nuestra Señora del Rosario) was inaugurated in 1783, although there has been a church on the site since 1600, and it is famous for its organ often used for recitals.

One block north, at Moreno 350, the **Museo y Biblioteca Etnográfico J. B. Ambrosetti** ⑰ (open Feb–Dec Wed–Sun 2.30–6.30pm) has the largest archeological and ethnographic collection in Argentina, including a 1,200-year old mummy and ceramics from the pre-Columbian era. The early 19th-century building was formerly the Law Faculty of the University of Buenos Aires.

The **Museo Nacional del Grabado** ⑱ (open Mon–Fri & Sun 2–6pm) at Defensa 372 offers exhibitions of works by contemporary and 19th-century engravers, and includes a library.

Map on pages 142–3

The basilica of **Santo Domingo** *contains four British flags captured during the British invasions of Buenos Aires in 1806 and 1807, as well as two Spanish flags taken by General Belgrano during the wars of independence.*

San Telmo – bohemian Buenos Aires

Like Greenwich Village in New York, **San Telmo** used to be one of the city's more run-down areas, until history, architecture, and low rents in the 1960s caught the attention of artists and intellectuals who began to revive the area. Attractive studios, restaurants, and antique shops began to replace the decaying tenements. An open-air Sunday flea market in the central plaza has brought in

BELOW: an antique shop in San Telmo.

enough tourists to nourish the new business ventures. While San Telmo is now one of the principal tourist stops, the neighborhood maintains its historic authenticity and its vitality. **Plaza Dorrego**, the site of the Sunday flea market, is proof of this. Weekdays, it remains a fascinating spot, where old people who have lived all their lives in the *barrio*, many of whom still speak with an Italian accent, meet to talk and to play chess and *truco*.

San Telmo grew during the 18th-century as a rest stop for merchants en route from the Plaza de Mayo to the warehouses along the Riachuelo. Next to the Plaza Dorrego was a trading post for imported goods. On adjacent streets, *pulperías* (bar/grocery stores) quickly sprang up to accommodate passersby.

Except for the Bethlemite priests who had established themselves in the San Pedro Church, the area's first residents were Irish, blacks, and Genoese sailors, whose rowdy drinking habits made the *pulperías* notorious.

In the early 19th century, many important families built their homes along **Calle Defensa**, which connects Plaza de Mayo and Plaza Dorrego. During this period, a typical home had three successive interior patios, and only the facade would change, as new architectural styles arrived. The first patio was used as living quarters, the second for cooking and washing, and the third for the animals.

In the 1870s, a yellow fever epidemic swept through San Telmo, killing more than 13,000 people during a three-month epidemic. At the time, it was widely believed that the fog off the Riachuelo carried the disease. Those who could fled San Telmo and built homes just west of the downtown area, approaching what is now called Congreso, and in the northern section, now called Barrio Norte.

In the 1880s and the subsequent three decades, San Telmo received poor European immigrants, particularly Italians, who were arriving in Argentina. Many of the old mansions and *chorizo* houses were converted into *conventillos* (one-room tenements that open onto a common patio), in order to accommodate the flood of new families.

Nineteenth-century homes in San Telmo were called chorizo *(sausage) houses because of their linear shape.*

BELOW: lace stall, San Telmo market.

Tango, jazz and eating out

A walk through San Telmo begins at the corner of Balcarce and Chile, the northern edge of the *barrio*. There are several of the city's oldest and most prestigious tango bars nearby (*see Travel Tips, page 353*).

Crossing Chile on Balcarce, you come to a two-block long cobblestone street called **San Lorenzo**. To the right are beautiful old houses, many now nightclubs. Others, some with interior patios, have been converted into apartments, studios and boutiques. At 319 San Lorenzo are **Los Patios de San Telmo**, a renovated house open to the public, which contains numerous artists' studios, and a bar. The brick and wood ceilings date back at least 200 years.

Balcarce continues across Independencia and is one of the prettiest streets in San Telmo for strolling, and for more live music venues. The next block is **Pasaje Giuffra**, another narrow, cobblestone street, where many of the old *pulperías* used to be.

Further down, **Carlos Calvo** is an attractive street with numerous restored colonial houses, several of which have been converted into elegant restaurants. Half a block past Carlos Calvo at 1016 Balcarce is the old home of the Argentine painter **Castagnino**, whose murals from the 1950s adorn the ceiling of the Galerías Pacífico shopping mall on Florida. After he died, his son converted Castagnino's home into an art museum.

Map on pages 142–3

On this same block on the right is the **Galería del Viejo Hotel** (1053 Balcarce), another old *conventillo* that has been renovated and now serves as an arts center. Two stories of studios open onto a central plant-filled patio. Visitors may wander through the complex and watch the artists at work. Weekends are the best time to visit.

Calle Humberto 1 is the next block. Turning right, you come upon the old **Iglesia de Nuestra Señora de Belén** ❶. The church was built by Bethlemite priests in 1770, and was temporarily occupied by the British invaders in 1807. Next door, at Humberto 1 378, is the ghoulish **Museo Penitenciario Nacional** ❷ (Wed–Fri 3–6pm, Sun 11am–6pm), on the site of a former jail, which operated until the 1870s. This museum offers delights such as exhibitions of leg irons and other prison paraphernalia. Guided visits of the museum, which also offers occasional art exhibitions, can be arranged on request.

Sunny balcony of a café in San Telmo.

Across the street is Escuela G. Rawson, a former convent that is now a school. Next door is a plaque commemorating the site of an old *pulpería*, operated by a woman named Martina Cespedes. During the British invasion, Señora Cespedes and her daughters enticed British soldiers into their bar , tied them up and turned them over to the Argentine army. Although one of her daughters reputedly married a captured British soldier, the mother was eventually rewarded for her brave deeds with the title of Captain of the Argentinian Army.

BELOW: the baroque church of Nuestra Señora de Belén.

TIP

If, after visiting the flea market, you still want more open-air browsing, one block north of Plaza Dorrego, on Carlos Calvo, is San Telmo's Municipal Market, which sells fresh meat, fruit, and vegetables.

Sunday flea market

Finally, we are upon **Plaza Dorrego ㉑**, the center of San Telmo's commercial and cultural life. It is the site of the Sunday flea market, with junk jewelry, secondhand books, antiques, and some handicrafts. Surrounding the plaza are several restaurants, bars, and antique shops that are fun to wander through. Another charming shopping mall on Defensa is **Galería El Solar de French**. It has been redone in a colonial style, with flagstone floors, narrow wooden doors, bird cages, and plants hanging from wrought iron hooks along the patio.

Located two blocks south of the plaza, at Avenida San Juan 350, is the **Museo de Arte Moderno ㉒** (open Tues–Sun 11am–8pm free on Wed closed Feb). The museum is housed in the former Massalin y Celasco cigarette factory, an attractive building with a brick facade. It houses the Ignacio Pirovano collection of major 20th-century painters, as well as temporary exhibitions of international art.

Parque Lezama is just four blocks south of Plaza Dorrego on Defensa. Many believe that this little hill was the site of the first founding of the city. Later it was the home of Gregorio Lezama, who converted it into a public park. By the end of the 19th century, it was an important social center, with many amenities such as a restaurant, a circus, a boxing ring, and a theater. Today, the park is somewhat run-down, and the view is no longer attractive due to the surrounding construction and heavy traffic. However, the old mansion still holds nostalgic memories and has been converted into the **Museo Histórico Nacional ㉓** (open Tues–Sat 1.30–5.30pm), the national history museum at Defensa 1600. One of the museum's highlights is a room decorated with the furniture from the house in France where General San Martín ended his days.

BELOW: colorful clutter of a typical La Boca house.

La Boca

The working-class neighborhood of **La Boca** ㉔ is at the southern tip of the city, along the Riachuelo Canal. The *barrio* is famous for its houses made from sheet-iron and painted in bright colors, and for its history as a residential area for Genoese sailors and dock workers in the 19th century.

La Boca came to life with the mid-19th century surge in international trade and the accompanying increase in port activity. In the 1870s, meat-salting plants and warehouses were built, and a tramway facilitated access to the area. As the city's ports expanded, the Riachuelo was dug out to permit the entrance of deep-water ships. Sailors and longshoremen, most of whom were Italian immigrants, began to settle in the area.

One painter's influence

The famous painter Benito Quinquela Martín took up the theme of color, traditional to his neighborhood, and made it his own. Quinquela was an orphan, adopted by a longshoreman family of La Boca at the turn of the 20th-century. As an artist, he dedicated his life to capturing the essence of La Boca. He painted dark, stooped figures, set in raging scenes of port action. In one of his works (which Mussolini reputedly tried unsuccessfully to buy from him with a blank check), an immense canvas splashed with bright oranges, blues, and black, men hurriedly unload a burning ship.

Neighborhood residents took pride in their local artist, and were influenced by Quinquela's vision of their lives. They chose even wilder colors for their own homes, and a unique dialogue grew between residents and artist.

Quinquela took over an alleyway, known as the **Caminito**, decorated it with

Map on pages 142–3

The sheet-iron homes that can still be seen throughout La Boca and across the canal in Avellaneda were originally built from materials taken from the interiors of abandoned ships by Genoese sailors.

BELOW: graffiti inspired by art.

murals and sculpture, and established an open-air market to promote local artists. The brightly painted homes and colorful laundry hanging out to dry provide the background to this charming one-block alley. There are small stands, manned by the artists themselves, where watercolor paintings and other works of art are displayed for sale.

A walking tour

A stroll through La Boca begins at the Caminito. Heading north from the river, it is worth walking around the block and back to the riverside to get a sense of the normal residential street. The tin houses were not created for tourists but are, in fact, comfortable homes. Most have long corridors leading to interior apartments, and are graced by wood paneling. The cobblestone streets are shaded by tall sycamore trees, and elevated sidewalks are some defense against frequent flooding.

The **Vuelta de Rocha**, where the Caminito begins, consists of a small triangular plaza with a ship's mast. It overlooks the port area, which may be more accurately described as a decaying shipyard and you may be accosted by the foul odors of the canal.

Fundación Proa is a small modern, museum with changing contemporary art exhibits and a cafe and terrace with good views of the waterfront. A new Malecón promenade leads from the Vuelta de Rocha along the river and is a good place for a stroll.

East along Pedro de Mendoza, the avenue parallel to the canal, at No. 1835 is the **Museo de Bellas Artes de La Boca** (open Tues–Sun 10am–6pm), the neighborhood's very own fine arts museum. The top floor was used by Quinquela as

an apartment studio. Many of his most important paintings are here, and one may also see the modest apartment he used in his last years. The museum is a fun stop, if only to get the view of the shipyard depicted in his paintings

Map on pages 142–3

Rowdy cantinas, rowdy soccer

Just past the Avellaneda Bridge is **Calle Necochea**, where rowdy *cantinas* contrast with the sedate restaurants in other areas of Buenos Aires. These lively music and dance clubs were originally sailors' mess halls, and their high spirits recall the jazz clubs of New Orleans.

Brightly colored murals of couples dancing the tango, speakers set out on the sidewalk blaring loud music, and somewhat aggressive doormen who compete for the tourist dollar, may combine to frighten off those who are not prepared. But the scene is not as seedy as it might appear. Families from the interior of the country are there for a festive night out. Old people are singing their favorite tunes and dancing amid balloons and ribbons. And the idea that a night out on Calle Necochea is a celebration of sailors returning home is definitely preserved. Much of the action is concentrated between calles Brandsen and Olavarria *(see page 360)*. Two blocks west is **Avenida Almirante Brown**, the main commercial street in La Boca renowned for its excellent pizzerias.

Bar mural in La Boca.

La Boca also boasts the country's most famous soccer team, **Boca Juniors**, and their stadium, La Bombonera ("the candybox"), located in the heart of the neighborhood, draws fans from all over the city. Diego Maradona, the internationally famous soccer star who carried Argentina to victory with his spectacular goals in the 1986 World Cup, played here.

BELOW: hopeful future Maradonas practicing in the park.

Puerto Madero

Back at the Plaza de Mayo, and east toward the river, is the vibrant, renovated docklands area of **Puerto Madero** ㉕. Walking from Plaza de Mayo, cross Avenida Alem, where at Sarmiento and Alem, two blocks east of the plaza, you'll find the **Correo Central** (Main Post Office), an ornate French-style building (open Mon–Fri 10am–8pm). Crossing Avenida Madero and Avenida Alicia Moreau de Justo, you will finally reach the string of renovated port buildings that runs from Avenida Córdoba at the northern end to the Buenos Aires-La Plata Highway at the southern end. The original waterfront port buildings, constructed by Eduardo Madero in 1887, have been turned into fancy office blocks and restaurants, where you can have a very elegant meal or a coffee. While this is the in place for lunch or dinner, the restaurants to be found here are among the most expensive in Buenos Aires – and not necessarily the best.

The Puerto Madero neighborhood has a pedestrian walkway extending the length of the port, and also includes yacht clubs and most of Buenos Aires' most modern tower blocks, in addition to the 19th-century port buildings. The most technologically advanced buildings in the area are the Telecom Tower and the Fortabat Tower, both near the Córdoba end of the district. At Dock 3, the **Fragata Sarmiento** (open daily 9am–9pm), is a 19th-century Argentine Navy frigate now serving as a museum. The ship, built in England in 1897, still has its original woodwork and furniture. The area is constantly being developed and Madero Este on the eastern side is now the site of a stylish Philippe Starck apart-hotel.

A short distance away, to the east of Puerto Madero, is the **Reserva Ecológica Costanera del Sur** ㉖ (open daily 8am–7pm; free admission), a large open green

BELOW: Cafe La Biela, in Recoleta.

CAFE LIFE

The social life, and to a great extent the business and cultural life of Buenos Aires revolves around cafes, or *confiterías*, as they are known in Argentina. "*Meet me at the confitería*" is the typical response to an invitation to go to the cinema or the theater, as well as to clinch a business deal or simply to get together for a chat. A coffee or a cognac in a favorite *confitería* is also the standard ritual for ending a night out on the town.

There are cafes on almost every street corner and they range from the most elegant to modest and cozy gathering places where neighbors exchange greetings or employees from nearby offices take a break to read the daily paper. Visitors to Buenos Aires often comment that only Paris rivals the city as a true "cafe society."

Historically, the rise of the cafe as an institution came from the high proportion of male immigrants, who were either single or whose wives stayed behind. These men came to the cafes for companionship, a smoke, or a game of dominos. Gradually, many cafes became associated with a particular clientele. Each political, artistic, and social group laid claim to its own cafe, so that even today many of the events that mark Argentine history were first discussed among friends or foes over a *confitería* table.

space along the river which has been a nature reserve since 1986. There are four lakes and a revamped esplanade which make it an attractive area for walking. The reserve, which is very popular at weekends, is home to many species of waterbirds and mammals.

Returning to Plaza de Mayo and facing west, the view down Avenida de Mayo to the National Congress is spectacular, and the 15-block walk is a wonderful introduction to the city. The avenue was inaugurated in 1894 as the link between the executive branch and the Congress, most of which had been completed by 1906. It was originally designed to imitate a Spanish avenue, with wide sidewalks, gilded lamp posts, chocolate shops, and outfitters' emporiums, and old Zarzuela theaters. Today, however, there is a mixture of influences with local adaptations that defy classification. As in much of the city, "neoclassical", "French", "Italian", and "art nouveau" are terms that do not adequately describe the special combination of influences seen here. Nor is there a traditional coherence from one building to the next; ornamental buildings stand side by side with others that are simple and austere.

Ornamental lunch

There are several well-known restaurants and cafes along the way, including **Cafe Tortoni** (825 Avenida de Mayo), a historic meeting place for writers and intellectuals. Apart from the famous customers said to have frequented the cafe, the ornamental interior makes the place worthy of at least a quick glimpse. Marble tables, red leather seats, bronze statues, and elaborate mirrors create the most regal of atmospheres. In the evenings the cafe hosts various theater and music shows, the most common being tango or jazz.

Map on pages 142–3

A menu from Cafe Tortoni, the most famous cafe in Buenos Aires.

BELOW: the red-brick renovation of Puerto Madero.

The Spanish-style **Teatro Avenida** ㉗, inaugurated in 1908, is at Avenida de Mayo 1222. Closed down since 1979 as a result of a fire, the building has been renovated and was re-opened in 1994. The beautiful 1,200-seat theater offers regular theatrical and musical performances, usually by Spanish companies or with a Spanish theme, and it is also used for conferences.

Avenida de Mayo ends at the Plaza Lorea, just before the Plaza del Congreso.

Plaza del Congreso is used as the zero kilometer mark for maps of Argentina.

Pizzas, pigeons and politics

The next block is the **Plaza del Congreso** ㉘. The plaza is a wonderful place for people-watching on warm summer evenings. Old and young eat pizza and ice-cream on the benches among the pigeons, enjoying the civilized atmosphere. There is a dramatic fountain with a galloping horse and little cherubs, and at night, classical music booms out from below the falls. There is a monument above the fountain that honors "two congresses" – the 1813 assembly that abolished slavery, and the 1816 congress of Tucumán that declared the country's independence. In the past several years, it has also been the site of a white tent in which public schoolteachers have maintained an ongoing hunger strike in protest at miserable education salaries. Similarly, every Wednesday since the early 1990s there has been a demonstration by senior citizens in front of Congress, protesting at the starvation-level pensions and the failure of the government to increase minimum monthly pensions despite repeated promises.

The green-domed **Palacio del Congreso** ㉙ houses the Senate on the south side and the House of Representatives on the north (Rivadavia entrance). The green color was not in the original plans when the building was inaugurated in 1910 for the centenary of the May Revolution – the dome was made of copper which over time assumed its present green shade. Congressional sessions, which normally run from May 1 to September 30, are open to the press or those with a pass, available at the annex of the House of Representatives across Rivadavia. Guided tours in Spanish are available Mon, Tues, Thur, and Fri at 11am and 5pm. The interior is decorated with appropriate pomp: large paintings, bronze and marble sculptures, luxurious red carpets, silk curtains, and wood paneling. The central hall (Salón Azul) is especially impressive, lying under the dome and including a huge two-ton crystal chandelier dating from 1910. Next to the Salón Azul is the Salón de los Pasos Perdidos, where delegations are received and where former Argentine presidents have lain in state. The building also boasts an extensive library, open 24 hours a day, Monday–Saturday.

BELOW: the Obelisk is at the center of the city's nightlife.

Across Rivadavia is a modern wing of the **House of Representatives**. Work began in 1973, but halted with the military coup of 1976. With the return to democracy in 1983, building resumed, and the wing was inaugurated in 1984.

The street that never sleeps

Congress is located at the corner of Rivadavia and Callao. Callao runs north from Rivadavia, and four blocks down is **Avenida Corrientes**, another principal street for *porteños*. Some of its bustle has recently been hijacked by Sante Fe, which has a very American feel, but Corrientes appeals to those who support local rather than imported culture. So, while there are neon lights, fast food restaurants serving good local cuisine, movie theaters, and music stores on Corrientes, the atmosphere is intellectual rather than gaudy.

There are little bookstores everywhere, *kioscos* (newspaper stands) with a wide selection of newspapers, magazines, and paperbacks, and old cafes where friends gather for long talks. The international and national films on show also reflect the serious interests of the moviegoers; you'll find European art-house cinema here, whereas Santa Fe is more likely to feature the latest Hollywood hit. The bookstores are traditionally one of Corrientes' greatest attractions. They are single rooms, open to the street, selling both secondhand and new books. Some patrons come to hunt for old treasures, or the latest bestseller. Others use the bookstores as a meeting place. The stores stay open way past midnight, and, unlike other Buenos Aires shops, you may wander in and out without being accosted by aggressive salespeople.

Coffee and culture

Another endearing feature of Corrientes and adjoining streets is the cafe life. There are hundreds of old cafes, with tall, wood-framed windows that are left open when it's warm. A small table next to the window permits the lone thinker to gaze at the street life, and to write or read in a relaxed atmosphere. But going out for coffee in Buenos Aires is also a social encounter. Even if it is a *licuado* (fruit and milk shake) that you finally indulge in, "having a coffee" means an intimate moment with a friend. And without a doubt, the nicest aspect of these coffee breaks is that the waiter will never hurry you.

Map on pages 142–3

TIP

Rivadavia (allegedly the longest street in the world) is a key street in Buenos Aires, dividing the city into two; street names change at its crossing and numbering begins here as well.

BELOW: the National Congress building.

TIP

For a taste of
Corrientes of years
past, go to **La Giralda**
on the 1400 block.
Here the white-coated
waiters serve the
house specialty of
chocolate y churros
(thick hot chocolate
and delicious hot, fried
sugary dough sticks).

On the 1500 block of Corrientes, next door to each other are **Liberarte** and **Librería Gandhi**. These are both combinations of bookstore, cafe, and performance space, where the artsy and the intellectual gather to browse for books, sip coffee, or take in poetry readings, plays, or music. Both are open in the evening.

Free culture

At Corrientes 1530 is the **Teatro Municipal General San Martín ⓷**. This chrome and glass building was inaugurated in 1960 and is the largest public theater in Argentina, with five stages and an estimated half a million spectators each year. There is a year-round program of free concerts, plays, film festivals, lectures and musical performances here, and the theater has a permanent company; there is also a contemporary ballet company and a group of puppeteers. Within the building, you'll also find the Leopoldo Lugones cinema, offering film retrospectives, international cinema, and avant garde works.

In the block behind the theater, at Sarmiento 1551, is the **Centro Cultural San Martín ⓷**, a sister building with an equally important flurry of cultural activity. The **City Tourism Bureau** is on the fifth floor, where you can pick up maps, hotel information, event listings, and a schedule of free, guided city tours.

The tradition of free concerts, seminars, and other cultural activities is one of the most striking aspects of life in Buenos Aires. If anything, the activity has gained momentum in recent years, despite the economic crisis, and was undoubtedly boosted by the 1980s return to democracy *(see page 69)*. For visitors, both these centers are a fine introduction to the contemporary cultural scene in Buenos Aires and the rest of the country.

Plaza Lavalle is another center of activity in the area. It is two blocks north

BELOW:
a quiet period
in Cafe Tortoni.

of Corrientes at the 1300 block. The **Federal Justice Tribunals** are at one end of this historic plaza, and the internationally renowned Teatro Colón is at the other. The plaza first served as a dumping ground for the unusable parts of cattle butchered for their hides. In the late 19th century, it became the site of the city's first train station, which later moved to Once. In the plaza today there is a beautiful statue and fountain commemorating Norma Fontenla and José Neglia, two dancers from the Colón ballet killed in a plane crash with nine other members of the ballet troupe in the 1970s.

Colón opera house

The **Teatro Colón** ㉜, Buenos Aires' opera house, occupies the entire block between Viamonte, Lavalle, Libertad, and Cerrito (part of 9 de Julio). It is the symbol of the city's high culture, and part of the reason Buenos Aires became known in the early 20th century as the "Paris of Latin America". The theater's elaborate European architecture, its acoustics – which are said to be near perfect – and the quality of performers who appear here, have made the opera house internationally famous.

Three architects took part in the construction of the building before it was finally finished in 1907. The original blueprint, however, was respected. It is a combination of styles – Italian Renaissance, French, and Greek. The interior includes colored glass domes and elaborate chandeliers. The principal auditorium is seven stories high and holds up to 3,500 spectators. There is a 612 sq. meter (6,590 sq. ft) stage on a revolving disk that permits rapid scenery changes.

Well over 1,000 people are employed by the theater. As well as its role as an opera venue, it is also the home of the National Symphony Orchestra and the National Ballet. In a recent rehaul that cost millions of dollars, a huge basement was added, creating storage space for the sets, costumes, and props and working space for the various departments.

The Colón's season runs approximately from April to November. An interesting guided tour of the opera house is available in Spanish and English, Monday to Friday, on the hour, from 11am–3pm, Saturdays, 9am–noon. Also within the Colón, with the entry on Viamonte 1180, is the **Museo del Teatro Colón**, which includes original costumes and props as well as documents, and the **Museo de Instrumentos Antiguos**, with a collection of antique musical instruments (both mueums open Mon–Fri, 9am–4pm; Sat 9am–noon). In addition, there is also a library, with a wealth of material on opera and classical music (open Mon–Fri 9.30am–5pm).

One block from the front of the Colón, along the Plaza Lavalle, is the beautiful **Sinagoga Central**, the principal synagogue of Argentina's 1 million-strong Jewish community (open Mon–Fri 8am–6pm). In front of the synagogue a series of concrete barriers has been erected, like most other synagogues and buildings linked to the Buenos Aires Jewish community: this came in the aftermath of the 1992 car bombing of the Israeli Embassy and the 1994 car bombing of the Jewish mutual society AMIA, in which 84 people were killed. Barricades to prevent cars from parking and the

Map on pages 142–3

A modern sculpture at the Centro Cultural General San Martín.

BELOW: baroque-style rooftops overlooking Plaza Lavalle.

One of the treasures of the Teatro Colón is its central chandelier. Made in France, it measures 7 meters (23 ft) in diameter, holds 700 light bulbs and weighs 2½ tons.

deployment of permanent guards are aimed at preventing further such attacks. Within the synagogoue is the **Museo del Israelita** ❸ (open Tue–Thur 4–6pm). This small museum has a collection of religious artifacts and objects documenting the history of the Jewish community in Argentina.

Turning right off Libertad onto Córdoba brings you to the beautiful Spanish-style **Teatro Nacional Cervantes** ❸, inaugurated in 1921, designated the National Theater in 1933 and declared a national monument in 1995. The theater, which has three stages – the principal, large hall with red velvet seats and curtains and abundant gilt decoration; the 150-seat Sala Argentina, used for chamber music; and the presently closed Salón Dorado – has been remodeled on several occasions. Within the theater is the small **Museo del Teatro Nacional Cervantes** (open Mon–Fri 1–6.30pm), which includes exhibits on Argentina's most important actors, costumes, programs, and manuscripts from important plays.

World's widest avenue

You could not have missed **Avenida 9 de Julio** at the 1000 block. The world's widest avenue, according to the Argentines, is 140 meters (460 ft) from sidewalk to sidewalk. Everything about it is big – big billboards, big buildings, big *palos borrachos* (drunken trees) with pink blossoms in the summertime, and, of course, the big Obelisk.

The military government of 1936 demolished rows of beautiful old French-style mansions to build this avenue. Much of the central block is now occupied by parking lots. The only mansion to survive was the **French Embassy**; its occupants refused to move, claiming it was foreign territory. There is a sad

BELOW: the opulent Teatro Colón.

view of its barren white wall facing the center of town, testimony to the tragic disappearance of its neighbors.

Map on pages 142–3

The **Obelisco** ❸, which rises sharply up towards the clouds at the intersection of Diagonal Norte, Corrientes, and 9 de Julio, was erected in 1936 in commemoration of the 400th anniversary of the first founding of Buenos Aires. Three years after the monument was erected the City Council voted 23 to three to tear it down. However, the order was not taken seriously since the obelisk still stands today.

Pedestrian thoroughfares

Crossing 9 de Julio on Corrientes you enter the heart of the Buenos Aires business district. Here, it is worth going up to Lavalle, one block north, since the best stretch of Corrientes is back across 9 de Julio, as far as Callao. Lavalle, like Florida several blocks down, is a brash pedestrian street. At night, it is filled with young moviegoers, since in a four-block stretch there are many movie theaters. This is despite the fact that in recent years, a number have been closed down or turned into bazaars or evangelical temples. As more cinemas have been built in neighborhood shopping centers, the temptation to go downtown has been reduced. There are also pizza parlors, cafes, restaurants, and several shopping malls. Lavalle is the main gay cruising street in the city.

Books, burgers, and art

Avenida Florida, also closed to motor vehicles, is the principal shopping district downtown. The promenade, punctuated occasionally with *kioscos* and potted shrubs, is packed with shoppers throughout the day, as well as folk musicians,

BELOW: the broad expanse of Avenida 9 de Julio.

There are two tourist information booths at either end of Florida, one being at the junction with Diagonal Roque Sáenz Peña and the other between Córdoba and Paraguay.

pantomime artistes, and others passing the hat. There is a leisurely pace here, and, because of the crowds, it is not a good route for anyone needing to get somewhere in a hurry.

The shopping on Florida is slightly more expensive than in other districts downtown, although the posh end of the street is between Corrientes and Plaza San Martín; between Corrientes and Rivadavia, Florida becomes decidedly more cut-price. As elsewhere, most shops are one-room boutiques, many in interior shopping malls that exit onto adjacent streets. They sell clothes, leather goods, jewelry, toys, and gifts. Leather continues to be the best buy for foreigners. **Centro Cultural Borges** on Viamonte and San Martín was constructed in 1995. It is a theater and arts venue which commemorates, rather than features, the great writer.

The most centrally located mall is the **Galerías Pacífico**, between Viamonte and Córdoba. It is part of an early 20th century Italian building that was saved from demolition because of the frescoes on the ceiling of its great dome. These are the work of five Argentine painters: Urruchua, Bern, Castagnino (*see page 160*), Colmeiro, and Spilimbergo. Renovated in 1990, its spacious, air-conditioned interior provides a welcome relief from the bustle of Florida, with a good selection of shops, cafes, and craft stalls.

There are also cafes along Florida, which offer a chance to relax from the busy street. The street ends at the entrance to **Ruth Benzacar Gallery** (1000 Florida). It's literally an underground art gallery, dedicated to Argentine contemporary artists. At the southern end of Florida, toward Plaza de Mayo is the financial district. Tall banks and exchange houses line the narrow streets.

BELOW: Galerías Pacífico shopping mall on Florida.

The northern quarter

The northern district, which includes the Retiro, Recoleta, and Palermo *barrios*, is the city's most expensive residential and commercial area. Elegant mansions built at the turn of the 20th century are immediately reminiscent of Paris, although the architectural styles are actually a mixture of different influences.

Until the end of the 19th century, this area was unpopulated, except for a slaughterhouse on the site of the Recoleta Plaza. Much of the area was under water. In the 1870s, following the yellow fever epidemic, many wealthy families from the south moved north.

Great changes came in the 1880s when President Roca began a campaign to turn Buenos Aires into the Paris of Latin America. Prominent Argentines had traveled to the French capital and were deeply influenced. They brought back materials and ideas for the transformation of Buenos Aires into a cosmopolitan city.

Roca's policies were and still are controversial. Critics supported a more nationalistic policy, oriented toward the development of the interior of the country. And yet, unquestionably, what was called the "Generation of the 80s" was responsible for making Buenos Aires the great city that it became.

A walking tour of the northern area begins at the eastern edge of the city center, where Florida ends at the corner of Plaza San Martín. At the northern end of Florida is **Plaza San Martín** ㊱, one of Buenos Aires' ritziest neighborhoods. Facing the tree-filled plaza, at the corner of Santa Fe and Maipú, is the **Palacio Paz y Museo de Armas** ㊲, formerly the residence of the Paz family (founders of the newspaper *La Prensa*) and now housing the Círculo Militar. The French-style building, partially modeled on the Louvre Museum in Paris, is of architectural interest for its ornateness, while the Arms Museum houses a series of uniforms used by the Argentine Army, as well as antique weapons. The museum is open Tues–Fri 3–7pm; closed Jan and Feb. The only part of the Círculo Militar open to the public is the library–Mon–Fri 9am–7pm.

Across Plaza San Martín at the end of Florida is the **Edificio Kavanagh** ㊳, built in 1935 and one of the most striking buildings in Buenos Aires, as well as the tallest in the city at the time of its inauguration. The building, with 105 apartments, is notable for its narrow front and terraced façade. Behind it, at San Martín 1039, is the **Basílica del Santísimo Sacramento** ㊴. Opened in 1928, it is the church of the majority of Buenos Aires' most traditional families, and particularly popular for weddings.

Within the Plaza San Martín itself is the black marble monument to Argentine soldiers killed in the Falklands/Malvinas war, modeled on the Vietnam war memorial in Washington. Across Libertador is **La Torre Monumental** ㊵ (open Wed–Sat noon–7pm) or "La Torre de los Ingleses", on Plaza de la Fuerza Aérea, donated by British residents to celebrate the centenary of the 1860 May Revolution. It includes four clocks whose faces measure 4.5 meters (nearly 15 ft) in diameter. The tower is open to the public.

On one side of the plaza is the **Retiro** train station, which includes the Mitre,

Map on pages 142–3

British-style post box on Florida.

BELOW: the Ruth Benzacar Art Gallery, on Florida.

Belgrano and Sarmiento suburban railroads, and, at the far end, the renovated Retiro bus terminal, where most long-distance buses arrive and depart. The Retiro train station was constructed in 1908 on the basis of the style of British train stations of the period; it is now sadly deteriorated.

To one side of the Retiro station, along Libertador, is the **Museo Nacional Ferroviario** ❹ (open Tues–Fri 10am–5.30pm). This museum is housed in a rather dilapidated converted warehouse and contains old locomotives, documents, and other memorabilia illustrating the former glories of the Argentine railroad network. Outside is an eccentric collection of modern art sculptures created out of scraps of train and car parts. On the other side of the plaza is the modern, 24-story Sheraton Hotel, and still further to the south, a series of high-rise mirrored glass and chrome office buildings known as the **Torres Catalinas**, completed in the late 1970s. Just to the west of Plaza San Martín, at Suipacha 1422, is the **Museo de Arte Hispanoamericano Isaac Fernández Blanco** ❷ (open Tues–Sun 2–7pm; tel: 4327 0272 to arrange a guided tour in English), located in a former stately home and including collections of colonial and post-independence artwork and silver objects from all over South America.

Chic shoppers

Before setting off to visit the Recoleta, those interested in shopping may want to detour to Avenida Santa Fe, one of the principal commercial districts. The busiest area is between Callao and 9 de Julio avenues. Here, there are innumerable shopping malls, replete with little boutiques selling clothing, shoes, chocolates, leather goods, linens, china, and jewels. But perhaps the greatest attraction is watching the young *porteños* from Barrio Norte, decked out in the

BELOW: lining up for the bus outside Retiro train station.

Map
on pages
142–3

latest Parisian styles, and simply out for a sunny stroll. The Alteneo bookshop has relocated here, at No. 1860, from Florida, and is known as **El Alteneo Gran Splendid**. It is now the largest bookstore in Latin America.

Evita's final resting place

The **Recoleta**, often referred to as Barrio Norte, is adjacent to Retiro on the northern side. A 20-minute walk from San Martín Plaza, along elegant Avenida Alvear to the Recoleta Cemetery provides a pleasant introduction to what some *porteños* call their golden years (1880–1920).

The **Cementerio de la Recoleta ㊸** (open daily 7am–6pm) is the burial ground for the rich and famous, and the most expensive property in the country. Entering the gates, you have the sense of walking into a city in miniature, and, in fact, it provides an architectural and artistic history of Buenos Aires from its inauguration in 1882. The nation's great leaders, as well as their enemies, are buried here.

The history of the place should be indisputable, since the tombs and cadavers are material proof. Yet the schisms of the rest of Argentine society are reflected here, not only in terms of the conflicting architectural styles, but, astonishingly, in disagreement about who is buried here and why. For example, one of the most visited tombs is that of Evita Perón.

Nevertheless, despite the fact that she is listed in the cemetery's own map-guide, tourism officials have been known to deny that Evita is buried here, explaining that she is not of the "category" of people entombed in the Recoleta. In fact, she is buried here with other members of the Duarte family, 9 meters (30 ft) underground to keep her enemies from stealing her body, as happened in 1955.

Exclusive enclaves

Many of the city's most sumptuous palaces lie along Avenidas Tres Arrollos and Alvear. The **French Embassy** at 9 de Julio and Alvear is hard to miss, not only because of its luxurious appearance, but because it is the only building left standing in the middle of the wide avenue. Two blocks further, at 1300 Alvear, is **Plaza Carlos Pellegrini,** where two other great mansions, the **Brazilian Embassy** and the exclusive **Jockey Club,** are located.

Some of the best-quality and most expensive shops are situated along **Alvear**. At 1777 and 1885 there are elegant malls, ideal for window shoppers. And at the 1900 block is the stately **Alvear Palace Hotel,** which also has its own arcade of chic boutiques.

Running parallel to Alvear one block down the hill toward Avenida Libertador is **Posadas**, where at the 1200 block you'll find **Patio Bullrich**, probably the most exclusive shopping mall in Buenos Aires. This former slaughterhouse *(see page 187)* stretches through to the next street, and houses not only stores and boutiques, but a cinema and various cafes. Directly across from it lies the modern **Caesar Park Hotel**.

Also parallel to Alvear, but on the other side to Posadas, runs **Avenida Quintana**, which ends at the **Plaza Ramón Cercano** and the Recoleta Cemetery.

BELOW: Edificio Kavanagh on Plaza San Martín.

Among the many trees shading the street cafes opposite the Recoleta Cemetery is a giant rubber tree (Ficus macrophylla), brought here from Australia more than 100 years ago.

Here, you can browse in more boutiques, or stop for croissants and coffee at **La Biela** or **Cafe de la Paix**, two of the city's traditional social gathering sites, or one of the other numerous sidewalk cafes and modern American-style theme restaurants overlooking the plaza. This is one of the places to see and be seen among the Argentine wealthy and beautiful.

And, just to the left, along the pedestrian street **Ortiz** (which merges with **Junín** after a couple of short blocks), are some of the more renowned restaurants of the city, most with indoor and outdoor seating. Under the shade of a giant rubber tree, you have a view of the entrance to the Recoleta Cemetery; the handsome Pilar Basílica, an American baroque convent which is now used as a cultural center; and a series of attractive and well-kept parks and gardens.

Despite its modern-day refinement, the Plaza Ramón Cercano, has a very gory past. It used to be the sight of a *hueco de cabecitos*, a dumping ground for heads of cattle slaughtered for their hides. As in the case of other *huecos*, a little stream flowed past the area, where other waste was also thrown. The meat was not consumed, and black women were reputedly employed to drag away the carcasses.

The stream was piped underground in the 1770s and the Recoleta priests began to fix up the area, converting it into an orchard and vegetable garden. Until the 1850s, the Río de la Plata ran up to the edge of the plaza, covering what is now Avenida del Libertador. Under Rosas' administration this area began to be filled in. It was not until the 1870s that the population, mostly the wealthy, started to migrate to this northern *barrio*.

The **Iglesia de Nuestra Señora de Pilar** ㊹ was built between 1716 and 1732. Subsequent restorations have been faithful to the original Jesuit simplicity of its architects, Andres Blanqui and Juan Primoli. Many of the building materi-

BELOW: a deli counter at the Patio Bullrich shopping center.

als, such as wrought-iron gates and stone, were brought from Spain. It may be recalled that there is no rock in Buenos Aires, since the city lies on part of the pampas, and it was not until much later that stone was transported from an island in the delta. Among the historic relics contained in the church is a silver-plated altar, believed to have been brought from Peru. Like many other colonial churches during the British invasions it was used as a hospital by foreign soldiers. Today, it is where some of the city's elite get married.

The **Centro Cultural Recoleta** ❹❺ (open Tues–Fri 2–9pm, Sat and Sun 10am–9pm), just next door to the church, is housed in a former convent. There is always a flurry of activity inside this large arts center, which features a changing program of photography, painting, and sculpture exhibits, plus a theater, and dance and music performances. And on Sundays, the grassy plaza which slopes down towards the river fills with people enjoying one of the largest arts and crafts fairs in the city.

Parks and patriachs

Down the hill from the Recoleta is Avenida del Libertador, and on the far side, before you reach Avenida Figueroa Alcorta, there is a series of parks and gardens that are great for joggers interested in seeing more than the pretty woods and fields of Palermo. On the way down the hill is one of the most spectacular of Buenos Aires' monuments, a mounted statue of **General Alvear**.

Alongside the monument is the **Palais de Glace** ❹❻, a late 19th-century exhibition center, that has since been used as an ice-skating rink and cabaret and nightclub and is once again an exhibition center again. The complex has housed the National Fine Arts Salon since 1932, and was re-modeled as the

Map on pages 142–3

BELOW: the Iglesia de Nuestra Señora del Pilar.

National Exposition Rooms in 1978. The Palais de Glace offers an ongoing series of temporary exhibitions (open daily 2–9pm).

Two blocks away at Libertador 1473 is the National Fine Arts Museum, the **Museo Nacional de Bellas Artes** ❼ (open Tues–Fri, 12.30–7.30pm; Sat and Sun 9.30am–7.30pm). It contains some 10,000 works, including the best collection of 19th- and 20th-century Argentine paintings in the country, as well some excellent paintings and sculpture by major foreign artists, including Rembrandt, El Greco, Goya, Degas, Gauguin, Rodin, Manet, and Monet.

Almost at the end of this row of plazas is the **Chilean Embassy**. Behind it lies one of the prettiest public gardens in the area. Nearby is the reconstructed house, **Grand Bourg** (open Mon–Fri 9.30am–5pm), from France, where the hero of the Independence Wars, General José de San Martín, spent the last 10 years of his life. In front of the building a series of statues represent some of the liberation fighter's closest fellow campaigners.

Sign of the Automovil Club Argentino (ACA), the motoring organization, whose headquarters are on Avenida del Libertador 1850.

BELOW: the Paseo del Rosedal, one of Palermo's parks.

Erasing the past

On Libertador, between Aguero and Austria, you will find the **Biblioteca Nacional** ❽, the national library which was under construction for 30 years and only inaugurated in 1992. The building is located on the site of the former Unzué Palace, which became the presidential palace and was torn down in 1955 because the military government considered it "contaminated" by the fact that Perón had lived there (and Evita died in the building). A statue of Evita was erected in the plaza in 1999.

The concrete library has several million books and a newspaper library, with extensive reading rooms and park space outside with benches for readers. It

also contains exhibits including a first edition of Don Quixote and a desk used by the novelist Jorge Luis Borges, once director of the library (guided tours in Spanish Mon–Sat 3pm).

Maps:
Area 142
City 181

Palermo's palaces

The neighborhood of the rich and famous, **Palermo Chico**, is just around the bend. In fact, you'll have to weave around several bends in order to get a sense of this exclusive neighborhood. It is a cozy nest of palaces, which are set off from the rest of the city by its winding streets that seem to exclude those from outside its boundaries. An assortment of movie stars, sports heroes, and diplomats make up this unusual community.

The area was built up together with the Recoleta area in the 1880s. Many of the old French-style mansions are now used as embassies, since the original owners have been unable to maintain such an exorbitant standard of living. There are also many new wood- and brick-built homes with classic red-tile roofs, but apart from their well-kept gardens, they can hardly compete with the great stone palaces.

One of those classic palaces can be found at Libertador 1902. The **Museo Nacional de Arte Decorativo** and **Museo Nacional de Arte Oriental** ⑲ (open Tues–Sun 2–7pm) is located in a French-style mansion, primarily in Louis XVI style, which contains European and Oriental paintings, porcelain, and sculptures.

Also in Palermo Chico, at Libertador 2373, is the **Museo de Motivos Argentinos José Hernández** Ⓐ (open Tues–Fri 2–7pm; Sat–Sun 10am–6pm), which contains a spectacular collection of 19th-century silver pieces, including the traditional *gaucho* tack and tools of the trade, and an exposition of

BELOW: roller-blading in a Palermo park.

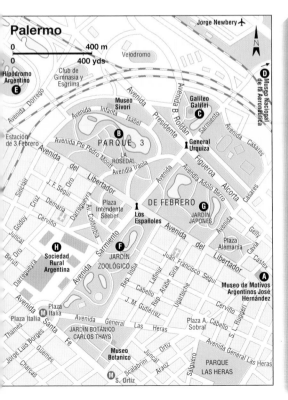

Statue of General Urquiza on Avenida Sarmiento and Figueroa Alcorta.

BELOW: the Museo Nacional de Arte Decorativo.

crafts from the interior of the country on sale to the public. There is also a library specializing in Argentine folklore.

The rest of Palermo is known for its parks and gardens, although there are other quite beautiful residential sections. There are hundreds of hectares of exotic vegetation that include strange juxtapositions of pines and palms. And you can enjoy an equally eclectic array of entertainment.

Parks and gardens

Few cities in the world have an infrastructure like Buenos Aires for recreation, and this is undoubtedly a key to understanding *porteños*. In the parks of Palermo, the frenzy of the city subsides and *porteños* refuel with the oxygen from the sumptuous vegetation. There are families picnicking, men working out with their buddies, young couples in the grass who have escaped the stern supervision of their parents, and, of course, lots of babies. The parks are a constantly changing scene of people, bicycles, and dogs. As Buenos Aires has relatively little open green space in comparison with other cities of similar size, the series of parks and woods in Palermo is a very welcome relief. At the same time, the neighborhood is less crowded with large apartment buildings and office blocks than much of the city, with some areas still dominated by one- or two-story houses in late 19th-century style.

A pleasant but lengthy jaunt through Palermo may begin in Palermo Chico. But the heart of the park area, **Parque 3 de Febrero ❸**, is six blocks further down Figueroa Alcorta Avenue from the tip of Palermo Chico.

The park includes 400 hectares (1,000 acres) of fields, woods, and lakes. There are several points of interest near and within it. These include a zoo,

Map
on page
181

botanical gardens, tennis courts, and a golf course, as well as polo and horse-back riding facilities. Many people, however, simply come to sprawl out on the well-trimmed grass to begin work on their tans before hitting the beaches of Mar del Plata or Punta del Este.

To the right on Avenida Sarmiento is the **Planetario Galileo Galilei G**, which sits next to a small artificial lake. The planetarium features a changing astronomy show on Saturday and Sunday at 3pm, 4.30pm, and 6pm.

The intersection of Figueroa Alcorta and Avenida Sarmiento (not to be confused with Calle Sarmiento downtown), the wide avenue that crosses the park, is marked by an enormous statue of General Urquiza, who became president when he overthrew Rosas in 1852. Past Figueroa Alcorta is the Costanera Norte, where the metropolitan airport Aeroparque is located. Nearby at Rafael Obligado 4500 is the **Museo Nacional de la Aeronáutica D** (open Tues–Fri 8am–noon, Sun; 2–6pm in winter Tues–Fri 8am–noon, Sun, 3–7pm in summer), which has an exhibition of military aircraft in service from 1937 to 1973.

To the left on Sarmiento is **Avenida Iraola**, which leads to the heart of Palermo's parks and lakes. There are paddle boats for hire, and a storybook pedestrian bridge that leads to rosebush-lined gravel paths with stone benches every few yards. Ice-cream vendors also sell warm peanuts, sweet popcorn, and candied apples, and still others specialize in *choripánes* (sausage sandwiches) and soda. A cafe overlooks the most crowded area of the lake.

The enclosed park beside the lake is called La Rosedal and is open 8am–7pm daily. Iraola weaves around the lake and back to Libertador and Sarmiento, where another large monument marks the intersection. This one was a gift from the Spanish community, and is surrounded by a pretty foun-

BELOW: the *hipódromo* in suburban San Isidro.

Map on page 181

Eco-friendly waste disposal unit.

BELOW:
welcoming waiter.
RIGHT:
traffic along
Avenida 9 de Julio.

tain pool. Heading back down Avenida Sarmiento and taking a left on Avenida Libertador are two of Palermo's other attractions. The **Hipódromo Argentino E**, or horserace track, is located at the corner of Libertador and Dorrego, and races are usually held on Monday and Friday, starting around 3 or 4pm. Across the street is the **Campo de Polo**, the attractive polo fields where in springtime the Argentine elite come to take in afternoon matches. Walking down Dorrego you can catch a glimpse through the bushes surrounding the fields.

Kiddies and creatures

Avenida Sarmiento continues up away from the parks and cul de sacs at **Plaza Italia**. Here at the intersection is the entrance to the **Jardín Zoológico F** (open Tues–Sun 9.30am–6pm), a pleasant zoo with a variety of monkeys and birds native to South America. Although renovated in the 1990s, some find the conditions for the animals disturbing. The **Jardín Japonés G** (Japanese Garden) is across the avenue. Extraordinarily lush botanical gardens, with fish ponds spanned by white, wooden footbridges, provide a pleasant spot for strolling.

Across Sarmiento from the zoo's main entrance is the **Sociedad Rural Argentina H**, an exhibition complex run by the powerful association of Argentina's large-scale farmers. Their biggest event is the Exposición Rural, a cattle, horse, and agro-industries show, but many other events are held here for the general public as well, from auto shows to tributes to foreign countries.

Plaza Italia is at the intersection of Las Heras, Santa Fe, and Sarmiento avenues. The plaza holds no special charm except for its intense activity. Weekends in the area are especially fun. To the right down Avenida Santa Fe there is a street fair known as the "hippie market." Here, the individual stands are often run by young beard-and-sandal types, who make the ceramic mugs and ashtrays, leather shoes, belts, and handbags, the jewelry, and the embroidered and tie-dyed clothes you see on sale. On the last block, the stands sell secondhand books and magazines.

Walking south from Plaza Italia along Serrano (now Jorge Luis Borges) gives an image of the residential part of Palermo, full of small plazas, family homes, trendy restaurants, and cafes. Some six blocks down Serrano is the Plazoleta Julio Cortazar, an especially trendy spot filled with bars and a few ethnic restaurants. Unlike the rest of the northern *barrios* of Buenos Aires, Palermo is less exclusive, with pockets of wealth surrounded by middle-class homes, gypsy communities and the intellectual elite.

Past Palermo to the west (accessible on Line D of the subway) is the *barrio* of Belgrano, a well-to-do neighborhood that also has a thriving nightlife and social scene. Belgrano, characterized largely by expensive high-rise apartment buildings, also includes the so-called Barrancas de Belgrano, a green hill which stands out in Buenos Aires' general flatness, as well as the **Museo Sarmiento**, at the corner of Cuba and Juramento. ❑

THE ARCHITECTURE OF BUENOS AIRES

With its grand nationalistic monuments and colorful neighborhood back streets, the capital reflects the country's turbulent history

The eclectic architecture of Buenos Aires was once described as being composed primarily of architectural styles which are painful to the eyes. Although its sometimes garish attempts to resemble Paris or New York do somewhat justify this description, Buenos Aires still boasts beautiful buildings ranging from more austere colonial styles to baroque, neo-classical, rather fantastic French designs, and inventions which blend these styles and could be described as purely *porteño*. The city center and hyper-fashionable Puerto Madero accommodate tall steel and glass office buildings with all the latest technology, jockeying for space with the old docks of the port area and with classic and increasingly unkempt public buildings.

A DIFFERENT PERSPECTIVE

Look down on the city from a tall building, or look at the side and back of the buildings whose impressive facades first meet the eye, and the difference is striking; the elaborate facades are virtually stuck on to square, unadorned buildings which often resemble rabbit hutches more than stately homes or *belle époque* buildings. The importance given to the facade in comparison with what lies behind it gives a clue to a wider *porteño* way of thinking.

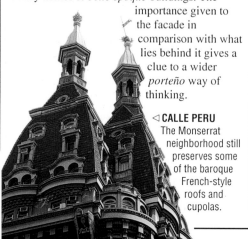

◁ **CALLE PERU**
The Monserrat neighborhood still preserves some of the baroque French-style roofs and cupolas.

▷ **CALLE CAMINITO**
Colorful Caminito in the southern La Boca *barrio* (neighborhood), whose brightly painted houses recall the first Italian immigrants.

△ **NATIONAL MONUMENT**
The slim, distinctive profile of the Kavanagh Building, which in the 1930s was Latin America's first skyscraper.

△ **DON'T CRY FOR ME...**
It was from Government House, known as the Casa Rosada, that Perón and Evita addressed their followers in the Plaza de Mayo.

▷ **STUNNING THEATER**
The spectacular Teatro Colón, an acoustically near-perfect temple to music and dance realized in gilt, crystal, marble, and velvet.

TEMPLES OF SHOPPING

As in other world cities, the shopping mall has become increasingly a social and cultural reference point in Buenos Aires, with a rising number growing up in and around the city in the past decade. Some malls have been installed in old and renovated buildings, such as Patio Bullrich in a beautiful building which was once a slaughter-house; Galería Pacífico in a one-time railway station; or the Abasto shopping center in the former central fruit and vegetable market. One of the most popular purpose-built malls is the Alto Palermo mall, located at the upmarket corner of Santa Fe and Coronel Diaz. Alto Palermo is a two-block long steel and glass-roofed structure spread over three stories. While Alto Palermo offers a number of clothing stores, its principal attractions, and those of other "shoppings", probably lie in the food hall and cinemas that represent the hub of social activity. Among the movie houses and chic boutiques are fast-food outlets, from McDonald's to a kosher deli, offering a place to meet, eat, see, and be seen – one of the most beloved pastimes of *porteños*.

◁ **HEART OF THE NATION**
The elegant Cabildo, where Argentine independence took its first steps in 1810, and the Plaza de Mayo, scene of many protests.

△ **HEROIC STATUE**
The Liberator, José de San Martín, contemplates his elegant surroundings in the leafy Plaza San Martín from his charging steed.

◁ **WATER WORKS**
The outrageously elaborate Obras Sanitarias building was the headquarters for the state water and sewage company and is now a national monument.

AROUND BUENOS AIRES

Despite the enormous sprawl of the capital city, it's relatively easy to head out for a day or so – to a quiet ranch in the country or to an elegant riverside resort

Map on page 190

From Buenos Aires there are many possibilities for trips to nearby small towns in the pampas, north along the river to the delta and its islands, or east along the coast as far as the provincial capital, La Plata. Most of the attractions described below can be seen in a day, but if you are in need of a longer break from the city bustle, a good range of accommodations is available.

Suburban side trips

Among the attractive northern suburbs easily reached by train from Retiro or by bus are Olivos (where the presidential residence is located), and San Isidro. Both are also served by the Tren de la Costa railroad, an elaborate sightseeing line which leaves from Retiro and ends at the huge Parque de la Costa amusement park in Tigre, on the Río Luján. Passengers can use one ticket to get on and off at any of the stations en route, many of which are linked to shopping malls, riverside restaurants, and sports clubs. **Olivos ❶** has a couple of yacht clubs and a number of elegant European-style residences, as well as outdoor tea rooms and fresh air. Fishing can be done here, from a jetty managed by the local fishing club, the Club de Pescadores which also operates catamaran cruises, sailing downriver as far as the delta on weekends and public holidays.

To the north, **San Isidro ❷** has an important horse-racing track, belonging to the Jockey Club and inaugurated in 1935. The Hipódromo de San Isidro is on Avenida Santa Fe, at the junction with Márquez, flanked by the golf course and polo club. Races are on Wednesday and Saturday 3–9pm; Sunday 2–9pm. Both Olivos and San Isidro are located along the continuation of Avenida del Libertador and have traditionally been home to most of Buenos Aires' English-speaking community.

Up the delta

Tigre ❸ is an old town situated at the mouth of the delta. Fruit brought by boat from the northern provinces is deposited here en route to Buenos Aires. But the principal economic activity revolves around the summer tourists and weekenders who come to fish, row, water ski, and cruise the winding channels that flow past hundreds of little islands. While it is only 28 km (17 miles) from downtown Buenos Aires, the air is clear, the vegetation subtropical, and the rhythm of activity less hurried. There is almost no crime, and it is said that the dogs never get sick because of special immunities gained from drinking the brown river water. There's a recommended fruit market, **Puerto de Frutos**, at Sarmiento 160 which takes place daily and is joined by a lively crafts market at weekends.

After touring the charming plant-filled residential area of the town, you should head for the main drag along the

LEFT: peaceful reflection at La Plata cathedral.
BELOW: one of the many waterbirds seen in the delta.

TIP

Empresa Cacciola
operates guided tours
to Isla Martín García.
The full-day cruises
depart from Tigre daily
at 7.30am, returning
at 7pm, and include
lunch on the island
(tel: 4394-5520).

riverside, **Paseo Victorica**. Old English rowing clubs and *parrillas* (steak restaurants) line the street. There are several small docks where you can pick up rides on *lanchas* (taxi boats). Several larger ferries run two-hour cruises, which leave from the dock next to the train station. They also operate a regular daily service through the delta, allowing passengers to alight at various points and continue or return by the same or another company. Boats may also be rented for floating parties, and there is a ferry that crosses over to the Uruguayan beaches.

A train runs from the Retiro station to downtown Tigre, taking about 45 minutes. Or bus No. 60 starts in Constitución and winds through downtown to reach Tigre. Ask before getting on the bus because there are many different routes, and be prepared for a long journey. You can get more information on bus services from Tigre town hall, tel: 4512-4497/8; or the tourist office, tel: 4512-4498.

Unless you are planning a visit, don't get on board the **Tren de la Costa** which also goes to Tigre, but drops you off in the middle of the **Parque de la Costa** at the Delta station. A new amusement park set in 16 hectares (40 acres), the park, with its mock Victorian buildings, includes rides, concerts, and other live performances. For more information on the park and the train, tel: 4732-6300.

Island reserve

Three hours from Tigre by boat is the **Isla Martín García** ❹, the largest in the Delta. The island, which was once a fortress and center of naval battles in the wars of independence, and where presidents Hipólito Yrigoyen, Juan Perón, and Arturo Frondizi were once briefly detained, is now a nature reserve with a wide variety of flora and fauna including waterbirds and deer. The island also has a small historical museum, a hotel with a good restaurant, and a modern lighthouse.

BELOW: sunset at
Chascomús.

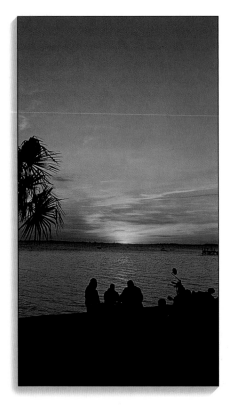

Around Buenos Aires

Luján

One of the oldest cities in the country, **Luján ❺**, is visited today by millions of Argentine tourists every year because of its religious importance. It lies 63 km (40 miles) west of Buenos Aires, along the Luján River. Trains leave from the Once station, and take two hours, stopping at every little town in the pampas along the way.

Map on page 190

The **Basílica Nuestra Señora de Luján** is a magnificent gothic structure, built over a period of 50 years and completed in 1935. The great attraction is a statue of the **Virgen de Luján**, which is housed in its own chapel behind the main altar. Legend has it that the statue was sent by wagon from Brazil, and the wagon wouldn't continue until the virgin was taken off. Here she has remained, and now she is the patron saint of Argentina. Each October, hundreds of thousands of young Catholics make a pilgrimage from Buenos Aires, arriving on foot in honor of the saint.

The Luján River runs through the city, and in colonial times boats heading to the northwest were checked here for contraband. When there have been no recent rains, the river is a place of recreation for residents and tourists.

Field of sunflowers by the roadside on Ruta 8.

There are several museums in Luján. The **Complejo Museográfico Enrique Udaondo**, in a beautiful old colonial building, shows relics of Argentina's customs and history. In an annex is the **Museo del Transporte**, which has an interesting collection, mostly of horse-drawn carriages but also a flying boat, *Plus Ultra*, which was the first plane to cross the South Atlantic, in 1926. Both museums are open Wed–Fri noon–6pm, Sat and Sun 10am–6pm. There is also the **Museo de Bellas Artes** (open daily 1–6pm), in Parque Florentino Ameghino, dedicated principally to contemporary Argentine art.

BELOW: horseracing at San Isidro.

On national and religious holidays there are *gaucho* competitions on horseback that are quite spectacular. Most of the competitors are in fact descendants of *gauchos* and now work as farm hands, although costumes and saddles are saved for these special occasions.

Gaucho country

Cannon outside the Ricardo Güiraldes Gaucho Museum in San Antonio de Areco.

Some 50 km (30 miles) further northwest of Buenos Aires, on RN8, is the town of **San Antonio de Areco ⑥**, a typical town of the cattle-raising area of the pampas. There are a number of *estancias* (farm estates) here which can be visited, including the **Estancia La Porteña** where famous author Ricardo Güiraldes (who wrote the *gaucho* classic *Don Segundo Sombra*) once lived. The **Ricardo Güiraldes Gaucho Museum** (open Wed–Mon 10am–5pm) includes extensive grounds on the river with numerous indigenous plants, while the **Gaucho Silver Museum and Workshop** at Alvear and Alsina is open daily 8.30am–12.30pm and 3–8pm.

In the second week of November, San Antonio de Areco celebrates Tradition Week, with *gaucho* shows, horse races and breaking, and *gaucho* parades. Several *estancias* in the area offer visits and accommodations, as well as *gaucho* shows and traditional *asados (see page 362).*

Heading South

BELOW: Estancia Los Patricios, San Antonio de Areco.

There are also a number of possible outings to the south of Buenos Aires that offer fresh air, green space, and other attractions. Passing **Ezeiza**, the area which includes both the international airport and the wide open spaces of the local forests, is the small pampas town of **Lobos ⑦**, about 95 km (59 miles) from Buenos Aires on RN3. The town is known primarily for its *laguna*, a large lake used for fishing and windsurfing, and as the possible birthplace of Juan Perón.

The house in which Perón was said to have been born, located at Buenos Aires 1380, is the **Museo Juan Domingo Perón** open Wed–Sun 10am–noon and 3–6pm, containing some of the ex-president's personal effects, including a letter written to Evita from his prison cell on Martín García.

Some 120 km (75 miles) south of Buenos Aires on Route 2, going toward Mar del Plata, is the city of **Chascomús ⑧**, located on the largest of the chain of lakes south of the capital. The attractive colonial city is the center of a prosperous agricultural region, and its buildings are well-preserved and stand on wide tree-lined streets with green plazas. The Laguna de Chascomús offers fishing, boating, water skiing, and other watersports, while the Chascomús Riding Center offers horse rides.

The town has a well-developed tourism infrastructure (the **Tourist Office** is located at Costanera España, on the *laguna*, and is open daily 9am–6pm) and has a variety of attractive restaurants along the lake front offering fresh fish (primarily *pejerrey*) and *parrillada mixta*. There are a number of *estancias* offering accommodations and shows for tourists, as well as the **Fortín Chascomús** fort (tel: 03241-424-993), scene of battles against the Araucanians in 1780.

La Plata

A 1½-hour train ride south from Buenos Aires' Constitution train station will take you toward La Plata. Just beyond the city, you pass through an industrial belt populated by poor, working-class people. Shanty towns line the tracks.

Traveling by road, some 38 km (24 miles) from Buenos Aires, where routes 1 and 14 split, is an *estancia* that used to be owned by the Pereyra family. It was expropriated by Perón and transformed into a recreational park, where working-class people who live in the area can come to relax. Adjacent is a zoo, where the animals run wild and visitors can drive safari-style through the countryside.

La República de los Niños, a marvelous recreational center for children, lies 14 km (9 miles) further south. Built by Evita Perón, it celebrated its 50th anniversary in 2001.

A few more miles down Route 1, you'll reach the city of **La Plata ❾**. Despite being only 56 km (35 miles) south of Buenos Aires, it is representative of many provincial cities in Argentina. The capital of the province of Buenos Aires, life is less frantic here and the city's inhabitants enjoy an independent political and cultural life.

The city was founded in 1882 by Dr Dardo Rocha, and conceived by Pedro Benoit, who planned its tidy layout with its numbered horizontal/vertical streets, and diagonal avenues. Just off Plaza San Martín is the Legislatura, the Palacio del Gobernio, and the Pasaje Dardo Rocha, a large cultural center. The gothic Catedral de La Plata is on the Plaza Moreno, and across the plaza you'll find the Palacio Municipal. One block away, between calles 9 and 10, is the Teatro Argentino.

The **Paseo del Bosque** is a series of pretty parks in the center of the city, with lakes, a zoo (actually much more complete than the Buenos Aires zoo), an observatory, and a theater, **Anfiteatro Martín Fierro**. The Paseo del Bosque is also home to the **Museo de Ciencias Naturales** (open daily), which was founded in 1884. This museum has many fascinating geological, zoological, and archeological exhibits, and is considered the best of its kind in all of South America. The **Museo Provincial de Bellas Artes** (open Mon–Sat), at 525 Calle 51, has an excellent collection of Argentine paintings and sculpture.

Uruguayan excursion

About 45 minutes north of Buenos Aires, across the river in Uruguay, is the attractive riverside town of **Colonia del Sacramento**, founded by the Portuguese in 1680. The colonial district – the Barrio Histórico – has been decreed a site of World Heritage status by UNESCO. It has renovated Portuguese and Spanish mansions, several of which have been coverted into museums, including the restored 18th-century viceroy's palace; and its picturesque cobbled squares and the old parish church make for a pleasant visit.

A return trip from Buenos Aires can easily be made in one day. Buquebus, with offices at Córdoba 867, offers frequent hydrofoil services from its terminal at the southern end of Puerto Madero. ❏

Map on page 190

Chascomús is the birthplace of Dr. Raul Alfonsín, former president of Argentina (1983–89).

BELOW: main plaza of San Antonio de Areco.

MAR Y SIERRAS

*The Atlantic coast is the playground for Buenos Aires'
rich and beautiful set, while inland in the* sierras *is some fine
countryside for walking, cycling, and horseback riding tours*

Map
on page
198

If your interests tend at all toward the sociological and anthropological, then this is the place to come. Here along the extensive Atlantic coast, where the hills roll down to the sea (giving rise to the popular name Mar y Sierras) is an array of resorts for all tastes and bank accounts. Here one can see the Argentines at play.

Although their country is enormous, and has an astonishing variety of appealing destinations, few Argentines explore it. Instead they head for the beach. Year after year, they return to the same spot, often renting the same changing *cabaña* (beach hut) every time. This fostering of a second home leads to a real sense of community in each resort. Families who may live far apart during much of the year see each other each summer, watch each other's kids grow up, and keep up-to-date with the community gossip.

Along these beaches, the older folks pass the day playing the card games of *truco* and canasta, while the young swim and play paddle ball and volleyball. Young women pose in their *cola*-less bikinis (this translates as tail-less; the backsides of these suits are strikingly short on fabric), and everyone seems relaxed and happy to escape the mania of city life.

PRECEDING PAGES:
an off day near Mar
del Plata.
LEFT: checking
the nets.
BELOW: Mar del
Plata beach.

The Argentines are fiercely proud of their riviera. Keen competition exists among all the resorts of the South Atlantic, and some of Argentina's hot spots consider themselves rivals of such places as Punta del Este, in Uruguay. Fashions are kept up to the minute, and many fads actually start here. Those of the smart set insist on being seen here at least once during the summer season.

So, if your exposure to Argentine society has been mostly to people burdened with the pressures of *porteño* life, it's not a bad idea to visit the coast, where everybody is smiling. It's not a bad spot to take a vacation either.

Coastal developments

The main strip of this popular vacation coast extends from San Clemente del Tuyú to Mar del Plata, the hub of the Atlántica area. Though founded late in the 19th century, Mar del Plata was at first a resort for well-to-do *porteños*, i.e. for those residents of Buenos Aires who could afford the 400-km (250-mile) journey to the then solitary cliffs near Punta Mogotes. Early on, this journey was made by train, and later by car. Only in the mid-1930s did Mar del Plata really start to boom. This was due mainly to two developments: the opening of the casino, with its 36 roulette tables (in those days the largest gambling place in the world), and the paving of the Ruta Nacional 2, which brought Mar del Plata to within four hours by car from Buenos Aires. The road has been repaved and

Waiting for the afternoon catch.

widened, cutting the journey time further. With the construction of still another road along the coast (Ruta Provincial 11), smaller seaside resorts started to sprout up north and south from Mar del Plata. Before long, each of these places acquired a character of its own; some preferred by the elderly, others by youth, some by those who like rock music, and some by the lovers of smooth tango dancing.

By road, train, or airplane

Until fairly recently, an excursion to the vacation coast was a small adventure. Muddy roads made access to many of the smaller villages very difficult, but today the entire coastline is easily reached. While the roads are now excellent, be warned that there are four toll stops between Buenos Aires and Mar del Plata and the roads can get very crowded during weekends and holidays. For one person traveling alone, it's cheaper to go by long-distance buses which serve most of Mar del Plata's sprawl, or even by air: in summer, services are inexpensive and frequent, and you can often pick up special promotional offers. Most flights con-

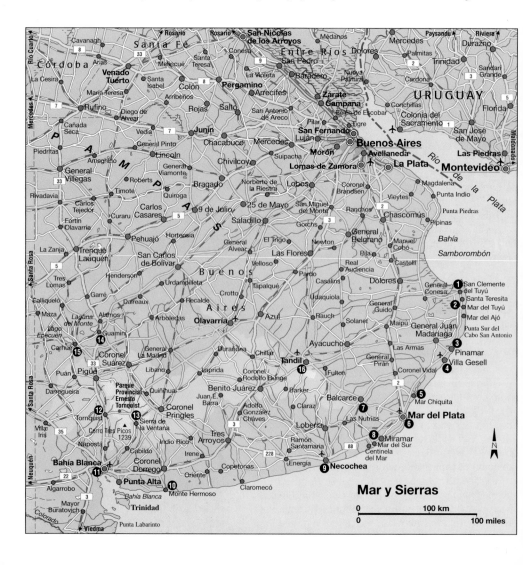

Mar y Sierras

nect Buenos Aires and Mar del Plata, but some of the smaller resorts can be reached by air, including Santa Teresita, Pinamar, Villa Gesell, Miramar, and Necochea. Traveling by rail, Mar del Plata and Miramar can be reached by the Roca train which departs from Constitución station in Buenos Aires twice a week, taking less than six hours to make the journey south.

Fishermens' retreats

Heading south on Ruta Provincial 11 from Buenos Aires, the first resort town is **San Clemente del Tuyú ❶**, located at the northern point of **Cabo San Antonio**, the most easterly point of continental Argentina. It is adjacent to Bahía Samborombón, the muddy mouth of the Río Salado and other, smaller rivers of the pampas. The bay is rich with fish that come here to feed.

Mundo Marino is one of the few "marine worlds" in South America, and is particularly popular among fishermen who arrive hoping to catch the *corvina negra* or *corvina rubia*, fish used in soups and stews and regarded as a delicacy. There are numerous well-equipped campsites, as well as many other sports facilities.

A small stretch of land juts out between the bay and the ocean, an area called **Punta Rasa**. Here you can visit the **El Faro San Antonio** (open daily 9am–7.30pm), an iron lighthouse built in 1890 which, at 63 meters (207 ft) high, offers remarkable views. Also in Punta Rasa is an ecological reserve for migratory birds, which visit in spring and autumn on their journey between Alaska or Canada and Tierra del Fuego. The Estación Biológica Punta Rasa became the "wings over the bay" visitor center in 1997 with an impressive audiovisual show on local migratory birds.

A further 22 km (14 miles) south on Ruta 11 is another well-developed resort town, **Santa Teresita**. In addition to the popular beach, long fishing pier, and many seafood restaurants, there is a golf course, horseback riding, and various campgrounds.

Heading south on Ruta 11, you'll find resort towns one after the other, in a rather developed 26-km (16-mile) stretch of coastline. **Mar del Tuyú ❷** is the capital of the so-called Coast municipality, which includes all the following towns: Costa del Este, Aguas Verdes, La Lucila del Mar, Costa Azul, San Bernardo, and Mar de Ajó. Mar del Tuyú itself is a small, quiet resort, most popular for its swimming and fishing off the pier. The resorts attract many tourists, but the beaches are wide and services abundant. San Bernardo is the largest resort, with high-rise condominiums and hotels.

Most visitors to this area come to swim, sunbathe, and walk along the narrow beach beside the high sand dunes, but many others come to fish. This, however, is simply for sport; when it comes to mealtime, most of these visiting fishermen retire to one of the area's countless tiny seafood restaurants, many of which specialize in Italian fare.

South from Mar de Ajó, the beach becomes increasingly solitary. The spaces between settlements become wider, and you can find more stretches of isolated pristine shore.

 Map on page 198

TIP

To the west of San Clemente del Tuyú is a wildlife sanctuary which is one of the last remaining habitats of the once numerous pampas deer and an important resting area for migratory birds.

BELOW: one of the girls of summer.

Shipwrecks, sand dunes, and lighthouses

Along this part of the coast you can see many old lighthouses made of iron and brick. Previously mentioned is El Faro San Antonio, in San Clemente. Another is near Punta Médanos, a rather barren and rocky area without many facilities, which also reportedly boasts a number of past shipwrecks, at the southern tip of Cabo San Antonio. The lighthouse here, built in 1893, stands 59 meters (194 ft) tall amid sand dunes *(médanos)*, after which the place is named. The dunes cover an enormous stretch of coastline between Mar de Ajó and Pinamar, some of them now covered in vegetation but others still forming, and reaching up to 30 meters (98 ft) high.

Still more lighthouses can be found halfway to Mar del Plata (Faro Querandi), on the southern outskirts of Mar del Plata (Faro Punta Mogotes), and at Monte Hermoso. Some of these towers are over a century old, and many of them have shared in the area's long and fascinating history of maritime adventures and misfortunes. They are well worth a visit, from both an architectural and a historical point of view, although some may be under repair and closed to visitors. In a walk along the beach you will frequently encounter the stranded and disintegrating hull of some old windjammer or steamer.

Probably one of the loveliest of all the urban areas along the Costa Atlántica is the one that comprises Pinamar, Ostende, Valeria del Mar, and Cariló.

Pinamar ❸ is a very fashionable spot which recieves large numbers of tourists in January and Feburary. It is bordered by a pine forest, and the scent of the pines mixed with the salty sea air gives the town a bracing atmosphere. There are no sand dunes at Pinamar, which makes access to the beach easy, even by car. Accommodations range from four-star establishments down to modest, if not

One of this area's many shipwrecks was the Anna, *a steamship from Hamburg. In 1894 it hit a sandbank near Punta Médanos, where it remained until 1967, when it was scrapped. One of the ship's masts was salvaged, however, to be used as a flagpost for the lighthouse.*

BELOW: beachfront at Mar del Plata.

budget *hosterías* and *hospedajes* (hostels). Although hotels of all categories are available all year round, most people come for two weeks or a full month and therefore choose to rent an apartment at prices which are much cheaper than that of the most humble hostel. These apartments may be rented on the spot, or in advance in Buenos Aires. Pinamar is the most urban development along this part of the coast, with a number of high-rise apartment blocks and discos, which makes it a good spot for young people. Its range of sporting activities include everything from horseback riding to windsurfing.

Upmarket elegance

The greater Pinamar area includes **Ostende** and **Valeria del Mar**, where some very high dunes are to be found. A casino, formerly located in Pinamar, is now just outside Valeria, on Ruta 11, the main road running parallel to the coast. A short distance south of Valeria, **Cariló** is a country club-style community dotted with elegant villas and shaded by pines, which also has a wide beach and some of the most beautiful and unspoiled wooded areas left on the coast. Cariló also has a tiny, attractive, and up-market town center, with shops and restaurants constructed in Alpine style.

About 20 km (12 miles) south of Cariló lies **Villa Gesell** ❹. Founded by Carlos Idaho Gesell in 1940, the town was forested with pines with the intention of maintaining a small and tranquil tourist spot. Except for Avenida 3, its streets are still constructed of sand, which absorbs water better; trucks pass on a daily basis to water it all down. The town, with a long and very wide beach, also has a forestry reserve including a museum and archive with photos and documents relating to the foundation of the city. Outside the center is a horse-

Map on page 198

TIP

The Pinamar region is a sports-lover's paradise, with golf courses, horseback riding centers and even a "Tennis Ranch" run by former Argentine champion, José Luis Clerc.

BELOW: the Museo de Automovilismo Juan Manuel Fangio, Balcarce.

Soaking up the summer sun.

back riding school, which offers classes and guided outings and there is year-round fishing for shark, mackerel and other fish from the pier. Villa Gesell is especially popular with young people, due to its many bars, discotheques and skating rinks; and it also has several excellent campsites.

The main attraction between Gesell and Mar del Plata are the shady campsites at **Mar Chiquita ❺**, which is a small cluster of hotels and restaurants on the edge of a salt-water lagoon, and **Santa Clara del Mar**. Both, however, are some distance from the beach.

Pearl of the Atlantic

Shortly before you reach **Mar del Plata ❻**, the landscape changes dramatically. Approaching the city on the coastal Ruta 11, the high cliffs of Cabo Corrientes and the downtown skyscrapers built upon this rocky peninsula seem to grow from the sea like a *fata Morgana* (mirage). It is a truly striking first impression which, as one gets closer, becomes no less impressive.

Mar del Plata is proudly called *La Perla del Atlántico* (the Pearl of the Atlantic) by its 700,000 residents. Accommodations range from first-class hotels to apartments available for short-term lease all year round. The city has well-groomed plazas, parks, boulevards, and several golf courses. Beyond the beaches and the sun lies perhaps the biggest attraction for the 3 million summer visitors, the colossal **Casino** where, you can try your hand at roulette, poker, *punta banca*, and other games. There are also several theaters, which feature mostly comedies,

BELOW: the circus big top comes to Mar del Plata.

Another major pastime in Mar del Plata is to see and be seen. In the past all of fashionable Buenos Aires felt obliged to be seen here at least once a year. In recent years, however, tourism has been somewhat reduced by the availability

of cheap beach vacations in Brazil, Mexico, and the Caribbean, and latterly, by recession. Nevertheless, during the peak of the season the boutiques and galleries of **Calle San Martín** and the adjacent streets still bustle late into the night with the tanned and the beautiful.

Map on page 198

International events

Mar del Plata has a number of important events throughout the year, such as the National Ocean Festival (first week of January), with a number of sporting events, the National Fishing Festival and Regatta in February, the International Film Festival in March, the International Jazz Festival in April, and the National Film Festival in November. In summer, its beaches are so crowded that the sand virtually disappears, although further from the center the beaches are somewhat less populated. A good place to observe the beautiful people and the locals is the Rambla, a wide pedestrian walkway which runs along the Bristol beach in the center of the city, past the Gran Hotel Provincial and the Casino.

A visit to Mar del Plata would not be complete without sampling the area's specialties. At the fishing port, with its red and yellow boats along the quays, a raft of restaurants in the area serve good, fresh fish and seafood. You might also like to take the opportunity to buy well-made inexpensive woolens here, made by the locals during the winter months.

Some 60 km (37 miles) inland from Mar del Plata on Ruta 226 is the city of **Balcarce ❼**, with 35,000 residents. The area is more hilly than most of the province of Buenos Aires, and Balcarce lies in a valley near La Brava. The city houses a satellite land station, of which a guided tour can be organized with the **EMTUR** tourist office in Mar del Plata. The **Museo de Automovilismo Juan Manuel Fangio** (open daily 10am–8pm, Mar–Dec until 6pm) in Balcarce is named for the town's most famous citizen, the five-time world champion racing driver who died in 1995. The museum contains many of Fangio's prizes as well as one of his racing cars, the Mercedes Benz Flecha de Plata. Near Balcarce are the the Ojos de Agua caves as well as Laguna La Brava, a well-known fishing spot.

Solitary beaches

From Mar del Plata, the coastal road runs past the Punta Mogotes lighthouse (where there is a popular beach lined with seafood restaurants) toward Miramar. The scenery along this 40-km (25-mile) stretch is very different from that at the northern end of the Costa Atlántica. Instead of dunes and sandy beaches, the sea is met by cliffs. The road runs along the very edge, offering travelers a splendid view of the ocean, and the spectacle of Mar del Plata disappearing into the distance.

About halfway between Mar del Plata and Miramar is Chapadmalal, where the presidential vacation residence is located. The area has a tourism complex opened in the 1950s by the Eva Perón Foundation for students, pensioners, and low-income families, which has a privileged position on a quiet beach and is still much in demand.

TIP

While in Mar del Plata, be sure to try one of the famed *alfajores marplatenses*. These are biscuits filled with chocolate or caramel, and are a favorite for afternoon tea.

BELOW: on the crest of a wave.

Miramar ❽ is infinitely less developed and much quieter than Mar del Plata, yet the main beachfront is overshadowed by towering apartment buildings. But the beach is very wide here and it's not difficult to escape the crowds. There is plenty of open space for many outdoor sports, including bicycling, horseback riding, tennis, jogging, or just walking. For a break from the sand and surf, Miramar boasts a lovely, large, wooded park, Vivero Florentino Ameghino, complete with picnic spots and walking trails.

Between Miramar and Necochea, the seaside resorts become sparser. Along this 80-km (50-mile) section of shoreline, there are only three places with facilities for vacationers: Mar del Sur (which has beautiful, deserted and windswept beaches), Centinela del Mar, and Costa Bonita.

At **Necochea ❾**, a pleasant city 125 km (78 miles) from Mar del Plata, the Río Quequén empties into the sea. There is a large port, from where fishing excursions depart daily, a developed beachfront, and a proper city center. Beyond the beach, an interesting trip is 15 km (9 miles) up the river to the Parque Cura Meucó, where you can relax and enjoy the small waterfalls.

There are even fewer developed beaches south of Necochea. **Claromecó**, about 150 km (93 miles) to the south, is one of the most attractive.

Peace and quiet

One place that is highly recommended is **Monte Hermoso ❿**, some 110 km (68 miles) further down the coast. Visited by Darwin during his voyage on the *Beagle*, and since then well known for its wealth of fossils along the shore, Monte Hermoso has a broad beach of fine white sand, shady campsites, and a venerable lighthouse. The lack of crowds make this peaceful place well worth

BELOW: the docks at Bahía Blanca.

exploring. There is a large YMCA campsite just outside Monte Hermoso, which also offers hotel accommodation, and the town has an artisans' market. Sunbathing opportunities may, however, be limited by the fierce wind which sweeps the area most of the time, as the southern coast of Buenos Aires is much less protected from South Atlantic winds than the eastern coast. It is here, at Monte Hermoso, that the Argentine vacation coast ends.

About 90 km (56 miles) further along the southern coast from Monte Hermoso, and some 660 km (410 miles) southwest of Buenos Aires on Ruta Nacional 3, is the city of **Bahía Blanca ⓫**. Located on the largest bay in southern Argentina, it is a major industrial center and port. The most important civic buildings are located on the **Plaza Rivadavia**, including the town hall, cathedral, court buildings, library, and the newspaper offices of *La Nueva Provincia*.

The city has several interesting museums. The **Museo Municipal de Ciencias** (open Tues–Fri 9am–noon and 4–8pm Sat–Sun 3–6pm), on Alsina 425 is a natural history museum with some interesting exhibits. The **Museo del Puerto**, on Guillermo Torres 4131 (open Mon–Fri 9am–noon, Sat–Sun 3.30–7.30pm; closed Jan) contains old photographs and other memorabilia of the town's industrial past. In the **Mercado Victoria** area, formerly the central export market for hides and wool, there remains an English neighborhood of houses constructed in the 19th century by the railway companies for their English employees.

Into the *sierras*

Some 80 km (49 miles) north of Bahía Blanca, and entering the *sierras* area of the province, is the small town of **Tornquist ⓬**, founded in 1883 and filled with pines and attractive gardens. The Santa Rosa de Lima church is made of

Map on page 198

BELOW: grazing livestock in the *sierras*.

Map on page 198

stone and especially pretty. Nearby is the former residence of Ernesto Tornquist (an important 19th-century businessman responsible for much of the early development of the Atlantic coastal resorts), for whom it is named. The estate includes a castle of medieval design, a copy of Chateau Amboise in the French Loire valley. Close to Tornquist is the **Parque Provincial Ernesto Tornquist**, which has an ecology center containing information on its flora and fauna, from where guided tours of the park can be made. The Cerro Bahia Blanca mountain and the Toro cave grotto are found in the park.

Beyond the park to the south on Ruta 72 is the attractive town of **Sierra de la Ventana ⓭**, the principal tourist center in the area. Surrounded by three rivers, the town has beaches, walking sites, and campgrounds, as well as a golf course. It is also a center for the production of herbs, and visits to herbal plantations can be arranged at the tourist office, as well as guided walking, bicycle or riding excursions in the mountains. The town is located in the sierra, and the Confitería El Mirador offers panoramic views of the area. Nearby is **Cerro Tres Picos**, the highest mountain in the pampas area at 1,239 meters (4,065 ft).

Lagoons and lakes

North of Tornquist, on Ruta 33, is **Guaminí ⓮**, in the southwest of Buenos Aires province close to the border with La Pampa. The town, a central fortress in the Conquest of the Desert in the 1870s, is located on the Laguna del Monte. One of the largest lagoons in the province, it has a beach and fishing clubs, as well as an island with an antelope reserve. In the town itself, the former fort (now the police station) and the **Museo Histórico** (open daily, 3–8pm) are worth a visit. Some 40 km (25 miles) further west lies **Carhué ⓯**, also originally a fort, whose principal architectural attraction is the art deco municipal building. Carhué is located near **Lago Epecuén**, a large saltwater lake known for its curative properties, which swallowed up the nearby town of Villa de Epecuén during the 1985 floods.

The principal city in the *sierras* is **Tandil ⓰**, located some 160 km (99 miles) north of Necochea. The city was founded in the early 19th century and is an important tourist center, especially in Holy Week, when celebrations are held at Mount Calvary and the Passion Play is enacted.

Tandil found fame as the site of the "moving rock", a 300-ton stone which perched precariously on the edge of a cliff, and trembled for some 30 years before finally falling in 1912. Efforts to return the stone to its original site failed, but its memory is still widely celebrated. Tandil has a large park and lake (Lago del Fuerte) nestling at the foot of the hills in the south of the city. The city houses the **Museo Tradicionalista Fuerte Independencia** (open Tues–Sun 4–8pm), which includes exhibits from the history of life in Tandil, such as a hansom cab and carriages. In the *sierras* around the city are several *estancias*, which offer accommodations as well as a range of day visits with outdoor activities. The luxurious **Estancia Acelain**, 50 km (31 miles) from Tandil, has an Andalusian-style mansion, pool and gardens (*see page 349*). ❑

BELOW: school transport.
RIGHT: fishing boats in Mar del Plata.

THE CENTRAL SIERRAS

Map on page 220

This landlocked region offers some exquisite Jesuit architecture in and around the historic city of Córdoba, as well as excellent outdoor activities in the surrounding countryside

The province of Córdoba could in many respects be considered the heartland of Argentina. It lies about midway between the Andes and Buenos Aires and the Atlantic coast. Beyond geography, Córdoba represents much that Argentina is known for. Its economy is based not only on farming and ranching, but also on commerce and agro-related and automotive industries.

Approaching Córdoba from the east, one drives across miles and miles of stunningly flat pampas before reaching the gentle waves of the central *sierras*. Along the open plains or in the hidden valleys one may stumble upon a variety of characteristically Argentine scenes: a vast herd of the country's famous grass-fed cattle, or an animated scene of *gauchos* branding cattle in a rough-hewn country paddock, or a farm specializing in the breeding and training of world-class racing horses and polo ponies.

Aside from the chance encounters, there is much that the traveler can set out to see and do here. The city of Córdoba, Argentina's second largest, holds some of the country's finest examples of colonial architecture, both secular and religious. The province's mountain landscapes, embellished by numerous lakes, rivers, and streams, are an ideal environment for trekking, horseback riding, water sports, and fishing, among other options.

During the summer, the village of Villa Carlos Paz, near the provincial capital, becomes the country's second-biggest tourist destination after Mar del Plata. Here, as in other quaint mountain villages, summer visitors have their choice of several cultural and musical events. The most famous are the folk festival in Cosquín and the Oktoberfest beer festival organized by the German community in Villa General Belgrano.

PRECEDING PAGES: symmetrical church facade in Córdoba **LEFT:** gilt ceiling of Cordoba Cathedral. **BELOW:** modern sculpture in Villa Dolores.

Historic Córdoba

The city of Córdoba dates back to colonial times. One of the oldest cities in the country, it was founded by Jerónimo Luis de Cabrera in 1573. Cabrera came from Santiago del Estero in the north, following the Río Dulce, and settled his people by the Río Suquía. It is interesting to note that when information about these new, not yet settled areas was recounted in Peru by the early adventurous surveyors, some of the characteristics that have made Córdoba attractive were already mentioned. It was said that these lands had low mountains, plenty of fish in the many streams and rivers, an abundance of wild birds and animals (rheas, deer, pumas, armadillos, otters, hares, partridges, and much more), beautiful views, and weather like Spain.

In these few words lay the allure, the charm of the Córdoba region, the same charm which draws Argentines to visit the hundreds of little towns, inns, and campgrounds every year.

Grinding stone and mortar of the Comechingones.

When Cabrera arrived in the Córdoba region in 1573, it was populated by three principal indigenous groups: the Sanavirones in the northeast, the Comechingones in the west, and the Pampas in the plains.

Though a few confrontations did take place between the Spanish and the indigenous peoples, the latter were labeled "peaceful and cooperative" by the Spaniards, a commentary dictated by the contrast between these groups and other very bellicose tribes of the northwest, south, and east of the country.

The Pampas were nomadic groups who roamed the plains. The Sanavirones and Comechingones lived in caves or crude adobe houses surrounded by thorny bushes and cactus fences. They were organized in tribes led by *caciques* (chiefs) and they lived by hunting, gathering, and agriculture. Their religion centered around the sun and the moon, and there were three or four main languages and many dialects in the area. It is estimated that there were between 12,000 and 30,000 people in the area at the time of the Spanish conquest.

The discovery by the Spaniards of metal sources and stone for quarrying in the mountains more than justified in their eyes the foundation of a new city.

One hundred years after its foundation, Córdoba manifested the characteristics which are still seen as its trademark. The little village had flourished religiously and culturally. By that time it boasted an astonishing number of churches, chapels, and convents erected by the Jesuits, the Franciscans, the Carmelites, and others; it had a Jesuit-run university, one of the oldest in the country, erected in 1621 (now called the Universidad Nacional de Córdoba); the local economy was supported by a variety of agricultural products (corn, wheat, beans, potatoes, peaches, apricots, grapes, and pears) and by extensive and ever-growing herds of wild cattle.

BELOW: the church of Candonga, in the *sierras* of Córdoba.

The mountains and "the tree"

In Córdoba one finds the stark juxtaposition of the impossibly flat pampas with the rolling *sierras*, the first mountain chain one encounters when moving west toward the Andes. As one approaches across the plain, the hills appear like great waves breaking on a beach.

There are three chains of mountains in the western part of the province of Córdoba, all of which run parallel to each other, from north to south. They are the Sierra Chica in the east, the Sierra Grande in the center, and the Sierra del Pocho (which turn into the Sierra de Guasapampa) in the west. The highest peak in the province is Champaquí, which reaches a height of 2,884 meters (9,462 ft). The Sierras de Córdoba are neither as high nor as extensive as many of the other mountain formations east of the Andes. Their easy accessibility, their beauty, their dry weather, magnificent views, and good roads, as well as the myriad of small rivers and water courses have established for Córdoba a strong reputation as an ideal spot for rest and recuperation.

Most of the rain falls in the summer and is heavier in the eastern section where the hills look very green and lush. In truth the vegetation on these hills is mostly of the *monte* type: bushes and low thorny thickets. Toward the piedmont of the eastern hills, larger trees grow in greater abundance. Among these trees, the friendly *algarrobo* deserves special mention. From prehistoric times right up to the present it has been used by the local populations as a shade-giving tree, and as a source both of fruit and wood for fence posts and for fires. The fruit is used to make various foodstuffs, including *patay*, a hard, sweet bread. The *algarrobo* is also one of the trees most resistant to drought, and because of all these virtues, it is sometimes simply called "the tree" by the locals.

Map on page 220

The city of Córdoba was founded on 24 June 1573, as Córdoba La Llana de la Nueva Andalucía, a likely reference to its sunny Mediterranean climate.

BELOW: the rocky landscape around La Cumbrecita.

Bird songs

The fauna of the region is not as rich as when the Spaniards first arrived, but is still plentiful enough in some hidden areas to support seasonal hunting. Pumas or American lions still roam the hills but are few and isolated. Guanacos are not a common sight around most of the vacation resorts but can be seen toward the higher western areas. Hares abound and are hunted and eaten, as are partridges and vizcachas. Several types of snake can be found, including rattlesnakes and coral snakes, but the steady invasion of most places in the mountains by residents and visitors has decreased their numbers. Foxes are also occasionally seen, and there are countless species of birds, including condors, in the area.

The rich wildlife in this region attracts many visitors – these days most are armed only with cameras and binoculars.

Córdoba has a dry continental climate, with cooler, wetter weather in the *sierras* and warmer and drier weather in the plains to the south and east of the province. Though the summer, with its hot days and cool nights, is the favorite season for most visitors, the winter is not without its charm. Because the rains are seasonal, occurring in spring and summer, the views change dramatically.

Across the flats

The easiest access to the city and province of Córdoba is from the south and east. Leaving from Buenos Aires, the visitor has the choice of traveling by plane, bus or car. Buses are fast, offer a wider variety of schedules and are modern, spacious, and comfortable units. There are several companies that make the Buenos Aires–Córdoba run with options to stop in Rosario and a few other large towns (which takes under 9 hours).

If the trip from Buenos Aires is made by land, there are two main ways to go to Córdoba. The shortest is via Rosario, a city of over 1 million inhabitants

BELOW:
bright young
sparks in Córdoba.

located 300 km (185 miles) northwest of Buenos Aires, using Ruta 9 *(see page 230)*. The other choice is using Ruta 8, a slightly longer but quieter and quainter road, which runs parallel to the south, passing through some traditional agricultural towns such as San Antonio de Areco *(see page 192)*, Pergamino, Venado Tuerto, and Río Cuarto. In both cases, the visitor will pass through miles and miles of pampas (plain, flat, and very rich terrain) dotted with small towns and huge plots planted with corn, wheat, soya, and sunflower. Everywhere there are enormous herds of cattle (Aberdeen Angus, Hereford, Holando-Argentina) and horses. The roads are quite good and offer the basic commodities (hotels, small restaurants, cafés, gas stations) in almost every town along the way.

Córdoba can also be reached easily from the west (either Santiago, the Chilean capital, or Mendoza) by plane and bus and from the north (Santiago del Estero, Salta, Tucumán, Jujuy) by plane, bus, and train. All buses arrive at the **Terminal de Omnibus**, located at Boulevard Reconquista 380.

Spanish grid

The city of **Córdoba** ❶ is the second-largest in the country, with a population of approximately 1.3 million. The basis of its economy is agriculture, cattle, and the car industry. Its key location, at the crossroads of many of the main routes, established its early importance and fostered its rapid growth. Although Buenos Aires, with its excessive absorption of power and people, has always tended to overshadow the rest of the country, Córdoba and its zone of influence is the strongest nucleus of resistance found in the vast interior of Argentina.

Córdoba, like most Spanish-settled cities, was designed with a rectangular grid of streets, with the main plaza (Plaza San Martín), the cathedral, and the main

Maps:
Area 220
City 216

TIP

The airlines Aerolíneas Argentinas, Austral, and Southern Winds have several daily flights from Buenos Aires to Córdoba which take about an hour.

LEFT: the cathedral.
BELOW: El Arco, Córdoba.

TIP

If you are planning a trip to the country, make sure to visit Córdoba's provincial tourist office, the Dirección Provincial de Turismo, at Tucumán 360, which offers a wide range of information about the nearby *sierras*.

buildings in the city center. It is therefore easy for tourists to find on a map the different sites of historical, architectural, or artistic interest within the city.

Because many of the early buildings of Córdoba were either religious or educational, time and progress have spared a great number of them, leaving visitors and residents with a rich treasure-trove of colonial chapels, churches, convents, and public buildings amid the modern surroundings.

There are several different tourist offices, including downtown, at the airport and inside the bus terminal. The main office for city tourism is located in the **Recova del Cabildo Ⓐ** (open Mon–Fri 8am–9pm, Sat–Sun 9am–1pm and 3–7pm), Independencia 30, with information about walking tours, special events, museum exhibits, maps, and historical background.

Church circuit

The religious *circuito* (circuits being the various tours that are recommended by the city tourist office) covers most of the oldest colonial religious

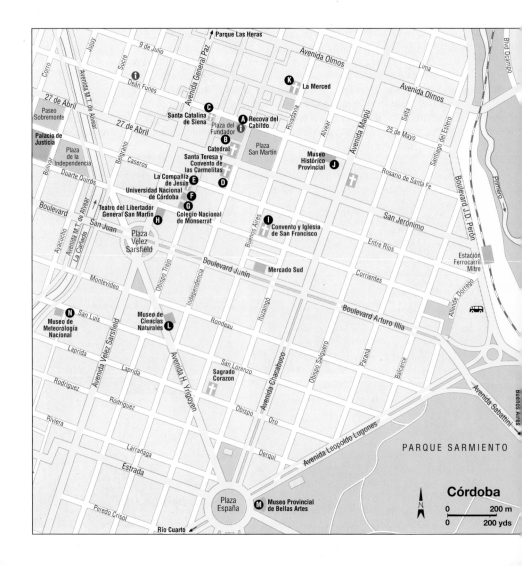

buildings. An ideal walking tour around the city center, which you can make unaccompanied or with a guide, begins at Plaza San Martín. Though its site was originally decided on in 1577, the final consecration of the **Catedral ❸** took place in 1784, after collapses, interruptions, and changes. These delays account for the many artistic styles visible in the architecture. It has been described by the architect J. Roca as having a classic Renaissance portico and a baroque dome and steeple, with influences of indigenous origin in its towers. A large wrought-iron gate completes the picture. The cool, shady interior of the church, located on the western side of **Plaza San Martín**, is divided into three large naves, separated from each other by wide, thick columns (which replaced the smaller original columns that were not strong enough to support the building). The main altar, made of silver, is from the 19th century; it replaced the original baroque altar which is now in the church of Tulumba.

El Cabildo, Córdoba.

The church and convent of **Santa Catalina de Siena ❻** (open at Mass hours: Mon–Sat 7am, Sun 8am 9am, and 7.30pm), located behind the cathedral, off the pedestrian street Obispo Trejo and at the end of the Pasaje Cuzco, was founded in 1613 by a wealthy widow, Leonor de Tejeda y Mirabal, who converted her home into the province's first convent. The current building dates from the end of the 19th century, and is noted in particular for its dome.

The **Iglesia de Santa Teresa y Convento de las Carmelitas ❼** (Church and Monastery of the Carmelite Nuns, also called Las Teresas) (open at Mass hours: 8am daily) was founded in the early 17th century. It was completed in 1717 but was heavily renovated during the latter half of the 18th century and many of the buildings date to this later period. The main altar has a large baroque sculpture of Santa Teresa de Jesús and the wooden choir is an example of fine woodwork. In the monastery there is a religious art museum, the Museo de Arte Religioso, in which many of the objects once belonging to the cathedral are now exhibited. The entrance is on Calle Independencia and the complex is located opposite the cathedral.

BELOW:
the narrowest
building in the
world, Córdoba.

The Jesuit complex

Built on the original site of a small shrine, dating from 1589, the Jesuit complex is located on Calle Caseros, two blocks from the cathedral. It was declared a World Heritage Site in 2000.

The group of buildings is made up of the church, the Capilla Doméstica and the living quarters. Originally it also encompassed the Colegio Máximo and the university, both of which are now national institutions.

The church, **La Compañía de Jesús ❽** (open Mon–Sat 8am–7pm, Sun at Mass hours) dates to the 17th century. One of its notable details is an arch made of Paraguayan cedar, in the shape of an inverted boat's hull, fitted with wooden pegs. The church interior is lined with cedar beams and the roof is made up of beams and tiles. The tiles were joined with a special glue, which after 300 years is still tightly weatherproof. Many of the baroque altars, including the one made of cedar, date to the 18th century and the Carrara marble work on the walls is 19th century.

The Capilla Doméstica is also from the 17th century. Here, the ceiling was constructed of

wooden beams, and canes tied with rawhide, which were placed between the beams and then plastered and covered with painted cloth.

Within the Jesuit complex is located the **Universidad Nacional de Córdoba ⓕ** (Rectory of the University of Cordoba, open Mon–Fri 8am–9pm, Sat 8am–noon). Opened in 1613, it is the oldest university in the country. The rectory includes the university library, as well as cloisters, gardens, and a monument to university founder Bishop Trejo y Sanabria.

Another academic institution located within the Jesuit complex is the traditional **Colegio Nacional de Montserrat ⓖ** (Montserrat National College) (open Mon–Fri 8am–9pm during term), a secondary school which until 1998 was open only to boys. The college was founded by Ignacio Duarte Quirós in 1687, and since 1907 has been a dependency of the University. The building was reconstructed in 1927 and is primarily notable for the clock tower at one end, as well as a mural by Claudio Boggino in its central salon (open Mon–Fri, mornings only).

Across from the Montserrat on Duarte Quirós, between Velez Sarsfield and Obispo Trejo, is the **Teatro del Libertador General San Martín ⓗ**, formerly known as the Teatro Rivera Indarte and constructed in 1887. The theater, which is considered to have outstanding acoustics, still offers performances and includes the **Museo del Teatro y de la Música** (open Mon–Fri 9am–noon), with photographs, scores, and programs from the history of the theater.

The **Convento y Iglesia de San Francisco** (Church and Convent of Saint Francis) ⓘ is located at the corner of Calles Buenos Aires and Entre Rios, two blocks from the cathedral. The land for the church was given to the Franciscan Order by the founder of the city, Jerónimo Luis de Cabrera. The first chapel was

BELOW: Paseo de las Flores, one of Córdoba's pedestrianized shopping streets.

built in 1575; this original chapel and a second one which replaced it no longer exist. The current structure was initiated in 1796 and finished in 1813. Within the complex, the room named Salon de Profundis is original.

Map on page 216

Ethnic artifacts

Also worth mentioning is the **Museo Histórico Provincial ❶** (Provincial History Museum, open Tues–Fri 9am–1pm and 3–7pm, Sat–Sun 10am–1pm), an outstanding example of colonial residential architecture, located in the mansion of the Marquis de Sobremonte, the last colonial mansion left in the city, on calles Rosario de Santa Fe and Ituzaingó, three blocks from the cathedral. The building was constructed in the 18th century and occupied by the governor of Córdoba. It hosts a large collection of indigenous and *gaucho* artifacts, old musical instruments, ceramics, and furniture.

Renowned 19th-century French landscape architect Carlos Thays was responsible for the layout of Parque Sarmiento in Córdoba, as well as designing other city parks in Mendoza, Tucumán, and Buenos Aires.

Located in the corner of 25 de Mayo and Rivadavia, only three blocks from the cathedral, is the **Basílica de La Merced ❸**. The present building was finished in 1826 over foundations dating from the1600s. The main altar, executed in 1890, and the polychrome wooden pulpit from the 18th century are two of the outstanding attractions of the interior.

In the southern part of the city is the huge **Parque Sarmiento**, near the Barrio Nueva Córdoba and the **Ciudad Universitaria**, which houses all of the university's faculties in buildings of different eras and designs. The park has a lake with two islands, a Greek theater, a zoo, and the Córdoba Lawn Tennis Club. It was designed in the late 19th century by French landscape architect Carlos Thays.

Beyond the city center

The **Museo de Ciencias Naturales ❶** (open Mon–Fri 9am–noon; with daily guided tours), located at Yrigoyen 115, includes exhibits on geology, botany, paleontology, and zoology relating to the history and flora and fauna of the province.

At Parque Sarmiento's main entrance, located on Plaza España, is the **Museo Provincial de Bellas Artes ❹** (open Tues–Sun 4–7pm), opened in 1916 and offering special art exhibitions, a library, and cultural activities. Another Fine Arts museum, the **Museo de Bellas Artes Dr. Génaro Perez** (open Tues–Fri 9.30am–1.30pm and 4.30–8.30pm, Sat–Sun 10am–8pm), is located in the Palacio Garzón, on the Paseo de la Ciudad two blocks north of the Cathedral and has permanent exhibitions of Argentine three-dimensional art.

To the west of the center, near the canal at San Luís and Belgrano, is the **Museo de Meteorología Nacional ❶** (National Meteorology Museum and Observatory; open Tues–Fri 9am–1pm and 3–7pm, Sat 8.30am–12.30pm), founded in 1871 by President Sarmiento and Argentina's principal observatory.

Another huge park, located on the western edge of the city, is the **Parque San Martín**, located by the Río Suquía and close to the Córdoba stadium and the University of the Environment. This beautiful park, also designed by Carlos Thays, includes the **Centro de Arte Contemporáneo** (open Tues–Sun 4–8pm),

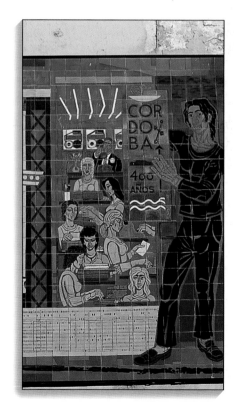

BELOW: mosaics in Basílica de la Merced, Córdoba.

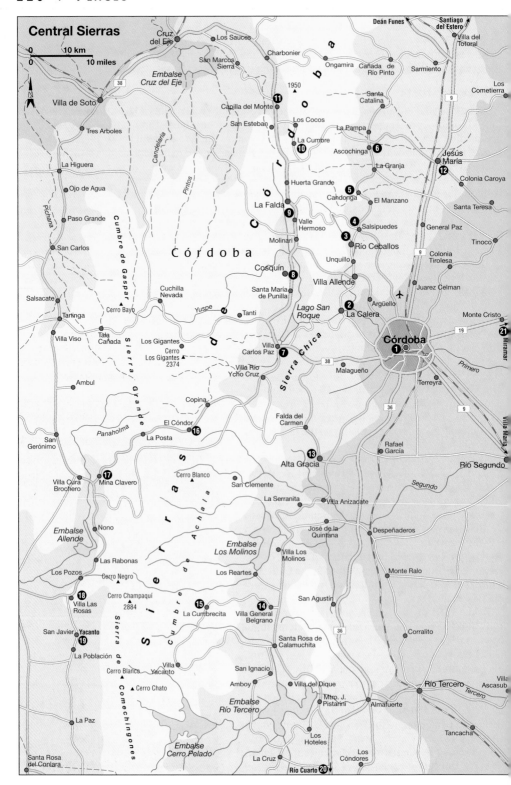

which exhibits permanent as well as temporary works of modern art; an exhibition center, and a camp ground. Also by the river is the **Parque Las Heras**, extending from the Centenario Bridge to the Antártida Bridge, which includes a monument to famous tango singer Carlos Gardel.

Maps:
Area 220
City 216

The contemporary city

Córdoba might be better known for its colonial charm, but the modern city also has much to offer visitors. A few blocks from the city center is **La Cañada**, the tree-lined canal that runs through town, a lovely place to walk in the evening or at quiet times of day. On Saturday and Sunday there is an art and crafts fair on the corner of La Cañada and A. Rodriguez. The Rincón de los Pintores (the Painters' Corner) is a gallery devoted to the work of local artists, and is located inside the Centro Muncipal de Exposiciones Obispo Mercadillo at Rosario de Santa Fe 39. *Peatonales* (pedestrian streets) in the city center are lined with cafés, bookstores, and boutiques – popular sites for university students. This is a good place to sit and relax, do some window shopping, or watch people strolling by. Also closeby are numerous movie theaters showing current releases.

Córdoba has many popular street cafes.

Village *fiestas*

Once you have had your fill of the city of Córdoba, a trip to the surrounding country is highly recommended, if you have the time. The local tourism authorities have laid out a number of routes which will lead the dedicated traveler up into the mountains, along paved and unpaved roads to tiny villages, lakes, streams, campsites, and spectacular views. While these routes can be undertaken by public bus, private transport is necessary to really explore the area.

BELOW: a Germanic-style cafe in Villa General Belgrano.

THE JESUITS IN CORDOBA

During the 17th and 18th centuries, the city of Córdoba was the spiritual and administrative center of the Jesuit movement in the Americas, whose activities covered all of north and west Argentina and much of central South America.

The chief goal of the Jesuits was a spiritual one – to convert the heathen souls of the indigenous population and to further the religious education of their brotherhood. However, as they attracted an increasing number of native converts into their missions, the Jesuits developed their own economic system, abolishing forced labor and replacing it with a productive, communal economy.

With a steady flow of new missionaries from Europe, together with large donations of money and property, the Jesuit "empire" grew spectacularly. The highly skilled communities built fabulous missions, comprising churches, residences, and *estancias*, filled with finely-crafted furniture, ironwork, and silverware. By the time of their expulsion in 1767 by Spain's King Carlos III, the Jesuits had established a network of centers in and around Córdoba, including La Calera, Estancia Santa Catalina, Jesús María, and Alta Gracia *(see map on opposite page)*, the remains of which can be visited today.

TIP

Laguna Azul is a popular bathing pool, converted from a disused quarry, near the Mal Paso Dam on the Río Suquía, outside La Calera.

Side trips from Córdoba

Among the shorter day excursions from Córdoba is **La Calera** ❷, some 15 km (9 miles) to the west of the city and now one of the dormitory communities for those working in the city. Located at the foot of the *sierras*, La Calera stands near the Mal Paso Dam on Río Suquía, which offers attractive views over the reservoir. Within La Calera, surrounded by former limestone quarries started in the 17th century, are the ruins of a Jesuit Chapel and of the former lime mills and furnaces. The town also has a municipal beach on the river, which gets extremely busy in the summer.

About 40 km (25 miles) to the north of Córdoba is **Río Ceballos** ❸, a delightful town in the *sierras* and also home to many of those working in the city. The Ceballos River runs through the center of town, set among green hills, and at the far end of the town is La Quebrada reservoir and park. Slightly farther up (or about two hours' walk on foot) is the Cascada del Aguila waterfall and the Cascada de los Hornillos waterfall. Río Ceballos also has a casino and is a popular summer watering hole for those seeking a quieter get-away than the night life of Villa Carlos Paz. Between La Calera and Río Ceballos are a number of other purely residential towns such as Villa Allende and Unquillo, which are well worth passing through because of their attractiveness.

One of the most popular areas is **El Valle de la Punilla**, which extends north from the city of Córdoba on Ruta 38 toward **Cruz del Eje**. This route passes through or near most of the small resort towns of the region. Among these towns is **Salsipuedes** ❹, about 30 km (19 miles) north of Río Ceballos. The town is located in an area of great natural beauty and has a riverside beach area for tourists. Passing Salsipuedes, after about another 20 km (12 miles) brings

BELOW: a river running slowly through the *sierras*.

you to the tiny village of **Candonga ❺**, located on the dirt road on the way to Cerro Azul. There is an 18th-century chapel here, the **Capilla de Candonga**, which was formerly part of the Santa Gertrudis Jesuit *estancia*. A larger Jesuit site is located in **Ascochinga ❻**, north of Salsipuedes on a road that offers great natural beauty and a great selection of German pastry shops. Ascochinga has the former Jesuit **Estancia Santa Catalina**, including a church and cemetery and the ruins of a seminary. The complex can be seen from outside (the key to the church can be requested from the caretaker) and is an exceptional example of colonial architecture from the early 18th century.

To the west of Córdoba is **Villa Carlos Paz ❼**, famous for its busy nightlife, its casinos, restaurants, and clubs, and the sports activities centered around San Roque lake. This town surprises the visitor, with its handsome chalets, comfortable hotels, and streets packed day and night with tourists (during the high season).

Music festivals

About 18km (11 miles) directly north of Carlos Paz is **Cosquín ❽**, a quaint village famous for its Argentine and Latin American folk music and dance festival in the second half of January *(see page 358)*. Another 15 km (9 miles) north along the narrow, well-paved road brings you to the village of **La Falda ❾**, which holds a festival celebrating the folk music of Argentina's immigrants, along with tango, in the first week of February. At other times of the year, golfing, swimming, horseback riding, and sailing can be enjoyed. La Falda has an archeological museum and a museum of miniature locomotives.

About 11 km (7 miles) further north lies **La Cumbre ❿**. This town, on Río San Gerónimo, offers excellent trout fishing from November to April, as well

Map on page 220

The town of La Cumbre is noted for its well-tended gardens and large brick buildings, built by English immigrants.

BELOW: the Jesuit complex at Alta Gracia.

German immigrants in Villa General Belgrano celebrate a hearty Oktoberfest every year.

as golf, tennis, and swimming facilities. Its altitude of 1,142 meters (3,768 ft) creates a very pleasant climate and it has become known as a writers' haven. In 1999 it hosted the Paragliding World Cup and achieved international fame.

Another 15 km (9 miles) along the same road (106 km/66 miles from Córdoba) will take the visitor to **Capilla del Monte ⓫**, a town which celebrates its Spanish Festival in February. You can enjoy hiking, rock climbing, swimming, and serenity in this town in the heart of the *sierras*.

Cutting across country to the east for some 65 km (40 miles) on to Ruta 9 brings you to the large town of **Jesús María ⓬**, also associated with the Jesuits. The Jesuit **Estancia Jesuitica San Isidro Labrador**, on the outskirts of the town, comprises a church, residence, and museum (open daily). There is another former Jesuit school in town, the **Casa de Caroya**. The city also has a national festival of folklore and rodeo, held in the first half of January at an amphitheater next to San Isidro Labrador.

Gaucho games, *mate*, and cakes

Ruta 5 south of Córdoba will lead you to another tourist haven, **El Valle de Calamuchita**, which lies between La Sierra Chica and La Sierra Grande.

Arriving in **Alta Gracia ⓭**, one finds a charming, prosperous town which welcomes tourists but is not overwhelmed by the kinds of crowds found in Carlos Paz. One of the main attractions is the Jesuit complex, a veritable jewel of colonial architecture, containing the Iglesia de la Merced (open during Mass hours) and the Residencia Jesuítica (open daily, admission fee). In 2001, the **Museo Casa de Ernesto Che Guevara** (open daily) was opened. The legendary revolutionary hero spent his teenage years here when a doctor recommended the town's dry air for his asthma.

BELOW: handicrafts for sale in the *sierras*.

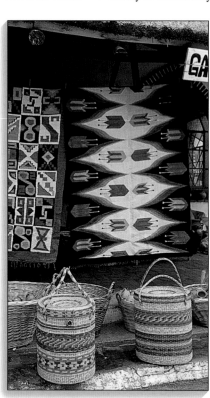

A short excursion into the hills behind Alta Gracia toward La Isla, on the Río Anizacate, leads over a passable dirt road, past small farms with spectacular views of the beautiful river. With luck, somewhere along this route, or another in the *sierra* region, you just might come upon a group of locals branding their cattle and be invited to eat a barbecue *(asado)*, drink strong red wine, and throw the *taba* (a *gaucho* game of chance played with the left knee bone of a horse).

Leaving Alta Gracia behind and returning to the main route, continue on south and enter the Sierras on a well-paved but winding road. Twenty picturesque kilometers (12 miles) later the Embalse Los Molinos appears. This is a favorite spot for the people of the region to practice various aquatic sports, or have a meal by the dam, high above the lake.

Another 20 km (12 miles) brings you to **Villa General Belgrano ⓮**, a town purportedly founded by seamen from the ill-fated Graf Spee, who chose not to return to Germany. Villa General Belgrano has a decidedly German character, with its charming chalets and well-kept gardens. As might be expected, the town celebrates an Oktoberfest during the first week of that month. And don't leave town without sampling some of the famous homemade cakes. A bit further to the south is the Embalse Río Tercero, part of a series of seven lakes beginning with Los

Map
on page
220

Molinos, all of which offer beautiful mountain scenery. Embalse Río Tercero is the largest lake in the area. The town of Embalse at the tip of the lake offer reasonable tourist facilities.

The tiny town of **La Cumbrecita** ⑮ is nestled at the foot of Las Sierras Grandes, 40 km (25 miles) down an unpaved road west of Villa General Belgrano. Visitors will find many nature paths just outside town, crossing small rivers and waterfalls, and meandering among varied plant life, including a small forest of cedar, pine, and cypress trees. La Cumbrecita is relaxing and quiet, with attractive houses and gardens along the side streets. On the road between Villa General Belgrano and La Cumbrecita there's a view of **Cerro Champaquí**, at 2,884 meters (9,461 ft), the highest peak in the *sierras* of Córdoba, and which can be climbed on foot or on horseback (around two hours in the latter case).

A more tranquil part of the *sierras* is the valley of Traslasierra (which means behind the mountains), reached by taking **El Camino de las Altas Cumbres** to the west, on the other side of the mountains from the La Punilla and Calamuchita valleys. On this road there is a panoramic view from **El Cóndor** ⑯, a lookout point at the site of the former Hotel El Cóndor. Some of the towns worth visiting in Traslasierra are Mina Clavero, San Javier, and Cura Brochero.

Mina Clavero ⑰ is located at the meeting of the Panaholma and Mina Clavero rivers, and houses the **Museo Piedra Cruz del Sur** (open daily in summer only), a museum of minerals, which has stone carvings and other crafts for sale. Further south is the former tobacco town of **Villa Las Rosas** ⑱, on the Río Gusmara, with a beach area. South of Villa Las Rosas is **Yacanto** ⑲, an upmarket resort with grand summer houses and an exclusive hotel complex, the Hotel Yacanto, with its own golf course. Yacanto is located outside San Javier, a town crossed by canals, located at the foot of Cerro Champaquí.

Further exploration

The Sierras of Córdoba offer countless possibilities to explore off the main tourist routes, following dirt roads to quiet villages in the mountains.

In the south of the province is the large city of **Río Cuarto** ⑳, located on the river of the same name, close to the southern lake district around Río Tercero and some 220 km (137 miles) from the city of Córdoba. Río Cuarto has a 19th-century cathedral located on Central Julio Roca, as well as the **Museo de Bellas Artes** (open daily), with an important collection by local and national artists; and the **Museo Histórico Regional** (open daily except Mon), housed in a building dating from 1860, covering local history from the pre-Columbian era to the present day.

In the north of Córdoba province, on the shore of **Laguna Mar Chiquita**, is the resort town of **Miramar** ㉑ (open Mon–Fri 7am–2pm), which offers water sports, a center for balneotherapy, and the Reserva Provincial at Laguna Mar Chiquita, an important wetlands area for overwintering shorebirds; the area has been made a Provincial Natural Reserve and Hemispheric Site of the Organization of Reserves for Beach Birds. ❑

BELOW: a rocky riverbed near La Cumbrecita.

THE NORTHEAST

This long sliver of land, squeezed in between Uruguay, Brazil, and Paraguay, is home to the famous Iguazú Falls, as well as ruins of Jesuit missions and a clutch of lesser-known natural attractions

Map on page 230

As with everywhere else in Argentina, the distances in the northeast are considerable. Here, the major tourist attractions are few and far between and hurried visitors tend to fly to Iguazú and skip the rest. In so doing, they miss an overland journey that can be really worthwhile. The best way to do this journey is in a car, so that you can spend time in selected spots, although public transportation is quite extensive and reliable.

The two principal sites in Misiones – the 275 impressive and thundering cascades of Iguazú Falls and the Jesuit ruins at San Ignacio – should not be missed. Neither should the 2-km (1¼-mile) wide Moconá Falls on the Uruguay River on the border with Brazil. On the way to Moconá are 40 smaller cascades accessible by jungle paths in the Central Highlands, and the charming town of Oberá, a jumping-off point for expeditions to the falls.

Along the road to Misiones, in the slow-paced and friendly towns in Entre Ríos and Corrientes, there are churches, modest museums, and even small private zoos to see. In between the towns, across a variety of terrains, there are provincial and national parks, such as the Parque Nacional El Palmar near Colón in Entre Ríos, with rare palm trees and abundant wildlife.

But the most interesting park and nature reserve of all is the Esteros del Iberá lagoon and wetlands in Corrientes province, where intrepid travelers can see hundreds of bird and animal species, and look alligators and boa constrictors in the eye from small boats paddled by former poachers turned park rangers. (The ex-poachers' change of heart has a purely capitalistic motive: their salaries make it more profitable for them to protect the animals than to hunt them.)

Along the way, you can always break up the trip with a visit to a citrus farm, or a *yerba maté* plantation, to sample a gourd filled with the green tea that is Argentina's national drink.

Fantasy ferry journey

From 1550 to about 1920, the rivers of northeast Argentina were the safest, cheapest, and best way to see the country. For more than 350 years, vessels navigated the rivers, carrying goods, settlers, explorers, officials, and, in later years, tourists.

Today, however, the vast majority of visitors to this region travel by road or air. Nevertheless, everything of any interest in northeast Argentina is on or close to a river, so one approach to getting to know this area, on paper at least, would be to use the river system to explore this corner of the country. On this hypothetical journey one will embark in Buenos Aires.

Soon after setting sail, the vessel will have to find the navigable mouth of the Paraná, as the river splits up

PRECEDING PAGES: waiting for the last boat home.
LEFT: the steaming Iguazú Falls.
BELOW: a barefoot Corrientes *gaucho*.

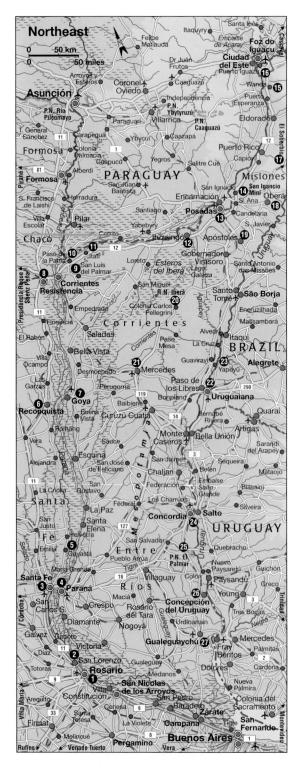

into many channels when it joins the Río de la Plata, forming a huge delta. Suburban **Tigre** is the gateway to this maze of waterways lined with weekend houses, each with its own small jetty. Here people have a restful time fishing, boating, or just getting away from the nearby metropolis. The delta has a life of its own from Monday to Friday: there are permanent residents, fishermen, citrus growers, and pulp-wood producers, all of whom lead the gentler and slower-paced life of river dwellers. Hotels and guest houses are plentiful.

Upriver, **Zárate** is the site of a huge road and rail bridge complex which, when completed in 1979, at last joined Mesopotamia to Buenos Aires and made obsolete the double ferry connection which was susceptible to interruption by flood and drought water levels and was a fearful hassle.

On then to **Rosario** ❶, a large grain port which was once the second city in the country, though *Rosarinos* may still debate the "once" bit. It is a large city, with a population of more than 1 million, although it suffered a major loss of population following the decline of its port, once the nation's second after Buenos Aires. Nevertheless, the port was privatized in the mid 1990s and is again becoming a major hub of activity.

Rosario is not particularly geared toward visitors, but the early 20th-century and art deco architecture in the center of town gives some idea of its history. A pedestrian precinct in the city center passes through some of the oldest and most architecturally mixed parts of town. It is also worth visiting the monument to the national flag, the **Monumento a la Bandera**, which consists of a sweep of steps, an obelisk backed by a series of arches, and an eternal flame.

North to Santa Fe

Some 32 km (20 miles) upstream, on the western shore, is **San Lorenzo** ❷, and the **Convento de San Carlos**, built at the end of the 18th century and famous for being the site of a battle in the War of Independence. Here, on February 3, 1813, the Argentine hero San Martín was pinned under his fallen horse. A Sergeant Cabral saved him, but in so doing was himself fatally wounded. The tree under which he died still stands in the grounds of the convent as a symbol of self-sacrifice.

Rosario is in the province of **Santa Fe**. It is by far the most important city in that province, but it is not the capital, a fact that *Rosarinos* dislike intensely. This honor goes to **Santa Fe ❸**, a city some way upstream and the next port of call. First founded in the early 1500s, somewhat north of its present location, it was lost early on to disease and indigenous harrassment. The new city was founded in 1573. Today, Santa Fe is a pleasant provincial town, steeped in tradition, but with modern amenities and little pretense. On the corner of Amenábar and San Martín is the ancient but beautiful church of **San Francisco**, surrounded by monastic buildings that house the province's **Museo Histórico** (open Mon–Fri 8am–noon, Sun 9am–noon and 4–7pm).

The town center also includes the **Catedral Metropolitana**, constructed in the 1750s, and at San Martín 1490 is the **Museo Provincial de Bellas Artes** (open Tues–Sun 10am–noon and 4–8pm). Here you will find a large collection of some 2,000 works of art by native and foreign artists. The city hosts a folklore festival of music and dance in the first week of February.

From Santa Fe there is a tunnel under the Río Paraná to the city of **Paraná ❹**, capital of the province of Entre Ríos. Paraná has fine parks, lovely buildings and churches, and views across the river. Inland, the undulating landscape is dotted with woods of native acacias and cut into chunks by smaller rivers and streams. Santa Fe, on the other shore, sits in lowlands as flat as a pancake, surrounded by lakes, marshes, and rivers. Its hinterland is all fenced off into square fields, with regularly spaced towns and villages.

Jungle ruins

About 80 km (50 miles) upstream near **Cayastá ❺**, old Santa Fe slept of oblivion until it was rediscovered in the 20th century. Previously hidden by vegetation of centuries' growth on the low bank of a small branch of the river, slowly and gently it is being uncovered. Though it was a small town and entirely built of adobe (stone of any kind is hard to find in the pampas), there were something like seven churches or religious orders represented here and it is an important historical site, although tourist facilities are minimal. Cayastá also offers panoramic views of the San Javier river and islands.

In the north of Santa Fe province is **Reconquista ❻**, a town of some 55,000 people where the late 19th-century port is currently undergoing renovation and a rise in shipping due to the dredging of the Paraguay and Paraná rivers. The large **Plaza 25 de Mayo** in the town center has a monument to the city's founder, General Manuel Obligado.

Passing into the province of Corrientes, the second-largest city is **Goya ❼**, located on the Río Paraná and a well-known draw for *surubí* (a large tropical catfish) angling enthusiasts, as well as the headquarters of the local Philip Morris cigarette manufacturing subsidiary, Massalin Particulares. Goya has a 19th-century

Map on page 230

San Martín's cell and final resting place, San Lorenzo.

BELOW: Monumento a la Bandera, Rosario.

Gauchos *on an empty back road in Corrientes.*

BELOW: Convento de San Carlos, San Lorenzo.

cathedral on the Plaza Mitre, river walks, and the **Capilla del Diablo** (on Ruta 12, in Colonia Carolina, ask owners for permission to enter), constructed by immigrants in the early 20th century and featuring a carving of the Virgin Mary in a block of carob wood, as well as additional carvings including serpents and other apparently diabolical designs.

There is still a ferry in operation between Reconquista and Goya, and for those interested, the trip across gives you a good feel for the entire stretch of the Paraná River. It takes from four to six hours and goes along a network of waterways, wending between islands with wooded shores.

A bridge links the cities of **Resistencia 8**, capital of Chaco province (and once named Eva Perón) and **Corrientes**, capital of the province of the same name. The latter, on the east bank, sits high, while Resistencia lies among the swamps. Neither is high on most tourist agendas, but Corrientes does have a locally popular carnival during the last days before Lent, with floats, music, dancing, and fancy-dress. About 25 km (15 miles) inland from Corrientes, the small town of **San Luis del Palmar 9** has retained the flavor of colonial times and is well worth a visit.

A short distance beyond Corrientes, you reach the confluence with the Río Paraguay. It is about here, at **Paso de la Patria 10**, that fishermen from all over the world congregate to try for dorado, the "fightingest fish in the world". Lodging, boats, guides, and equipment are available from July to November.

Pilgrims' progress

Incongruous and totally out of the blue, the huge church dome at **Itatí 11** can be seen from up to 24 km (15 miles) away across the plains. This dome is said to be the "most impressive" after St Peter's in Rome. It tops the basilica where

THE RUINS OF SAN IGNACIO MINÍ

Among the 30 or so Jesuit missions whose remains have survived in northeast Argentina, San Ignacio Miní is the largest and best preserved. For its historic and architectural importance, the site has been declared Patrimonio Histórico Cultural de la Humanidad by UNESCO.

Founded in 1610 on what is now Brazilian territory in the north of Misiones province, San Ignacio suffered continual slave raids from the Portuguese colony and was forced to move twice, finally settling in its current location near Posadas, by the Río Paraná, in 1696.

Throughout the 18th century the mission grew to become one of the most important in the region, inhabited by more than 3,000 Guaraní converts. Following the expulsion of the Jesuits in 1767, however, San Ignacio, along with all the missions, fell into decline until, in the 19th century, it was destroyed and its occupants ejected.

Miraculously, much of the original complex has survived today, aided by some careful restoration work. Entering San Ignacio via a wide, tree-lined avenue, visitors are confronted by the towering red sandstone walls of the church and adjoining buildings. Encroaching vegetation drapes some outlying ruins and a nightly *son et lumière* show recreates the atmosphere of the Jesuits' glory days.

many pilgrims converge to venerate the miraculous Virgin of Itatí, housed in the adjoining shrine. For sheer bad taste it is hard to beat the local *santerías*, which sell plaster statues of the virgin and saints, and other religious articles.

The gigantic hydroelectric dam, **Represa Yacyretá**, has become the chief tourist attraction of the once-sleepy Corrientes town of **Ituzaingó ⑫**, some 330 km (205 miles) east of Resistencia, which is recommended for its beaches, zoo and fishing. The multi-million dollar dam meant nearly 50,000 people were forced to relocate. Free tours are available several times daily.

Just southwest of Posadas, the character of the river changes; the wide, shallow sweeps change to a boxed-in area between steep, high banks in rolling country. Upstream from here, the river cuts through a basalt flow originating some 1,290 km (800 miles) away in Brazil. Here, even the soil changes; the red lateritic soil of Misiones province deceives one into thinking it is quite fertile, as the vegetation here is very lush. This is, however, an illusion: the constant fall of leaves makes its own rich compost right on the forest floor.

Map on page 230

Jesuit missions

Another 140 km (87 miles) upstream is **Posadas ⑬**, the provincial capital of Misiones, with some 250,000 inhabitants. Posadas' dwindling Paraguayan market is open every day at calles San Martín and Roque Pérez, while a bridge crosses the river to Encarnación in Paraguay itself. The city has the nearest main airport to the increasingly popular Iberá wetlands *(see page 238)*.

The Jesuits were the real pioneers in Misiones; indeed, it is from their work that the province gets its name. They arrived early in the 17th century, and proceeded to settle and convert the Guaraní natives. They soon began to be pushed around,

Prize dorados drying in the sun.

BELOW: the Jesuit ruins of San Ignacio Miní.

first by slave traders in the area and then by the Iberian governments, first Portugal, then Spain. They were finally expelled in 1777, and left behind them the mission buildings and lots of unprotected and slightly Christian souls.

Some 20 km (12 miles) southeast of Posadas is the small town of **Candelaria**, which has a beach area on the Río Paraná, as well as the Jesuit ruins of Nuestra Señora de Candelaria o Purificación, which was founded in 1689 and was the Jesuit seat in the area until the order's expulsion. A few kilometers further north on Ruta 12 are the towns of **Santa Ana** and, 30 km (19 miles) away, and **Loreto**, both of which also have Jesuit ruins dating from the same period. In addition to the ruined missions, Candelaria has both natural forests and planted eucalyptus and pine plantations, as well as the **Parque Provincial El Cañadón de Profundidad**, with a river, waterfall, canyon, and small campsite.

Of the 12 mission ruins that have been restored to date in Misiones, the best-known is **San Ignacio Miní** ⓴ (open daily 7am–7pm, with a *son et lumière* show at 7pm in winter and 8.30pm in summer), 55 km (34 miles) east of Posadas on Ruta 12. It is best to amble around the ruins at dawn or dusk, when you can be alone and when the light plays wonders on the red stone. It is then that you can commune with the spirit of what was begun in the name of humanity.

Northern settlers

Some of the villages of Misiones have a flavor peculiar to themselves. Wooden houses and churches are made from local materials, but the ideas which inspired them came from northern Europe –the origin of most of the settlers. Immigrants from Germany, Poland, Switzerland, Sweden, and France settled in this area, which accounts for the fair-haired people seen everywhere.

BELOW: bird's-eye view of the *Garganta del Diablo* (Devil's Throat) of the Iguazú Falls.

Shortly before reaching Puerto Iguazú on the trip north from Posadas, and located on a bend in the Paraná River, is the small town of **Wanda ⓯**, where semi-precious stones are mined. The town is famous for its stone crafts, and has a commercial center where artisans sell regional crafts.

One finally disembarks in **Puerto Iguazú ⓰**, the head point of navigation, now that the Itaipú Dam has closed off the Paraná and since the Río Iguazú has its own natural barrier. This small town is fully geared for tourism, with a number of hotels, restaurants, taxis, exchange houses, and so on. As a town, it has little to save it from mediocrity, but it just happens to be the nearest settlement to the **Parque Nacional Iguazú** and the world-famous **waterfalls**.

An alternative to staying in Puerto Iguazú is to cross the border into Brazil, where its twin town **Foz do Iguaçu** offers better accommodations and restaurants, although these are no better value than those on the Argentine side. The more spectacular close-up views of the falls are on the Argentine side, where the entrance fee includes a lot more for your money.

Iguazú Falls

Amidst a spectacular jungle setting, the **Cataratas del Iguazú ④** lie on the Río Iguazú, which runs along the border of Brazil and Argentina. It is often said about this magnificent site that Argentina provides the falls and Brazil enjoys the view. Certainly the 550 meters (600 yards) of walks on the Brazilian side give the visitor a marvelous panoramic view of most of the falls but this is at something of a distance. The simple solution, if you are torn for choice but have enough time, is to visit both sides, which can be done in a day.

On the Argentine side, the falls can be experienced from a number of angles.

*Maps:
Area 230
Falls 235*

Lookout tower over the Iguazú Falls in the national park.

BELOW: walkway perilously close to the rim of the falls.

Iguazú Falls

The lush forest around the falls is brimming with fauna and flora, such as this bromeliad.

The lower falls circuit is perhaps the most beautiful 1,000 meter walk in the world and should be done clockwise. It leads to the start of the **Isla San Martín** boat trip, which is free and recommended as it allows one to get right into the heart of the spectacle.

By far the most magnificent walk is the one right across the upper river, from Puerto Canoas to the **Garganta del Diablo** (the "Devil's Throat"), where the water plunges the entire 70 meters (240 ft) off the basalt flow into the cauldron below. Late afternoon till dusk is the best time to see the Garganta, both for the lighting at that hour and to see the flocks of birds that swoop through the billowing mists on their way back to their nests for the night.

The park has many trails into the sub-tropical rainforest surrounding the falls. If you are attentive and lucky, there's a good chance of seeing some of the exotic wildlife that inhabits the area. At the **Visitors' Center** ❽ you can get lists of the local mammals, birds, and plants. In 2001, a gas-powered, silent train service was completed. Leaving every 20 minutes from the Visitors' Center, it takes passengers to the start of the two walking trails. A US$18-million-dollar project also included improvement to facilities and the construction of a large car park.

The **Hotel Internacional** ❿ is located on the premises of the park, and offers easy access to all the sites.

Iguazú and Itaipú dams

The Río Iguazú is some 900 km (540 miles) long above the falls and has been dammed. The forest clearing in the watershed permits the immediate runoff of rain, so the river floods, runs dry, runs dirty, "pulses" (due to week-day industrial energy demands) and, in general, behaves in a way unnatural to the trained eye. The stunning natural setting, however, offsets any disappointments.

The **Represa Hidroeléctrica Itaipú**, on the Río Paraná, 20 km (12 miles) north of Puerto Iguazú, is a joint enterprise between Brazil and Paraguay. Free guided tours (Mon–Sat at 8am, 9am, 10am, 2pm and 3.30pm) are well worth it, especially if one of the sluice gates is opened, creating a cascade of water to rival that of Iguazú.

Bitter tea

To return to Buenos Aires on the Río Uruguay would be impossible, due to the river's rapids. The first obstacle encountered is the **Moconá Falls**, some 230 km (143 miles) south by road, which are best viewed from the Brazilian side of the river. To see the falls, the nearest town is **El Soberbio** ⓱, which is also known as the national capital of essential oils, its principal export. The tiny town, founded only about 50 years ago by German and Italian immigrants, is located on the Río Uruguay on the site of three river basins and three hill ranges. El Soberbio has both hotels and campsites, and you can arrange trips in small boats to the Moconá Falls; by crossing to Porto Soberbio in Brazil, the trip can also be made by land in good weather. The falls themselves are within the Parque Provincial Moconá, an ecological reserve, and consist of a 3-km (2-mile) long series of waterfalls of up to 12 meters (40 ft) high.

Yerba maté plantations

There are two towns of interest in the southwest of Misiones. **Oberá** ⑱, about 90 km (56 miles) east of Posadas on Ruta 5, has settlers from many European countries. The second-largest city in Misiones, with a population of around 42,000, Oberá has a number of European-style buildings, especially of German influence, and the town hosts the National Festival of the Immigrant in its Parque de las Naciones. The city also houses the Museo de Ciencias Naturales Florentino Ameghino (natural science museum), on Barreyro and José Ingenieros (open Tues–Fri and Sat am only), as well as the Wendlinger bird sanctuary, on Haití and Díaz de Solís, containing native and foreign species.

About 100 km (60 miles) to the southwest of Oberá – and founded some 300 years before, in 1638 – lies **Apóstoles** ⑲, the capital of the *yerba maté* industry. The *yerba maté* tree is of the holly genus *(Ilex)*, though there the similarity ends. Its leaves are used in many South American countries to make a strong tea, sometimes called Argentina's national drink. Apóstoles has the **Museo y Archivo Histórico Diego de Alfaro** (open daily), on Belgrano 845, which includes exhibits on prehistoric culture, the Jesuits, the colonial period, and fine arts of the region.

Near Apóstoles are the Jesuit missions (*reducciones*) of **Santa María la Mayor** and **San Javier**. Santa María was one of the most important Jesuit missions in Argentina, after San Ignacio Miní *(see box on page 232)*, and was also one of the wealthiest, with extensive livestock and crop production. At present, the mission is permanently open to visitors as an archeological site, although it lacks tourist infrastructure and restoration plans have made little progress. San Javier, which was founded first in 1629, was an important cultural center with the first printing press

The majority of the nation's favorite drink, yerba maté, *is produced in large plantations in Misiones and Corrientes.*

BELOW: spectacled caiman in the Iberá wetlands.

Maps:
Area 230
Falls 235

Insectivorous plants in the Iberá Lagoon, which allegedly keep the mosquito population down.

in South America, and later became a fortress against attacks by slave traders from Brazil. The mission, on the outskirts of the small town of the same name, is located on the Río Uruguay, and the town also has a sugar mill and distillery.

Back in Corrientes province, **Gobernador Virasoro** is characterized by its red soil and its fields of *yerba*, as well as the raising of cebu cattle. The town, founded in the late 19th century, was originally a posting stage for courier services between Santo Tomé and Posadas, and later the home of the Nordeste Argentino train station of Vuelta de Ombú, the town's original name.

Wetlands wildlife

On the eastern edge of the **Esteros del Iberá** (Iberá marshlands) is the tiny town of **Colonia Carlos Pellegrini ⑳**, which has a couple of lodges and a camp ground on the Iberá Lagoon and has been named an "ecological village" due to the nature of its buildings, constructed primarily of wood and adobe. The town also has bungalows and cottages to rent, making it a good base to visit the **Reserva Provincial del Iberá**. This huge area runs from Ituzaingó on the Río Paraná to Chavarría in the south, and accounts for nearly 15 percent of Corrientes province. It offers varied scenery, including a series of lagoons, forests, and many native species of plants and animals, including water fowl, alligators, and capybaras (huge rodents). Iberá is considered one of the most important, unspoiled ecosystems in Argentina, with reserves for endangered species such as foxes and swamp deer. The animals are being bred to preserve the species and may be quite tame within the reserves. The best way to view the wildlife is to stay at one of the lodges near the lagoon, where you can organize boat excursions *(see page 350)*, or enquire at the visitors' center just outside Carlos Pellegrini.

BELOW: Palacio de San José, near Colón, former residence of President Urquiza.

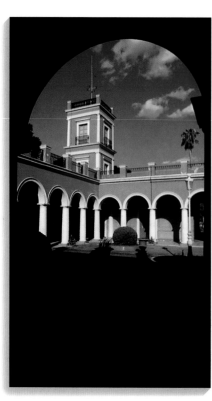

About 50 km (30 miles) south of Iberá is the city of **Mercedes ㉑**, a livestock breeding center, which hosts an annual livestock exposition as well as regional craft exhibitions. Within the city is the artisans' cooperative **Fundación Manos Correntinas** (corner of San Martín and Salta), which sells leather, stone, wood, and woolen crafts, as well as fine work in silver or bone. The city has museums of natural science (the largest in the area) and history, while the Nuestra Señora de las Mercedes church, on the main Plaza 25 de Mayo, includes a collection of fine robes, jewels, and a silver crown.

Some 76 km (47 miles) southeast of Mercedes, on the Río Uruguay and on the border with Brazil, is **Paso de los Libres ㉒**, a main transport route for the Brazilian port of Porto Alegre. The city has a casino, close to the main Plaza Independencia, and the Laguna Mansa, with camping and swimming facilities. It is located in one of the principal rice-growing areas in Argentina.

Yapeyú ㉓, some 60 km (37 miles) northeast of Paso de los Libres, was originally a Jesuit mission and later a Spanish garrison which was burned to the ground by the Portuguese in 1817. Its claim to fame is that the Argentine hero and liberator, José de San Martín, was born here. His father was a Spanish officer stationed at the garrison. The Templete Histórico Sanmartiniano, on Alejandro Aguado, displays some of San Martín's personal effects (open daily).

Concordia and Colón

Concordia is a large rural city about 450 km (280 miles) south of Yapeyú on Ruta 14, and is the center of the now ailing citrus industry. When the **Embalse Salto Grande** dam just north of the city was planned, the Río Uruguay flowed clear. By the time the dam was finished, however, the river had become muddy due to deforestation. There is a question as to how long the dam will remain operative; it now effectively serves as a sedimentation tank although tours are availabe.

Heading south, you'll find the **Parque Nacional El Palmar** ㉕, which protects the 800-year-old yatay palms for which the park is named. Facilities for staying overnight are limited to camp sites in the park and a motel in **Ubajay**, the nearby village. There are a number of interesting walking trails in the park, and some rare species of animals.

Colón is an old meat-packing town. A few kilometers to the west you will find the **Palacio de San José** (open daily), the former residence of General Justo José de Urquiza, who is famous for having ousted Juan Manuel de Rosas, the 19th-century dictator. The house is maintained as a National Historic Monument; its opulence has faded but it is still impressive.

About 30 km (18 miles) south of Colón is **Concepción del Uruguay** ㉖, situated on the Río Uruguay. Founded in 1783, it was one of the first provincial cities to join the rebels after the 1810 revolution against Spain, and also saw the beginning of the uprising led by General Urquiza against Rosas in 1851. The pronouncement by Urquiza was made at the pyramid located in the center of the **Plaza Francisco Ramirez**, where the casino and the **Basílica de la Inmaculada Concepción** are also located. The basilica was constructed in 1857 on the orders of Urquiza, who is buried here, and is noted in particular for its organ.

The city also has the **Museo Histórico Delio Panizza** (open daily), on Galarza and Supremo Entrerriano. Housed in a colonial residence, it contains a collection of colonial exhibits. Close to Concepción is the Banco Pelay beach and campground, with water sports and horseback riding.

Gualeguaychú ㉗, south of Concepción, is one of the largest cities in Entre Ríos province and is famous for its carnival, which takes place during Lent and is the largest in Argentina. The city has an annual week-long carriage parade starting on October 12, considered a provincial festival. It also has folklore and horse breaking shows throughout the year. The colonial city was sacked by the Italian nationalist Giuseppe Garibaldi in 1845, then residing in Uruguay and a supporter of anti-Rosas forces, and includes a number of interesting buildings such as the Cathedral, located on Plaza San Martín, the **Museo de la Ciudad** (open Tues–Sun), on San Luis and Jujuy, and the **Museo Arqueológico** (open Mon–Sat), housed in the city's cultural center, on 25 de Mayo 734.

Just before the rail and road bridge at **Brazo Largo**, which crosses over to **Zárate** 140 km (87 miles) to the south, there is a side road east to **Paranacito**, a good place to get a feel for the marshy delta terrain.

A little down-river, but out of sight, is the city of Buenos Aires, where one would disembark at the end of our imaginary journey. ❑

The amount of concrete used in the construction of the Itaipú Dam (see page 236) is equivalent to building a two-lane highway from Lisbon to Moscow, according to company literature.

BELOW: park ranger at Parque Nacional El Palmar.

THE NORTHWEST

This extensive territory was home to Argentina's earliest settlers, and it contains some of the country's most rugged mountain landscapes

Map on page 244

The northwest of Argentina is in large part a colorful, wind-sculpted montane desert traversed by green river valleys. Blessed with as many minerals as rock colors, it is the epicenter of Argentina's colonial and pre-Columbian cultures; its elevation and dry, sunny climate have made it an ideal agricultural region for settlers over the past 10,000 years. The Calchaquí Valleys, named after one of the pre-Inca tribes that inhabited the region, occupy a 17,500 sq. km (6,800 sq. mile) area in the provinces of Salta, Catamarca, and Tucumán, that is home to small farmers and artisans. There are interesting yet modest ruins scattered throughout the northwest; historical museums and monuments, traditional foods and music, and arts and crafts still made using ancient techniques. This is the most traditional region of Argentina, and the area where the size and influence of the indigenous population is still relatively considerable.

Sometimes known as the NOA (Nor Oeste Argentino), this is a large area, comprising the provinces of Jujuy, Salta, Tucumán, Santiago del Estero, and Catamarca, which can be grouped into three distinct regions. The best known are the *quebradas*, the arid, high *precordillera* (foothills of the Andes), characterized by painted desert hillsides, cacti and dry shrubs, deep canyons, and wide valleys. In stark contrast, the *yungas*, or subtropical mountainous jungle, are identified by dense vegetation, misty hillsides, and trees draped in vines and moss. Finally, there is the *puna*: cold, high-altitude and practically barren plateaux close to the Chilean and Bolivian borders.

PRECEDING PAGES: the church of El Carmen, Salta. **LEFT:** multicolored corn on the cob. **BELOW:** a typical church of the northwest.

Salt flats and volcanoes

The southernmost region covered in this section, **Catamarca** offers stark geographical and historical highlights. This province has the greatest altitude differences imaginable; toward Córdoba and Santiago del Estero in the east, the vast **Salinas Grandes** salt flats are barely 400 meters (1,300 ft) above sea level, while in the west, near the Chilean border, the **Ojos del Salado** volcano reaches the vertiginous height of 6,864 meters (22,520 ft), making it the highest volcano in the world.

In the capital, **San Fernando del Valle de Catamarca ❶**, points of interest include the Catedral Basílica, containing the famous wooden Virgin of the Valley, discovered being worshiped by Amerindians in the 17th century; the convent of San Francisco; archeological and historical museums; and a permanent arts and crafts fair, best known for rugs and tapestries, located a few blocks from the center. The area around the central Plaza 25 de Mayo, including the Casa de Gobierno and the cathedral, is exceptionally pretty, with an attractive plaza full of citrus trees and views of the surrounding mountains.

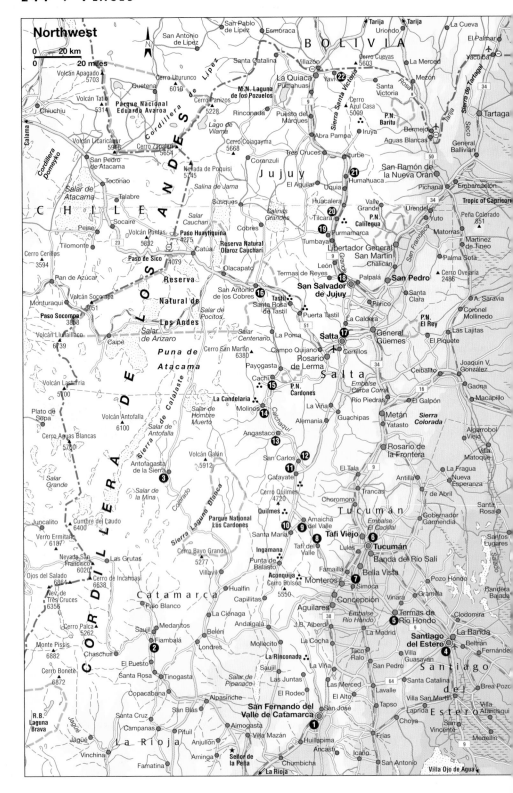

Map on page 244

Around San Fernando del Valle de Catamarca

The country around the capital is lovely, and several side trips are worth mentioning. Ruta 4 winds up north through hills and canyons, passing the two small towns of **El Rodeo** (37 km/23 miles) and **Las Juntas** (another 15 km/9 miles), both with services for visitors and recreational activities, including beach and water sports in a green valley setting. Heading east out of town on Ruta 38 is the well known **Cuesta El Portezuelo**, a winding road climbing out of the valley and up the lush mountainside, offering stunning views of the valley below.

Some 7 km (4 miles) to the north of the capital is **La Gruta de la Virgen del Valle**, where the Virgin of the Valley was discovered, and further along Ruta 32 is the **El Jumeal** dam *(dique)*, with fishing and a scenic view of the city. On Ruta 41, also north of the city, is a series of 19th-century chapels along the Río Valle, leading to the **Las Pirquitas** dam, forming a huge and beautiful lake used for fishing and water sports and offering spectacular views.

Frozen stream beds on the puna.

Time permitting, a trip to the old indigenous settlements scattered on Ruta 40 is highly recommended. The road crosses the province through a series of valleys and riverbeds, surrounded by dusty mountains. These towns are now slightly more developed than they were hundreds of years ago, and their small museums, traditional chapels, and the spectacular landscape make for a worthwhile trip. The most visited of these towns are **Tinogasta**, **Belén**, and **Santa María**. Look for the thermal spas along the route, one of the most developed being at **Fiambalá ❷**, 48 km (30 miles) north of Tinogasta. Fiambalá, which is also famous for its weaving, is an oasis surrounded by vineyards. Its thermal spa is located 15 km (9 miles) to the east of the town, in a ravine with waterfalls, and has been used for its curative waters since pre-Columbian times.

BELOW: vicuñas crossing a salt flat on the altiplano.

For the adventurous, there is **Antofagasta de la Sierra ❸**, about 250 km (155 miles) north of Ruta 40, located in the *puna* region of northern Catamarca. The remote Antofagasta is 3,500 meters (11,482 ft) above sea level and nearby are lagoons, volcanoes, and salt flats. High-quality textiles can be bought here, especially during March, when a craft and agricultural fair is held in the town.

Dusty flats

To the east of Catamarca lie the dusty flats of Santiago del Estero province. The capital of the province, bearing the same name, was founded by the Spanish in 1553, making it the oldest continuously inhabited city of the region. The city of **Santiago del Estero ❹** is also home to the first university established in Argentine territory, and some very attractive colonial buildings remain near the central plaza.

There is not much to see in this region beyond *algarrobo* (carob) forests and cotton fields. However, there is one major attraction: **Termas de Río Hondo ❺**. Near an artificial lake, which offers a variety of sporting activities, the city and thermal spa of Río Hondo has developed into one of the most fashionable spas in Argentina, with upmarket (though not particularly good) restaurants, luxury hotels, and even convention facilities. Life here is as bustling in winter as it is on Mar del Plata's beaches in the summer months.

TIP

Running northwest of San Fernando, Ruta Nacional 40 and Ruta Provincial 43 leading to Antofagasta de la Sierra cross some of the remotest parts of the northwest. Facilities are very limited and road conditions variable, so seek local advice before you set out.

BELOW: the sun-baked scenery around Salta.

A tropical garden

Not far from Río Hondo the dusty desert gives way to a subtropical spectacle which surprises everybody who visits Tucumán for the first time. Here the almost endless aridity and scenic boredom of Santiago del Estero, Formosa, and the Chaco provinces is replaced abruptly by a cornucopia of tropical vegetation. It is for this reason that the province of Tucumán – the smallest of the 24 Argentine federal provinces – is popularly known as the Garden of the Republic. This climatic and visual contrast is most vividly marked along the Aconquija range, which has several peaks of more than 5,500 meters (18,000 ft). The intense greenery is juxtaposed with snow-capped peaks. The best time of year to visit is in winter (June–August), when the weather is usually warm and dry; in the summer months it is often stiflingly hot and heavy rains are common. Favored with copious rainfall, the province of Tucumán is one of the loveliest in Argentina. On the plains, farming, and tobacco and sugar cane cultivation are the major economic activities. Around Tucumán, the provincial capital, one finds the smoky *ingenios* (sugar mills) which became in the 1830s the province's first industry and remain the principal economic source.

In addition to its very visible colonial past, **Tucumán ❻**, previously known as San Miguel de Tucumán, is the only city in the northwest with a very large immigrant population, especially of Italian, Arab and Jewish settlers. As a result, it has traditionally been a thriving commercial center with a pace of life more similar to Buenos Aires than to the slower-paced cities of the north. It was also the first industrial center in the northwest which, together with its historical past as the main commercial center between Buenos Aires and Bolivia and Peru, make it a fairly cosmopolitan and very lively place.

The spacious **Parque 9 de Julio**, the baroque **Casa de Gobierno**, and several patrician edifices, together with a number of venerable churches, are reminders of the town's colonial past. This may best be appreciated by visiting the **Casa de la Independencia** (open Mon–Fri 9am–1pm and 4–6pm, Sat and Sun 9am–1pm). In a large room of this stately house, part of which has been rebuilt, the Argentine national independence ceremony took place on July 9, 1816.

Among the other museums worth a visit in Tucumán (that is its name now) are the **Museo Histórico de la Provincia** (open daily), located in the house of 19th-century president Nicolás Avellaneda; the **Museo Folklórico** (open daily), also including a craft shop and a restaurant; the **Museo Provincial de Bellas Artes** (open daily except Mon); and the **Casa Padilla** (open Mon–Fri), located next to the Casa de Gobierno, also offering crafts for sale.

The principal colonial churches in Tucumán, all of them (like the museums) located close to the central **Plaza Independencia**, are the **Cathedral**, **San Francisco Church** (open daily), both located on the plaza; **Santo Domingo Church** (open Mon–Fri), on 9 de Julio and also operating as a school; and **La Merced**, on the corner of 24 de Septiembre and Las Heras, which houses a famous image of Tucumán's patroness, the Virgin of Mercy.

Local crafts and cooking

In the area near the main plaza and La Merced, on and around 24 de Septiembre, are various craft shops and a number of restaurants offering exquisite examples of regional cooking. The regional specialties include *empanadas* (meat pies) filled with diced beef, chicken, or occasionally tripe, as well as a number of corn-based dishes such as *humita* (a stew made of

Map on page 244

TIP

Tucumán's Casa de la Independencia puts on a nightly *son et lumière* show, re-enacting the city's key role in Argentina's independence (Wed–Mon 8.30pm).

BELOW: baking bread in a traditional adobe oven.

corn, squash, onion, tomato, and spices), *locro* (a heavier corn-based stew which contains pig's feet and other cuts of pork and beef), and *tamales* (corn meal and shredded pork, wrapped in corn husks and boiled). In the artisans' shops, watch out for the black ceramics which are a regional traditional, often using pre-Incan designs, usually depicting the tatú, an animal similar to the armadillo.

Some high-quality local handicrafts can be bought in Tucumán's craft fair.

Parque 9 de Julio

Tucumán has a lively cultural output, with a fine university (most of whose buildings are located in the Parque 9 de Julio), a cultural center located on 25 de Mayo which offers daily lectures, debates, films and theatrical activities, a theater, and a casino. East of the city center is the elegant **Parque 9 de Julio**, designed by French landscape architect Carlos Thays in 1916, and including a lake, rose garden, polo ground, and show jumping arena, theater, tennis club, an Italian garden, various cafes, and the house of Bishop Colombres, the early 19th-century bishop of Tucumán who founded the sugar industry. The house contains the **Museo de la Industria Azucarera** (open daily), which contains exhibits illustrating the process of sugar production. The beautiful park makes a relaxing break from the rather rushed pace of the city. However, care should be taken, especially after dark.

A few blocks to the south of the park, is one of the most modern bus terminals in Argentina, which offers services to cities throughout the north and center of the country and as far afield as Buenos Aires. It also includes a shopping mall with restaurants and cinemas. An international airport is located 8 km (5 miles) east of town.

BELOW:
Tucumán Cathedral.

Side trips

However, it is not so much the town but its surroundings which make Tucumán worth an extended visit. Short excursions are highly recommended to **Villa Nougués** and to **San Javier**, high up in the Aconquija range. Both are summer resorts with hotel and restaurant facilities and splendid walks, and San Javier, at the top of the mountain, has a huge statue of Christ the Redeemer, university facilities, and a panoramic view. Both sites offer a splendid view of Tucumán, its outskirts, and the extensive sugar cane and tobacco fields. En route to Villa Nougués and San Javier, one passes through the pretty suburb of Yerba Buena, a rural setting where many of Tucumán's elite have their estates.

A visit to nearby **El Cadillal**, with its dam, artificial lake, archeological museum, and restaurants (where fresh *pejerrey* fish is served) is quite pleasant. Guided tours are available to some of the local sugar mills *(ingenios)*.

Once finished with the sightseeing tours in and around Tucumán, you may choose between two different roads to carry on toward the north. One choice is the main Ruta Nacional 9, which passes by Metán and the Rosario de la Frontera spa and then winds through dense scrub forest and bushland to Salta and from there to Jujuy. But perhaps the better choice is to leave Tucumán, heading south. Passing through sugar cane fields, past several sugar mills, and the large town of Monteros, you come to **Simoca** ❼, "the sulky capital of Argentina," where on Saturdays the locals travel to town in their horse-drawn sulkies and offer produce, crafts, freshly prepared spices, and home cooking at a weekly fair which should not be missed.

From there, the road west travels toward **Acheral**. From Acheral, a narrow paved road starts climbing up through dense tropical vegetation, until it reaches a pleasant green valley, which is frequently covered by clouds. The winding road (not recommended for novice drivers) is spectacular, with lush sub-tropical vegetation, steep cliffs, waterfalls, and a river at the bottom of a ravine. Nearly half way to Tafí del Valle is a stopping place called **El Indio**, with a giant statute of an Amerindian, spectacular panoramic views, and a number of artisans, many offering high-quality craft items. The valley is dotted with tiny hamlets, the principal one being the old aboriginal and Jesuit settlement of Tafí del Valle.

Stone circles

Tafí del Valle ❽, situated in the heart of the Aconquija range at an altitude of 2,000 meters (6,600 ft), is considered the sacred valley of the Diaguitas, who, with different tribal names, inhabited the area. The valley is littered with clusters of aboriginal dwellings and dozens of sacred stone circles.

By far the most outstanding attractions at Tafí are the menhirs or standing stones. These dolmens, which sometimes stand more than 2 meters (6 ft) high, were assembled at the **Parque de los Menhires**, close to the entrance of the valley, by the government of General Antonio Bussi, moving them from their original positions and thereby destroying the chance to study their archaeological significance.

Also prior to entering Tafí is the La Angostura dam and lake, in an idyllic mountain setting. The town of

Map on page 244

TIP

In spite of its relatively cool mountain climate, most businesses in the northwest retain the *siesta* custom inherited from Spain, and close from noon until about 5pm.

BELOW: El Anfiteatro, an eroded river gorge near Cafayate.

Tafí itself, with a dry and cool mountain climate, is a favorite retreat for local residents, with beautiful views, coffee houses, and artisan crafts, foods, (especially cheeses) and sweets.

From Tafí, a dusty gravel road winds up to **El Infiernillo** (Little Hell), at 3,000 meters (10,000 ft) above sea level. Just past this point the landscape changes dramatically once again, from rolling grass-covered mountains to the desert highlands.

Local tradition has it that at **Amaicha del Valle ❾**, 56 km (35 miles) north of Tafí del Valle, the sun shines 360 days of the year. Some hotel owners are so fond of this bit of lore that they reimburse their guests if an entire visit should pass without any sun at all. The local handwoven tapestries and the workshops certainly merit the visit. The town is a favorite vacation spot for residents of Tucumán, many of whom have weekend homes here. It has a permanent population almost exclusively of indigenous origin, which is the only indigenous community in Argentina to have been given the titles to its traditional lands (by the Perón government in the early 1970s). Although Amaicha tends to be hot during the day throughout the year, the high altitude and sparklingly clear air make it cold at night even in summer: a sharp change in temperature which is refreshing and requires warm clothes, even at the height of summer.

In February every year, the traditional indigenous **Fiesta de la Pachamama** (Mother Earth Festival) is celebrated here, to give thanks for the fertility of the earth and livestock. An elderly local woman is chosen to play the part of the Pachamama, dressing up and offering wine to all participants. A recent rise in tourist interest has made the week-long festival somewhat more commercial, but it sticks to tradition and offers ritual ceremony, music and, dance.

BELOW: improvized see-saw.

Sun-blessed valleys

Leaving Amaicha you enter the colorful, sun-blessed **Santa María** and **Calchaquí** valleys, fertile landscapes fed by rivers of the same names. Together these valleys constituted one of the most densely populated regions of pre-Hispanic Argentina. Shortly after Amaicha, the road splits into two . To the left (the south) one soon reaches **Santa María ❿** (in Catamarca province), with its variety of fine artisan products and wines, and its important red pepper industry. In recent years the town has experienced a boom as a result of the huge Bajo La Alumbrera gold and copper mine nearby.

However, still better is to go straight ahead toward the north. Soon after you reach Ruta Nacional 40 (the same Ruta 40 recommended for exploring Catamarca, and Argentina's longest road), a short approach road leads to the archeological ruins of **Quilmes**, one of the country's most important indigenous sites *(see box on page 252)*.

On goes the journey through forlorn villages like **Colalao del Valle** and **Tolombón** to **Cafayate**, leaving Tucumán province and crossing into Salta.

Shady patios

Though situated only 260 km/160 miles (about 3½ driving hours) from Tucumán, **Cafayate ⓫** should be earmarked in advance as a place to spend at least one night. There is more to Cafayate than the cathedral, with its rare five naves; its small museums of archeology and wine cultivation; several *bodegas* (wine cellars), tapestry artisans, and silversmiths. It is the freshness of the altitude of 1,600 meters (5,300 ft) and the shade of its patios, overgrown with vines, that really enchant the visitor. The surroundings of this tiny colonial town

The cardón or candelabra cactus, a familiar site in the northwest.

BELOW: Parque de los Menhires, Tafí del Valle.

are dotted with vineyards and countless archeological remains. In Cafayate, the exquisite white wines made from the Torrontés grape are produced, with guided tours of its vineyards a popular tourist attraction.

Two ways to Salta

There are two routes which lead from Cafayate to Salta. To the right, along Route 68, the road winds through the colorful **Guachipas Valley**, also called **La Quebrada de Cafayate**. Along this valley, water and wind have carved from the red sandstone a vast number of curious formations which delight the traveler at every bend. It is a pleasant drive of less than four hours (about 180 km/112 miles), and is especially ideal for those who are in a hurry.

Others, who have more time and who are equally interested in natural beauty and history, could choose the longer route, following Ruta Nacional 40. It snakes along the scenic **Calchaquí Valley**, which is irrigated by the Calchaquí, one of Argentina's longest rivers.

Every one of the many romantic villages along the Calchaquí Valley deserves at least a short sightseeing walk, in order to gain an appreciation of the fine colonial architecture and Hispanic art still largely preserved in this region. A stop at **San Carlos ⑫**, not far away from Cafayate, is especially worthwhile. This sleepy spot is said to have been founded no fewer than five times, first by the Spanish conquistadors as early as 1551, and later by waves of missionaries.

Soon after San Carlos the road becomes even more winding. From the chimneys of humble houses lining the way, the tempting aromas of traditional dishes is frequently perceivable. The observant traveler may smell *locro* and *puchero* (meat and vegetable stews), *tamales* (ground maize pasties), or

BELOW:
Humahuaca,
Jujuy province.

QUILMES

This vast stronghold of the Calchaquís, located in the Calchaquí valley, near Santa María, once had as many as 202,500 inhabitants, and was the last indigenous site in Argentina to surrender to the Spanish, in 1667.

The Calchaquís were farmers, cultivating a large area of land around the urban settlement, and they developed an impressively integrated social and economic structure. This undoubtedly helped their long resistance of the Spanish – both the invasion and conversion to Christianity.

Quilmes is a paradigm of fine pre-Hispanic urban architecture. Its walls of neatly set flat stones are still perfectly preserved, though the roofs of giant cacti girders vanished long ago. Local guides take the visitor to some of the most interesting parts of this vast complex, its fortifications (requiring quite a steep climb), its residential area, its huge dam, and its reservoir.

At the foot of the ruins is a small museum and a craft shop with very beautiful ceramics and tapestries for sale. The ruins are open daily from 9am–5pm, and within the complex there is a hotel and simple restaurant which is interesting for having maintained the architectural style and low profile of the ruins very successfully (although controversial for being built on part of the ruins themselves).

mazamorra (a hot drink made from corn meal and sugar), as well as fragrant bread being baked in the adobe ovens that are hidden behind the dwellings.

The route briefly leaves the river bed and crosses the impressive **Quebrada de la Flecha**. Here, a forest of eroded sandstone spikes provides a spectacle, as the play of sun and shadow makes the figures appear to change their shapes. **Angastaco ⓭**, the next hamlet, was once an aboriginal settlement, with its primitive adobe huts standing on the slopes of immobile sand dunes. In the center there is a comfortable *hostería*. Angastaco lies amid extensive vineyards, though between this point and the north, more red peppers than grapes are grown.

Molinos ⓮, with its massive adobe church and colonial streets, is another quiet place worth a stop. *Molino* means mill, and one can still see the town's old water-driven mill grinding maize and other grains by the bank of the Calchaquí River. Across the river is an artists' cooperative, housed in a beautifully renovated colonial home, complete with a large patio, arches, and an inner courtyard. The local craftspeople sell only handmade goods, including sweaters, rugs, and tapestries. At **Seclantás** and the nearby hamlet of **Solco**, artisans continue to produce the traditional handwoven *ponchos de Guemes*, red and black blankets made of fine wool that are carried over the shoulders of the proud *gauchos* of Salta.

Cactus church

By far the loveliest place along the picturesque, twisting Calchaquí road is **Cachi ⓯**, 175 km (108 miles) north of Cafayate. Cachi has a very old church with many of its furnishings (altar, confessionals, pews, even the roof and the floor) made of cactus wood, one of the few building materials available in the area. Across the

Map on page 244

BELOW: eating out in Bermejo, near Salta.

The llama, sturdy beast of burden throughout the Andes.

square lies the archeological museum (open Mon–Sat), probably the best of its kind in Argentina. With the permission of the museum's director, visitors are allowed into the vast aboriginal complex at **Las Pailas**, some 18 km (11 miles) away and partially excavated. This is one of countless archeological sites in the Calchaquí region, which was densely populated before the arrival of the Spanish.

Here, as in Cafayate, you may decide to stay for more than just one night. An ACA Hostería is situated magnificently atop a hill above old Cachi.

So clear is the air here that the mighty **Cerro Cachi** (6,300 meters/20,800 ft) seems to be within arms' reach. Inhabitants of this region are said to benefit from the crisp mountain air, and many live to a very old age.

For closer views of Mount Cachi and a glimpse of the beautiful farms and country houses, be sure to visit **Cachi Adentro**, a tiny village 6 km (4 miles) from Cachi proper. Ruta Nacional 40 at this point becomes almost impassable, although you can visit the sleepy village of **La Poma**, 50 km (30 miles) to the north and partly destroyed by an earthquake in 1930. But the main tourist route runs to the east over a high plateau called **Tin-Tin**, the native terrain of the sleek, giant *cardón*, or candelabra cactus. The **Parque Nacional Los Cardones** was designated a national park in 1997 to protect the endangered and distinctive cactus.

Some 90 km ⑯ (56 miles) to the north of La Poma is the town of **San Antonio de los Cobres** ⑯, although the road is in bad condition and frequently impassible. The town is situated at 3,775 meters (12,385 ft), and is the final destination of the spectacular tourist **Tren a las Nubes** ("cloud train"), which makes a one-day trip from Salta to San Antonio once a week *(see page 346)*. Also nearby, on Ruta 51, is the pre-Inca city of Santa Rosa de Tastil, discovered in 1903 and dating from the 14th century. There is a small museum at the site, whose care-

taker also offers guided tours around the ruins (open Tues–Sat 9am–5.30pm).

Down the spectacular **Cuesta del Obispo Pass**, through the multicolored **Quebrada de Escoipe** and over the lush plains of the Lerma Valley the road stretches to Salta. From Cafayate to Salta, via Cachi, without stopovers, it is a demanding eight-hour drive.

Colonial gems

Salta , known as "Salta the beautiful," is probably the most seductive town of the Northwest, due both to its setting in the lovely Lerma Valley and to the eye-catching contrast of its old colonial buildings with its modern urban architecture. Salta is very proud – not to say snobbish – with respect to its colonial heritage, and many *Salteños* consider themselves to be the only true *criollos* (native Argentines of Spanish parentage) "untainted" by generations of immigrants. The city is the most formal in dress and behavior in the region, and is the largest in northern Argentina, making it a good base to explore the area which offers many opportunities for adventure tourism.

Salta cradles some valuable colonial gems, such as the Convento de San Bernardo (not open to the public), the Iglesia de San Francisco, and the Cabildo (city hall). The **Catedral Ⓐ**, completed in 1882 and located on the Plaza 9 de Julio, houses the remains of heroes of the independence such as General Martin Miguel de Güemes. Opposite the cathedral on the plaza is the **Cabildo y Museo Histórico del Norte Ⓑ**, dating originally from 1626 and which used to house the government of the vice-royalty until 1825. It was the seat of provincial government until the end of the 19th century. With its graceful row of arches, the Cabildo is particularly famous for the 16th-century statues of the

Maps:
Area 244
City 256

TIP

In the whole northwest region many roads are impassable during the rainy summer season (approximately Christmas to Easter). Fall and spring (April–May and September–November) are the most advisable times for a visit.

BELOW: a religious procession in Jujuy.

TIP

An excellent way to pass an evening in Salta is at a local *peña*, where traditional food is served and folk music is performed live by local musicians. Among the city's best places are Balderrama and La Casona del Molino.

Virgin Mary and *Cristo del Milagro* (Christ of the Miracle), washed up from a Spanish shipwreck on the Peruvian coast and credited with having performed miracles such as stopping a 1692 earthquake. The Cabildo also houses a very fine historical museum (open daily except Mon), which has ten rooms of archeological and colonial artefacts.

Art and history museums

Two blocks from the Cabildo, on the corner of Florida and Alvarado, is the **Museo de la Ciudad ⓒ** (open Mon–Sat), once the residence of the Hernandez family. Dating from 1870, it now houses the museum of the city of Salta. Also on Florida, at No. 20, is the **Museo de Bellas Artes ⓓ** (open daily except Mon), located in the 18th-century Arias Rengel residence, the most important building left from the vice-regal period. The house has been restored, and the museum has a fine collection of American art, including from the Jesuit Missions, in particular from local and Argentine artists.

Another residence from the colonial period, the **Museu Uriburu ⓔ** (open daily except Mon), located on Caseros one block from San Francisco, has been renovated and houses a museum of the colonial era. Also in this area are a number of artisans' shops, primarily selling silver and alpaca products of high quality (the locally crafted silver, alpaca, and wooden *maté* holders are especially beautiful).

A few blocks further east of Museu Uriburu, on the corner of Caseros and Santa Fe, is the beautiful **Convento de San Bernardo ⓕ**. The convent, which is closed to visitors, has been occupied by the Carmelite Order since 1846, and is built around four cloisters with roofed galleries. The adjoining church is a

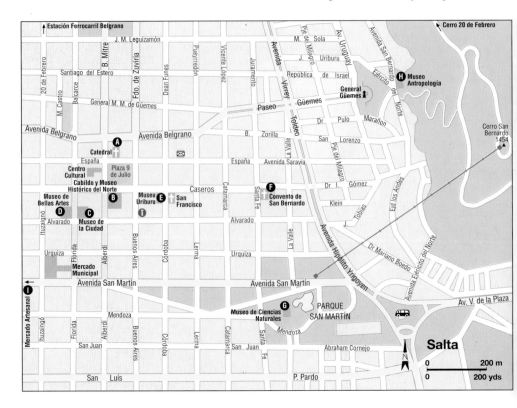

less elegant and more solid building, part of which remains from the original construction, which was destroyed by an earthquake in 1692, although the unadorned tower is thought to date from the 18th century.

Located a few blocks southeast of the Plaza 9 de Julio is the large **Parque San Martín**, which includes a statue by famous Tucumán sculptress Lola Mora; and at Mendoza 2, the **Museo de Ciencias Naturales Ⓖ** (open daily) has exhibits of native plant and animal life from Salta and Jujuy, including examples of the tatú, a local type of armadillo, and of fossils of earlier fish and plant species.

The **Museo de Antropología Ⓗ** (open daily except Sat), on Ejército del Norte and Polo Sur, contains a chronology of the cultural history of the northwest and, in particular, an exhibition of pieces from Santa Rosa de Tastil, including weavings and a stone on which the "Tastil dancer" was carved. Also well worth a visit is the **Mercado Artesanal Ⓘ** (open daily 8am–8pm), located three blocks southwest of the Plaza 9 de Julio, with handicrafts by some of the indigenous tribes living in the vast province of Salta.

A superb view of the city can be enjoyed from atop **Cerro San Bernardo**, which can be reached by cable car from Parque San Martín; the cable car runs Mon–Fri 2–8pm, Sat–Sun 11am–1pm and 3–7pm.

Convento de San Bernardo, Salta.

A great railway journey

The Tren a las Nubes (train to the clouds) is now run purely for tourists, and is one of the highlights of Argentina. It is one of the last remaining "great railway journeys" of South America. The train, fully equipped with dining car, bar, guide, and stewardess, leaves Salta's main station at 7 o'clock in the morning and enters the deep **Quebrada del Toro** gorge about an hour later. Slowly, the

BELOW: the church of San Francisco, in Salta.

train starts to make its way up. The line is a true work of engineering art, and doesn't make use of cogs, even for the steepest parts of the climb. Instead, the rails have been laid so as to allow circulation by means of switchbacks and spirals. This, together with some truly spectacular scenery, is what makes the trip so fascinating.

After passing through **San Antonio de los Cobres**, the old capital of the former national territory, Los Andes, the train finally comes to a halt at **La Polvorilla Viaduct** (63 meters/207 ft high and 224 meters/739 ft long), an impressive steel span amid the breathtaking Andean landscape. At this point the train has reached an altitude of 4,197 meters (13,850 ft) above sea level.

From here the train returns to Salta, where it arrives in the late evening, after a round-trip of 272 km (169 miles), taking about 14 hours. Unfortunately, El Tren a las Nubes only runs from March through October, making the journey about two to six times a month. For more details, look at www.trenubes.com.ar. Tickets can be purchased in both Salta (Caseros 431, tel: 4310-4984) and Buenos Aires (Esmeralda 1008, tel: 4311-4282).

Jungle retreat

Parque Nacional El Rey is located in the heart of the *yungas* or subtropical jungle region, 80 km (50 miles) from Salta. It's a natural hothouse with tropical vegetation as dense and green as one can find almost anywhere in South America. Visitors who come to fish, study the flora and fauna, or just to relax, will find ample accommodations; there is a clean *hostería,* some bungalows, and a campground. The park is only accessible by car or prearranged transportation from Salta, and the best time to visit is between the months of May and October.

BELOW: Carnival in Purmamarca.

Parque Nacional Calilegua, located on 76,000 hectares (188,000 acres) in Jujuy province. Calilegua is primarily tropical *yunga* forest, like El Rey, although as the altitude climbs the topography changes to mountain jungle, mountain forest, and eventually mountain plains. The park has a campsite, several rivers, and a wide range of wildlife, including wild boar and jaguars, in an exceptionally diverse ecosystem. In 2000, environmental groups lost their fight to stop a gas pipline being constructed through the park.

Jujuy

From Salta, a winding but wonderful mountain road, **La Cornisa**, takes you in about an hour and a half, to **San Salvador de Jujuy** ⑱. Don't miss the extraordinary gilded pulpit in the **Catedral** Ⓐ (open daily), carved by the local inhabitants. The cathedral dates from 1611, although most of the current building was completed in 1765 after being destroyed by an earthquake late in the 17th century. In addition to its famous pulpit, the cathedral has a beautiful chapel dedicated to the Virgin of the Rosary, as well as an outstanding 18th-century painting of the Virgin Mary. The tourist office is located nearby, at Belgrano 690.

Among the other attractions of this colonial city are the **Casa de Gobierno** Ⓑ, across the **Plaza General Belgrano** from the cathedral. The classical building, completed in 1920, houses the first Argentine flag and coat of arms, created by independence hero General Belgrano and donated to the city in 1813. The Salón de la Bandera where the flag is on display is open Mon–Fri 8am–noon and 4–8pm. The front of the Casa de Gobierno has four statues, representing Peace, Liberty, Justice, and Progress, by Lola Mora, the Tucumán artist who was once director of plazas and parks in Jujuy. Facing the Casa de Gobierno is the **Cabildo y Museo Histórico Policial** Ⓖ, a 19th-century building re-constructed after it was destroyed by an earthquake in 1863. The Cabildo houses the city's police department and a small museum (open daily 8am–1pm and 3pm–9pm; free admission), which includes exhibits on the police's anti-drugs campaign.

Two blocks from the Cabildo, on Belgrano and Lavalle, is the beautiful church of **San Francisco** Ⓓ (open daily 6.30am–noon and 5.30–9pm), situated on the site since the beginning of the 17th century, although the current building, maintaining the traditional style of Franciscan churches, dates from the 1920s. The church has a famous pulpit carved on the basis of traditional designs from Cusco in Peru and a notable wooden statue of St Francis – known locally as San Roque. Within the church is the **Museo de San Francisco** (open daily 8am–noon and 5–8.30pm), including the 13 stations of the cross painted in Bolivia in 1780.

The local religious imagery is particularly notable for its rather gory nature, primarily because life for the indigenous communities who originally inhabited the area was so hard that early missionaries had to depict the sufferings of Christ and other religious figures in exceptionally horrific terms in order to make an impression on the locals. Statues in particular are prone to depict gaping and bloody wounds with more enthusiasm than is usually the case.

Maps:
Area 244
City 260

Church bell tower, Casabindo.

BELOW: Easter procession in Tilcara for the Virgin of Copacabana.

Among the other interesting museums in Jujuy are the **Museo Histórico Provincial** (open Mon–Fri 8am–noon and 4–8pm, weekends 9am–1pm and 4–8pm), located in a 19th-century residence in which the hero of the Argentine union General Lavalle died in 1841 after his defeat by the federalists at the battle of Famaillá. The museum contains exhibits of 19th-century dress, as well as religious works of art, and a room is dedicated to the independence movement, including weapons captured in the battle of Suipacha.

Two blocks away, also on Lavalle, is the **Museo Arqueológico Provincial** (open daily), where exhibits including stone, ceramic, and metal objects from the region are on display. The oldest church in Jujuy is **Capilla de Santa Bárbara** dating from 1777 and including a collection of 18th-century religious paintings. Two blocks away, on Calle Lamadrid, is the **Teatro Mitre**, constructed in 1901. The Italian-style theater was restored in 1979. Two blocks to the east is the Mercado Municipal. The French-style railway station is located two blocks from the Plaza Belgrano, on Gorriti and Urquiza, while the bus terminal is a few blocks south of the Río Chico Xibi Xibi at the corner of Iguazú and Dorrego.

City park

Several blocks to the west of the plaza is the **Parque San Martín**, the city's only park which, although smaller than those of other Argentine cities, contains a swimming pool, as well as a housing complex and a restaurant, La Mirage. Near to the park, on Bolivia 2365, is the **Museo de Mineralogía** (open Mon–Fri 9am–1pm), which belongs to the provincial university's geology and mining faculty. The museum has exhibits of the mineral wealth of the province, including the history of its tin and iron mining tradition as well as its gold deposits.

BELOW: fresh produce at Jujuy's Mercado Municipal.

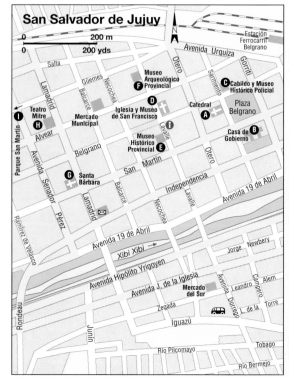

A few miles from town, one can visit the **Termas de Reyes** spa, located in a narrow valley. The visit offers beautiful views of the city and of mountains and lakes in the area, as well as the opportunity to indulge in thermal bathing.

Maps:
Area 244
City 260

The colorful Quebrada

Ruta 9 climbs steadily up, and before long, the sun breaks through. Here, a wide and highly distinctive *quebrada* (gorge) is dominated by the Río Grande. This river receives torrential and often destructive rains in the summer, when the colors of the valley wall become more intense and delineated. The Quebrada de Humahuaca valley has been used for 10,000 years as an important passage for transporting both people and ideas between the Andean highlands and the plains below. In 2003 it was made a World Heritage Site.

Purmamarca 19, a tiny village with the striking **Cerro de los Siete Colores** (Hill of the Seven Colors) towering behind the old adobe church. Around the shady square, local vendors sell wood carvings, handwoven carpets, and herbs to cure every possible ailment. After a short ride you come to **Tilcara 20**, famous for its huge pre-Columbian *pucará* (stronghold), built on a hill in the middle of the valley. The **Museo Arqueológico** (open daily) on the main plaza has a pre-Inca mummy and various other artifacts from Bolivia, Chile, and Peru. There is also a botanical garden, with specimens from the *puna* (high plateau).

At **El Angosto de Perchel** the Quebrada narrows to less than 200 meters (650 ft) and then opens into a large valley. Wherever the available water is used for irrigation, tiny fields and orchards give a touch of fresh green to the red and yellow shades of the river banks.

Floral painting from Tilcara's Easter festivities.

BELOW: a cemetery in the Quebrada de Humahuaca.

Map
on page
244

TIP

South of Humahuaca, at Huacalera, a monument marks the exact point of the Tropic of Capricorn (23 degrees and 27 minutes south of the Equator).

BELOW: Iglesia de Candelaria, Humahuaca.
RIGHT: El Tren a las Nubes, Salta.

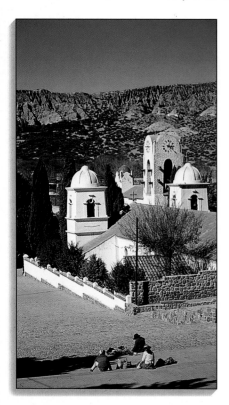

Desert chapels

At last one reaches the town of Humahuaca, which takes its name from an aboriginal tribe and gives it in turn to the surrounding valley.

Humahuaca ㉑ lies at almost 3,000 meters (9,000 ft), so move very slowly to avoid running out of breath. Also avoid eating heavily or drinking alcohol prior to ascending: a cup of sweet tea is more beneficial at this altitude. Here one finds stone-paved and extremely narrow streets, vendors of herbs and produce near the railway station, and an imposing monument commemorating the Argentine War of Independence. The museum of local customs and traditions is worth a visit. Most travelers pay only a short visit to this fascinating place, but a stay of several days is truly worthwhile, as many side trips can be made from here.

Some 9 km (6 miles) outside the town are the extensive archeological ruins of **Coctaca**. The true significance of this site is still largely unknown although scientists are studying it, and its secrets may soon be revealed. Other options include a journey to **Iruya**, a hamlet cradled amid towering mountains, 75 km (47 miles) from Humahuaca. An even more adventurous trip would be to **Abra Pampa** and from there to the **Monumento Natural Laguna de los Pozuelos**, where you can see huge flocks of the spectacular Andean flamingo, and vicuña herds grazing near the road. Near Abra Pampa there is a huge vicuña farm.

Here in the heart of the *puna* or *altiplano* (with an average altitude of 3,500 meters/11,500 ft), are some of the most interesting villages in the northwest, in a region inhabited for thousands of years before the arrival of the Spanish, and occupied by the Incas during the expansion of their empire southward from Bolivia. Many of the isolated villages have surprisingly large and richly decorated colonial churches, including those at Casabindo, Cochinoca, Pozuelos, Tafna, and Rinconada. None of these are right on Ruta 9, but can be reached by smaller access roads that wind through the peaceful countryside. Ruta 9 continues all the way to **La Quiaca**, at the Argentine border, opposite the Bolivian town of Villazón.

Glowing gilding

Finally, as if saved for a happy ending to this excursion, there remains one of the most sparkling jewels of Argentina: the ancient **Iglesia de Nuestra Senora del Rosario y San Francisco**, in Yavi.

The tiny village of **Yavi ㉒**, on the windy and barren high plateau near the Bolivian border, lies protected in a small depression, about 15 km (9 miles) by paved road to the east of La Quiaca. Between the 17th and 19th centuries, Yavi was the seat of the Marqués de Campero, one of the wealthiest Spanish feudal positions in this part of the continent. Though the chapel here was originally built in 1690, one of the later marquesses ordered the altar and pulpit to be gilded. The thin alabaster plaques covering the windows create a soft lighting which makes the gilding glow (open Tues–Sun 9am–noon and 3.30–6pm). This precious historical monument makes a fine conclusion to a rewarding journey through the plains and valleys and over the mountains of the Northwest. ❑

THE CUYO

Map on page 268

*The west-central area of Argentina is its main wine-growing region.
It is also the location of South America's highest peak, Aconcagua,
fashionable ski resorts, and whitewater rafting activities*

A rgentina is the fifth-largest wine producer in the world, and the Cuyo is the heart of that industry. The vines are nurtured by the melting snows of the Andes, and the mountains themselves add colorful drama to the scene. Every March, the grape harvest is celebrated in the *Festival de la Vendimia* in Mendoza, but a visitor at any time of the year can tour the *bodegas* (wine cellars) and sample the excellent wines. The cities of the area are some of Argentina's oldest, and although most have been rebuilt in modern times to repair damage caused by earthquakes, you can still learn a lot about Argentine history in the many regional museums. Opinions differ as to exactly what area is covered by the Cuyo, but in this section we include all the provinces from Mendoza in the south, through San Luis, to San Juan and La Rioja in the north.

Nestled high in the Andes is Aconcagua, the highest mountain in the world outside Asia. There are also numerous ski resorts in the area, most notably Las Leñas, which is becoming increasingly popular as an off-season vacation and competition site for skiers from the Northern Hemisphere. Mendoza's mountains and rushing white-water rivers have made it an adventure center attracting mountain climbers, rafters, hikers, and trail riders from around the world.

San Juan's wines are generally of lower price and quality than those of its neighbor Mendoza. Other points of interest are the shrine to La Difunta Correa and the Reserva Provincial San Guillermo, home to guanacos, vicuñas, rheas, and condors. The largest nature reserve in the region is the Reserva Provincial Ischigualasto, which incorporates the Valle de la Luna and the Parque Provincial Talampaya in neighboring La Rioja province. You will find these and many more scenic attractions along the winding mountain passes and tree-lined country roads of the Cuyo.

Colonial history

In the mid-16th century the Spanish colonies along the western coast of South America sought to expand their territories beyond the Andes, to the east, in what is today Argentina. They were driven by reports that these lands held a vast wealth of gold, similar to what had been found further to the north. Several of the early Chilean efforts at settlement were wiped out by repeated Amerindian attacks. Conquistadors from Peru had better luck, staking their claims to the north. In 1553, Francisco de Aguirre founded Santiago del Estero for the Spanish viceroyalty of Peru. It is the oldest surviving settlement in all of Argentina *(see page 38)*.

The explorers from Peru went on to found the towns of San Miguel de Tucumán (on a site earlier established by the explorers from Chile), Salta, and Xiu

PRECEDING PAGES: a shady road outside Mendoza. **LEFT:** the Cuyo's Andean backdrop. **BELOW:** a vineyard owner shows off his raw materials.

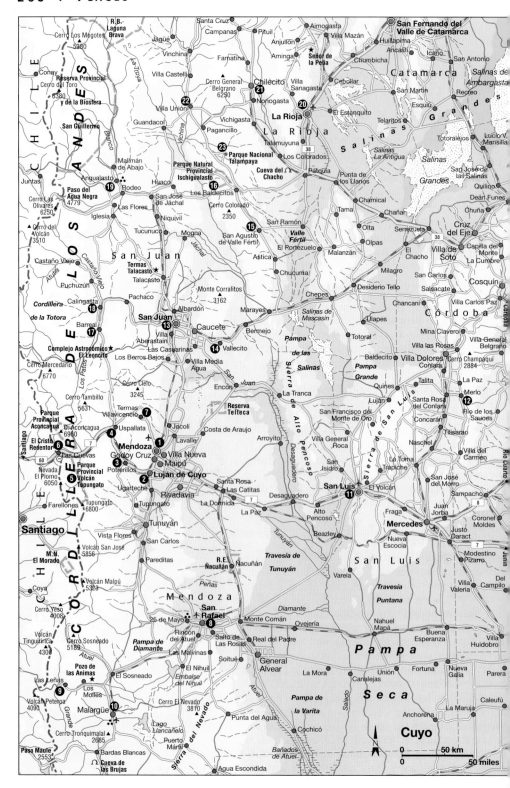

Xiu (Jujuy). The Chileans were finally successful in establishing their domain further to the south, in the Cuyo region, parallel to Chile's central valley. Although this eastern side of the Andes was barren and arid (Cuyo means "desert land" in the dialect of the local Huarpe indigenous culture), it was cut through by rivers flowing down from the melting snows of the high Andean peaks.

Map on page 268

First cities

The first permanent settlement in the Cuyo was established at Mendoza, a site chosen for its location across from Santiago at the eastern end of the Uspallata Pass, the major access through the Andes in the region. Pedro de Castillo founded the town in 1561, and named it for Hurtado de Mendoza, the governor of Chile. Not long after, the town was relocated several miles to the north.

In 1562, Juan Jufre founded San Juan, to the north of Mendoza, and a third town, San Luis, was started to the west in Chile, in 1598.

The Spanish Crown established the eastern viceroyalty of Río de la Plata in 1776 to accommodate the growing importance of the port of Buenos Aires. At this time, the Cuyo and the Peruvian holdings to the north passed to the jurisdiction of the new territory. However, the Cuyo remained isolated from the east for many years, and its strongest economic and cultural ties were with central Chile.

The isolation was broken in 1884, with the completion of the transcontinental railroad, and today the region is well integrated into the Argentine economy. It is the center of the country's wine industry, and a whole array of fruits and vegetables are grown for eastern markets. The area has also proved to be rich in mineral wealth, although not in gold that the early explorers had hoped to find.

The region is the major supplier for the nation's vital petroleum industry, and uranium, copper, and lead mines are scattered throughout the mountains. One of the principal sources of provincial income in Mendoza is hydro-electricity; there are several hydroelectric projects, and the reservoirs created by the dams have made this a popular recreational area. People come for the skiing (best between June and October) and the civilized pleasures afforded by the hot spring spas and *bodegas*.

An Inca mummy, found in Panquegua, near Mendoza, is kept at the city's Museum of Natural History and Anthropology.

Mendoza

Today, the Cuyo comprises the provinces of Mendoza, San Juan, San Luis, and La Rioja. The largest city is **Mendoza ❶**, with a population of 600,000, located 1,060 km (659 miles) due west of Buenos Aires. Although it was founded in 1561, little remains today of the town's original colonial architecture.

The whole region is periodically racked by earthquakes, some of them quite severe. One such quake, in 1861, killed 10,000 and completely leveled Mendoza, and rebuilding was done with an eye to averting further disaster. Another in January 1985, left 40,000 homeless. The last major quake happened in 1997.

In spite of Mendoza's relatively modern appearance, it has a long history, of which its residents are very proud. It was from here, in 1817, that General San Martín launched his march with 40,000 men across the Andes to liberate Chile and Peru. The wine industry began in earnest in the mid-19th century, with

BELOW: Mendoza in the mid-19th century.

Snacks on wheels in Mendoza.

the arrival of many Italian and French immigrants. This was due in large part to the progressive thinking of a series of Mendozan governors who took positive steps to attract immigrants. Among other things, they paid agents at the port of Buenos Aires for each immigrant transported to the province; in particular, qualified engineers and vintners who were responsible both for designing the irrigation system that made cultivation possible in the desert province, and for the planting of vineyards and the construction of wineries. The strength of the wine industry, which has reached world-class standard for fine wines, is reflected in the annual grape harvest festival (**Festival de la Vendimia**), held late February to early March and featuring a beauty contest, fireworks, dances, and *son et lumière* shows in an Andean setting. Although wine remains a substantial part of the economy, it was the growth of the petroleum industry in the 1950s that brought real prosperity to the town.

Among the airlines serving Mendoza are Aerolíneas Argentinas and LAPA (ARG) from Buenos Aires and Córdoba, Lan Chile from Santiago, and Dinar and Andesmar from the Argentine north. El Plumerillo Airport is located 5 km (3 miles) to the north of the city. A large number of long-distance bus lines link Mendoza with virtually all parts of Argentina, as well as Chile; all buses arrive and depart from the bus terminal east of the city center, at Avenida Gobernador Videla and 25 de Mayo.

A clean and cultural city

While Mendoza is nothing like the metropolis that Buenos Aires is, it has its own charms, and a wealth of cultural activity. Transplanted residents from the capital boast a happy conversion to the more relaxed pace of Mendoza. *Mendocinos* often claim that the province is the most civilized in the country, with an unusually modernist and democratic tradition based on the concept that the successful development of the province is the result of the efforts of the inhabitants, rather than of the generosity of nature. The city is arguably the cleanest and certainly one of the most modern in the country, nestled at the foot of the mountains and offering a wide range of cinemas, theater, concert halls, and other cultural activities.

BELOW: a blaze of lupins brightens up a city park.

The atmosphere of the town is certainly conducive to relaxation. The waters of the region have been put to good use, and the arid landscape has been transformed into a lush oasis. Some of the irrigation canals dug by the original Amerindian inhabitants are still in use, and many more have been added since. The city's low buildings lie along wide, tree-lined streets, where channels of running water keep the temperature an agreeable measure below that of the surrounding desert, although in summer Mendoza has an extremely hot, desert climate. Even in winter, when the *zonda* wind storms sweep the city, the temperature can rise to Saharan levels.

Most homes have well-tended gardens, and there are parks throughout the city that serve the dual interests of recreation and safety in case of an earthquake. In the midst of the plentiful shade, it is astonishing to realize that all the millions of trees have been planted by the city's residents and developers. Not one of the poplars, elms, or sycamores is native to the region. Beyond and above all this greenery, to the west lie the Andes, which provide Mendoza with a spectacular backdrop of changing hues throughout the day.

Theaters and museums

At the center of the city of Mendoza is the **Plaza Independencia**. Several important buildings flank the plaza; the oldest is the **Legislatura Provincial** (Provincial Legislature), which dates from 1889. Opposite this, on the northwestern corner is the 1925 **Teatro Independencia**, where theatrical and musical performances are held. In the center of the plaza, located underground, are the **Museo Municipal de Arte Moderno** Ⓐ (open daily), a small gallery exhibiting modern works by local artists, with occasional temporary exhibitions; and the Teatro Municipal Julio Quintanilla, which puts on theatrical performances at weekends. Around the corner, at Sarmiento and 25 de Mayo, is the provincial **Casino**, part of the same complex as the Teatro Independencia and Plaza Hotel. There is also an artisans' market on the eastern side of the plaza, facing Calle Patricias Mendocinas, where crafts are on sale Friday to Sunday.

Running east from the plaza, past the Provincial Legislature and the Stock Exchange, is the pedestrian Paseo Sarmiento, a lively place in the evening, with a number of attractive shops and outdoor cafes, populated by occasional street musicians. This leads to Avenida San Martín, Mendoza's main street.

Mendoza has a good selection of museums and other sites of interest. The **Museo del Pasado Cuyano** Ⓑ (open Mon–Fri, summer only, 9am–12.30pm), located at Montevideo 544, two blocks south of Plaza Independencia and housed

EN VINAGRE DULCE

Mendoza's grapes are not only used to make wine but are also used in some local delicacies, such as garlic cloves preserved in sweet grape vinegar.

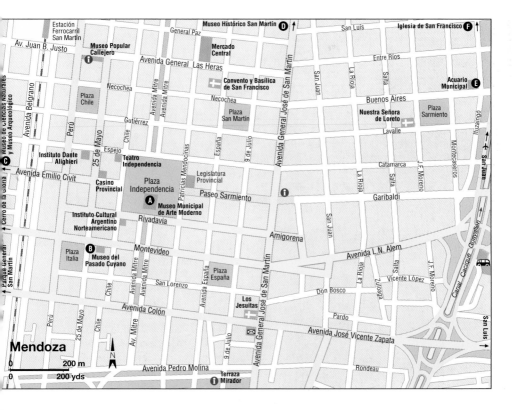

BELOW: taking it easy in Mendoza's Parque San Martín.

in a residence dating from 1873, includes the Historical Studies Board, as well as an exhibition on General San Martín, a collection of artifacts from Mendoza's history, and a series of religious art and an arms collection. Archeology, anthropology, and paleontology buffs should enjoy the **Museo de Ciencias Naturales y Museo Arqueológico** ☉ (open daily except Mon), located outside the city center in Parque San Martín, at Las Tipas and Prado Español. The museum contains some pre-Columbian ceramics, along with a small folkloric collection, and includes archeological and zoological collections. The **Museo Histórico San Martín** ☉ (open Mon–Fri), at Avenida San Martín 1843, houses a collection dedicated to the general and his accomplishments.

Located underground at the junction of Ituzaingó and Buenos Aires, south of Parque O'Higgins, is the **Acuario Municipal** ☉ (open daily). The aquarium has one of the most important collections of fresh- and salt-water fish in Latin America, including species from both the Atlantic and Pacific, and aquatic animals such as giant sea turtles. The aquarium breeds some rare species not usually bred in captivity, and it makes a very interesting visit, especially for children.

Shady plazas

Mendoza has a number of plazas, of which the **Plaza España** is probably the most attractive. Donated by the Spanish government in the 1940s, the Plaza España recreates an Andalusian square, complete with fountains and painted tiles imported from Spain; tile scenes include depictions of the founding of Mendoza in 1561. The plaza is one of four which form an extended square some three blocks distant from the Plaza Independencia, the others being Plaza Italia, Plaza Chile and Plaza San Martín. The latter is located in the heart of the banking dis-

trict, and has tall, shady trees and a statue of the Liberator. To the east of the city center, located near the aquarium and snake house, and two blocks south of the Parque Bernardo O'Higgins and the Teatro Municipal Gabriela Mistral, is another square, **Plaza Sarmiento**, flanked on its southwestern side by the Nuestra Señora de Loreto Church, which was rebuilt after being destroyed by an earthquake in 1861, and renovated in 1957.

North of Plaza Sarmiento, the **Plaza Pedro de Castillo**, formerly the Plaza Mayor, marks the site of the original, 16th-century city center, now preserved as the Area Fundacional. On the northwestern side of the plaza are the ruins of the **Iglesia de San Francisco** . Founded by the Jesuits in the 18th century as the Iglesia de Loreto, the church was destroyed by a massive earthquake in 1861, which flattened the whole city. Also on this plaza is the **Museo Histórico del Area Fundacional** (tel: 061-425 6927; open Mon–Sat 8am–8pm, Sun 3–10pm), a comprehensive, modern museum containing exhibits and models of the original city and other archeological objects.

Behind the rather unattractive **Casa de Gobierno**, located within the Civic Center to the south of the city center, is the **Museo del Vino Giol**, an extension of the nearby state-owned winery. It is small, but has wine-tasting events and some interesting old photographs. A variety of leather crafts and other items can be picked up at the **Mercado Artesanal**, at Lavalle 97.

In this desert climate, hot summer days are followed by pleasantly cool nights, and there are restaurants which offer dining al fresco. **La Bodega del 900**, on the outskirts of town, has a dinner show on its patio, and a small wine museum in its cellar. There are several cafes and nightclubs perched along the foothills to the west. One of the most pleasant of these is **Le Per**, open until quite late, with its patio overlooking Mendoza.

Parque San Martín

On the western edge of the city lies **Parque San Martín**, crowned by the Cerro de la Gloria (Glory Hill). Located at the foot of the Andes, the 420-hectare (1,038-acre) park has facilities for a wide variety of sports, including a soccer stadium built for the World Cup and a yacht club with an artificial lake. It was designed by French landscape architect Carlos Thays at the end of the 19th century, and has fine statues (most of them copies of well-known French sculptures); it also houses the Universidad Nacional del Cuyo. Further up the hill is the **Jardín Zoológico** (City Zoo; open Tues–Sun 9am–6pm), with shaded walkways between open-air cages, which are pleasantly set among ponds, caves, and rockeries. The zoo contains some 700 animals, both indigenous and foreign species, including orangutans and lions.

At the top of the **Cerro de la Gloria** sits an ornate statue, the **Monumento al Ejército Libertador**, complete with bolting horses and Liberty breaking her chains. Bas-relief around the statue's base depicts various scenes of the liberation campaigns. The site also provides an excellent overview of Mendoza.

Behind the hill, in the southwestern corner of the park, is the **Teatro Griego Frank Romero Day**, an amphitheater built in 1940, and site of many of the

Map on page 271

TIP

There are several tourist information offices around Mendoza; the main Centro Municipal de Información Turística, a kiosk at the corner of San Martín and Garibaldi, is quite helpful (open Mon–Fri 9am–12.30pm and 4–8pm).

BELOW: Maipú, outside Mendoza.

Frieze of the grape harvest, Luján de Cuyo.

city's celebrations, including the grand spectacle of the *Festival de la Vendimia* (Grape Harvest Festival). First held in 1963, this large festival takes place every year in February or March, and lasts over three or four days. During the first few days there are street performances and parades, and a queen of the harvest is chosen. The finale is a somewhat overproduced extravaganza, with dancing, fireworks, and moving light shows. This is Mendoza's annual opportunity to show off its hard-earned wealth.

Just to the south of Mendoza, in the town of **Luján de Cuyo** ❷, is the Museo Provincial de Bellas Artes Emiliano Guiñazú, on Avenida San Martín 3651 (open daily except Mon). The museum is known as the Casa de Fader as it was inaugurated on the birth date of Spanish painter Fernando Fader, who lived in Mendoza for some years in the early part of the 20th century. Fader's murals decorate some of the walls of the museum, formerly the summer residence of Emiliano Guiñazú. The museum includes formal gardens, as well as collections of foreign and Argentine artists, local landscape painters, and an exhibit of Fader's work.

Mendoza's *bodegas*

Scattered across this fertile plain are nearly 2,000 different vineyards, some of which are small family operations, others huge and state-owned. All of this cultivation is made possible through an extensive network of irrigation channels, laid in pre-Columbian times and extended during the colonial era. The area is blessed with a heady combination of plentiful water, sandy soil, a dry climate, and year-round sunshine, which makes for enormous grape yields.

The first vines were planted in the Cuyo by Jesuit missionaries in the 16th century, but production really took off in the mid-1800s with the arrival of Italian

BELOW: the pass at Villavicencio.

and French immigrants. Many of them simply worked as laborers in the fields, but a knowledgeable few contributed European expertise that greatly refined the industry. Toward the end of the 19th century, Mendoza was finally linked by rail with Buenos Aires and, by the 1920s, with the opening up of many more vineyards, the region had become one of the world's leading wine producers.

A number of vineyards are right on the outskirts of Mendoza. Tours can be arranged through a travel agent, but a more pleasant way to make the rounds is by getting a map, renting a car, and finding them yourself *(see page 284)*. This provides the opportunity to meander down the lovely country lanes lined with poplars and wildflowers, and to get a sense of the Cuyo's lifestyle. Local cycling fanatics are out in packs and, with luck, you might even catch sight of old men playing a lazy afternoon game of *bocci* (bowls).

Day-trip to Chile

One of the most spectacular trips to be made from Mendoza is up the **Uspallata Pass** to the border with **Chile**. It is an all-day excursion of some 210 km (131 miles), passing through the flat, irrigated oases and climbing to over 3,000 meters (9,840 ft) beyond Puente del Inca, in the shadow of Cerro Aconcagua. Organized coach tours are available from Mendoza, but hiring a car will allow you to avoid being herded around. Either way, you should start early in the morning to allow enough time to see all the sights en route.

However, unless you're carrying on through Chile, driving independently is only recommended outside the winter months (July–September). Although the roads are paved throughout, conditions in the upper reaches are often icily treacherous during these months, and snow and rock slides are common.

Map on page 268

La Virgen de la Carrodilla, patron of the grape harvest.

BELOW: the Puente del Inca, a natural rock bridge.

At any time of year it is worth taking some warmer clothes for these cooler altitudes. Also be aware that altitude sickness can be a problem, as you climb from 750 meters to 2,500 meters (2,500 ft to 8,200 ft). Those requiring visas for Chile should get them in Mendoza, as they will not be issued at the border.

You begin the trip by heading south from Mendoza on Route 7 to **Luján**. Turning right at the town square, you get onto Highway 7, which carries you up into the pass. This stretch of road, the Camino de los Andes, is part of the vast Pan-American Highway. Throughout the centuries, even before the time of the Incas, the pass was used to cross the mountains.

Immediately the landscape becomes more barren as you leave behind the irrigated greenery of the lowlands to follow the Mendoza River up the valley. Trees give way to scrub and the occasional bright flower.

The Potrerillos Hotel was the base for the Dutch soccer team during the 1978 World Cup, hosted (and won) by Argentina.

The first spot you will pass in the valley is the **Cacheuta Hot Springs**, located at a lovely bend in the river in the grounds of the Centro Climático Termal Cacheuta (Cacheuta Thermal Springs Center; reservations, for which you'll need a doctor's prescription, in Mendoza, tel: 061-431 6085).

Thirteen km (8 miles) beyond is **Potrerillos ❸**, a scenic oasis where many *Mendocinos* have summer homes to escape the heat. The **Potrerillos Hotel** has terraced gardens overlooking the valley, along with a swimming pool and facilities for tennis and horseback riding. There is also a campsite nearby. Up from Potrerillos, at the end of a side road, is the modest ski resort of **Vallecitos**. The resort is open from July to September. Continuing up the valley for another 105 km (65 miles), you reach the town of **Uspallata ❹**, set in a wide meadow. Further up again, the valley widens at Punta de Vacas (Cattle Point), where long ago the herds were rounded up to be driven across to Chile. It is at Punta de Vacas that you

BELOW: the Río Mendoza, near Potrerillos.

submit documentation if wishing to continue across the border. About 10 km (6 miles) beyond Punta de Vacas lies the ski resort of **Villa Los Penitentes**, which has a ski school, and several hotels and restaurants. Buses bring skiers up for day trips from July through September. Across the valley is the strange formation for which the resort is named; tall rock outcroppings look like hooded monks (the penitents) ascending toward the cathedral-like peak of the mountain. In winter, wind-swept ice on the rocks heightens the illusion.

Aconcagua

Off to the left of the road, a few kilometers further on, is a desolate, melancholy sight: the Cementerio de los Andinistas is a small graveyard for those who have died in the attempt to scale nearby Cerro Aconcagua. A couple of kilometers beyond this is the **Puente del Inca**, a natural stone bridge made colorful by the sulfurous deposits of the bubbling hot springs beneath it. There is a hostel used particularly by Aconcagua expeditions, as well as gift stalls selling an unusual line in souvenirs – objects solidified in the mineral waters.

Just a few kilometers up the road lies the most impressive sight of the whole excursion. There is a break in the wall of rock and, looking up the valley to the right, you can see the towering mass of **Aconcagua**, at 6,960 meters (22,834 ft) the highest peak in the Western Hemisphere. Horseback rides and trekking expeditions to Aconcagua are arranged in the summer months from Puente del Inca, for periods of three to ten days. Another important trekking site is **Parque Provincial Volcán Tupungato ❺**, located just south of Puente del Inca and dominated by the 6,800-meter (22,310-ft) Tupungato Volcano, surrounded by glaciers and also served by organized treks of three to 15 days.

Aconcagua means "stone watchtower" in the Huarpe dialect. It is perpetually blanketed in snow, and its visible southern face presents a tremendous 3,000-meter (10,000-ft) wall of sheer ice and stone. The clear mountain air creates the illusion that Aconcagua lies quite close to the road, but the peak is actually 45 km (28 miles) away. You can walk as far as **Laguna de los Horcones**, a green-colored lake at the mountain's base. Most expeditions tackle the northern face. The best time to attempt the climb is mid-January to mid-February. Further information can be obtained in Mendoza at the Club Andinista (F.L. Beltrán 357, tel: 061-4319 870), or on the Aconcagua website (www.aconcagua.com).

Christ the Redeemer

The last sight to see before heading back is the statue of Christ, which marks the border with Chile. On the way there, the road passes the town of **Las Cuevas**, where the road branches. To the right is the tunnel for road and rail traffic to Chile (passenger rail service has been suspended due to lack of customers). To the left is the old road to Chile, which climbs steeply over rock and gravel to **La Cumbre Pass**, at an altitude of 4,200 meters (13,800 ft). At the top is the 8-meter (26-ft) high statue of **El Cristo Redentor ❻**, erected in 1904, in commemoration of an international border pact signed with Chile. It is most interesting for

Map on page 268

The statue of El Cristo Redentor, *on the Argentine-Chilean border, was transported in pieces by rail from Buenos Aires, and made the last leg of its journey by mule.*

BELOW: the south summit of Cerro Aconcagua.

River rafting on the Río Mendoza is suitable for all ages, with no experience necessary. Day-trips are organized by several agencies in Mendoza.

BELOW: World Cup skiing competition at Las Leñas.

the bits of colored rag tied onto it by visitors, in hopes of having prayers answered. The best reward for having made it up this far is the view over the mountains. In every direction, the raw steep peaks of the Andes reach up, the tips still catching the late afternoon sun. The perfect cap for the journey is to catch sight of a condor soaring at this lonely altitude, so keep your eyes open.

Jet-set skiers

Another day trip from Mendoza is to **Villavicencio** ❼, the hot spring spa 45 km (28 miles) to the northwest along Ruta 52. The road continues on until it reaches the mountain pass at Uspallata, but this portion is not paved.

If you're heading south toward Patagonia, it is worth stopping at the agricultural oasis of **San Rafael** ❽, some 240 km (150 miles) south of Mendoza. Nearby hydroelectric projects have created reservoirs, which have become centers for vacationers. The river fishing here is said to be excellent. San Rafael is Mendoza's second-largest city, as well as one of its most modern. Like in the city of Mendoza, local residents have kept the desert at bay through planting hundreds of trees and creating parks. The city is on the Río Diamante; there is a park and campsite with a small zoo on an island in the middle of the river, as well as the **Museo de Historia y Ciencias Naturales**, a small but eclectic museum with five rooms on botany and zoology, geology, anthropology, history, and local folklore (open daily). In the city center, on Bernardo de Irigoyen 148, is the **Museo de Bellas Artes**, with a small exhibition of art (open business hours, Mon–Fri). Some 92 km (57 miles) to the south of San Rafael is Mendoza's largest hydroelectric plant, El Nihuil, which has a dam and reservoir where water sports such as windsurfing and fishing are practiced.

Skiing at Las Leñas

To the southwest of San Rafael, in the **Valle Hermoso** (Beautiful Valley), is the ski resort of **Las Leñas** ❾. This is becoming quite the place for the chic set of both hemispheres to meet between June and October. It has 45 km (28 miles) of dry powder slopes and has accommodations for 2,000 people. Charter flights bring skiers from Mendoza to the nearby town of **Malargüe** ❿, where buses take them the rest of the way. The city of Malargüe, located on the site of a mid-19th century fort, is a smallish oil town well known for its *gaucho* crafts. In the former Estancia La Orteguita at the entrance to the city is the **Museo Regional** (open daily 8am–8pm), a small museum with three rooms containing historical, archeological, and mineralogical exhibits.

San Luis and watersports

Although **San Luis** ⓫ does not really merit an extra trip, it lies on the road between Buenos Aires and Mendoza, so those going overland may want to rest here for a day or so. The town sits at the northwest corner of the pampas, and was a lonely frontier outpost; it retains a faintly colonial atmosphere, with some interesting buildings such as the restored 18th-century Convento de San Domingo, on Plaza Independencia. Recently, however, industrial promotion schemes offering tax breaks to companies investing in the province have created a significant industrial base in the area around the city.

Several resorts clustered around reservoirs in the San Luis province are popular with anglers and windsurfers. On Ruta 1, which leads to the Sierras de Córdoba, is the spa resort of **Merlo** ⓬. With a particularly sunny, dry, and mild micro-climate, Merlo offers a range of hotels, holiday chalets, casinos, a river, and attractive surrounding country. It is this region's most popular tourist destination. The resort becomes especially crowded during Semana Santa (Holy Week) and the winter holiday period. While it has few buildings of great architectural or historical interest, the town offers a well-developed tourist infrastructure, with activities such as horseback riding, trekking, climbing, and hang gliding all available locally.

San Juan

The town of **San Juan** ⓭ is 177 km (106 miles) north of Mendoza along Ruta 40. An earthquake on January 15, 1944 leveled the town, and it has been completely rebuilt since then. It was Juan Perón's theatrical and highly successful efforts to raise funds for the devastated town that first brought him to national prominence, and which incidentally first brought him into contact with the actress Eva Duarte, later to become his second wife and famous as Evita Perón. Unfortunately, the town's architecture is on the whole very modern and not especially attractive.

San Juan is a major center of wine production, although the bulk of its production is of the table variety rather than fine wine; in general the quality of its wines is lower than that of Mendoza or Salta. However, the city is most famous for being the birthplace of Domingo Faustino Sarmiento (1811–88), the noted historian and educator who was president of the

Map on page 268

TIP

The area around Merlo has several quarries containing onyx, marble, and rose quartz; the town of La Toma, to the northeast of San Luis, specializes in green onyx. These stones can be purchased inexpensively locally.

BELOW: pre-Columbian milling stone, Talampaya National Park.

republic from 1868 to 1874. His former home, on the corner of Avenida San Martín and Sarmiento is the site of the **Museo Histórico Sarmiento** (open Fri–Tues), which has nine rooms around two patios, containing various items of furniture and personal effects. There is also the **Museo de Ciencias Naturales** (open Mon–Fri, Sat am only), which is near the Parque de Mayo, close to the intersection of 25 de Mayo and España. Besides the usual natural history exhibits, this museum also has an important collection of fossils from the Parque Natural Provincial Ischigualasto – better known as Valle de la Luna *(see page 281)* – which date from 200 million years ago.

On the other side of the city center, to the east, on the corner of Avenida General Rawson and General Paz, is the **Museo Histórico Provincial** (open Tues–Sun 9am–1pm), which houses a large collection, primarily of 18th- and 19th-century crafts and artwork, weapons, silver, furniture, and clothing. Located in the former warehouses of the General Belgrano railroad is the Mercado Artesanal Tradicional (traditional artisans' market; open Mon–Fri 8am–9pm), specializing in weaving and other rural crafts.

Climbing and rafting

To the west of San Juan is the Sierra de Tontal, with peaks of around 4,000 meters (13,120 ft), which involve less strenuous climbs than those of the Mendoza peaks. You can inquire at the local tourist office about the possibility of white-water rafting on the area's rivers *(see also Travel Tips, page 364)*. Some 30 km (18½ miles) away to the west lies the Embalse de Ullum (dam and reservoir) on the Río San Juan, in a pleasantly contrasting green setting. The dam has a hydroelectric plant and the reservoir is used for various water sports.

BELOW: roadside shrine to La Difunta Correa.

THE TRUCKDRIVERS' SHRINE

In 1841, in the course of the civil wars between federalists and unitarians, Deolinda Correa was forced to leave San Juan after the death of her husband, and to make the trek north toward La Rioja through the desert with her infant son. Deolinda was later found dead in the desert, although the baby was found to be alive and still able to nurse from his dead mother's breast.

Many years later, at the end of the 19th century, herdsmen stumbled across Deolinda's grave while they were searching for their cattle lost in a storm. They prayed for her assistance in recovering their herd and were astonished when the next morning they found them on a nearby hill. The herdsmen built a crude chapel by Deolinda's grave to show their gratitude and soon the story spread, attracting hopeful pilgrims.

Thus was born the shrine to Deolinda Correa, to whom miracles are popularly attributed, although she has not been canonised by the Catholic Church. A chapel has been erected on the spot, to the east of San Juan, and La Difunta (The Deceased) Correa has become the patron of road travelers and truck drivers, with visitors to the shrine leaving a bottle of water at her grave. At Easter and Christmas it is not uncommon for 200,000 pilgrims to visit the tomb.

About 60 km (37 miles) to the east of San Juan, on Ruta 20, is the small village of **Vallecito** ⓮ and the shrine to La Difunta Correa, one of the most visited religious sites in the whole of South America *(see box on previous page)*.

About 250 km (155 miles) to the northeast of Vallecito, along Ruta 141 and Ruta 510, is the Valle Fértil, where the town of **San Agustín de Valle Fértil** ⓯ lies in the middle of a desert oasis surrounded by vineyards and citrus groves, which are irrigated by the adjacent San Agustín reservoir.

Valle de la Luna

San Agustín del Valle Fértil is the gateway to the **Parque Natural Provincial Ischigualasto** ⓰ (including the World Heritage Site of Valle de la Luna), about 75 km (47 miles) to the southeast. This extensive park covers a 62,000-hectare (153,000-acre) area, which includes the Parque Provincial Talampaya in La Rioja, set in a large natural depression where constant erosion by wind and water through millennia has sculpted a series of sandstone formations of strange shapes and an abundance of colors. Beyond its beauty, the Valle de la Luna has great geological and paleontological significance. In prehistoric times (even before the birth of the Andes) this area was covered by an immense lake, surrounded, during the triassic period, by a rich fauna and flora. A 2-meter (6-ft) long reptile, the Dicinodonte, was one of the most typical inhabitants of the area. Sixty-three different species of fossilized animals have been found here.

The small town of **Barreal** ⓱ lies 94 km (58 miles) to the west of San Juan, amid spectacular scenery. The drive there takes some three hours, via Ruta 12, along a difficult mountain road. Barreal lies at 1,650 meters (5,410 ft) above sea level, on the banks of the Río Los Patos and flanked by birch trees. It is the

Map on page 268

Precariously balanced rock formation in the Valle de la Luna.

BELOW: the Valle de la Luna.

TIP

If you are visiting La
Unión, try *patero*, the
local white wine, a
homemade variety,
produced in the tradi-
tional way, crushing
the grapes underfoot.

region's main tourist center, with trekking and other outdoor activities organized locally. North of Barreal, on Ruta 412, is the Calingasta Valley, reached
after passing through the Cerros Pintados ("Painted Hills"), which show a
spectacular array of white, green, and red coloration. The town of **Calingasta**
⑱, in the middle of the valley at the joining of four rivers, is an important
center for local fruit cultivation, primarily apples and tomatoes, and in the past
gold, silver, and copper were mined and smelted in the area.

San Guillermo Wildlife Reserve

Some 200 km (120 miles) to the north of Calingasta is the small town of
Angualasto ⑲, located in a grape- and wheat-growing oasis between two
mountain ranges. The town's **Museo Arqueológico Municipal Luis Benedetti**
(open Tues–Sun, 8am–1pm and 3–7pm) houses a 400-year-old mummy, as well
as other archeological exhibits. The town is close to the **Reserva Provincial y
de la Biosfera San Guillermo**, devoted to the preservation of regional fauna,
primarily vicuñas and guanacos. The park lies at over 3,000 meters (9,840 ft)
above sea level and is accessible only by 4x4 vehicles. For much of the year, the
area is extremely cold and wet, and is best visited in the summer. Information
on access and guides can be obtained from the tourist office in Angualasto.

About 150 km (93 miles) further north, via San José de Jachal on Ruta 40,
brings you to the arid province of La Rioja, also a wine-producing province,
although on a lesser scale than Mendoza and San Juan. La Rioja is primarily
famous as the birthplace of the 19th-century federalist *caudillo* Facundo Quiroga
and of late 20th-century president Carlos Menem.

The provincial capital, **La Rioja** ⑳ is a small city situated in the desert,

BELOW: Cerro
Aconcagua (6962
meters/22,841 ft),
the highest peak in
the Americas.

whose principal architectural interest lies in the church of **Santo Domingo**, the oldest building in Argentina. Dating from 1623, it is also the only colonial building left in this city. Located in an Italian style 19th-century mansion two blocks from the main plaza is an important artisans' market (open Tues–Sun) offering crafts in leather, wood, silver, and ceramics, as well as woven textiles. The city also has a **Museo Folklórico** (open Tues–Sun), one block away from the artisans' market along Pelagio Luna, with fascinating exhibits of pre- and post-colonial life in the province, as well as a room devoted to provincial mythology. About 130 km (81 miles) northwest of La Rioja, in a valley between the Los Colorados and Sañogasta mountain ranges, is **Chilecito ㉑**, the second-largest city in the province and the center of its wine industry (controlled by the Menem family). A cable car leads from a station in the south of the city to the former La Mejicana copper mine. Between 1904 and 1929 the cable car linked the copper refinery with the railroad, although both the mine and the railroad have long since ceased to operate.

Map on page 268

Condors are often spotted soaring on the thermals around this region's highest mountain valleys.

Canyons and condors

The modern town of **Villa Unión ㉒** lies at the entrance to the Vinchina valley, parallel to that of Chilecito, and separated by the Sañogasta mountain range. It is reached by the road through the dramatic Cuesta de Miranda pass, and is a popular base for visiting some interesting sites in the vicinity.

Some 65 km (40 miles) to the north of Villa Unión is the small town of **Villa San José de Vinchina**, which has been inhabited since pre-Columbian times. It has an old water mill and dotted around the area are six unusual flattened mounds, painted with multicolored, 10-pointed stars which were thought to have been used as ritual sites. One of the stars can be seen just outside the town, across the Río Vinchina.

Also worth a visit is **Jagüe**, a tiny hamlet 37 km (23 miles) to the north of Vinchina, cradled at the foot of the giant **Volcán Bonete** (5,943 meters/19,500 ft), on the old muletrack that connects the green meadows on the Argentina side with the Chilean mining towns in the southern Atacama Desert.

The main destination from Villa Union though, and a suitably dramatic conclusion to this tour of the Cuyo, is the **Parque Nacional Talampaya ㉓**, a 270,000-hectare (667,000-acre) area 65 km (40 miles) to the southeast, which has some of the most spectacular scenery in Argentina. The park is set in an impressive gorge with cliffs towering to more than 145 meters (480 ft), and is full of amazing rock shapes carved by centuries of wind. The area was occupied by the Diaguita culture, which left behind innumerable rock paintings and engravings that can still be seen on some rock faces, offering a fascinating archeological contrast to the impressive geological formations of the canyon. A wide variety of animals, including foxes, hares, pumas, and guanacos also inhabit the park, and look out for condors soaring high above the gorge, whose nests are perched on the cliffs. Although private vehicles are not allowed within the park, there are guides with their own vehicles who run excursions (*see Travel Tips, page 364*). ❑

BELOW: a scenic road through the Cuyo country.

BODEGA HOPPING IN THE CUYO

With enormous industrial plants and friendly, family-based enterprises, Mendoza has vineyards galore, and tastings are positively encouraged

There are more than 1,290 vineyards in the Mendoza region, which produce 80 percent of the country's wines, Many of them offer tours and the chance to sample and buy wine. Local agencies organize excursions to many of the vineyards, some of which are listed here:

Bodega Lopez,
Carril Ozamis 375, Maipú, tel: 97-42406
Guided tours, Mon–Fri 8–11.30am/1–4pm.

Museo del Vino Bodega La Rural,
Montecaseros s/n, Coquimbito, tel: 97-43590.
Includes a museum, open Mon–Fri 9am–6pm.

Bodega Trapiche,
Mitre y Nueva Mayorga, Coquimbito,
tel: 97-42388. Guided tours, Mon–Fri
10am–4.30pm.

**Museo Nacional del Vino y Antigua
Bodega La Giol**,
Carril Ozamis 914, Maipú, tel: 497-6777.
Guided tours daily, Sat am only, Sun pm only.

Bodega Chandón,
Km 29, Agrelo, tel: 490-9900.
Guided tours daily.

Bodega Fabre Montmayou,
Roque Saenz Peña s/n, Lujan de Cuyo,
tel: 98-42330.
Guided tours,
Mon–Fri, by
appointment.

▷ **DIVINE ORIGINS**
Argentina's first
wine producers
were 16th-
century Jesuit
missionaries,
who planted
the vines to
make
communion
wine.

△ **FABRE MONTMAYOU**
This family-based, high-
quality winery was
founded in the early
20th century by a
Frenchman, Hervé
Joyaux Fabre.

▷ **DRINKING HABITS**
Argentina is the world's
fifth-largest wine producer.
Its export market is
growing, but most
wine is kept for
domestic consumption.

◁ **STUNNING BACKDROP**
The foothills of the Andes overlook Mendoza's vineyards, providing not only a spectacular setting but also a crucial supply of fresh mountain water.

△ **PEST CONTROL**
Rose bushes planted next to the vines are prone to pests and diseases, giving early warning to protect the precious grape crop.

▽ **ANTIQUE ARTEFACTS**
Several *bodegas* in the Mendoza area have their own museum, displaying hand-operated machinery and tools used in the past.

▷ **GRAPE VARIETY**
Argentina's best wines are the reds, and the most widely planted grapes are the Italian Bonarda, as well as Malbec, Cabernet Sauvignon, and Pinot Noir varieties.

THE PICK OF THE BUNCH

The most popular destinations for *bodega* hoppers are the major, streamlined operations at Peñaflor (producers of Trapiche), and Chandón. The best time to visit is during the March harvest, when the roads are clogged by trucks spilling over with grapes. Visitors are taken on a standard tour through the areas where the various stages of production take place (English-speaking tour guides can also be arranged). Huge oak casks are set on rollers as an anti-seismic precaution.

One of the less-visited but more interesting *bodegas* is La Rural, with a small but fascinating museum. This winery, whose brand is San Felipe, retains a lot of charm, with its original pink adobe architecture.

Cuyo Vineyards map

Espejo
Panqueua
Las Heras
El Plumerillo
Zanjón Bermejo
Mendoza
Villa Nueva
Estancia Guaymallén
Rodeo de la Cruz
Godoy Cruz
Confín
7
Gobernador Benegas
Luzuriaga
La Puntilla
General Gutiérrez
San Luis
Garrodilla
Bodega López
Bodega La Rural
Bodega Trapiche
7
Zanjón
Bodega Fabre Montmayou
Museo Nacional del Vino y Antigua Bodega La Giol
Maipú
Luján de Cuyo
Pescara
Bodega Chandón
Agrelo

Cuyo Vineyards

0   2 km
0   2 miles

PATAGONIA

At the very end of the South American subcontinent lies the land that Magellan and his chronicler Pigafetta, while grounded on a desolate coast during the winter of 1520, named Patagonia

Map on page 292

This wild and isolated terrain has figured prominently in the exotic fantasies of many armchair adventurers through the ages. From whale-watching and out-of-the-way ranch stays to deep green lakes and the crashing icy waters of Tierra del Fuego, Patagonia inspires.

Even though this large triangle of land comprises roughly a third of Argentina, one is still surprised by the wide range of spectacles that are contained here, and there are three World Heritage sites in the region. It has some of the hemisphere's highest peaks, forests of strange primeval trees, several of the world's most noteworthy glaciers, although sadly these are retreating due to global warming, and fossil-rich coastal cliffs that were explored by Charles Darwin. The abundance of rare wildlife is astounding, and, for the athletic traveler, Patagonia has some of the most challenging skiing and mountain climbing to be found.

At the top of the wedge-shaped territory are the provinces of Neuquén and Río Negro, the former famed for its ancient *araucaria araucana* (monkey puzzle) forests and Mapuche reservations, and the latter for the Alpine-style town of Bariloche in Parque Nacional Nahuel Huapi. Both provinces border on trout-rich Lago Nahuel Huapi, have their own ski resorts, and offer summer hiking, horseback riding, mountain climbing, and water sports.

Further south, Chubut flaunts the marine fauna of the Valdés Peninsula and an exotic cultural mix comprising the Mapuches and the customs of the Welsh communities of the coast and the montane hinterland. Puerto Madryn's Golfo Nuevo is Argentina's scuba-diving capital and is home to the southern right whale during the winter and fall months. Santa Cruz, at the tip of the Patagonian wedge, is the country's second-largest and least-inhabited province, in addition to harboring some of nature's most imposing glaciers, a large petrified forest that is 150 million years old, and numerous cave paintings more than 10,000 years old.

Bold explorers

Ferdinand Magellan, Pedro Sarmiento de Gamboa, Francis Drake, and Thomas Cavendish are just a few of the many explorers who set foot on this land. Here, on these dismal shores, European law and customs gave way to the most violent passions – revolts, mutinies, banishments and executions were common. In 1578, in the Port of San Julian (now the town of Puerto San Julian in Santa Cruz province), Sir Francis Drake used the same scaffold Magellan had used to hang his mutineers half a century before.

Sarmiento de Gamboa founded the first settlements in 1584, naming them Nombre de Jesus and Rey Felipe, on the Strait of Misfortunes. His first encounter with the native inhabitants should have sounded a

PRECEDING PAGES: high Andean snow fields; Cerro Norte and Río Onelli. **LEFT:** Perito Moreno glacier. **BELOW:** Argentine Mapuche woman.

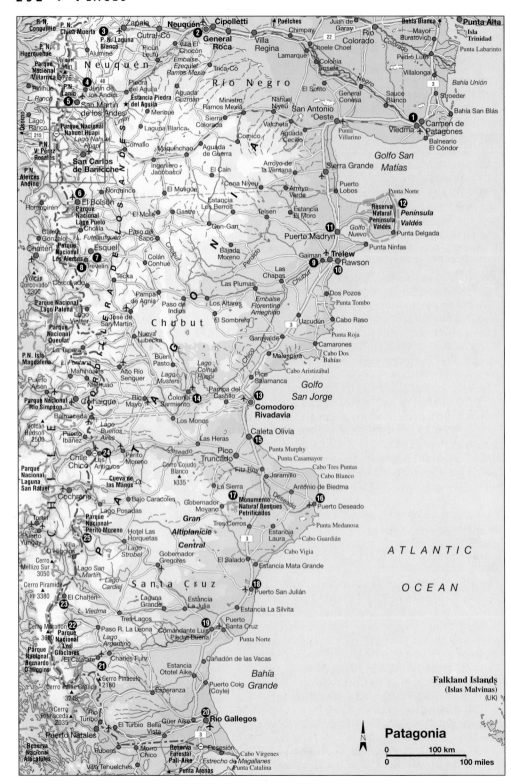

Patagonia

Map on page 292

warning: "Ten naked indians approached us and pronounced words of welcome in an unknown language. The Chief, trying to prove their friendship, took a long arrow and swallowed it till it almost disappeared down his throat; when he slowly took it out, it was covered in blood." Two years later, Thomas Cavendish, the English privateer captain, found the survivors of this expedition wandering on the deserted coast, and after spending four days there, gave it the desolate name of Port Famine.

Stretching westward from the white cliffs on the coast lie the vast plains and mesas that remained unexplored for centuries. The Jesuits were among the few who, driven by the spell of the "lost city of the Caesars," dared to take a look at the endless plateau. They came from Chile, across the Andes, and never ventured far from the mountains. In 1670, they founded a mission in a remote place, on the shores of Lago Nahuel Huapi. It didn't last long. The indigenous community had a premonition that they would be doomed if the Spanish found their secret trails across the Andes, and so murdered most of the missionaries.

The origin of the name Patagonia, according to some historians, comes from the name given to the natives because of their big feet (pata is Spanish for an animal's foot, -gón is a common affix for "big").

The desert conquest

The early inhabitants of this land were, from the start, part of the exotic spell that attracted the first settlers, but soon became an obstacle to their purposes. They had been there long before the white man arrived and they stood their ground. The bravest were the Mapuches, a nomadic tribe who lived on both sides of the border in the northern part of Patagonia. For 300 years they led a violent lifestyle on the plains by stealing and plundering the larger *estancias* (ranches) of the rich pampas, herding the cattle over the Andes and selling them to the Spaniards on the Chilean side.

BELOW: beautiful Magellanic fuchsia.

STIRRING PATAGONIAN PROSE

Nobody has ever expressed more precisely than British naturalist Charles Darwin the emotions that remote Patagonia stirs in a visitor. Darwin, back in England after sailing five years on the *Beagle*, wrote, "In calling up images of the past, I find that the plains of Patagonia frequently cross before my eyes; yet these plains are pronounced by all wretched and useless… Why then… have these arid wastes taken so firm a hold on my memory?"

Since Darwin's time, Patagonia has attracted a steady stream of foreign writers. In the 19th century, Argentine-born William Henry Hudson wrote *Idle Days in Patagonia*, a poetic narrative of his youth spent discovering the flora and fauna of the region.

But perhaps the best-known modern account of the place and its people is Bruce Chatwin's *In Patagonia*, which captures the essence of Patagonia through his meetings with local inhabitants encountered during his travels. "So next day, as we drove through the desert, I sleepily watched the rags of silver cloud spinning across the sky, and the sea of grey-green thornscrub lying off in sweeps and rising in terraces and the white dust streaming off the saltpans, and, on the horizon, land and sky dissolving into an absence of color."

*Mapuche jewelry,
now produced
primarily for the
tourist industry.*

In 1879, the Argentine army, under General Roca, set out to conquer the land from the Amerindians. The campaign, which lasted until 1883, is known as the Conquest of the Desert. It put an end to years of Amerindian dominion in Patagonia and opened up a whole new territory to colonization. The natives vanished: some died in epic battles, others succumbed to new diseases, and others simply became cowhands on the huge *estancias*. Fragments of their world can still be found in the land, in the features of some of the people, in customs, and in religious rituals still performed on Amerindian reservations.

European settlement

When the Amerindian wars ended, colonization began. The large inland plateau, a dry expanse of shrubs and alkaline lagoons, was slowly occupied by people of very diverse origins: Spaniards, Italians, Scots, and English in the far south, Welsh in the Chubut Valley, Italians in the Río Negro Valley, Swiss and Germans in the Northern Lake District, and a few North Americans scattered throughout the country.

These people inherited the land and reproduced in the far south a situation similar to the American West. Ports and towns developed on the coast to ship the wool and import the goods needed by the settlers. Large wool-producing *estancias* were established on these plains. To the west, where the plains meet the Andes, several national parks were designated to protect the rich natural inheritance, to develop tourism, and to secure the national borders.

BELOW: Carmen de Patagones in the early 19th century.

The Patagonian towns grew fast. Coal mining, oilfields, agriculture, industry, large hydroelectrical projects, and tourism attracted people from all over the country and from Chile, transforming Patagonia into a modern industrial frontier

land. Some people came to start a quiet new life in the midst of mountains, forests, and lakes. In the Patagonian interior, descendants of the first sheep-breeding settlers and their ranch-hands still ride over the enormous *estancias*.

Map on page 292

A few geographical facts

With defined geographical and political boundaries, Patagonia extends from the Río Colorado in the north, more than 2,000 km (1,200 miles) to Cabo de Hornos at the southernmost tip of the continent. It covers more than 1 million sq km (400,000 sq miles) and belongs to two neighboring countries, Chile and Argentina. The final agreement on this long, irregular, international border took a while to come by and was not an easy matter to settle. Although the land was still unexplored, there were times when both countries were almost on the brink of war. Fortunately, it never reached that point, due to the common-sense of both governments. An historical example of this attitude was the meeting of the Chilean and Argentine presidents in 1899 in the Straits of Magellan. In 1978, a similar diplomatic encounter was carried out in Puerto Montt, Chile, where both countries agreed on the last stretch of undefined boundary, which concerned some small islands in the Beagle Channel. The Argentine part of Patagonia includes approximately 800,000 sq km (308,000 sq miles), and can easily be divided into three definite areas: the coast, the plateau, and the Andes.

The population density of Patagonia averages fewer than three inhabitants per sq km (less than one per sq mile), compared to more than 2,500 people per square km (more than 1,000 per sq mile) in Buenos Aires.

The change of seasons

Seasons are well defined in Patagonia. Considering the latitude, the average temperature is mild; winters are never as cold and summers never as warm as in similar latitudes in the northern hemisphere. The average temperature in

BELOW: horseback trekking above Lago Nahuel Huapi, near Bariloche.

TIP

There are only two
main roads in
Patagonia: Ruta 40,
which runs down the
Andes, and Ruta 3,
which follows the
coast. Many smaller
roads link the coast to
the mountains, but not
many are paved, so
you may have to
choose between a
smooth but longer
journey or a quick but
bumpy dirt road.

Ushuaia is 6°C (43°F) and, in Bariloche, 8°C (46°F). Even so, the climate can turn quite rough on the desert plateau. There, the weather is more continental than in the rest of the region. The ever-present companion is the wind, which blows hard all year round, from the mountains to the sea, making life here unbearable for many people.

In spring, the snow on the mountains begins to melt, alpine flowers bloom almost everywhere, and ranchers prepare for the hard work of tending sheep and shearing. Although tourism starts in late springtime, most people visit during the summer (December to March). During this period, all roads are fit for traffic, the airports are open and, normally, the hotels are booked solid.

The fall brings changes on the plateau. The poplars around the lonesome *estancias* turn to beautiful shades of yellow. The mountains, covered by deciduous beech trees, offer a panorama of reds and yellows, and the air slowly gets colder. At this time of the year, tourism thins out. Parque Nacional Los Glaciares, in the far south, closes down for the winter. While the wide plains sleep, the winter resorts on the mountains thrive. San Martín de los Andes, Bariloche, Esquel, and even Ushuaia attract thousands of skiers, including many from the northern hemisphere who take advantage of the reversal of seasons.

Northern Patagonia

The northern boundary of Patagonia is the **Río Colorado**. The steppe starts further north and extends through inland Patagonia and the coast, down to the Straits of Magellan. Near to the mouth of the Río Negro, which runs parallel to the south of the Colorado, are the twin towns of **Carmen de Patagones** and **Viedma ❶**, on opposite banks of the river. Carmen de Patagones is one of the

BELOW:
fall comes
to the plains.

oldest Spanish settlements in Patagonia, founded in 1779. The first settlers lived in constant fear of being invaded by foreign powers seeking to conquer Patagonia. In the mid-1980s, President Raúl Alfonsín launched a project to make Viedma the new capital of the Argentine Republic – the Argentine Brasília – on the southern end of the continent, a symbol of the gradual shifting of economic and political interest. But as the cost of moving the capital from Buenos Aires became clear, the plan was quietly forgotten.

Fertile fruit orchards

Nearby, you can see the caves used for shelter by the first settlers. Where the river meets the sea, there is a sea lion colony similar to the many others along the coast. **Puerto San Antonio Este**, the port from where all the fruit production of the valley is shipped to foreign countries, lies 180 km (110 miles) to the west, and nearby is **Las Grutas**, a popular seaside resort with extensive sandy beaches. The warm, clear waters here make it a popular destination for divers; game-fishing and whale-watching are also popular.

The **Río Negro** flows through an oasis of intensive agriculture, which stretches for more than 400 km (250 miles). The valley itself is a narrow strip of fertile land, in sharp contrast to the desert surroundings that threaten to swallow it. Anyone interested in visiting agricultural areas specializing in growing fruit (apples, pears, grapes), should not miss this place. Fruit farms, juice factories, and packing establishments give an intense economic life to this oasis.

Traveling inland along the Río Negro, past cultivated strips of land that alternate with steppe, you arrive at a string of cities: **Neuquén ❷**, Cipoletti, General Roca, and Villa Regina, some 540 km (330 miles) from the coast. These are the

Map on page 292

The black-necked swan, a common sight in Patagonia's Lake District.

BELOW: winter comes to the mountains.

region's most important cities, forming a rare ribbon of urbanization, interspersed with fruit orchards. The main road here is heavily used, but traffic thins out markedly beyond Villa Regina.

The northern Lake District

Going west from Neuquén to the Andes, you come to the northern limit of the Patagonian Lake District, an enormous area of beautiful lakes and spectacular mountain peaks, which stretches 1,500 km (900 miles) down the Andes, from Lago Aluminé in the north to Parque Nacional Los Glaciares in the south. One can divide this region into two sections, the northern and southern Lake Districts. The zone that lies in between is sparsely populated and traveling is a challenge to be taken on only by the most adventurous.

January and July are the most popular months for visitors, reflecting the vacations in Buenos Aires. However, apart from May and June, which tend to be rainy months, the area has its attractions in all seasons. There are many tours available to local landmarks and abundant opportunities for hiking, climbing, fishing, and horseback riding in summer, or skiing and snowboarding in winter.

The northern Lake District covers the area from Lago Aluminé southward to Lago Amutui Quimei. It encompasses a 500-km (300-mile) stretch of lakes, forests, and mountains divided into four national parks. From north to south is the Parque Nacional Lanín and the nearby towns of San Martín de los Andes and Junín de los Andes; Parque Nacional Nahuel Huapi and the alpine-style resort of Bariloche; Parque Nacional Lago Puelo and the village of El Bolsón; and, farthest south, Parque Nacional Los Alerces with the town of Esquel. This region connects to the so-called Lake District in Chile.

The 19th-century English explorer George Muster wrote At Home with the Patagonians (1871), *about his six months' journey through the region with a group of Amerindians. The book is still hailed as the most complete description of the Patagonian interior and its people.*

BELOW: the road to Bariloche.

Entering the Lake District from the north, the first place of interest you'll reach is the **Parque Nacional Laguna Blanca ❸**. The park lies just to the southwest of Zapala, which is about 185 km (115 miles) west of Neuquén on Ruta 22. It includes a large lake, and is home to hundreds of interesting birds: the prime attractions are the black-necked swans, which gather in flocks of up to 2,000 birds. Flamingos are also part of the scenery, and the surrounding hills give shelter to large groups of eagles, peregrine falcons, and other birds of prey. There is a visitor's center at the park, and a campsite. There are infrequent buses to the park from the nearest town, Zapala, 35 km (22 miles) away, which has an information office.

Traveling southwest from Neuquén along Ruta 237, after about 76 km (47 miles) you'll come to the huge Embalse E. Ramos Mexía. This reservoir is an impressive sight, created by building a dam across the Río Limay, and is now one of the biggest hydroelectric plants in the country.

Monkey puzzles and trout

The area around Lago Aluminé is well known for its Amerindian reservations where you can find handicrafts such as ponchos and carpets. This area is also home to one of the most peculiar-looking trees in the world, the *araucaria araucana* or monkey puzzle. This prehistoric tree, which grows at considerable altitudes, still has a primeval look to it. Its fruit, the *piñón*, which can be boiled and eaten, was a treat for the indigenous peoples on their way across the Andean trails.

Parque Nacional Lanín, near the town of San Martín de los Andes, covers 3,920 sq km (1,508 sq miles) and gets its name from the imposing Lanín volcano, on the border with Chile. The volcano soars to 3,776 meters (12,388 ft), far above the height of the surrounding peaks.

The national park is noted for its fine fishing; the fishing season is from mid-November through mid-April. The rivers and streams around the small town of **Junín de los Andes ❹** are famed for their abundance and variety of trout. Fly-casters come from around the world to fish for the brook, brown, fontinalis, and steelhead. The best catch on record is a 12-kg (27-lb) brown trout – the average weight for this fish is 4–5 kg (9–11 lbs). Although Junín has several good restaurants and hotels, most anglers prefer the several fishermen's lodges located in the park.

Parque Nacional Lanín is also well known for hunting. Wild boar and red and fallow deer are the main prey in the fall rutting season. The national park takes bids for hunting rights over most of the hunting grounds, and local farm owners make their own agreements with hunters. For information, contact the tourist office in San Martín de los Andes.

Guided tours, by bus or boat, depart from **San Martín de los Andes ❺**, a small, well-manicured, exclusive town at the eastern end of Lago Lacar. Fishing and hunting, and mountain climbing guides are available, as well as car rentals, a good range of accommodations and two interesting Mapuche museums. Also recommended is a trip to lakes Hue-

Map on page 292

TIP

A Pase Verde allows entry to four national parks at a reduced rate, available from national park offices.

BELOW: a good day's catch.

Wily Patagonian fox
(zorro patagónico).

chulafquen and Paimun and the majestic Lanín volcano, fringed by a forest of araucaria or monkey puzzle trees.

Cerro Chapelco, at 2,441 meters (8,000 ft) and 20 minutes or so by car from San Martín, is one of the country's most important winter sports centers. The ski season here runs from mid-June to mid-October.

Three roads link San Martín de los Andes with Bariloche. The middle (shortest, but unpaved) road runs across the Paso del Córdoba through narrow valleys where the scenery is beautiful, especially in the fall when the slopes turn to rich shades of gold and deep red. This road reaches the paved highway at Confluencia. From here, if you turn back inland, you come to the **Estancia La Primavera**, with its trout farm. To the dismay of locals who used to fish here, it is now private property, belonging to US media tycoon Ted Turner. Returning to the paved road to Bariloche, you follow Río Limay through the Valle Encantado, a valley of bizarre rock formations, also skirting the Rincón Grande, a ring of steep escarpments formed by river erosion, creating a striking natural amphitheater.

The third road from San Martín is the famed **Ruta de los Siete Lagos** (Route of the Seven Lakes). This road, of which about half is paved, takes you past beautiful lakes and forests and approaches Bariloche from the northern shore of Lago Nahuel Huapi. In summer, all-day tours make the trip from Bariloche to San Martín, combining the Paso del Córdoba and the Ruta de los Siete Lagos.

Switzerland in Argentina

BELOW:
gauchos on the
Patagonian steppe.

Jan Carlos de Bariloche , in the middle of Parque Nacional Nahuel Huapi, is the real center of the northern Lake District. Buses, trains, and planes arrive daily from all over the country and from Chile, across the Paso Puyehue.

Bariloche, as it is commonly called, has a very strong Central European influence; most of the first settlers were of Swiss, German, or Northern Italian origin. These people gave the city its Alpine atmosphere, with Swiss-style chalets, fondue restaurants, and chocolates. However, something tells you that you are not in Europe; boats are seldom seen on the huge Lago Nahuel Huapi, the roads are swallowed in the wilderness as soon as they leave the city, and at night there are no lights on the opposite shore of the lake.

The town has grown rapidly in recent decades, spreading along the foot of **Cerro Otto**. This long ridge offers a good introductory walk, or take a cable-car ride to the top, where there are splendid views of the town, the lake, the surrounding park and a revolving café. There are also pleasant woodland walks descending the far side of the ridge to Arelauquen and the quiet Lago Gutiérrez.

The best way to begin your tour of Bariloche is by visiting the **Museo de la Patagonia** (open daily) in the Civic Center. This building and the Hotel Llao Llao were designed by architect Exequiel Bustillo in his own interpretation of traditional Alpine style, and they give Bariloche a distinctive architectural personality. The museum has displays on the geological origins of the region and of local wildlife. It also has a stunning collection of indigenous artifacts, which chronicle the demise of local tribes.

Regional buys

Chocolates, jams, ceramics, and sweaters are among the most important local products. The large chocolate industry has remained in the hands of Italian families and a visit to some of the downtown factories is worthwhile. So is a visit to the ceramics factory, where you can watch the artisans at work. Sweaters

Map on page 303

BELOW: Cerro Lanín.

CROSSING THE ANDES

While you are in the northern Lake District there are various options for crossing over to Chile. From Bariloche, if you want to reach Puerto Montt on the Pacific coast, try the old route first used by the Jesuits across the lakes. This day-long journey combines short bus rides with leisurely boat crossings of lakes Nahuel Huapi, Frías, Todos los Santos, and Llanquihue, through marvelous settings of forests and snow-capped volcanoes.

While the lake crossing has the advantage of escaping normal traffic, the road through the Puyehue Pass, northwest of Bariloche, gives views of Lago Correntoso and Lago Espejo. Over the border, the Parque Nacional Puyehue offers the opportunity to sample thermal springs and mud baths, or to explore the temperate rainforest.

Further north, via San Martín de los Andes, is the little-used Hua-Hum Pass. A small car ferry carries you the length of Lago Pirihueico with its steep-forested sides and glimpses of the Choshuenco volcano, and at the far end a road continues into the village of Choshuenco.

More northerly still, beyond Junín de los Andes, is Paso Tromen. This much higher and sometimes closed in winter, but affords wonderful views of the Lanín volcano and the native *araucaria* (monkey puzzle) forests.

are for sale everywhere, as are locally produced jewelry and handicrafts.

Bariloche has many accommodations, ranging from cozy inns to luxury hotels. The local cuisine reflects the area's large population of settlers from Germany and Italy, with specialties such as fondue and trout, venison and wild boar.

Lakes, forests, and mountains

There are some excellent excursions to choose from in the Bariloche area: 17 km (11 miles) southwest is the **Villa Cerro Catedral **, one of Argentina's largest and most important ski centers, also with fine walking trails on the mountainside and around Lago Gutiérrez. The base of the ski lifts is at 1,050 meters (3,465 ft) above sea level, and a cable-car and chair-lifts take you up to a height of 2,010 meters (6,633 ft). The view from the slopes is absolutely superb. The ski runs range in difficulty from novice to expert, and cover more than 25 km (15 miles) and there are full facilities. The ski season runs from the end of June to September. Snowboarding, bungee jumping, and paragliding are also possible.

Another 10 km (6 miles) further south is **Villa Mascardi**, a small tourist resort on the shore of Lago Mascardi. Picturesque boat cruises are available from here across the turquoise waters of the lake toward Monte Tronador, the highest peak in the national park, at 3,478 meters (11,411 ft). The mountain can also be visited via a long and winding scenic drive. Between lakes Gutiérrez and Mascardi lies the watershed of rivers draining into the Atlantic and the Pacific oceans. Past Pampa Linda, where there is one hostel, and approaching the mountain, you pass the Black Glacier, so-called because of all the muddy debris churned up onto the surface of the glacier. Another route from Lago Mascardi goes to lakes Fonck and Hess, both popular fishing spots, with camping

"It is not the imagination, it is that nature in these desolate scenes, for a reason to be guessed at by and by, moves us more deeply than in others.

– W. H. HUDSON
(Anglo-Argentine naturalist, 1841–1922)

BELOW: San Martín de los Andes.

sites. En route, you pass the lovely Cascada Los Alerces, which cascades for some 20 meters (66 ft) over drenched, mossy rocks. A number of these routes operate one-way systems allowing only ascent or descent within certain times, in order to regulate peak season tourist traffic, so you'd be advised to check the details at the Bariloche tourist office if traveling independently by road.

Map below

Llao Llao Peninsula

One of the most popular half-day excursions from Bariloche is the so-called Circuito Chico, or small circuit. This takes you westward along the shore of the lake and up to the Punto Panorámico, with its breathtaking views over the water toward Chile. It is a rare building that could blend into, even enhance, such a magnificent landscape, but the **Hotel Llao Llao ⓓ** at the base of the Península Llao Llao, is equal to the challenge. The enormous, Apine-style hotel was built in 1939, and in 1995 was the setting for a summit meeting of presidents of the Americas, including Cuba's Fidel Castro.

Continuing the circuit, farther round the lake is **Bahía López**, a tranquil inlet where it is often possible to see condors circling the huge bulk of Cerro López overshadowing the bay. There is a well-defined path leading up this mountain as far as the mountain refuge, with a more rugged track thereafter up to the summit ridge. On the road back to Bariloche you will pass the Cerro Campanario chairlift at Km 17. Although much lower than lifts at Cerro Otto or Catedral, the views are unrivaled and well worthwhile.

At the far end of Lago Nahuel Huapi, en route to Chile, **Puerto Blest ⓔ** is host to much through traffic. Few stay, however, so outside these brief flurries of traffic it is a place of exceptional peace and beauty. There is a small hotel, a

One of Bariloche's tempting chocolate shops.

BELOW: Bariloche's Civic Center.

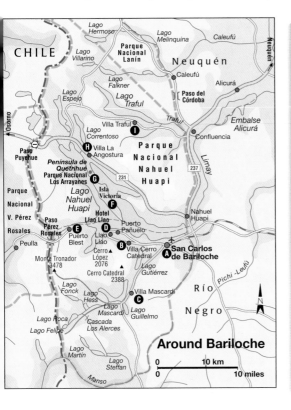

Around Bariloche

pleasant walking trail to the Cascada Los Cantares, and a warden to give directions for more demanding walks. You can visit Puerto Blest and Isla Victoria by catamaran excursions across Lago Nahuel Huapi from Puerto Pañuelo.

Bambi's forest

Isla Victoria ❻, on Lago Nahuel Huapi, is renowned for its *arrayanes*, rare trees related to myrtles, found only in this area and in the Parque Nacional Los Alerces *(see page 306)*. The story goes that a visiting group of Walt Disney's advisors were so impressed by the white and cinnamon colored trees here that they used them as the basis for the scenery in the 1942 film *Bambi*. Most visitors to the island come in groups on the catamaran excursions, but you require only a little ingenuity to discover the beauties of the island away from the crowds.

Extending from the northern shore of the lake is the Península de Quetrihue. containing the **Parque Nacional Los Arrayanes ❼**, dedicated to protecting the rare *arrayán* trees, some of which are 300 years old and 28 meters (92 ft) high. Boat excursions to Isla Victoria often stop at Quetrihue, allowing time to walk in the park. You can also reach the Península de Quetrihue from **Villa La Angostura ❽**, a small, quietly chic resort at the far end of the lake. There is a good selection of hotels, camping sites, and other amenities in the vicinity, which has been developed to cater to the tourist overflow of the nearby skiing center of Cerro Bayo.

Another popular excursion heads east from Bariloche, then north through the Valle Encantado, until turning off at Confluencia for **Villa Traful ❾**. The small town is famous for the excellent salmon fishing in Lago Traful, as well as for some inspiring hiking and horseback riding in the surrounding countryside.

BELOW:
above the clouds
at Cerro Catedral.

The road continues through the town, climbing to a commanding viewpoint high above Lago Traful and takes a scenic route back through Villa la Angostura. This circuit, predictably described as the Circuito Grande (large circuit), covers some 240 km (149 miles) and is offered as a full-day excursion from Bariloche.Most travel agencies in Bariloche offer a variety of bus and boat excursions visiting the above-mentioned sites, but if you fancy something a little more energetic to tap this area's vast potential for outdoor pursuits, visit the Club Andino, the city's specialist mountaineering organization (see page 364).

Maps,
pages
292 & 303

Hippie refuge

El Bolsón ❻ is a small town 130 km (80 miles) south of Bariloche, situated in a narrow valley with its own microclimate. Beer hops and all sorts of berries are grown on small farms. Hippies favored El Bolsón in the 1960s, today leading peaceful lives on farms perched in the mountains. Some 20 km (12½ miles) south of El Bolsón, and bordering Chile, is the serene **Parque Nacional Lago Puelo** (237 sq km/92 sq miles), established in 1937 as an annex to nearby Parque Nacional Los Alerces. Another angler's paradise, the park has mountains covered with ancient forests of deciduous beech trees and cypresses and more than 100 species of birds. Basic camping facilities are available by the lakeshore, with some marked trails.

Handicrafts market at El Bolsón.

The gringo outlaws

Further south, on the road to Esquel, you come across the beautiful **Cholila Valley**, a little-known area where in early summer the fields are carpeted in blue by wild lupins. This was the place chosen by Butch Cassidy and the

BELOW: Hotel Llao Llao, on Lago Nahuel Huapi.

Sundance Kid, the US outlaws made famous by George Hill's 1969 movie starring Paul Newman and Robert Redford. Butch and Sundance sheltered temporarily in Cholila, while they were on the run from Pinkerton's agents. A letter sent by them to Matilda Davis in Utah, dated August 10, 1902, was posted at Cholila. After their famous hold-up of the Río Gallegos Bank in 1905, they were again on the run, until they were finally killed by the Bolivian police. Other members of the gang who stayed on in this region were ambushed and killed, years later, by the Argentine constabulary.

From Cholila, the road going south splits in two. Ruta 40 turns slightly to the east, through the large Estancia Leleque, alongside the narrow-gauge railroad, until it reaches Esquel. The other route to Esquel takes you right into **Parque Nacional Los Alerces**. This park covers 2,630 sq km (1,012 sq miles) and is less spoiled by towns and people than other parks are in this region. Summer visitors to the park stay at camping sites and fishermen's lodges around **Lago Futalaufquen**. One tour you should not miss is the all-day boat excursion, which leaves in the summer from Puerto Chucao to Lago Menéndez, the largest lake in the national park. There are outstanding views of **Cerro Torrecillas** (2,200 meters/7,260 ft) and its glaciers, and be sure to see the huge *Fitzroya* trees (related to the American redwood), some of which are over 2,000 years old.

The Old Patagonian Express

As you get closer to Trevelín and Esquel you begin to leave behind the northern Lake District. This area is strongly influenced by Welsh culture, as a sizeable community of Welsh people settled here in 1888 after a long trek from the Atlantic Coast along the Chubut Valley *(see page 310)*.

Traveling 167 km (104 miles) south of El Bolsón on Ruta 40 and Ruta 258 brings you to **Esquel ❼**, an offshoot of the Welsh Chubut colony. The town, with 32,000 inhabitants, lies to the east of the Andes, on the border of the Patagonian desert. In its remote location, on the edge of the desert, Esquel has the feel of a town in the old American West. You are as likely to see people riding on horseback here as in cars. Sometimes the rider will be a *gaucho* dandy, all dressed up with broad-brimmed hat, kerchief, and *bombachas* (baggy pleated pants). Several times a year, principally in January, a rural fair is held in Esquel. People come from miles around to trade livestock and agricultural supplies. In town, several stores *(talabarterías)* are well-stocked with riding tackle and ranch equipment. Ornate stirrups and hand-tooled saddles sit next to braided, rawhide ropes and cast-iron cookware. This was once goose-hunting country, but the rare local species have since become protected.

Esquel's railway station is the most southerly point of the Argentine rail network. The narrow-gauge railway (0.75 meters/2.48 ft), used to provide a regular service between Esquel and Ingeniero Jacobacci to the north. The train – La Trochita – was made famous abroad by US author Paul Theroux, in his book *The Old Patagonian Express*. These days it runs only a partial and intermittent schedule largely for the benefit of tourists. Nevertheless, if you happen to arrive

Many sheep farms in Patagonia (see box on page 308) are being bought out by large multinational enterprises, who buy the majority of their raw wool for processing abroad. Italian clothing magnate Luciano Benetton bought seven sheep farms in the region, totaling 20,000 hectares (50,000 acres).

BELOW: Cascada Los Césares, in the northern Lake District.

at the right time, there is no better way to get acquainted with Patagonia and its people than by a trip on this quaint little train which is pulled by an old-fashioned steam locomotive. For serious railway buffs, there are workshops open to visitors in El Maitén, providing a further glimpse of the romantic past.

In winter, Esquel turns into a ski resort, with **La Hoya Ski Center** only 15 km (10 miles) away. Compared with Bariloche and Villa Cerro Catedral, this ski area is considerably smaller and cozier but a range of rental facilities are available.

Trevelín ❽, 23 km (14 miles) southwest of Esquel, is a small village, also of Welsh origin. Its name in Welsh means "town of the mill." The old mill has been converted into a museum, the Museo Molino Viejo (open daily), which houses all sorts of implements that belonged to the first Welsh settlers, together with old photographs and a Welsh Bible. As in all the Welsh communities of Patagonia, you can enjoy a typical tea with Welsh cookies and cakes in several cafes in Esquel.

The "Beautiful Valley" of Chubut

Between the Atlantic Coast and Esquel lies the **Chubut Valley**. Only the lower valley, covering an area of 50 sq km (19 sq miles) is irrigated, while the rest is parched. The Welsh used this valley, which they called **Cwm Hyfrwd** (Beautiful Valley), to reach the Esquel/Trevelín area; a route described most romantically by Eluned Morgan in her book, *Dringo'r Andes (Climbing the Andes)*. Halfway down the valley, the river cuts through the plateau, forming an impressive canyon with red and white ravines named the Valle de los Altares and the Valle de los Mártires (Altars and Martyrs valleys). The latter refers to an ambush set by the Amerindians in 1884, in which a group of young Welshmen was wiped out. The lone survivor, John Evans, managed to escape, thanks to his

Map on page 292

La Trochita, *the Old Patagonian Express, one of the oldest steam trains still in operation in South America.*

BELOW: El Bolsón.

horse, Malacara, which leapt over the steep ravine. The graves of these unfortunate people, who are vividly described in Morgan's book, can still be seen alongside the road. Before coming to the lower valley, you will reach the **Dique Embalse Florentino Ameghino** and its artificial lake. The dam and the reservoir are nestled in a narrow rocky gorge, forming an impressive sight.

Sea lions at Punta Tombo

The lower Chubut Valley was the site of the first settlement established by the Welsh. The towns of Dolavon, Gaiman, Trelew, and Rawson developed here, and today they are surrounded by intensively cultivated lands.

Gaiman ❾ has an interesting museum similar to the one in Trevelín, the Museo Histórico Regional (open Mon–Fri 4–8pm), housed in the old train station, with a gift shop. The town is famous for its Welsh teas, which are offered by four leading *casas de té* (tea houses) in somber rooms crowded with evocative memorabilia of the first settlers. The *Eisteddfod*, the Welsh Arts Festival, which features singing and reciting, is held here every August. The river meets the sea close to **Rawson** ❿, the provincial capital city. Coming back from an excursion to Punta Tombo, in the afternoon, drive by the small fishermen's port at Rawson to watch the men as they unload their day's catch, and lazy sea lions grab whatever falls overboard.

Trelew is the most important city in the lower valley, and its airport is the gateway for visitors to the wildlife-rich Península Valdés area. Due to a program to promote industry in the 1980s, the population swelled here to 100,000. Its Welsh ambiance has faded and, apart from a leafy central square, it is not a particularly attractive city. One point of interest is a paleontological museum

THE BIG SHEEP BOOM

The first governor of Santa Cruz, Carlos Moyano, could find no one to settle in the desolate south of Patagonia. In desperation, he invited young couples from the Malvinas/Falklands to try their hand "on the coast," and the first sheep farmers were English and Scottish shepherds. They were soon followed by people from many other nations, mainly in central Europe, who remained behind after the 1890s gold rush. The sheep rearing proved hugely successful, and, by the 1920s, Argentinian wool commanded record prices on the world market.

The sheep in southern Patagonia are mainly Scottish corriedale, although some merinos have been brought from Australia, and two hardy new breeds have been developed for the region. Farm work intensifies from October to April, with lamb marking, shearing, dipping, and moving the animals to the summer camps. In the fall they are moved back to the winter camps and the wool around the eyes is shorn.

Shearing is usually done by a *comparsa*, a group of professionals who travel from farm to farm, moving south with the season. However, each farm has its own shepherds and *peones* (unskilled workmen) who stay year round, tending fences and animals.

marking the important dinosaur remains that have been found in Patagonia. The **Museo Paleontológico Egidio Feruglio** (open daily), on 9 de Julio 655, contains fossil remains of dinosaurs such as carnotosaurus, the only known meat-eating dinosaur, and the 65-million-year-old eggs of titanosaurus.

The Valdes Peninsula

Puerto Madryn ⓫ is a center for visitors to the Península Valdés and Punta Tombo. It is a spruce seaside town with extensive sands, and flamingos in the bay. The **Museo Oceanográfico y de Ciencias Naturales** (open daily), on the corner of Domecq and García Menéndez, is worth a visit for its collections of coastal and marine flora and fauna.

Don't miss the magnificent **EcoCentro**, Julio Verne 3784 (open Tues–Sun). where local marine life is fascinatingly explained in various interactive displays and exhibits.

Punta Tombo, 165 km (102 miles) south of Madryn (108 km/67 miles of which is dirt road), has the largest colony of Magellanic penguins in the world. The penguins arrive in September and stay until March. In this colony you can literally walk among thousands of these comical birds as they come and go along well-defined "penguin highways" that link their nests with the sea across the tourist path, and see them fish near the coast for their meals.

The **Península Valdés ⓬** is one of the most important wildlife reserves in Argentina and designated a World Heritage site in 1999. It is the breeding ground for southern right whales, elephant seals, and sea lions, and the nesting site for thousands of shore birds, including pelicans, cormorants, and oyster-catchers. Guanacos, rheas, and maras can all be spotted with sharp eyes. There

Map on page 292

One of Gaiman's Welsh-built solid brick houses, dating from the late 1800s.

BELOW: Cerro Guanaco, towering over the Río Negro.

The Welsh in Patagonia

Patagonia is partly pampas, largely desert and unrelentingly wind-blown, with only small areas of fertile soil and little discovered mineral wealth. Why would anyone leave the lush valleys and green hills of Wales to settle in such a place? The Welsh came, between 1865 and 1914, partly to escape conditions in Wales which they deemed culturally oppressive, partly because of the promise – later discovered to be exaggerated – of exciting economic opportunities, and largely to be able to pursue their religious traditions in their own language.

The disruptions of the 19th-century industrial revolution uprooted many Welsh agricultural workers; the cost of delivering produce to market became exorbitant because of turnpike fees, grazing land was enclosed and landless laborers were exploited. Increasing domination of public life by arrogant English officials further upset the Welsh. Thus alienated in his own land, the Welshman left.

Equally powerful was the effect on the Welsh people of the religious revivals of the period, which precipitated a pietistic religiosity that continued beyond World War I. For many, the worldliness of modern life made impossible the quiet spirituality of earlier times, and they saw their escape in distant, unpopulated areas of the world then opening up. Some had already tried Canada and the United States and were frustrated by the tides of other European nationalities which threatened the purity of their communities. They responded when Argentina offered cheap land to immigrants who would settle and develop its vast spaces before an aggressive Chile pre-empted them. From the United States and from Wales they came in small ships on hazardous voyages to Puerto Madryn, and settled in the Chubut Valley.

Although the hardships of those gritty pioneers are more than a century behind their descendants, the pioneer tradition is proudly remembered. Some remain in agriculture, many are in trade and commerce. Only a dwindling number of the older generation still speaks Welsh, but descendants will proudly show you their chapels and cemeteries (very similar to those in Wales), take you for Welsh tea in one of the area's many tea houses, and reminisce about their forebears and the difficulties they overcame. They speak of the devastating floods of the Chubut which almost demolished the community at the turn of the 20th century, the scouts who went on indigenous trails to the Andean foothills to settle in the Cwm Hyfrwd (the Beautiful Valley), the loneliness of the prairies in the long cold winters, the incessant winds, and the lack of capital which made all undertakings a matter of backbreaking labor.

Unfortunately, the old ways are being discarded in our modern technological era. The Welsh language will not long be spoken in Patagonia. But traditions are still upheld, and descendants of the Patagonian Welsh still hold Eisteddfods to compete in song and verse. They revere the tradition of the chapel even when they do not attend, and they take enormous pride in their links with Wales. ❑

LEFT: a Welsh farmer proud of his crop.

is an interpretive center and museum at the entrance to the peninsula (entrance fee) itself, which is a large wasteland, with the lowest point on the South American continent, 40 meters (132 ft) below sea level. Some 40,000 elephant seals are found along a 200-km (125-mile) stretch of coastline, the outer edge of the Valdés Peninsula – the only such colony accessible by land outside Antarctica. Most of the beach is protected but tourists have a chance to observe the wildlife from specially constructed viewing hides at **Punta Norte** and **Caleta Valdés**, where two reserves have been established. About 10,000 elephant seal pups are born each year from late August to early November.

Whale watching

Puerto Pirámides, 95 km (59 miles) from Puerto Madryn, was once a major center for whaling and trading in seal skins. In the 19th century there were more than 700 whalers operating in these waters. An international protection treaty was signed in 1935, and since then the whale population has recovered slowly, now standing at about 2,000. The whales come to breed near these shores around July and stay until mid-December. Whale watching is concentrated on mother and calf pairs and is organized by a few authorized, experienced boat owners from Puerto Pirámides *(see page 364)*. On shore, you can observe the sea lions and cormorant colonies from a viewing platform at the foot of the pyramid-shaped cliff that gives this location its name.

There are a couple of hotels and a shoreside camping site where you can wake to the sound of whales blowing in the bay. It is an ideal center for exploring the peninsula's other wildlife sites, too, although if you hire a vehicle, beware of the tricky driving conditions. On the small side road out of the peninsula stands a

Map on page 292

Years ago, huge quantities of salt were extracted from salt-pits on the Península Valdés, and shipped out from Puerto Madryn.

LEFT: a Welsh Bible in the chapel.
BELOW: a Welsh gravestone.

A preserved tree trunk in the Bosque Petrificado José Ormachea.

monument dedicated to the first Spanish settlement here, which only lasted from 1774 to 1810, when the settlers were forced to flee from the native warriors. Here too, is a sea bird reserve, the **Isla de los Pájaros**.

Oil country

Some 440 km (270 miles) down the coast south of Trelew is Patagonia's major city, **Comodoro Rivadavia** ⓭, with a population exceeding 160,000. Its airport has daily flights connecting the Patagonian cities and Buenos Aires.

In 1907, while a desperate search for drinking water was underway, oil was discovered here. Since then, this has become one of the most important oil-producing regions in the country, and the vast landscape is strewn with "nodding donkey" oil pumps. The town witnessed the immigration of Boers from the Transvaal and the Orange State in South Africa, who left their homeland in search of a new place to live after the Boer War. The first arrivals landed in 1903, under the leadership of Conrad Visser and Martin Venter. Although some returned to South Africa, there are still many of their descendants living in the region. Today, Comodoro Rivadavia is a typical Patagonian city, with flat roofs, tall buildings, fisheries, textile factories, and the ever-present Patagonian wind.

Colonia Sarmiento ⓮, 190 km (118 miles) west of Comodoro Rivadavia, lies in a fertile valley flanked by two huge lakes, lagos Musters and Colhué Huapi, which attract black-necked swans. Heading south from the valley for 30 km (19 miles), you reach the **Bosque Petrificado José Ormachea**, which has remains that are more than a million years old. This forest tells us much of the geological past of this land, which a long time ago was covered in trees.

BELOW: wildlife in action at the Península Valdés.

Santa Cruz

The Province of **Santa Cruz** is the second largest in Argentina but with the smallest population per square kilometer. Most of Santa Cruz is dry grassland or semi-desert, with high *mesetas* (plateaux) interspersed with protected valleys and covered with large sheep *estancias*.

Ruta 3, nearly all of which is paved, is the province's main coastal road. It follows the shoreline of Golfo San Jorge south to the oil town of **Caleta Olivia** ⓯, with its huge central statue of an oil worker, then climbs inland. After 86 km (53 miles), Ruta 281 branches off Ruta 3 for 126 km (78 miles) to the coastal port of **Puerto Deseado** ⓰, named after the *Desire*, flagship of the 16th-century English global navigator, Thomas Cavendish.

Virtually unknown for many years, Puerto Deseado is the home base for a number of ships which fish in the western South Atlantic. It is beginning to develop as a tourist center, particularly for its rich coastal wildlife. There are sea lion colonies at Cabo Blanco to the north, and Isla Pingüino to the south of the bay, where you might see yellow-crested penguins and the unusual Guanay cormorant, and where spectacular black and white Commerson's dolphins play with boats in the estuary just outside the town.

Back on Ruta 3, the next important stop is a pristine natural wonder, the **Monumento Natural Bosques**

Petrificados ⓱, just 80 km (50 miles) to the west of the highway. This enormous petrified forest occupies over 10,000 hectares (247,000 acres). At the edges of canyons and *mesas*, the rock-hard trunks of 150 million-year-old monkey puzzle trees stick out of the ground. Some trunks are 30 meters (100 ft) long and a meter (a yard) thick – among the largest in the world. A visit to this natural monument is for a day only; it closes at sundown, but there is a campsite at La Paloma, with a store.

Map on page 292

Explorers' remnants

About 250 km (155 miles) further south on Ruta 3 is the picturesque port of **Puerto San Julián** ⓲, also awakening to tourism, with several hotels and a small museum. Both Magellan (in 1520) and Drake (in 1578) spent the winter here and hanged mutineers on the eastern shore. Nothing remains there except a small plaque. Not far to the south of San Julián is the little town of **Comandante Luis Piedra Buena** ⓳, on the Río Santa Cruz, which was followed upstream by Fitzroy, Moreno, and other early explorers. Its main attraction is the tiny shack on Isla Pavón, occupied in 1859 by Piedra Buena, an Argentine naval hero. The island, on the river, is linked to the town by road bridge.

Downstream (29 km/18 miles) is the sleepy town of **Puerto Santa Cruz**, with its port, Punta Quilla, the base for ships that service the offshore oil rigs.

Gateway to national parks

The capital of the province is **Río Gallegos** ⓴, some 180 km (112 miles) south of Puerto Santa Cruz. It is a sprawling city of 80,000 on the south bank of the eponymous river, which has the third-highest tides in the world, at 16 meters (53

BELOW:
oil pumps in the
Patagonian South.

ft). At low tide, ships are left high and dry on mud flats. It is perhaps one of the most austere places in Argentina, but it has some historic appeal if you're interested in industrial heritage. There are several museums and signs designate historical spots. The enormous Swift meat packing plant has been abandoned, but the train yards, with several old engines, still receive coal from the Río Turbio, on the opposite side of the province. The town's main function for tourism however, is for visitors heading inland to the lovely scenic areas of El Calafate on Lago Argentino, the Parque Nacional Los Glaciares, and to Punta Arenas and the Parque Nacional Torres del Paine in Chile.

Moving southwest of Río Gallegos, Ruta 3 enters Chile near a series of rims of long-extinct volcanoes. One of these, Laguna Azul, is a geological reserve, 3 km (1½ miles) off the main highway near the border post.

Penguins and dolphins

Some 11 km (6 miles) south of Río Gallegos, Ruta 1 branches southeast off Ruta 3, over open plains to **Cabo Vírgenes** (129 km/80 miles from Río Gallegos) and Punta Dungeness (on the border with Chile) at the northeast mouth of the Strait of Magellan. Here you can see Argentina's second-largest penguin colony, home to some 300,000 birds, visit the lighthouse, and perhaps watch dolphins just offshore. Near the cliffs are the meagre remains of Ciudad Nombre de Jesús, founded by the Spanish explorer, Pedro Sarmiento de Gamboa in 1584. The road to Cabo Virgenes passes a couple of sheep farms: Estancia Cóndor, one of the larger *estancias* in the area, and a few kilometers beyond that is Estancia Monte Dinero, which has a separate guest house for visitors and which also offers wildlife trips to Cabo Virgenes (tel: 0966-426 900).

BELOW: the empty coastline of Santa Cruz.

Westward on Ruta 40

Western Santa Cruz is spectacular but desolate. The main route through it is on **Ruta 40** – the longest road in the country, snaking its way up through the northwest as far as the Bolivian border – and not a road to be taken lightly. Those who have traveled it from top to bottom are full of admiration for the rugged beauty of the country and are proud they have survived it. Ruta 40 is not even accurately detailed on most maps, including those of the prestigious Instituto Geográfico Militar. The best one is the ACA (Automóvil Club Argentino) map of the Province of Santa Cruz. In winter, some parts of the road may be inaccessible.

Southern Ruta 40 is a gravel road – rocky and dusty when dry, muddy when wet. Places marked on the map may consist of just one shack or may not exist at all. You must carry extra fuel and/or go out of your way at several places to refill. Sometimes small towns, or even larger ones run out of gasoline and you may have to wait several days until a fuel truck comes. In southwestern Patagonia there are gas stations only at Perito Moreno, Bajo Caracoles, Tres Lagos, El Calafate, and Río Turbio.

If you take any secondary roads, remember that there is no fuel available. You also need to carry spare tires, some food, and probably even your bed. There are few places to buy food or even a soft drink outside the larger towns. El Calafate is the main town of the southern Lake District, 313 km (194 miles) from Río Gallegos. Halfway there is Esperanza, a truck stop with a gas station and roadside snack bar; nearby is Estancia Chali-Aike which takes paying guests. Most of the drive is past ranches over the *meseta central*, coming to a high lookout at Cuesta de Miguez, where the whole of Lake Argentino, the mountains and glaciers beyond, and even Mount Fitz Roy can be seen.

Map on page 292

BELOW: the José Ormachea Petrified Forest Reserve.

El Calafate **㉑**, a town of about 3,200, nestles at the base of cliffs on the south shore of beautiful **Lago Argentino**, one of Argentina's largest lakes. An airport constructed in 2000 receives direct flights from Buenos Aires and this is the jumping-off point for the surrounding area, particularly to the Parque Nacional los Glaciares. On the eastern shore of Lago Argentino, at the edge of town, is Laguna Nimes, a small bird reserve, which is home to a variety of ducks, geese, flamingos, and elegant black-necked swans. Walking around the lake from here is tricky however, as the ground is boggy and criss-crossed with wide streams. Accommodations range from camp sites and a youth hostel to elegant hotels. There are several tourist agencies and a number of good restaurants. Large tour groups do the circuit – Buenos Aires, Puerto Madryn, El Calafate, Ushuaia, Buenos Aires – every week.

The Hotel Los Alamos, one of the best hotels in El Calafate and a typical example of the locally popular, Alpine-style architecture.

BELOW: El Calafate, on the shores of Lago Argentino.

Parque Nacional los Glaciares

Traveling 51 km (32 miles) west of El Calafate, along the south shore of the Península Magallanes, brings you to the **Parque Nacional Los Glaciares ㉒**, one of the most spectacular parks in Argentina. The southern Patagonian ice cap, which is about 400 km (250 miles) long, spills over into innumerable glaciers *(ventisqueros)*, which end on high cliffs or wend their way down to fjords. Just beyond the Península Magallanes, you can cross Brazo Rico in a boat for a guided climb on the World Heritage Site of the glacier of **Ventisquero Perito Moreno**. A few kilometers on, the road ends at the *pasarelas*, a series of walkways and terraces down a steep cliff, which faces the glacier head on. It's a magnificent sight, especially on a sunny day. Visitors line up along the walkways, cameras at the ready like paparazzi at the Oscar awards ceremony, waiting for a

chunk of glacier to calve off into the water with a resounding thunderous crack.

The Perito Moreno glacier advances across the narrow stretch of water in front of it until it cuts off Brazo Rico and Brazo Sur from the rest of Lago Argentino. Pressure slowly builds up behind the glacial wall until, about every three to four years, the wall collapses dramatically and the cycle begins again. The glacier has not advanced since 1988, however, leading scientists to question whether global warming is to blame: 90 percent of the world's glaciers are retreating. Old water levels can be seen around these lakes. Hiking too near the glacial front, is prohibited because of the danger from waves caused by falling ice.

Upsala Glacier

The second major trip from El Calafate is a visit to the **Ventisquero Upsala**, at the far northwest end of Lago Argentino. Boats leave every morning from Punta Bandera, 40 km (25 miles) west of El Calafate. In early spring, they cannot get near Upsala because of the large field of icebergs, so may visit Spegazzini and other glaciers instead. Some trips stop for a short walk through the forest to Onelli glacier. On the way back, stop at Estancia Alice, on the road to El Calafate. *Asados* (barbecues) and tea are available here, and shearing demonstrations are held in season. You may also see black-necked swans and other birds.

It is only a short distance across the Sierra Los Baguales from Parque Nacional Los Glaciares, Argentina, to Parque Nacional Torres del Paine, in Chile. From some spots near El Calafate, the Paine mountains can be seen. But there is no road through. Instead, you must backtrack to Puerto El Cerrito (at least that section is paved) and then take Ruta 40 again west and south to enter Chile either at Cancha Carrera or further south at Río Turbio. You can also fly back to Río Gallegos and fly on to Punta Arenas, in Chile, from where it is still a seven-hour drive north to the Paine National Park.

Some 230 km (143 miles) south of El Calafate, **Río Turbio** is a coal mining town little visited by tourists although it does have an airport and a small skiing center nearby. From here, Ruta 40 makes a winding loop across the bottom of the province, then heads east to meet Ruta 3 just west of Río Gallegos.

Monte Fitz Roy

Returning north, up Ruta 40 from El Calafate, at the far northern end of the Parque Nacional Los Glaciares are some of the most impressive peaks in the Andes, including Cerro Torre (3,128 meters/10,263 ft) and Monte Fitz Roy (3,406 meters/11,175 ft). In good weather Fitz Roy can be seen from El Calafate. The sheer granite peaks attract climbers from all over the world, who describe their experiences in the register at the northern entrance to the park.

The best base for visiting this part of the national park is the tiny village of **El Chaltén ㉓**, some 90 km (56 miles) west, off Ruta 40, above the western end of **Lago Viedma**. The village – whose name means "blue mountain," the Amerindian name for Fitz Roy – nestles in a hidden bowl at the foot of the mountain, with its glacier coming down off the Southern Patagonian Ice Field. This enchanting little place is well worth a visit, and is growing in popularity with

Map on page 292

A shop in El Calafate selling handmade chocolates – a local specialty.

BELOW: the Perito Moreno Glacier.

Map
on page
292

visiting trekkers and mountain climbers. It has a national park information office, as well as a range of accommodations including holiday bungalows and basic camp sites. There are two or three very small stores, no fuel, and no telephones. El Chaltén shuts down from April to October. In summer, there are two daily buses from El Calafate, 219 km (136 miles) to the south.

Continuing north on Ruta 40, at Tres Lagos, Ruta 31 leads northwest to **Lago San Martín** (called Lago O'Higgins in Chile). Estancia La Maipú is situated on the south shore, offering accommodations, horseriding and trekking activities.

About 560 km (348 miles) north of El Chaltén, the northwesternmost town in Santa Cruz province is **Perito Moreno**, a dusty place with little to offer. From here however, a paved road leads 57 km (35 miles) west to the small town of **Los Antiguos ㉔**, on the shore of Lago Buenos Aires. Small farms here produce milk, honey, fruit, and vegetables; the town has one hotel and a campsite. Three km (1½ miles) to the west, you can cross the Chilean border to the town of Chile Chico and other scenic areas near the Río Baker.

Cave paintings

South of Perito Moreno is the **Cueva de las Manos** (Cave of the Hands), a national historical monument and World Heritage Site located in a beautiful canyon 56 km (35 miles) off Ruta 40 from just north of Bajo Caracoles. Pre-Columbian cave paintings are found all over Santa Cruz, but those at Cueva de las Manos are the finest. The walls here are covered by 1,000-year-old paintings of hands and animals, principally guanacos (relatives of the llama). Numerous lakes straddle the Argentine–Chilean border in this region. Ruta 40 lies well to the east of the mountains. Any excursions to the lakes to the west, such as Lago Ghio, Pueyrredón, Belgrano, and San Martín, must be made along side roads; there are no circuits – you must go in and out on the same road. The road to Lago Pueyrredón leaves from Bajo Caracoles.

Parque Nacional Perito Moreno ㉕ (not to be confused with the town of the same name) is the next major stop, 72 km (45 miles) to the west of Ruta 40. In the distance is Monte San Lorenzo, the highest peak in Santa Cruz at 3,706 meters (12,150 ft). Within the park are lakes Belgrano and Burmeister. Near the latter is the Casa de Piedra, a strange rock formation with ancient paintings.

Buses and Planes

For most visitors to southern Patagonia and beyond, the best way to get there is by air. Major airlines stop only at Río Gallegos, but smaller airlines, such as Kaikén, El Pinguino, and ARC fly to various towns, especially El Calafate. Some towns have an aeroclub which will take visitors on local photographic flights. Several bus companies operate on Ruta 3 from Buenos Aires to Río Gallegos and from Gallegos there are daily buses to El Calafate and Punta Arenas, in Chile. There are no bus services to Tierra del Fuego; most people move across the Strait of Magellan by plane or by car via the ferry from Punta Delgada to Puerto Espora at the Primera Angostura (First Narrows), about two hours' drive from Río Gallegos, within Chilean territory. ❑

BELOW: Lago Espejo in the northern Lake District.
RIGHT: stacking hay in Chubut.

SAFARI TO THE SOUTHERN STEPPE

In the vast and lonely expanses of Patagonia, people are far outnumbered by the region's wild inhabitants, ranging from condors to cougars

From its harsh interior to its strikingly beautiful coast, Patagonia is tailor-made for wildlife watching. Grey foxes are a common sight almost everywhere, and the open steppe is home to Patagonian hares or *maras*, to rheas (relatives of the ostrich), and to the elusive puma or cougar. Patches of marshy ground are good places to watch southern lapwings – probably Patagonia's noisiest birds – while to the west, the foothills of the Andes offer a good chance to spot condors as they soar high overhead in search of food. However, for most visitors, Patagonia's biggest attraction is its coastal wildlife, and the best time to see it is during the southern spring and summer, when penguins, seals, and whales all gather along the shore to breed.

WHALE-WATCHING

Like seals and penguins, Patagonia's whales are animals of fixed habits, breeding at the same sites year after year. The Península Valdés is one of the most famous of them all, hosting over 10 percent of the world's southern right whale population for three or four months each year. With so many of these huge, docile mammals crowded into the peninsula's bays, the result is a wildlife spectacle not to be missed, and whale-watching boat trips can be organized locally.

▷ **UNDERGROUND OWL**
In a bleak, treeless landscape, burrowing owls raise their young under-ground. These birds feed by night and day, often on insects.

▷ **PENINSULA VALDES**
Despite its barren landscape, this peninsula in northern Patagonia is one of the country's richest sites for shore birds and sea mammals.

△ **RAPID EXIT**
With its strange bouncing run, the Patagonian hare or *mara* can speed along at 45 km/h (28 mph). True hares – from Europe – are also common here.

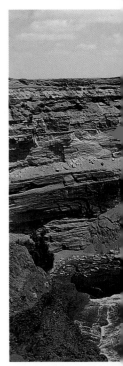

△ **SOCIAL BIRDS**
Huge rookeries of Magellanic penguins can be seen on the Península Valdés and the adjacent coastline.

▷ **TOP CAT**
Puma has one of the biggest ranges of any cat – Patagonia to western Canada.

WHERE TO SPOT THE WILDLIFE

Wildlife tourism is still in its infancy in Patagonia, but the locals are catching up fast. In towns like Trelew wildlife excursions to the coast are easy to pick up, although they are rarely cheap. Be aware also that the distances involved here can be very large: with day-trips especially, you may find that you spend a lot of time on the move.

The penguin breeding season runs from about October to March, with the down-covered chicks hatching from late November onwards. The biggest colony – and the most visited one by far – is at Punta Tombo. The colony at Cabo dos Bahías, further down the coast, is more time-consuming to reach, but offers the added attraction of other kinds of wildlife, including rheas and numerous guanacos.

In the Península Valdés, the whale-watching season extends from June to December – roughly from early winter to early summer. To make the most of this spectacular area it's worth staying here for several days.

◁ **ON THE ALERT**
Patagonian foxes are hunted mainly for their fur, but they still skillfully manage to survive in large numbers.

△ **LATE LUNCH**
A condor picks over a carcass high up in the Andes. These carrion-eating birds can be seen all the way down the Andes to the far south of Patagonia.

◁ **BLACK-NECKED SWANS**
These distinctive birds live mainly in freshwater lakes and marshes, although they occasionally feed on the coast.

THE UTTERMOST SOUTH

Wild and windswept Tierra del Fuego has been the ultimate challenge to travelers and explorers since the early days of global navigation and discovery

Map on page 328

Tierra del Fuego, the Land of Fire, lies at the southern tip of the South American continent. Beyond is only the icy mass of Antarctica. You really feel that you have reached the end of the earth here, in a wild, mysterious land. The very name evokes feelings of distance, fear of the elements, isolation, and loneliness. Shrieking gales, towering waves, desolation – these are some of the images of what is considered the extremity of the world. But the feeling of isolation should be an invigorating one, allied with a spirit of adventure.

In the days of sail, many people – the early merchants, explorers, and scientists – were able to claim that they had rounded Cape Horn. Some were shipwrecked there, but few stayed to settle. With the opening of the Panama Canal in 1914, fewer ships took the southernmost route. By then, Europeans had settled parts of Tierra del Fuego, but it was difficult for tourists to reach.

Over the past 35 years this has changed; Tierra del Fuego is now "in" for the discerning traveler. And although all the above images can be true enough, most visitors are pleasantly surprised by the uttermost south. The best months to visit are October to April.

Geography and climate

Eons ago, Tierra del Fuego rested under the sea. Then the land slowly rose up and mountains were formed as the great tectonic plates pushed together; the Fuegian Archipelago is one of the places in the world where this geological phenomenon can be seen most readily. Glacial ages came and went; at their height, most of what is now the Patagonian continental shelf was land. The waters of the Strait of Magellan broke through the tip of the continent some 9,000 years ago, isolating Tierra del Fuego from Patagonia.

Technically speaking, Tierra del Fuego includes all the land south of the Strait of Magellan and north of the Drake Passage, although only one island, the Isla Grande, is actually called Tierra del Fuego. Locally, the Isla Grande is known simply as "La Isla." It is surrounded, to the south and west, by a maze of mountainous islands, islets, channels, and fjords, most of them uninhabited and many unexplored.

The Fuegian Archipelago is well within the Subantarctic Zone. Its cool climate is dominated by the prevailing southwesterly winds which sweep in off the South Pacific and waters further south. These often gale-force winds can occur throughout the year but are strongest from the end of August to March (spring and summer). You can circle the globe at this point without meeting other land. Early sailors described this area as the "Roaring Forties, the Furious Fifties, the Screaming Sixties."

PRECEDING PAGES: Fuegian king crab rivals Alaska's in size and taste. **BELOW:** Isla de los Estados. **LEFT:** figurehead in Ushuaia's museum

The Andes, curving from northwest to east across the archipelago, ensure high rain over the western and southern islands, leaving less moisture for the northeastern plains. Temperatures along the Beagle Channel range from a record high of 30°C (86°F) in summer to a record low of about –14°C (7°F) in winter. Temperatures in the plains region are more extreme, but all of Tierra del Fuego lives in a perpetual "cool spring."

Exploration and settlement

Humans arrived on the archipelago in two ways. The earliest record is a 11,800-year-old site in northern Tierra del Fuego, occupied by nomadic hunters – people who, near the end of the last ice age, crossed the Magellanic land bridge before waters broke through it. In southern Tierra del Fuego, the oldest adaptation to a marine environment is a 6,000-year-old site at Tunel on the Beagle Channel, developed by canoe peoples. On the arrival of the Europeans, four cultural groups populated the area: the Ona (Shelknam) and Haush were the guanaco-hunters of the plains, while the Yahgans (Yámana) and Alaculuf were the spear-hunting canoe natives of the islands and channels. Eliminated mainly by white man's diseases, less than five pure members remain of the first three groups, although there are many mixed-people of mixed race.

The European exploration of Tierra del Fuego – first by Magellan in 1520, then by pirates, explorers, collectors, scientists, sealers and whalers, missionaries, seekers of gold, and merchants – is among the most fascinating in the world. Many tourists visit Tierra del Fuego because of childhood memories of stories of Drake, Cook, and Darwin, or the arduous, careful surveys of Fitzroy and King. One book, *Uttermost Part of the Earth* written by E. Lucas Bridges

Map of Tierra del Fuego, marking the southern limit of Ruta 3.

BELOW: back from the barber's.

in 1946, towers above the others as one of the world's great adventure stories *(see page 330)*. Bridges tells how his father, Thomas Bridges, began the Anglican Mission in Ushuaia (1869), explored unknown areas, worked with and taught the Yahgans and finally settled the first farm. The missionaries were followed by a coastguards' station, gold miners, sheep farmers, small merchants, oil workers, and all those needed to make up a modern town. In one short century, Tierra del Fuego has gone from a land of near-naked natives to a major tourist destination for cruise liners and in the past even occasionally a Concorde charter.

Map on page 328

Across the strait

Politically, Tierra del Fuego is split between Chile (to the west and south) and Argentina (north and east). The Argentine section is part of the Provincia de Tierra del Fuego, Antártida e Islas del Atlántico Sur, with its capital in the town of Ushuaia. The rough triangle that is Argentina's part of the Isla Grande covers some 21,340 sq km (8,300 sq miles).

Visitors arrive by several means. Aerolíneas Argentinas, Austral, and smaller airlines provide daily flights from Buenos Aires and other areas. Tourist ships visit Ushuaia briefly as part of longer cruises between Río de Janeiro, Buenos Aires, and the west coast of South America. Ushuaia, like Punta Arenas in Chile, is a jumping-off point for a number of ships to Antarctica.

Visitors coming by land must cross the Strait of Magellan by ferry, either at the First Narrows (a 20–30 minute barge crossing) or between Punta Arenas and Porvenir (a two- to three-hour crossing). There are no regular bus routes between Río Gallegos and Río Grande (charter services may be available), but there are two routes between Río Grande and Ushuaia.

BELOW: a sheep farm near Río Grande.

An Ona man, from
E. Lucas Bridges'
The Uttermost Part
of the Earth *(1946),*
the classic portrayal
of the Amerindians of
Tierra del Fuego.

BELOW: signpost
in Ushuaia.

Flora and fauna

Plant and animal life in this subantarctic climate is less varied in species than in warmer regions. Only six kinds of trees are found; the dominant three are species of Nothofagus or southern beech. Several kinds of shrubs produce beautiful flowers or edible berries. The most famous is the calafate *(Berberis buxifolia)*; legend says you will come back again if you brave its long thorns to eat the delicious, seedy berries. Most wildflowers are small but well worth searching for. Flowering plants and ferns total about 500 species, but some 150 of these have been introduced or naturalized.

Native land animals are few: the guanaco, Fuegian fox (or Andean wolf), bats, tucu-tucu, and mice. An abundance of introduced animals, such as beaver, muskrats, rabbits, and Patagonian foxes thrive here. About 200 species of birds are resident or visit. Surprisingly, this cool climate is also home to parrots (the austral conure), flamingos, and hummingbirds. The sea is highly productive in algae, with the result that 27 species of whale visit the archipelago.

Escaping the northern winter

Many visitors find the northern plains of Tierra del Fuego rather barren, but there is much to do and see. Those arriving by road must enter from Chile at **Bahía San Sebastián ❶**, where there is border control, a small *hostería* (reservations with the Argentine Automobile Club, ACA), a restaurant, and a gas station. Enormous mud flats, periodically covered by 11-meter (36-ft) tides, extend along the west of the bay. This is an important feeding area for thousands of small birds which escape the northern-hemisphere winter here; the entire coast is part of the Hemispheric Shorebird Reserve network.

Gold, fossils, and sheep

This is sheep-farming and oil country, where wells dot the grasslands and rolling hills. The eastern Strait of Magellan, in Chile, is peppered with oil platforms. Oil supply roads run in all directions, while sheep, cattle, guanacos, and wild geese graze among them. In winter, guanacos can be seen along any of the secondary roads. The best way to see them in summer is to drive north along the bay from the San Sebastián border post.

A 45-minute drive will take you to the base of the stony, super-barren **Península El Páramo**, but family groups of guanacos can be seen on the salt flats long before that. The base of the Páramo was once the main site of the gold rush (1887–98). Julius Popper set up his mining operation here and became the dictator of the northern plains. Today, nothing remains of his buildings, dredges, or cemetery.

Cliffs along the coast near Cabo Espíritu Santo and the roads near San Sebastián yield both marine and forest fossils, attesting to bygone eras. Sandstone hills farther south are littered with fossil shells and crabs. The plains may look yellow or brown and appear to have little life, but this is Tierra del Fuego's best sheep land. If you stop to look and listen, you will discover many birds. A short walk may reveal hidden wildflowers.

Going southeast toward Río Grande, **Estancia Sara**, Tierra del Fuego's second-largest sheep station, looks like a small town. In the old days, the *estancias* were essentially towns: each had its workshops, gardens, bakery, club, and library for the workmen. Before the days of oil, sheep farming was the main industry of northern Fuegia. Thousands of sheep, mainly Corriedale, covered the plains. The larger farms produced (and still do) world-class, prize-winning pedigree sheep. *Estancias* such as Sara once had 75 employees; low wool prices, higher wages and difficulty in finding good workmen has reduced that to 15.

Further south down Ruta 3 is the **Escuela Agrotécnica Salesiana**, which functions on the site of the Salesian Mission to the Onas, established in 1897. It is now a national monument. The original church and several other buildings have been restored; there is a small museum of artifacts and mounted birds.

Río Grande

The town of **Río Grande ❷** (population 56,000) is the center of the sheep and oil region, as well as the home of a number of companies producing television sets, radios, synthetics and other products – the result of a special 1972 law designed to bring development and more residents to this far reach of the republic. This produced a boom-town atmosphere in the 1980s.

Río Grande sprawls over the flat northern coast of the river. The wide, windblown streets overlook the waters of the South Atlantic. The Río Grande has silted up, allowing for little shipping. A wide bridge crosses it to the *Frigorífico*, a modern meat-packing plant on its southeast coast. Lambs from this freezer were once considered choice in Europe, but various difficulties have kept recent production low.

Río Grande has a cultural center, a number of video clubs, but no movie theater. The municipal

Map on page 328

TIP

A popular site for keen fossil hunters is Cabo Domingo, up the coast just to the north of Río Grande, and near to the Salesian Mission Museum.

BELOW: a glacial valley along the Beagle Channel.

Homesteads in Tierra del Fuego are sparsely scattered, with neighbors few and far between.

Museo de Ciencias Naturales e Historia (open daily, weekends pm only), on Calle Elcano near the sea, is well worth a visit.

This is Tierra del Fuego's fishing center. Trout (rainbow, brook, and brown) and salmon were introduced in the 1930s, and reach record sizes. Until recently fishing was open in all areas, permission being needed only to cross *estancia* land. Now access to this land can be gained only with guides and there is a charge. The Río Grande is ideal for sea-run brown trout. Best fishing times are January to March and upmarket *estancias* are the ideal choice as a fishing base.

Ruta 3 runs out on the opposite side of Río Grande from the bridge, circling southwest to cross another bridge and head toward Ushuaia. Near the airport, just west of town, Ruta C leads westward to **Estancia María Behety**, a picturesque village with an enormous shearing shed (room for 40 shearers), which is reported to be the world's largest. This local road then meanders northwest and west near the Chilean border. Some sections of this road are paved with fossils; muddier sections can become a quagmire in wet weather.

Back on Ruta 3, **Estancia José Menéndez** can be seen in the distance on the south side of the Río Grande. It is a picturesque old *estancia* set in grassy, rolling hills, and was the first farm in northern Tierra del Fuego. The original, like other large farms, has been divided up into five smaller *estancias*.

Forest and mountain

Near Estancia José Menéndez, rutas B, D, E, and F branch off to the west or southwest into the mountains, and cover steep hills, plains, forest, *vegas* (damp meadows) and *estancias* – fascinating for exploration, if you have time.

The gravel **Ruta B** leads westward, roughly parallel to the Río Grande, pass-

BELOW: headed for the shearer's.

WHAT'S IN A NAME?

The story goes that Tierra del Fuego (Land of Fire) got its name from early European explorers, who, when passing by on ships en route to riches further west, could see the landscape dotted with the campfires of the islands' original inhabitants.

This theory was expanded upon by Lucas Bridges (1874–1949), the son of an English missionary who spent his life in Tierra del Fuego and who wrote an account of frontier life among the Amerindians, *The Uttermost Part of the Earth*: "If a distant sail appeared, or anything else occurred to startle those who had remained at home, they [the Yahgan] would send out a signal to those away fishing by piling green branches or shrubs on the wigwam fire. At the sight of the black signal smoke the fishers would hurry back home. The early explorers of that archipelago would see these countless columns of smoke rising at short intervals for miles along the coast."

Perhaps the final word on the matter can be found in Bruce Chatwin's *In Patagonia*: "The fires were the camp fires of the Fuegian Indians. In one version Magellan saw smoke only and called it Tierra del Humo, the Land of Smoke, but Charles V said there was no smoke without fire and changed the name."

ing the farms Cauchicol, Despedida, Aurelia, San José, and San Justo, near the Chilean border. The *vega* lands are full of sheep and cattle, and the rivers with trout. *Kau-tapen* ("fishing-house" in Ona) on Estancia La Retranca and San José are exclusive fishing lodges.

Rutas D and **E** run parallel to each other going southwest from Ruta B and Estancia toward the mountains. Although very picturesque, there are no particular tourist facilities.

Ruta F winds almost south into the heart of Tierra del Fuego, up and down the steep glacial moraines to reach lakes Yehuin and Chepelmesh. There it joins **Ruta H**, which runs eastward from the Yéhuin over the hills to meet Ruta 3 near Estancia Indiana. There are several sawmills in the area and among the hills to the south. **Lago Yehuin**, favored for camping, and the Río Claro to the west are good fishing areas being developed for tourism.

South of Río Grande

Driving to Ushuaia along Ruta 3 is an education in ecology, for one goes from the flat sea coast through hilly, grassy plains and *vegas*, from low bush land on to scrubby deciduous forest (*ñire* or "low beech"); then, turning inland, the road climbs to healthier deciduous forest (*lenga* or "high beech"); up the mountain slopes nearly to the treeline, and then down on the south side of the mountains to thick forest interspersed with evergreen beech (*coihue* or *guindo)* and valleys filled with sphagnum swamps. Ruta 3 is paved from San Sebastián to near Tolhuin. All other roads are gravel.

Shortly after entering the northern forests, **Ruta A** runs eastward over high hills and grassy valleys to Cabo San Pablo, another favorite picnic spot. This road continues for some distance beyond San Pablo, as far as Estancia María Luisa, but it is not always in good condition. The eastern point of Tierra del Fuego is a mostly unused wilderness of forest, swamp, and mountain and can be reached only on foot, horseback, or helicopter.

Meandering southward, Ruta 3 follows the valley of the Río Ewan, gradually rising to a divide which separates the waters running into the South Atlantic from those of the Lago Fagnano or Kami, which flow westward into Chile to empty via the Río Azopardo into Seno Almirantazgo (Admiralty Sound).

The small town of **Tolhuin ❸** lies just north of the 100-km (60-mile) long Lago Fagnano, in the heart of the island. The word Tolhuin is the Ona name for a nearby heart-shaped hill. Take the back road out of town to the beach on Lago Fagnano, a popular site with fishing facilities, and a place for barbecues. Seen from here, the lake allegedly takes on a fascinating range of colors in different light conditions. Ruta 3 then follows the south shore of Lago Fagnano. The south coast of the lake has several small bays, formed when the land dropped during a 1949 earthquake. The highway turns inland past burnt-over forest and sawmills to wind up the mountains at **Paso Garibaldi**. Although sawmills here were once prosperous, pine imported from Chile is cheaper and generally used for construction. In the valley just north of the pass

Map on page 328

BELOW: the firebrush *(notro)* blossom, a commonly seen blaze of color on the hillsides.

lies the tranquil Laguna Escondida. Be sure to stop at the lookout on Paso Garibaldi to look north over Laguna Escondida and Lago Fagnano. This windswept spot attracts many local birds, and you can walk along the rocky lakeshore for a short distance, past beavers' dams and small farmsteads.

The Beagle Channel

South of the pass, the road curves downward to Rancho Hambre and the Tierra Mayor Valley. Ruta 3 runs westward through this valley and then southward through that of the Río Olivia to the Canal Beagle (Beagle Channel) and Ushuaia.

A branch road, **Ruta J**, turns sharply left at the bottom of the mountain to meander 50 km (30 miles) through the Río Lasifashaj valley to reach the Beagle Channel at Bahía Brown. Puerto Williams, in Chile, can be seen across the channel. The beach is lined with Yahgan shell middens, the circular heaps of discarded mussel shells that once surrounded their low shelters.

The road winds over hills above the Canal Beagle to **Estancia Harberton ❹**, the oldest farm in Argentine Tierra del Fuego, founded by the Reverend Thomas Bridges in 1886. Open to the public from October to April, the farm offers a guided walking tour of the property, which includes Tierra del Fuego's oldest nature reserve: a small wood with native trees. There are also some Yahgan kitchen middens and a model wigwam. Visitors can have tea in the original farmhouse by the bay. You can also visit Harberton by catamaran from Ushuaia (daily in summer), but traveling this way the stay at the farm is short.

Ruta J, the Ruta del Atlántico, winds eastward along the channel for some 30 km (18 miles) of spectacular views and hair-raising turns to finally reach **Estancia Moat**. This area, around Harberton and Moat is ideal for bird-

BELOW: a testimony to the force of the wind in Tierra del Fuego.

watching, with the opportunity to see steamer ducks, cormorants, oyster catchers, and perhaps an eagle or condor.

From Bahía Brown, a rather precarious road runs westward along the coast past several small farms and a fish hatchery to end at Estancia Remolino, built in the 1890s by the Lawrence family, but now almost abandoned.

Back on Ruta 3, the **Valle Tierra Mayor** is a winter sports center in a picturesque setting between the Sorondo and Alvear mountain ranges. It has several lodges for cross-country skiing, snowmobiles, and dog sleds in winter.

West of the Tierra Mayor valley lies the Valle Carbajal, between high mountains with views westward toward Chile. To the north is the Paso Beban, a long disused hiking trail. The road follows the Río Olivia along the west side of the beautiful **Monte Olivia**, where peat is harvested from swamps in the valley for sale in Buenos Aires. At last, the **Canal Beagle** appears in the distance.

At the mouth of the Río Olivia a rustic hiking trail follows the coast eastward to Estancia Túnel and eventually all the way to Harberton and points east. On the west shore of the river is the local government fish hatchery.

Ruta 3 turns westward on a new paved road above the city of Ushuaia, or you can follow the older gravel road along the coast.

Bright lights

The city of **Ushuaia** ❺ (population about 50,000) sits in a picturesque bowl on the southern side of the mountains, overlooking Bahia Ushuaia, the Canal Beagle, and Navarino and Hoste islands (both in Chile) to the south. To the east rise the peaks of the spectacular, pointed Monte Olivia and the Cinco Hermanos (Five Brothers). Ushuaia is the home of a large naval base, government offices, and stores for imported goods. It is a base for one or two farms, sawmills, a crab fishery, and a growing offshore fishing industry. It hosts several television and radio assembly plants, though these are gradually being phased out.

A simple triangular monument near the airfield marks the site of the **Anglican Mission** (1869–1907). Thomas and Mary Bridges (1870) and John and Clara Lawrence (1873) became the archipelago's first non-indigenous permanent residents. The official founding of the town was the establishment of a sub-prefecture (coastguard) in 1884.

Ushuaia's prison (1902–47) is now within the naval base. The octopus-shaped jail is open to the public and contains a small naval museum, the **Museo Maritimo y Presido de Ushuaia** (open daily in summer only), which includes fascinating miniature scenes from the earliest days of the discovery, exploration, and settlement of Tierra del Fuego.

Houses with decorative cornices built by prisoners are still scattered in the older part of town. A train once took inmates to fell trees in the outlying forests along the same route plied by the diminutive steam-powered Ferrocarril Austral Fueguino trains that today treat tourists to a 2½-hour excursion through Tierra del Fuego National Park.

A walk through the town's steep streets reveals a strange variety of architecture. The early wooden

Map on page 328

TIP

When it comes to nightlife, Ushuaia is no threat to Buenos Aires, but every year the Fuegian capital holds an all-night party on June 21, the longest night of the year, and an ice sculpture contest each August.

BELOW: crab traps and fishing boats by the shores of the Beagle Channel.

Plaque in Ushuaia commemorating the War of the Malvinas (Falkland Islands) in 1982.

houses covered with corrugated iron (to help prevent fires) with their prisoner-produced gingerbread decorations have a somewhat Russian flavor. They are intermingled with modern concrete structures, imported Swedish prefabs, and hundreds of small, wooden shanties. Usable land is in short supply in the small area hemmed in by mountain and sea; new houses climb the mountainsides, and many people live in poor conditions. Nevertheless, building and improvements are going on everywhere.

Ushuaia is much more geared to the tourist than Río Grande. There are a number of hotels and budget hostels, including two large ones on the mountain behind the town. The tourist office (open daily) on Avenida San Martín 674 provides information and brochures and has branches at the airport and port.

The restaurants of Ushuaia feature *róbalo* (mullet) and *centolla* (southern king crab) from the Canal Beagle. For those who prefer meat, *asado* (lamb, mutton, or beef roasted over an open fire) is another specialty.

Stores in Ushuaia pay only half the import duty that is charged in the rest of the country, and so focus on imported items (sweaters, jackets and china from Europe; cigarettes, whisky, and radios). There is little to buy that is native to Tierra del Fuego. There are several bookstores which sell books on the Fuegian area; these can also be bought at the museum.

The **Museo del Fin del Mundo** (open Mon–Sat, pm winter; daily in summer), on the corner of Maipú and Rivadavia, has information on the indigenous Yamana people, explorers' and missionaries' artifacts, and an attractive collection of (stuffed) local birds. Active historical research, especially of the eastern tip of the island, Península Mitre, is carried out from here.

BELOW: the fiery colors of autumn.

The **Museo de Maquetes Mundo Yamana** opened in 2002 on Gobernador Campos 267. It tells the story of the Yamana people who were wiped out by Europeans.

The world's southernmost research center, CADIC (Centro Austral de Investigaciones Científicas) at the southwest corner of the inner bay, on Malvinas Argentinas and Ruta 3 is usually not open to the public. Investigators study the marine life, geology, glaciology, climate, flora, hydrology, social history, anthropology, and archeology of Tierra del Fuego.

Tierra del Fuego National Park

A winding road climbs behind the town to the slopes of the **Montes Martial**, past two large hotels to a chair lift which goes up to the valley at the foot of the small, hanging Martial Glacier. In winter the lift takes you to ski slopes; in summer, the glacial hollow at the top of the lift is an ideal place to hike and see Andean flowers, such as the chocolate-scented *Nassauvia*, or even the rare mountain seed snipe. Part way down the road, a cross-country ski track leads over the rise to Ushuaia's first ski slope, a steep cutting on the forested mountainside to the northwest of town.

A 20-minute drive west of Ushuaia brings you to the **Parque Nacional Tierra del Fuego ❻**. The mountains are steeper and nearer the coast than at Ushuaia and points east. Near the park entrance, a road drops down to the channel at Ensenada, with native trees and Yahgan shell middens. To the north, the Río Pipo, with low falls, winds into the mountains. Further west, you catch a view of the Murray Narrows to the south, the narrow channel between Islas Navarino and Hoste through which came Master Murray of the *Beagle*. Further on is Lago Roca, a large lake hemmed by mountains, shared by Argentina and Chile. The park is ideal for birding and hiking, camping and kayaking. A small narrow-gauge train runs from near Ushuaia to the park, and several companies run a daily bus service. The road continues near the Chilean border, to end at Bahía Lapataia, which can also be reached by boat excursions from Ushuaia.

Map on page 328

Cruising the southern seas

Daily, three-hour excursions on the Canal Beagle aboard large catamarans visit the islands off Bahía Ushuaia to see colonies of sea lions, southern fur seals, cormorants, gulls, terns, and other birds. Longer trips go westward to Lapataia or eastward on the channel to see the Magellan penguins on Isla Yecapasela (Martillo) and visit Estancia Harberton. One local naturalist calls the Canal Beagle "a teeming cauldron of wildlife."

Several yachts based in Ushuaia's harbor offer a charter service to the Fuegian Channels, Cape Horn, Isla de los Estados, and Antarctica. One small yacht, the *Tres Marías*, does daily trips to the Islas Bridges off Ushuaia and is the only operator permitted to land on the islands. The Chilean chartered yacht *Terra Australis* cruises the Canal Beagle weekly from September to April, departing Punta Arenas on Sunday evening, and stopping at several points en route, including Ushuaia and sometimes Harberton, and returning Saturday.

The northwest arm of the Canal Beagle with its spectacular glaciers is only several hours by boat west of Ushuaia. It is impossible to get there from Ushuaia except on board the *Terra Australis,* or on one of the larger tourist cruise ships.

Large tourist cruise ships make the circuit of southern South America in summer (usually November to March). These leave from Río de Janeiro or Buenos Aires, visit Ushuaia and Punta Arenas, and go up through the Chilean channels to Puerto Montt or Valparaíso. There are usually only 4–6 hours in each port.

Cruise ships also visit Antarctica, part of whose territory is claimed by Argentina, Chile, and Great Britain. Regular sailings depart from Ushuaia or from Punta Arenas in Chile during the tourist season, which runs from late November to late February. Some cruises include a visit to the Falkland Islands/Malvinas or perhaps South Georgia (although travel connections from Argentina to these islands are not permitted at present.)

The Antarctic cruises last from 7 to 15 days, at least two of which are spent crossing the Drake Passage. Most are intensive learning experiences – naturalists and guest lecturers giving talks aboard and guided walks ashore. The emphasis is on history, geology, flora, and fauna. Activities ashore and aboard are controlled by the Antarctic Treaty Protocol to protect the environment. There is no question of these cruises being a rough ride, however. Many ships offer a full gourmet menu and accommodations tend toward the luxurious (*see Travel Tips, Page 341*). ❑

BELOW: braving the elements.
OVERLEAF: *gauchos* go home.

INSIGHT GUIDES
TRAVEL TIPS

☀ INSIGHT GUIDES Phonecard

One global card to keep travellers in touch. Easy. Convenient. Saves you time and money.

It's a global phonecard

Save up to 70%* on international calls from over 55 countries

Free 24 hour global customer service

Recharge your card at any time via customer service or online

It's a message service

Family and friends can send you voice messages for free.

Listen to these messages using the phone* or online

Free email service - you can even listen to your email over the phone*

It's a travel assistance service

24 hour emergency travel assistance – if and when you need it.

Store important travel documents online in your own secure vault

For more information, call rates, and all Access Numbers in over 55 countries, (check your destination is covered) go to **www.insightguides.ekit.com** or call Customer Service.

JOIN now and receive US$ 5 bonus when you join for US$ 20 or more.

Join today at

www.insightguides.ekit.com

When requested use ref code: **INSAD0103**

OR SIMPLY FREE CALL 24 HOUR CUSTOMER SERVICE

UK	0800 376 1705
USA	1800 706 1333
Canada	1800 808 5773
Australia	1800 11 44 78
South Africa	0800 997 285

THEN PRESS ⓪

For all other countries please go to "Access Numbers" at **www.insightguides.ekit.com**

* Retrieval rates apply for listening to messages. Savings based on using a hotel or payphone and calling to a landline. Correct at time of printing 01.03

(INS001)

powered by ⊛ **ekit**

"The easiest way to make calls and receive messages around the world"

CONTENTS

Getting Acquainted

Area: 2,780,400 sq. km.
(1,073,518 sq. miles)
Capital: Buenos Aires
Population: 37 million
Language: Spanish
Religion: mainly Roman Catholic
Time zone: Three hours ahead of GMT.
Currency: Argentine peso ($)
Weights and measures: metric
Electricity: 220 volts (50 cycles)
International dialing code: 54
(Buenos Aires 11)

Climate

Argentina, the world's eighth-largest country, spans from the deserts of Salta in the north to the glaciers of Patagonia in the south. Most of the country lies in the temperate zone of the Southern Hemisphere.

The northeast is humid and subtropical. The northwest is tropical but has a mild winter. The Pampas are temperate. The south has colder temperatures and rain most of the year. The rainfall varies in the Humid Pampa (which comprises the province of Buenos Aires, and some of the Córdoba and La Pampa provinces) from 99 cm (39 inches) in the eastern parts to about 51 cm (20 inches) in the areas near the Andes.

Summer months in Buenos Aires are indeed very hot and the majority of the people leave soon after Christmas for the beaches and mountain resorts. The city is almost empty during the months of January and February, when the heat and humidity can be overpowering.

Winter is generally pleasant, although July and August have very cold patches. Torrential rain is also common at this time, but is usually short-lived.

Government

The Republic of Argentina has a federal system, with 24 provinces and a strong central government, headed by a president. Legislative power is held by Congress, which is made up of the Senate, which has 63 members, and the Chamber of Deputies, which has 261 members, elected for a four-year term. After a 58-year period dominated by military rule and culminating in the horrific violence of the "Dirty War" of 1976–83, democracy returned to the country in the form of a radical government headed by President Raúl Alfonsín. The main political parties are the Partido Justicialista (PJ, Peronist Party); Unión Cívica Radical (UCR, Radical Party); and Frente del País Solidario (FREPASO, National Solidarity Front).

The constitution was reformed in 1994, allowing the president to serve two consecutive terms of four years.

In 2003 left-of-center Nestor Kirchner, a former lawyer, became president with only 22 percent of the vote after Carlos Menem pulled out of the race. In July 2003 Kirchner enjoyed 75 percent approval due to his radical reforms, which have earned him the nickname "Hurricane Kirchner". Indeed, when he was governor of Santa Cruz province he was accused of being a "caudillo", or strongman. The concern is that he will act in the same way while he is president, although this may be necessary to get the country out of economic disaster.

Economy

Although widely praised for bringing the heads of the last military junta to trial and for establishing the basis for a modern democracy, Alfonsín, who ruled as president from 1983–89, suffered the consequences of rampant inflation and fierce opposition from the trades union movement. His successor as president, the Peronist Carlos Menem, promised a new start for the country, with amnesties for imprisoned military leaders and a hard-headed program of economic reform and privatizations.

The most significant of his economic policies was the convertability plan, which pegged the Argentine peso to the US dollar and helped secure record low levels of inflation and high levels of growth by the late 1990s. But then the tide started turning for Menem. Unemployment, corruption in the government, and problems in the public services lent force to the opposition parties, which united in 1997 to form the Alliance and defeated Menem's Peronists in congressional elections that year.

The 4-year recession which began in 1998 led to the resignation of Menem's successor De la Rúa in December 2001.

In August 2001 the IMF made a controversial loan of $8 million and the economic crisis came to a head with the abandonment of the one-to-one currency peg with the dollar at the end of the year. Bank accounts were frozen in December 2001, and although this was lifted a year later, savings lost two thirds of their value and $20 billion was taken out of the country by the richest residents. December 20 2001 saw a violent protest in which hundreds of thousands of people took to the streets to protest at the economic crisis and 33 people throughout the country were killed.

The aim was to rid the country of corrupt politicians who had become rich at the expense of the starving Argentinians. During the following 18 days, the country had no less than 4 "revolving door" presidents and defaulted on its $95 million debt – the largest default in history. The peso was devalued in January 2002 and in May of the same year, tens of thousands across the country protested again against the worst economic crisis in Argentina's history.

In May 2003 Nestor Kirchner became Argentina's sixth president in 18 months. Sacking top officers in the police force, he promised to put increased control on state-owned banks and pension funds and to clamp down on tax evasion. Positive economic growth was seen in the beginning of 2003 – the first in 5 years – and is expected to rise 5 percent over the following year.

President Kirchner came to an agreement with the IMF and began negotiations for a 3-year debt relief program. In June 2003 Kirchner, along with the newly elected Brazilian president, Lula da Silva, pledged to work toward a common currency in South America. Together they plan to revive the Southern Cone Common Market – a trade bloc known as Mercosur.

Still 27 children die of hunger every day in a country which was once the food basket for Europe and North America. Argentina once boasted the highest wages in South America, but now has the highest unemployment in the continent and 37 percent of its population live below the poverty line.

Holidays & Festivals

The summer vacation season, when internal transportation and hotels are heavily booked, runs from January through March. The middle two weeks of July are the school winter vacation, during which period traveling is also very busy.

All government agencies as well as the banks close on the public holidays. These are listed below. With the exception of Christmas, New Year's, May 25, July 9, and December 8, holidays are observed on the closest Monday to allow for long weekends.

New Year's Day: January 1
Good Friday
Labor Day: May 1
Commemoration of First Government: May 25
Malvinas Day: June 10
Flag Day: June 20
Declaration of Independence: July 9
Death of San Martín: August 17
Columbus Day: October 12
Dia de la Tradición November 10. For several days leading up to this date there are *gaucho* parades in most towns throughout Argentina, with music and dance festivities.
Annunciation Day: December 8
Christmas Day: December 25

In addition to these national holidays, there are many provincial festivities around the country, which are celebrated with local folklore customs, music, and dancing. Details of some of these festivals can be found in the Places sections of this book.

In recent years, Buenos Aires has hosted three new festivals – an annual independent film festival in April, fashion week in March, and in September a biennial art festival.

Planning the Trip

Money Matters

Since the peso was devalued in January 2002, prices have fallen in dollar terms. At the time of writing the peso was trading at around 3.25 to the dollar, although economic uncertainty is likely to force the exchange rate even lower. A return to rapid inflation means that prices are rising along with the dollar, although the even faster rise of the dollar against the peso means that prices for foreign travelers are lower now than in recent years.

Dollars in small denominations are widely accepted, and there are *casas de cambio* (exchange houses) in the center of Buenos Aires around San Martin and Lavalle. American Express at Arenales 707 (Plaza San Martín) changes currency and travelers' checks.

Entry Regulations

All tourists to Argentina must have valid passports. In some cases only a tourist card is required, but this must be verified with a travel agent. EU and US citizens do not need a tourist visa.

What to Wear

Dressing in Buenos Aires for dinner is customary in the more expensive restaurants. Argentine men will always wear a suit or at least a sports coat with a tie. Women tend to be well dressed at all times.

More casual dress is common outside the work place or especially informal settings. Shorts are worn in the spring and summer in Buenos Aires and in tourist regions around the country to combat humidity.

Getting There

BY AIR

All international flights arrive at **Ezeiza International Airport** (EZE), 35 km (22 miles) from the center of Buenos Aires. Avoid the floods of taxi drivers who greet arrivals, and buy a ticket from the Remise (private car) foyer in the airport. A cheaper option is to go by airport bus (run by the Manuel Tienda León company, offices on Carlos Pellegrini 509. Tel: 4314 3636); this comfortable service runs hourly, takes 2 hours depending on traffic and drops you off in Plaza San Martín. From here, most hotels are a short taxi ride away.

Another airport, **Jorge Newbery**, is located within the city and is used mostly for local travel as well as for travel to and from bordering countries. The following are commonly used: Aerolíneas Argentinas, British Airways, Canadian Pacific, Air France, Aeroflot, Avianca, Iberia, Swissair, Lufthansa, Lan Chile, Varig. Local travel can be on Austral Airlines, Aerolíneas Argentinas, Dinar, ARG, and Southern Winds.

There is a departure tax of $70 to be paid on leaving the country.

BY SEA

There are only a few cruise ships that come to Buenos Aires. Most of these originate in Brazil or in Europe. The better-known cruises are with the Linea C Company, on their ships *Eugenio* and *Enrico*. These operate from December to March.

Another cruise ship, the *Pegasus*, from the Epirotiki Line, also operates from December to April. Antartur Lines has cruises from Ushuaia to the Antarctic and Tierra del Fuego. These only operate in January.

The US-operated Kapitan Dranitsyn also cruises around the Antarctic region and South Atlantic islands, with various packages on offer from November through March. Contact: Quark Expeditions Inc, 980 Post Road, Darien, CT 06820, USA. Tel: (203) 656 0499; toll free: (800) 356 5699; fax: (203) 655 6623. e-mail: quarkexpeditions@compuserve.com www.quark-expeditions.com

Australis (www.australis.com) has a new cruise ship, *Mare Australis*, which explores Patagonia and Tierra del Fuego on 3, 4, or 7-night journeys with a program of activities between October and April.

For more details contact a local travel agent or fax the tourist office in Argentina on (5411) 4313 6834.

OVERLAND

Most tourists do not arrive by land. However, for the adventurous type, this can be accomplished by bus or automobile. Bus service is available from Chile, Bolivia, Paraguay, Uruguay, and Brazil. Large air-conditioned buses are available for long-distance overland travel. Bus tickets do not usually have seat numbers, so it is worth getting on the bus in good time to make sure you have a seat. Also be warned that air conditioning is usually very powerful, so take a warm sweater, even during the summer months.

All international train services have ceased. Even the slower and less-reliable domestic connections have become increasingly unimportant, since the government withdrew state funding of the network in 1994, handing over the service to the provinces and private enterprises.

Traveling by automobile is possible. Most of the roads are paved but cautious driving is *essential*. There are speed limits posted. The **Automovil Club Argentino (ACA)**, located in Buenos Aires on Avenida Libertador 1850 (tel: 4802 6061/7061), is very helpful and can provide the traveler with maps and useful information. The Club offers a monthly membership, which entitles you to discounts for their wide range of goods and services: very good maps and travel literature, and extensive listings of hotels, hostels, campsites, and restaurants around the whole country.

Rutas de la Argentina are national and town maps provided

Tourist Information

Most Argentine embassies around the world provide basic tourist information facilities and will offer advice to travelers.
Australia: 1st Floor, Suite 102, MCL Tower, Woden, ACT 2606 Canberra. Tel: (26) 282 4555. Fax: (26) 285 3062. www.argentina.org.au
Canada: 90 Sparks Street, Suite 910, Ottawa, Ontario K1P 5BA. Tel: (613) 236 2351. Fax: (613) 235 2659. www.consargenmtl.com
Netherlands: Javastraat 20, The Hague 2585. Tel: (70) 365 4836. Fax: (70) 352 2161. www.mrecic.gov.ar
United Kingdom: 65 Brook Street, London W1Y 1YE. Tel: (020) 7318 1300. Fax: (020) 7318 1301. www.tourism.gov.ar
United States: New Hampshire Avenue NW, Washington DC 20009. Tel: (202) 9393 6400. Fax: (202) 332 3171. www.embajadaargentina-usa.org

In Buenos Aires, local and national tourist information can be obtained from: **Secretaría de Turismo**, Santa Fé 883, P.B., Buenos Aires. Tel: 4312 2232/5550. Fax: 4313 6834. www.sectur.gov.ar

There are several tourist information centers along Buenos Aires' pedestrian boulevard **Flórida**.

The English-language *Buenos Aires Herald* is a good source of information on where to visit.

free from tourist offices. **YPF**, the state oil company, also produces good road maps, available from gas stations.

Useful Addresses

TRAVEL AGENCIES

ASATEJ, Flórida 835, Floor 3, Office 315, Buenos Aires. Tel: 4311 6953. Fax: 4311 6840. One of the largest agencies, primarily aimed at students, but there's no age limit. Bright and cheerful office with notice-board brimming with items for sale, travel news, travelers seeking companions.
Eurotur, Viamonte 486, Buenos Aires. Tel: 4312 6077/8. www.eurotur.com Tours, transportation, and accommodations for individuals and groups throughout Argentina. English spoken; highly professional and recommended.
Eves Turismo, Tucumán 702, Buenos Aires. Tel: 4393 6151. Fax: 4393 6411.

Helpful and efficient for travel both within Argentina and abroad.
Kallpa Tours, Roque Saenz Pena 811, 2nd Floor, Suite B, Buenos Aires. Tel: (011) 4394 1830/ 1860. Fax: (011) 4326 2500. www.kallpatour.com This company specializes in wine and cultural tours, trekking, and horseback riding,

FOREIGN EMBASSIES IN BUENOS AIRES

Australia, Villanueva 1400. Tel: 4777 6580.
Canada, Tagle 2828. Tel: 4805 3032.
France, Santa Fe 846, 3rd Floor. Tel: 4312 2409.
Germany, Villanueva 1055, Belgrano. Tel: 4778 2500
Ireland, Suipacha 1380. Tel: 4325 5787.
United Kingdom, Dr Luis Agote 2412. Tel: 4803 7070.
United States, Colombia 4300. Tel: 4576 2222.

AIRLINE COMPANIES

DINAR, Tel: 0810-555-34627
Aerolíneas Argentinas/Austral, Tel: 4320 2000.
British Airways, Tel: 4320 6600.
Canadian Airlines, Tel: 4322 3762.
Lade, Tel: 4361 7071.
Pluna, Tel: 4342 4420.
United Airlines, Tel: 4316 0777.
Southern Winds, Tel: 0810 777 7979.

BUS COMPANIES

Ablo, Tel: 4313 2835. Travels to Córdoba province.
Anton, Tel: 4313 3078. Travels to the coastal cities.
Costera Criolla, Tel: 4313 3616. Travels to the coastal cities.
Chevalier Paraguaya, Tel: 4313 2349. Travels to Paraguay.
Expreso Silva, Tel: 4315 1652. Travels to the northern provinces.
Fenix, Tel: 4313 0134. Travels west to Chile.
Gral Urquiza y Sierras de Córdoba, Tel: 4313 2798. Travels to Córdoba.
La Internacional, Tel: 4313 3164. Travels to Paraguay and Brazil.
Micro Mar, Tel: 4313 3128. Travels to the seaside cities.
Onda, Tel: 4313 3195. Travels to Uruguay.
Pluma, Tel: 4313 3901. Travels to Brazil.
Tata, Tel: 4313 3836. Travels to the northern provinces and the border with Bolivia.

Business Hours

Monday to Friday, the business hours are from 9am to 7pm, and the banking hours from 10am to 3pm. In most of the country outside Buenos Aires, the stores open from 9am to 1pm and from 4pm to 7pm, almost invariably closing for the siesta, although local hours vary somewhat and should be checked.

Provincial Tourist Offices

Each of Argentina's provinces has a representative office in downtown Buenos Aires. Once you have decided on your destination, a visit to the province's *casa* can provide a wealth of information on hotels, restaurants, and excursions.

Buenos Aires (province), Av. Callao 237. Tel: 4371 7046.
Catamarca, Av. Córdoba 2080. Tel: 4374 6891.
Chaco, Av. Callao 322, 1st floor. Tel: 4476 0961.
Chubut, Sarmiento 1172. Tel: 4382 8126.
Córdoba, Av. Callao 332. Tel: 4373 2596/2538.
Corrientes, San Martín 333. Tel: 4394 7432.
Entre Ríos, Siupacha 844. Tel: 4328 2284/5985.
Formosa, Hipólito Yrigoyen 1429. Tel: 4381 7048/2037.
Jujuy, Av. Santa Fe 967. Tel: 4393 1295.
Mendoza, Av. Callao 445.

Tel: 4371 7301/0835.
Misiones, Av. Santa Fe 989. Tel: 4393 1211/1812.
Neuquén, General J.D. Perón 687. Tel: 4326 1188/0560.
La Pampa, Suipacha 346. Tel: 4326 1769/0511.
Río Negro, Tucumán 1916. Tel: 4371 5599.
La Rioja, Av. Callao 745. Tel: 4815 1929.
Salta, Av. Roque S. Pena 933. Tel: 4326 0321.
San Juan, Sarmiento 1251. Tel: 4382 5580/9241.
San Luis, Azcuenaga 1087. Tel: 4822 3641/0426.
Santa Cruz, 25 de Mayo 277. Tel: 4343 8478.
Santa Fe, Montevideo 373. Tel: 4375 4570.
Santiago Del Estero, Flórida 274. Tel: 4326 9418/7739.
Tierra Del Fuego, Av. Santa Fe 919.Tel: 4322 8855.
Tucumán, Suipacha 140. Tel: 4322 0564/0010.

Practical Tips

MEDICAL SERVICES

The health care in this country is good. Hospitals have trained personnel who have studied here and abroad. There are excellent specialists in most of the medical fields, who make it a point to attend international medical congresses, to inform themselves on the recent advances in medical science, and to bring these to Argentina.

Medical equipment is very costly, but all efforts are coordinated in order to maximize benefits.

In some sections of the country, the hospitals may not have up-to-date equipment, but what is available is adequate for an emergency situation.

Costs of medical care are difficult to establish because of the fluctuating economy.

PHARMACIES

Most pharmaceutical drugs can be purchased over the counter without a prescription. There is usually a pharmacist on duty. If you are prescribed any form of injections, the pharmacist offers this service. All over the country, pharmacies rotate a 24-hour service. A listing of the ones on duty and nearest to you appear in the local newspaper as "Farmacias de Turno."

The pharmacist can also recommend remedies for common ailments, flu, stomach disorders, headaches, etc.

HOSPITALS

British Hospital, Perdriel 74. Tel: 4304 1081.
German Hospital, Pueyrredon 1640. Tel: 4821 1700.
Dental Hospital, Pueyrredon 940. Tel: 4805 5521.
Eye Hospital Santa Lucia, San Juan 2021. Tel: 4941 5555.

SECURITY & CRIME

As in any other part of the world, the traveler must always be cautious and use a little common sense. When registering at the hotel, don't leave luggage unattended. Always keep your belongings close to you. If carrying valuables, ask to have them locked in a safe. Carry money in different parts of your clothing rather than all in a wallet or purse. Don't display large amounts of cash when making purchases, and always check your bill when handing over payment – quick exchanges of notes have been reported. Beware of pickpockets on the crowded pedestrian mall Flórida, although there are also plenty of police here.

Buenos Aires and most of the bigger cities are very much alive till the late hours of the night. But a little caution can prevent a bad experience. Don't walk on desolate streets and try not to walk alone. If driving, lock the car and don't leave any valuables in it. Avoid dining very late at trendy restaurants. Crime is on the rise, in line with poverty, mainly in the large cities. If you are held up, don't resist.

The main post office in Buenos Aires is located on Sarmiento 189, and operates Monday–Friday 9am–7.30pm. Other small post offices are located throughout the city. Your hotel is the best source for stamps and any other information you need.

The local papers are *La Nación*, *Clarín*, *Ambito Financiero*, *La Razón*, and *Página 12* (all in Spanish). National and international news in English is provided by the *Buenos Aires Herald*, which also has useful What's On listings for the city. There are newspaper and magazine stands on almost every city-center street corner, where foreign papers and magazines can also be found.

There are five television stations, and cable TV is widely available. Many of the programs are brought in from the US and Europe and clumsily dubbed into Spanish. A few are in English with Spanish subtitles.

There are numerous radio stations ranging from rock to tango. Radio Horizonte 93.5 FM offers a good selection of the latest international music. The BBC is available after 5pm (see the *Buenos Aires Herald* for details).

Aerolíneas Argentinas:
www.aerolineas.com.ar/
Flight schedules, costs, routings, and booking facilities, as well as general tourist information.
Argentine Youth Hostel Association:
www.hostelling-aaaj.org.ar/
Lists of hostels and tourist packages around the country, with prices and booking facilities.
Buenos Aires Herald:
www.buenosairesherald.com/
Local and international news; what's on in Buenos Aires; TV, video, and cinema listings.
Tango:
www.buenosairestango.com/
Tango shows in Buenos Aires and elsewhere; sound clips and live TV documentaries, books, magazines, interviews, and accommodations listings.
Tourist information:
www.liveargentina.com
A comprehensive site in several languages.
www.turismo.gov.ar
The site of the government tourist office. Lots of good pics, but they make the site slow to load, and there's not much text.

Dialing Codes

COUNTRY CODE (if dialing Argentina from abroad): 54

REGIONAL CODES

Don't dial the area code if calling the same area you are in. If calling from abroad, drop the first 0.

Bahía Blanca	0291
Bariloche	02944
Buenos Aires	011
Comodoro Rivadavia	0297
Córdoba	0351
Corrientes	03783
El Bolsón	02944
El Calafate	02902
El Chalten	02962
Esquel	02945
Jujuy	0388
La Plata	0221
La Rioja	03822
Mar del Plata	0223
Mendoza	0261
Merlo	02656
Neuquén	0299
Posadas	03752
Puerto Iguazú	03757
Resistencia	03722
Río Gallegos	02966
Río Grande	02964
Rosario	0341
Salta	0387
San Fernando	03833
San Juan	0264
San Luis	02652
San Martín de los Andes	02972
Santa Fe	0342
Santiago del Estero	0385
Trevelín	02945
Tucumán	0381
Ushuaia	02901
Viedma	02920
Villa Gesell	02255

INTERNATIONAL CODES

Australia	61
Bolivia	591
Brazil	55
Canada	1
Chile	56
France	33
Germany	49
Ireland, Republic of	353
New Zealand	64
UK	44
Uruguay	598
USA	1

Dial 00, and then the country code, followed by the number.

Telecommunications

Telephone

Since the service was privatized in 1989, it has been split between Telecom and Telefónica Argentina. Prices have fluctuated and, although they are becoming more competitive, telephone calls from Argentina are still among the most expensive in the world. However, the service is becoming much more efficient and the line quality is high.

International and national calls can be made from *locutorios*, or "call shops" throughout the country.

Local calls can be made from the blue phone booths found throughout the city. Phones accept coins or phone cards, which can be bought from *kioscos* (confectionery and tobacco booths).

Internet

The Internet can be used throughout the country. Connections are particularly good in cities and rates in Buenos Aires are the cheapest at only a few dollars an hour. Outlets come and go but there are some big chains, internet cafes where you can sip coffee and listen to music as you surf, as well as connections at larger airports and railway stations.

Getting Around

Buses

CITY TRANSPORT

The buses *(colectivos)* are a good and speedy way to get around Buenos Aires. The grid system of roads makes planning a journey relatively simple. It's worth investing in a *Lumi Guide*, which contains city maps and bus routes. Buses are cheap – for less than a dollar you can get from one end of the city to the other. It's best to have change when you board.

In most cities, there is a bus service that links the airport to the city center. In addition, each airline runs a minibus service that is coordinated with its flight schedule.

LONG-DISTANCE BUSES

The network of **long-distance buses** throughout Argentina is efficient, cheap, and comfortable. Distances involved often mean an overnight journey, but the well-paved roads should not hinder sleep and *coche camas*, or bed buses are as smooth as airplanes on wheels. *Comun* buses are cheaper and more basic than the higher-standard *diferencial*. Buses for destinations throughout the country leave from the Retiro Bus Station, opposite the Sheraton. The bus station has an information office on the 1st floor (tel: 4314 2323). Left-luggage lockers are available for a couple of dollars, payment by tokens on sale at kiosks in the station. The nearest subway station is Retiro on Linea C, entrance in the nearby Retiro train station.

Train to the Clouds

One of the most scenic trips in the country is the **Tren A Las Nubes** (Train To The Clouds), which makes the 136-km (85-mile) journey from Salta to San Antonio de los Cobres, 3,775 meters (12,385 ft) above sea-level, through the spectacular, dry mountainous area known as the Puna, ending at La Polvorilla viaduct. The recently renovated train offers tourist services only, with guides, stewardess, bar and restaurant facilities, during its 14-hour journey. The train leaves Salta at 7am, and the days on which it will run throughout the season are announced in April. In general, there is one service per week from April to June, three per week in July and August, two per week in September and October and one per week in November and December.

Train tickets may be obtained in Buenos Aires, at Esmeralda 1008 (tel: 011-4311 4282), or Esmeralda 320, 4th floor (tel: 011-4326 9626), and in Salta, at Caseros 431 (tel: 0387-4310 4984).

Trains

With the exception of a few tourist services, such as the *Tren a las Nubes (above)* passenger services around the country are virtually non-existent since the government privatized the network in 1994. Trains do run to the suburbs of Buenos Aires, however. There are four main train terminals in the city: **Retiro**. Tel: 4311 8074. For services to Delta Tigre, Capilla del Señor, and Bartolomé Mitre. **Constitución**. Tel: 4304 0028. For local trains. **Federico Lacroze**. Tel: 4553 5213. For excursions on a Scottish 1888 Neilson steam engine. **Once**. Tel: 4861 0043. For travel around Buenos Aires province. The ride from Olivos to Tigre along the coast provides excellent views of the River Plate.

Tren de la Costa, M.T. de Alvear 684. Tel: 4315 7778.

Subway

The Buenos Aires subway system, better known as the **SUBTE**, is usually the fastest and definitely the cheapest way to get around the sprawling city. The rides are quick, taking no more than 25 minutes, and the waiting time is about 3–5 minutes. A new subway line will connect parts of the city to the south of Avenida Rivaderia with the northern suburbs.

Private Transport

Remises

Remises are private automobiles, with a driver, that can be rented by the hour, excursion, day, or any other time period. A list of these can be located in the telephone directory or at the information desks of the hotels.
AAA Limousine, Viamonte 1620 piso 4. Tel: 4371 9107.
Plaza de Mayo, Azopardo 523. Tel: 4331 4705.

Car Rental

You can rent a car at the airport upon arrival, but it is better to book from home, especially during the high season. The following better-known car rental agencies have offices in Buenos Aires:
Avis, Cerrito 1257. Tel: 4326 5542.
Budget, Santa Fé 869. Tel: 4311 9870.
Hertz, Dr R. Rojas 451. Tel: 4312 1317.
Serra Lima, Av. Cordoba 3121. Tel: 4961 5276

Domestic Air Travel

Traveling by air in a country as big as Argentina is a good way to get from one region to the other, saving time on some long and, frankly mind-numbing journeys. The major local airlines are Austral, Aerolíneas Argentinas, LAPA, Dinar, and Lade. **Jorge Newberry Airport** or **El Aeroparque**, is Buenos Aires' airport for national traffic.

Aerolíneas Argentinas offer a special package to foreign visitors, called *Argentina Air Pass*. This is a booklet of 4, 6, or 8 coupons, each of which allows a segment of travel within Argentina. For example, one segment might be Buenos Aires to Río Gallegos one way, another might be B.A. to Mendoza; apart from Buenos Aires, a city can only be visited once. The *Argentina Air Pass* can only be bought in conjunction with an international air ticket, and is fully refundable if not used. There is no set time limit on using the coupons, although they are only valid for as long as the international ticket on which they are bought is valid. The price is US$400 for 3 coupons and US$100 for each additional coupon – which works out economically, since individual tickets are very expensive.

Change to Flight Prices

In fall 2002, the Government introduced a new pricing structure which means that all international travelers must purchase business class or first-class tickets for domestic flights bought in the country.

Ferries

Traveling by ferry to Uruguay is a good excursion away from the hustle and bustle of Buenos Aires. The most popular destinations are the historic port of Colonia, Montevideo, or the beaches of Punte del Este. The two main ferry companies are **Ferrylines** (Av. Córdoba and Maipú. Tel: 4315 6800) and **Buquebus**, which is

Tren de la Costa

Inaugurated in 1891 but only re-opened after 30 years' closure in 1995, this coastal train runs from Olivos to Tigre in the suburbs of Buenos Aires. Trains leave every 15 minutes, there are 11 stops and the full journey takes under 30 minutes. Tel: 4732 6000.

Taxis

Taxis are widely used by *porteños* and can often be the cheapest way to get around, particularly outside the rush hour and if you are sharing the fare with traveling companions. Taxis can be easily recognized (black with a yellow roof), and in Buenos Aires are readily available 24 hours a day. The meter registers a number that will correspond to the amount of the fare appearing on a list. These must be shown to the passenger by law. A small tip is usually given.

Radio taxis are ordered by telephone. "Remise" is a similar service but the cars are unmarked and the fare is calculated according to the distance traveled.

smarter and more efficient (Av. Córdoba 867. Tel: 4311 1159). The journey across the murky waters of the River Plate costs $64 for the slick 45-minute catamaran ride or $46 for the 3-hour trip by traditional ferry. (Should you wish to stay over in Colonia, a good hotel is the **Hotel Beltrán**. Tel: Uruguay 22955. It has pretty, leafy terraces, and rooms start at $40 a night.)

Where to Stay

Choosing a Hotel

Since the collapse of the peso, the cost of accommodations has dropped dramatically throughout the country. Like most destinations in the world, prices are considerably higher in the capital. In addition to hotels, there are also *hosterías*, *hospedajes,* and *pensiones*, all of which offer more basic but usually clean rooms at cheaper prices. Many of these places are often found near bus and train stations which, although may be noisy (ask for rooms at the back – *en el interior*), are convenient if you're traveling overland. The following is a selection of recommended places, including price ranges.

Hotel Listings

The following lists of accommodations around the country have been arranged by region, matching the order of the same regions covered in the Places section of this book. Price categories shown are all for one night in a double room in the high season, with no meals included unless otherwise specified.

BUENOS AIRES

Alvear Palace Hotel
Avenida Alvear 1891
Tel: (011) 4808 2100
Fax: (011) 4804 9246
www.alvearpalace.com
BA's most elegant hotel in the city's most chic neighborhood – Recoleta. French decor, several restaurants, tearoom, boutiques, health club, business center. **$$$$**

Caesar Park
Posadas 1232
Tel: (011) 4819 1296
Fax: (011) 4819 1290
www.caesarpark.com
Modern, large luxury hotel in the Recoleta. Lobby piano bar, three restaurants including elegant buffet, health club with pool. Popular with business set. **$$$$**

Carsson
Viamonte 650
Tel: (011) 4322 3551
Faded, charming elegance. **$$$**

Claridge Hotel
Tucumán 535
Tel: (011) 4314 7700
Fax: (011) 4314 8022
www.claridge-hotel.com
Very British, old-fashioned, centrally located. Health club with pool, penthouse suites with gardens, pleasant bar. **$$$$**

Crowne Plaza Panamericano
Carlos Pellegrini 551
Tel: (011) 4348 5000
Fax: (011) 4348 5250
www.crowneplaza.com
Located in the shadow of the Obelisco. Modern 18-floor twin towers, health club with rooftop pool, popular for conferences, excellent restaurant. **$$$$**

Four Seasons
Posadas 1086/88
Tel: (011) 4321 1200
Fax: (011) 4321 1201
Near the French Embassy and the Recoleta, large modern hotel in French style, with garden restaurant, lounge, health club, and outdoor pool. Popular with business people and visiting rock stars. **$$$$**

Gran Hotel Colón
Carlos Pellegrini 507
Tel: (011) 4320 3500
Fax: (011) 4320 3507
www.colon-hotel.com.ar
Across from Teatro Colón on 9 de Julio. Modern but cozy, luxury suites

Price Guide

Prices are all for a double room:
$$$$	$100 plus
$$$	$50–100
$$	$30–50
$	$30 or under

available with patio. Rooftop outdoor pool, restaurant. **$$$$**
Hotel Inter-Continental
Moreno 809
Tel: (011) 4340 7100
Fax: (011) 4340 7199
www.intercontinental.com
Four blocks from Plaza de Mayo in Monserrat, modern 19-story hotel, with restaurant/bar, health club, and indoor pool. Popular with business people. **$$$$**
Hotel Phoenix
San Martín 780
Tel: (011) 4312 4845
Fax: (011) 4311 2846
Faded old-world charm, fabulous large rooms, friendly staff, and a central location. **$$$**
Libertador
Avenida Córdoba 690
Tel: (011) 4322 8800
Fax: (011) 4322 9703
In the heart of the microcenter, bar and pool on the top floor, restaurant. Popular with business visitors and tourists. **$$$$**
Marriott Plaza Hotel
Flórida 1005
Tel: (011) 4318 3000
Fax: (011) 4318 3008
www.marriottplaza.com.ar

Elegant hotel on Plaza San Martín, favorite with visiting heads of state and royalty. Famous restaurant Plaza Grill, health club, outdoor pool. Central but quiet location, very comfortable, and excellent service. **$$$$**
Sheraton Buenos Aires
San Martín 1225
Tel: (011) 4318 9000
Fax: (011) 4312 9353
www.sheraton.com
Located in Retiro, 24-story highrise towers commanding magnificent view of the river and port area. Rooftop bar, international restaurants, tennis courts and pool; favorite with business set. **$$$$**
M.T. Alvear 902
Tel: (011) 4328 4751
Fax: (011) 4328 6476
Two branches with same ownership, highly recommended. Pleasant, modern, conference rooms available, and a bar. **$$$**
Hotel Crillon
Santa Fé 796
Tel: (011) 4310 2000
Fax: (011) 4310 2020
French-style antique building which has been refurbished; very modern

Price Guide

Prices are all for a double room:

$$$$	$100 plus
$$$	$50–100
$$	$30–50
$	$30 or under

inside, with many services for the business traveler, including 24-hour room service. Located on Plaza San Martín. **$$$**
Hotel Plaza Francia
E. Schiaffino 2189
Tel/fax: (011) 4804 9631
Classic brick-colored building, located in the Recoleta, near the Fine Arts Museum. Quiet, with a good breakfast served in your room if desired; highly recommended. **$$$**
Lafayette Hotel
Reconquista 546
Tel/fax: (011) 4313 9182
Conveniently located in microcentro, recently remodeled with English-style decor, restaurant and room service. **$$$**
Lancaster Hotel
Córdoba 405
Tel: (011) 4312 4061
Fax: (011) 4311 3021
Very European, fancy lobby, pretty sunlit rooms, nice bar/cafe. **$$$**
Orly Hotel
Paraguay 474
Tel: (011) 4312 5344
Basic rooms, good location. **$–$$**
Park Plaza Kempinski Hotel
Parera 183
Tel: (011) 6777 0200
Fax: (011) 6777 0290
www.parkplazahotels.com
On a quiet side street in the Recoleta; elegant classic European style, with 8 floors – each one dedicated to a famous painter. **$$$**
Recoleta Plaza Hotel
Posadas 1557
Tel: (011) 4804 3471
Fax: (011) 4311 7441
Attractive small French-style hotel in Recoleta, with a restaurant and room service. **$$$**
Gran Hotel Hispano
Avenida de Mayo 861
Tel: (011) 4345 2020
www.hispano.com

Youth Hostels in Argentina

Hostelling International Argentina (www.hostels.org.ar) runs youth hostels in the country, from Salta in the north to Ushuaia in the far south:
Salta: Backpackers, Buenos Aires 930. Tel/fax: (0287) 4423 5910.
Tilcara: Malka, San Martín, 400 m/yards from the square. Tel: (0288) 495 5197. Fax: (0288) 495 5200.
Iguazú: La Cabaña, Av. 2 fronteras 434. Tel: (02757) 420 564.
Villa Paranacito: Top Malo, Ruta 46, Km 18.2. Tel: (02446) 495 255.
Mendoza: Campo Base, Lavalle 2028. Tel: (0361) 445 7661.
Mendoza: Hostal Internacional Mendoza, España 343. Tel/fax: (0361) 424 0018.
San Rafael: Puesta del Sol, Deán Funes 998. Tel: (03627) 434 881.

Villa Carlos Paz: Acapulco, La Paz 75. Tel: (02541) 421 929.
Bariloche: Alaska, Av. Bustillo, Km 7.5. Tel: (03944) 461 564.
El Bolsón: El Pueblito, Barrio Luján, 1 km (⅔ mile) from Ruta 258. Tel: (03944) 493 560.
Puerto Madryn: Madryn HI, 25 de Mayo 1136. Tel: (03945) 474 426.
Esquel: Lago Verde, Volta 1081. Tel: (03945) 452 251.
El Chaltén: Patagonia, Av. San Martín 820. Tel/fax: (03962) 493 019.
El Chaltén: Rancho Grande, Av. San Martín. Tel/fax: (03962) 493 005.
El Calafate: Los Pioneros (450 m/yards from center). Tel: (03902) 491 243.
Ushuaia: Torre al Sur, Gobernador Paz 1437. Tel: (03901) 430 745.

One block from Plaza de Mayo and close to San Telmo, a renovated antique building, popular with European budget travelers. **$$**

Hotel Arenales
Arenales 2984
Tel: (011) 4821 0815
Comfortable, simple rooms, good service, located in Palermo. **$$**

Hotel Embajador
Carlos Pellegrini 1185
Tel/fax: (011) 4326 5302
Good location at 9 de Julio and Santa Fé, with modern, large rooms, and a cafe. **$$**

Hotel Impala
Libertad 1215
Tel/fax: (011) 4816 0430
www.hotelimpala.com.ar
Two blocks from Santa Fé shopping street and very near to Recoleta, this is modern, basic accommodation, with a cafe. **$$**

Hotel San Antonio
Paraguay 372
Tel: (011) 4312 5381
Charming, small, with air of old-fashioned European *pension*; good value. **$$**

Uruguay
Tacuari 83
Tel: (011) 4334 2788
Simple, inexpensive, and clean. **$$**

Waldorf Hotel
Paraguay 450
Tel: (011) 4312 2071
Fax: (011) 4312 2079
www.waldorfhotel.com.ar
Close to Flórida and Santa Fé shopping streets. Modern and comfortable, with a bar; larger rooms and suites. **$$**

Aparthotels and Suites

For longer visits to the capital, a good alternative is an aparthotel or suite hotel which give you the services of a hotel with the convenience of a furnished apartment, including a kitchenette. Prices per night range from $150 for a studio to $450 for a 3-room apartment.

Feir's Park All-Suites Hotel
Esmeralda 1366
Tel: (011) 4327 1900
Fax: (011) 4327 1935
One block from Libertador in elegant neighborhood, with room

service, pool, healthclub, business center; option of connecting suites.

Plaza San Martín Suites
Suipacha 1092
Tel: (011) 4328 4740
Fax: (011) 4328 9385
Between Plaza San Martín and 9 de Julio. Newly built and modern, with a health club and room service.

Suipacha y Arroyo Apart Hotel
Suipacha 1359
Tel: (011) 4325 8200
Fax: (011) 4325 1886
Situated in an upscale neighborhood near Libertador and 9 de Julio, with good service, a health club and outdoor pool, patio and garden, and garage facilities.

Torre Cristóforo Colombo Suites
Oro 2747
Tel: (011) 4777 9622
Fax: (011) 4775 9911
In Palermo, two blocks from US embassy. A modern tower, with rooftop bar, restaurant, healthclub, and outdoor pool. The standard of service is excellent.

Ulises Recoleta
Ayacucho 2016
Tel: (011) 4804 4571
Fax: (011) 4806 0838
Across from the Alvear Palace in the Recoleta, this is a European-style classic building with only 25 apartments (including a Penthouse suite); antique furnishings and a welcoming atmosphere. **$$$**

MAR Y SIERRAS

Mar del Plata

Hotel Sheraton
Alem 4221
Tel: (011) 4318 9390/
(0223) 499 9000
South of city center, facing the golf course. Usual 5-star amenities. **$$$$**

Gran Hotel Provincial
Bd. Marítimo 2500
Tel: (0223) 4915949
Fax: 4915894
Traditional "grand hotel" with a large number of rooms and a very good restaurant. **$$$**

Hotel Bisonte
Belgrano 2609
Tel: (0223) 492 6028

One block south of the Cathedral; recommended. **$$$**

Gran Hotel Continental
Córdoba 1929
Tel: (0223) 492 1300
www.granhotelcontinental.com.ar
Mid-range hotel; recommended. **$$$**

Gran Hotel Dora
Buenos Aires 1841
Tel: (0223) 491 0033
Close to the casino, two blocks from the beach. **$$**

Compostela
Belgrano 2561
Tel: (0223) 495 2796
$$

San Jorge
Alsina 2353
Tel: (0223) 451 3895
Inexpensive mid-range hotel. **$**

Tandil

Estancia Acelain
54 km (33½ miles) North of Tandil
Tel: (01) 4322 2784
Luxurious rooms in Spanish-style mansion, set in beautiful grounds, offering horseback riding, polo, boating, hunting, and fishing. Full board only. **$$$$**

Estancia la Montaña
50 km (31 miles) South of Tandil, near the Río Quequen Chico
Tel: (01): 4342 8417
Californian-style ranch, offering a wide range of outdoor activities:

Beach Resorts

The traditional Atlantic seaside resorts don't fit the European idea of a restful beach holiday. **Pinamar**, **Villa Gesell**, and **Mar de la Plata** are besieged by millions of *porteños* during the hot summer months, and the huge hotel complexes are fully booked. It's party time and discos and bars everywhere are packed until sunrise.

In winter, however, these holiday resorts become ghost towns. Quiet, undeveloped beaches are only to be found further south near **Bahía Blanca**. **Mar del Sur**, below Miramar, is a peaceful haven with 40 km (25 miles) of sandy beach.

horseback riding, polo, wildlife photo safaris. Full board only. **$$$$**

Villa Gesell
Hotel Bahia – Spa and Sea Club
Av. 1 between Paseos 108 and 109
Tel: (02255) 460 838
www.hotelbahia-gesell.com.ar
Modern 11-story block located on the beach with full spa facilities. **$$$**

Hotel Gran Internacional
Av. 1 and Paseo 103
Tel/fax: (02255) 468 747
www.hotelgraninternational.com
Beachside location. **$$$**

Hostería Mar Azul
Avenida 4, entre Paseos 106 & 107
Tel: (03255) 462 457
Basic but clean and very friendly family-run guest house in quiet residential area. Very comfortable; recommended. **$$**

CENTRAL SIERRAS

Gran Hotel La Cumbre
La Cumbre, Córdoba
Tel: (02548) 451 550
www.granhotellacumbre.com
Alpine-style, traditional family hotel in country resort 80 km (50 miles) north of Córdoba, with panoramic views. **$$$**

El Ciervo de Oro
Hipólito Yrigoyen 995,
Villa Carlos Paz
Tel/fax: (02547) 422 498
www.ciervodeoro.com.ar
A lovely lodge-type hotel right on Lago San Roque. Excellent food. **$$**

Residencial del Molino
Peru 281, Río Ceballos
Tel: (0251) 452 197
Friendly, clean, basic union-run hotel situated right on the river; excellent and inexpensive home cooking. **$**

THE NORTHEAST

Internacional Iguazú
Puerto Iguazú
Tel: (011) 491 800
Fax: (011) 491 848

Ugly building but five-star complex inside the national park, with tennis courts, pool, and great views. **$$$**

Las Orquídeas
Ruta 12, Km 5
Tel: (02757) 420 472
Comfortable and inexpensive with restaurant, in a great location outside Iguazú. **$**

Posada de la Laguna
Colonia Carlos Pellegrini,
Corrientes
Tel/fax: (03773) 499 413
E-mail: posadadelaguna@iberia.net
Very comfortable rooms; tranquil setting, with pool and great home cooking. Well situated for the Iberá wetlands, with the lagoon only meters away. Boat and birding trips organized with knowledgeable guides. Full board only. **$$$**

Estancia San Gará
25 km (14 miles) from Ituzaingó
Tel: (0786) 420 550; Buenos Aires tel: (01) 4783 698
Fax: (01) 4476 2848
Offers guided tours of the Iberá wetlands as well as horseback riding and local wildlife trips. Full board only. **$$$**

Hosteria Nandereta,
Colonia Carlos Pellegrini.
Tel: (0773) 420 155
www.nandereta.com
A comfortable lodge in the heart of the Iberá wetlands region. Air-conditioned rooms with private bathroom. Bar, restaurant, video and games room. Boat safaris and many other activities organized. Full board only. **$$**

THE NORTHWEST

Catamarca
Hotel Leo III
Sarmiento 727
Tel: (03833) 432 080
www.leo3.com.ar
One of the best in town, with restaurant. **$$$**.

Hotel Ancasti
Sarmiento 520
Tel: (03833) 431 464
Very traditional, comfortable, friendly, and low-key. Recommended. **$$**

Hotel Suma Huasi
Sarmiento 541
Tel: (03833) 432 595
Economical, but rooms near lounge can be noisy. **$**

Tucumán
Grand Hotel
Av. Soldat 380
Tel: (0381) 450 2250
Five-star hotel in Tucumán. Comfortable and central, with all facilities. **$$$**

Gran Premier,
Crisostomo Alvarez 510
Tel: (0381) 431 0385.
Comfortable, air-conditioned rooms; recommended. **$**

Hotel Garden
Crisóstomo Alvarez 627
Tel: (0281) 431 1246
Clean, comfortable, and reasonably priced. **$**

Beyond Tucumán
Hotel Termas de Reyes
Termas de Reyes
Tel: (03892) 235 500
Fax: (03892) 233 117
Telex: 66130 NASAT
Located about 19 km (12 miles) from the city, this hotel offers thermal baths in all rooms, good facilities and heated pool. **$$$$**

Hotel Ruinas de Quilmes
Amaichá del Valle
Tel: (03892) 421 075
Beautiful and extremely comfortable hotel, located at the ruins of the former Quilmes civilization and constructed and decorated in similar style. Very highly recommended and well worth the detour. **$$$**

Tilcara
Villar del Ala
Tel: (0288) 4794 8964
Intimate pleasant hotel, with good restaurant. Good base for exploring local countryside. Local excursions organized. **$$$**

THE CUYO

Mendoza
Reina Victoria Suites and Towers
San Juan 1127
Tel/fax: (0361) 425 9800

Luxury apart-hotel in the center of town, with pool, solarium, health club, and cafe. Comfortable air-conditioned rooms. **$$$**

Hotel Aconcagua
San Lorenzo 545
Tel: (0261) 420 4455
A few blocks from the main shopping area, with very modern architecture, pool, and air-conditioned rooms. **$$**

Hotel Internacional
Sarmiento 720
Tel: (0261) 425 5606
Large comfortable rooms. Recommended. **$$**

Hotel San Martín
Espejo 435
Tel: (0261) 438 0677
Recommended. **$$**

Hotel Imperial
Las Heras 88
Tel: (0261) 423 4671
Very basic, but a bargain. **$**

Potrerillos

Gran Hotel Potrerillos
Ruta 7, Km 50
Potrerillos
Tel: (02624) 482 130
Large, *estancia*-style hotel in extensive grounds on hillside overlooking the town. Rooms and apartments, with restaurant, bar, outdoor pool, tennis court, and other sports facilities. **$$$$**

Cabañas de Montaña
Complejo Turístico, Potrerillos
Tel: (02624) 483 100
Comfortable family cabins in beautiful countryside one hour from Mendoza, well situated for walking, horseback-riding, and whitewater rafting. **$$$**

Las Heras

Hostería Puente del Inca
Ruta 7
Tel: (0361) 438 0480
Fax: 4380 477
Secluded inn 2,720 m (8,920 ft) above sea level, with views of Aconcagua massif. **$$**

Luján de Cuyo

Hotel Termas Cacheuta
Ruta 7, Km 37, Cacheuta,
Luján de Cuyo
Tel: (03624) 482 082
Fax: (0361) 316 085

Excellent place for relaxing, surrounded by mountains. Good restaurant. Massage and spa facilities available. **$$$**

Salta

Hotel Salta
Buenos Aires 1
Tel: (0387) 4211 011
Fax: (0387) 4310 740
Traditional hotel with wooden balconies and all amenities, situated in the main square. **$$$**

Provincial
Caseros 786
Tel: (0387) 421 8400
Fax: (0387) 421 8993
Huge rooms, and a pool. **$$$**

Portezuelo
Avenida del Turista 1
Tel: (0387) 431 0104
www.portezuelo.com
Hotel in the hills with two pools and all facilities. **$$$**

Hotel Regidor
Buenos Aires 8
Tel: (0387) 431 1305
Good value and good facilities. Comfortable. **$**

Las Lajitas
Calixto Gauna 336
Tel: (0387) 423 3796
Modern and good value. **$**

Price Guide

Prices are all for a double room:

$$$$	$100 plus
$$$	$50–100
$$	$30–50
$	$30 or under

PATAGONIA

Posada Los Alamos
Moyano y Bustillo, El Calafate
Tel: (02902) 491 144
Fax: (02902) 491 186
www.posadalosalamos.com
Alpine-style lodge, very comfortable, with sports facilities, putting course, shop, bar, and excellent restaurant. **$$**

La Loma
B. Roca/15 de Febrero, El Calafate
Tel: (02902) 491 016
www.lalomahotel.com
Inexpensive and cozy. **$**

Los Notros
Parque Nacional Los Glaciares
Tel: (02902) 491 437
Overlooking Perito Moreno glacier with stunning views in the heart of the national park. Very comfortable. Half-board only. **$$$**

Hotel Tronador
Ruta 237, Km 19
Tel: (02944) 468 127
www.hoteltronador.com
Family-run hotel in a beautiful secluded setting on the shores of Lake Mascardi. **$$**

Hostería del Viejo Molino
Av. Bustillo 6400
Tel/fax: (02944) 441 011
Intimate hotel on Lake Nahuel Huapi, 6 km (4 miles) outside Bariloche. **$$**

Hotel-Bungalows Rupu Pehuen
Av Los Pioneros 4500
Tel: (02944) 441 456
In the suburb of Melipal, 4.5 km (3 miles) from Bariloche, with a swimming pool and tennis courts. **$$**

Hostería El Retorno
Ruta 258
Tel: (02944) 467 377
www.hosteriaelretorno.com
On Lake Guttierrez, about 10 km (6 miles) from Bariloche. Peaceful and attractive. **$$**

Hostería La Posada
Villa La Angostura
Tel: (02944) 494 450
Fax: (02944) 494 368
www.hosterialaposada.com
In its own secluded bay on the opposite side of the lake to Bariloche. **$$$**

Edelweiss Hotel
Av. San Martín 202, Bariloche
Tel/fax: (03944) 426 165
www.edelweiss.com.ar
A large hotel in the city with 100 rooms. Sauna, heated pool, fitness rooms, and a good restaurant. Combines tradition with modernity. **$$$**

Llao Llao Hotel and Resort
Tel/fax: (011) 4311 3432/3433
www.llaollao.com
One of the best located hotels in Argentina, approximately 29 km (18 miles) from Bariloche on the shores of Lago Nahuel Huapí, with own marina and golf course. **$$$$**

Hostería El Trebol
Cholila, Chubut
Tel: (03945) 498 055
Family-run hostel, with home produce and cooking. Hunting and fishing trips can be arranged with the proprietor. **$**

Price Guide

Prices are all for a double room:

$$$$	$100 plus
$$$	$50–100
$$	$30–50
$	$30 or under

TIERRA DEL FUEGO

Lago Escondido
Hosteria Petrel
60 km (37 miles) from Ushuaia on Ruta 3
Tel: (02901) 433 569
Very pleasant hostel by the foot of the lake. Good service and warm atmosphere. Breakfast included. Camping also available. **$$**

Rio Grande
Atlantida
Avenida Belgrano 582
Tel: (02964) 431 914/431 917
Fax: (02964) 431 915
Modern, functional, but popular, and the best in town. **$$$**
Posada de los Sauces
Elcano 839
Tel: (02964) 432 895
Fax: (02964) 432 430672
Comfortable hotel, with decent restaurant and bar.
Recommended. **$$$**
Los Yaganes
Avenida Belgrano 319
Tel: (02964) 430 822
Part of the ACA (Automovil Club Argentino) network. Comfortable rooms, with good but expensive restaurant. **$$**
Hospedaje Noal
Rafael Obligado 557
Tel: (02964) 427 516
Good-value option. **$**
Hospedaje Villa
San Martin 277
Tel: (02964) 422 312
Recommended budget hostel. Basic, clean basic facilities.**$**

Tolhuín
Albergue Libertad
Metet 321
Tel: (02901) 492 177
Backpackers' hostel with restaurant in this small village. **$$**
Hostería Kaiken
Ruta 2940 Km 3
Tel/fax: (02901) 492 208
A comfortable hostel a few kilometers south of Tolhuín, with a beautiful outlook on the shore of Lago Fagnano. With rooms and cabins for up to five people, restaurant (overpriced) and confitería. **$$**

Ushuaia
Las Hayas Resort Hotel
Camino Glaciar Martial Km3
Tel: (02901) 430 710–18
Fax: (02901) 430 719
www.lashayas.com
Located on a hill outside Ushuaia, with impressive views. Spa and pool. Runs a mini bus service to the city. **$$$$**
Hotel del Glaciar
Camino Glaciar Martial Km 3.5
Tel: (02901) 430 640
Fax: (02901) 430 636
Fantastic views and good service. Outside Ushuaia, but recommended. **$$$**
Cabo de Hornos
San Martín 899
Tel: (02901) 422 187
Pleasant and popular, with restaurant. **$$**
Hostal del Bosque Apart Hotel
Magallanes 709
Tel: (02901) 421 723
Pleasant hotel rooms with kitchens in city center. **$$**
Hotel Tolkeyen
Del Tolkeyen 2145
Tel: (02901) 445 315/6/7
www.hoteltolkeyen.com.ar
Excellent hotel outside town, fantastic views, very good service. **$$**
Hotel Ushuaia
Laserre 933
Tel/fax: (02901) 430 671/ 423 051/431 134/424 217
Modern, large, and pleasant hotel, though the neighborhood leaves something to be desired. Good service. Ten blocks to the center. **$$**

Torre al Sur
Gobernador Paz 1437
Tel: (02901) 430 745
www.torrealsur.com.ar
Very popular hostel for backpackers, with shared rooms. Good views and a friendly welcoming atmosphere. Kitchen for guests' use. Highly recommended. **$$**
Hostería Mustapic
Piedrabuena 230
Tel: (03901) 421 718
Old, simple, and one of the city's few inexpensive hotels. **$**
Hotel Cesar
San Martín 753
Tel: (02901) 421 460
www.hostal.com.ar
Central, with good service. Homey and friendly. **$**
Malvinas Hotel
Deloqui 615
Tel: (02901) 422 626
Clean, comfortable and quiet. Breakfast buffet. **$$**
Refugio del Mochilero
25 de Mayo 241
Tel: (02901) 436 129
Fax: (02901) 431 190
Another popular backpackers' hostel, with kitchen facilities, laundry and internet. **$**
Residencial Fernandez
Onachaga 72
Tel: (02901) 421 192
Small hostel, warmly recommended. **$**

Where to Eat

What to Eat

Argentina is well known for its beef, but in the past decade or so, the country has undergone something of a culinary revolution. Imaginative fusions, smart sushi restaurants, and exotic, authentic cuisine from around the world can be found – particularly in Buenos Aires (*see page 91*).

A typical meal would be *empanadas* (meat pastries, although the filling will vary according to the region), *chorizo* or *morcilla* (pork or blood sausage), and an assortment of *achuras* (sweetbreads), but this is only the appetizer. For the main course, a good *bife de chorizo* (T-bone steak), or *tira de asado*, or *lomo* are the most popular choices, accompanied by various types of salads. To finish off, one might choose a nice *flan* (custard), topped with *dulce de leche* and some whipped cream.

Throughout Argentina there are typical local cafes (*confiterias*), serving wonderful espresso, tea, soft and alcoholic drinks. A few of them, especially some famous traditional establishments in Buenos Aires, are highly recommended.

Restaurant Listings

BUENOS AIRES

Dining out is a favorite pastime of *porteños*, but the menu is not the only attraction. Restaurants are a place to socialize, to see and be seen, and share a bottle of wine until the wee hours of the morning. Nevertheless, *porteños* take eating seriously. A person could eat out every day of the year and still not savor the cuisine of all the restaurants of Buenos Aires. Dining out here is a delightful experience. Food, wine, and service are excellent, for the most part. A complete listing of all restaurants in the city would be impossible. A good gourmet guide is the *Guide to Good Eating in Buenos Aires*, published by the English-language *Buenos Aires Herald*. A list of recommended eateries follows, but there are hundreds of other good restaurants in the city, where the food is almost always fresh and well-prepared.

Restaurants in Buenos Aires open for lunch at noon, and for dinner around 8pm. But no one dines out in the evening before 9pm, with restaurants really coming alive between 10pm and 11pm. Weekends, restaurants stay busy well after midnight. Many restaurants close on Monday.

Regional Argentine
El Ceibal
Güemes 3402
Tel: (011) 4823 5807
Cabildo 1421
Tel: (011) 4784 2444
Great place to try specialties from Northern Argentina, including *locro* (stew with pig's feet and other meats), *humitas* (corn-based dish cooked in corn leaves), *tamales,* and *empanadas*. **$$**

La Payanca
Suipacha 1015
Tel: (011) 4312 5209
Northern Argentine food. Very central. Distinctive interior. Serves *locros* and *tamales*. **$$**

Indian
Katmandu
Córdoba 3547
Tel: (011) 4963 1122
Upmarket, authentic restaurant. **$$$**

French
Au Bec Fin
Vicente Lopez 1825
Tel: (011) 4801 6894
Classic French cooking in a splendid restored mansion; a Buenos Aires institution. Dinner only. Reservations. **$$$**

Catalinas
Calle Reconquista 875
Tel: (011) 4313 0182
Country French decor and innovative menu (rabbit with figs, fish with hazelnuts, grilled baby eels), including lots of seafood choices. Reservations. **$$$**

El Gato Dumas
Junín 1745
Tel: (011) 4804 5828
Offerings from the idiosyncratic master chef Gato Dumas include "ecstatic double chicken breasts" and "perfumes of crayfish and chicken." Reservations. **$$$**

Mora X
Vicente Lopez 2152
Tel: (011) 4803 0261
Menu created by the same culinary director of Au Bec Fin features informal French cooking and grilled meats. Stylish gallery atmosphere, mural-size paintings, and tall ceilings. **$$**

International
El Aljibe (Hotel Sheraton)
San Martín 1225
Tel: (011) 4318 9329
An exciting menu featuring beef and an eclectic range of dishes. **$$$**

Soul Café
Baez 248
Tel: (011) 4778 3115
Trendy bar and restaurant, with music. **$$**

Te Mataré Ramirez
Paraguay 4062
Tel: (011) 4832 7030
An excellent, original, international assortment of dishes, located in Palermo. Ideal for either a romantic evening or a business dinner. Specializes in dishes with aphrodisiac qualities. **$$–$$$**

Restaurant Prices

Categories are based on the cost of a meal for two people, with a bottle of house wine:

$$$	$40 or more
$$	$20–40
$	$20 or less

Italian and Mediterranean
(See also Pizzerias, page 355)
Bice
Av. Alicia de Justo 192
Tel: (011) 4315 6216
The original is in Milan, with ten more around the world, and the BA version in Puerto Madero. A very posh Northern Italian eatery, with modern twists on traditional pasta. **$$**

Campo del Fiori
Corner of Venezuela and San José, opposite Plaza Mayor
Tel: (011) 4381 8402
Nicely decorated family place where pasta is handmade in the middle of the restaurant. **$$**

Restaurant Prices

Categories are based on the cost of a meal for two people, with a bottle of house wine:

$$$	$40 or more
$$	$20–40
$	$20 or less

Fellini
Paraná 1209
Tel: (011) 4811 2222
Trendy and lively restaurant overlooking beautiful plaza, with interesting fresh and imported Italian pastas, gourmet pizzas, and specialty salads. **$$**

Teatriz
Riobamba 1220
Tel: (011) 4811 1915
Casual, warm atmosphere with a touch of elegance, also in Barrio Norte. Mediterrean menu with interesting pasta, chicken, and fish, and wonderful desserts. **$$**

Mexican
Cielito Lindo
El Salvador 4999, Palermo Viejo
Tel: (011) 4832 8054
Fairly good Mexican food at very expensive prices. **$$$**

Parrillas (Steakhouses)
Chiquilín
Montevideo 321
Tel: (011) 4373 5163
Specializes in Italian pasta, and Argentinian *asado*. **$$**

Des Nivel
Defensa 855/Estados Unidos
A spit-and-sawdust *parrilla* in San Telmo which serves mouthwatering steaks in a relaxed environment. Highly popular. **$$**

El Mirasol
Davila 202
Tel: (011) 4315 6277
Large upscale *parrilla* in posh Puerto Madero, with an elegant atmosphere. Reservations recommended. **$$$**

El Palacio de la Papa Frita
Lavalle 735
Tel: (011) 4393 5849
Popular place, serving typical meat dishes and excellent souffle potatoes. **$$**

La Chacra
Avenida Córdoba 941
Tel: (011) 4322 1409
Typical *asado* and *parrillada* restaurant with a touristy atmosphere; with meat roasting in the window for pedestrians to drool at. Huge portions. **$$**

La Estancia
Lavalle 941
Tel: (011) 4326 0330
Fun, classic *asado* restaurant in the heart of La City. **$$**

La Veda
Flórida 1
Tel: (011) 4331 6442
Another traditional establishment in La City. Basement floor, dark wood paneling, excellent steak au poivre. Tango dinner show most evenings. Reservations recommended. **$$$**

Munich Recoleta
R.M. Ortíz 1879
Tel: (011) 4804 3981
Popular for nearly forty years, for the lively atmosphere and great steak. Reservations are not accepted. **$$**

Río Alba
Cerviño 4499
Tel: (011) 4773 9508
Also in Palermo, a popular restaurant famous for brochettes, grilled fish, and enormous filet mignon steaks. **$$$**

Los Troncos
Suipacha 732
Tel: (011) 322 1295
Excellent meat and fruity wines at bargain prices. **$**

Confiterías (Cafes)

The traditional cafes of Buenos Aires are famous as lively neighborhood meeting places, offering not only good snacks and drinks, sometimes 24 hours a day, but also an eclectic mix of live music, poetry, and high-brow intellectual debate (*see box on page 166.*)

Café Tortoni
Avenida de Mayo 829
Tel: (011) 4342 4328
Built in 1848, with billiards, live jazz, poetry readings, and decaying grandeur. **$$**

Café La Paz
Corrientes 1599
Popular with students and intellectuals. Recently modernized, with a salad bar. Open until late. **$$**

Flórida Garden
Flórida and Paraguay
Traditional confitería and journalists' meeting place, serving a good range of sandwiches, cakes, and other snacks. **$$**

Ideal
Suipacha 384
Tel: (011) 4553 2466
Smart stylish meeting point for the elderly. Old-style confitería with polished marble floor and columns, now in decline. There is live music on Sunday evenings. (Open Mon–Fri 3–9pm.) **$$**

La Biela
Avenida Quintana 600
Tel: (011) 4804 0449
At the heart of Recoleta, very well-known. Attractive location opposite the Recoleta Cemetery, with outside tables. **$$**

La Giralda
Corrientes 1449
Delicious hot chocolate and churros in small, old-fashioned, wood-paneled cafe. **$$**

Richmond
Florida 468
Tel: (011) 4222 1341
Pleasant, English-style bar and tea room, now modernized but still retaining wood paneling, leather upholstered chairs, and hunting prints. **$$**

Pizzaerias

El Cuartito
Talcahuano 937
Tel: (011) 4393 1758
The closest BA comes to a sports bar, with clippings and photos covering the walls, soccer on the television, delicious pizzas, and cold beer. **$**

Los Inmortales
Corrientes 1369, Lavalle 746, Callao 1165
Small chain of legendary BA pizzerias where the decor is dedicated to the life and times of tango stars and the pizza is consistently good. Try the classic napolitana, covered with tomatoes and garlic. **$**

Spanish

El Globo
H. Yrigoyen 1199
Tel: (011) 4381 3926
One block from Avenida de Mayo, near Congreso. Try their *paella* or *puchero* (seafood stew). **$$**

Pedemonte
Avenida de Mayo 676
Tel: (011) 4331 7179
A favorite with BA politicians, with turn-of-the-20th-century decor, and featuring Spanish cuisine, pastas and grilled beef. Tango shows. Reservations. **$$$**

Plaza Mayor
Venezuela 1399
Tel: (011) 4383 0788
Specializes in Spanish seafood dishes. Situated in the independent-theater district, popular with the younger crowd and open late. **$$**

Tasca Tancat
Paraguay 645
Tel: (011) 4312 5442
Long, antique wooden bar, specializes in Spanish-style *tapas*. Closed weekends. **$**

Vegetarian

Dietética Córdoba
Córdoba 1557
Tel: (011) 4812 2685
Open lunchtime only, with an impressive buffet. In the same block is **La Esquina de las Flores,** also with a good selection and tasty vegetarian food. **$**

Ever Green
Vegetarian restaurant chain with inexpensive lunch buffets. reasonably extensive vegetarian and macrobiotic menu. Locations include Tucumán 666 and Sarmiento 1728. **$$**

Los Sabios
Corrientes 3733
Tel: (011) 4864 4407
Vegetarian Chinese food. **$$**

Tulasi
Marcelo T. de Alvear 628
Local 30
Tel: (011) 4311 0972
Located off leafy Plaza San Martín, this cafe is a good, inexpensive, lunch place, offering a selection of Indian food. **$**

Valle Esmeralda
Esmeralda 370
Tel: (011) 4394 9266
Self-service, lunches only. **$$**

Yin Yang
Paraguay 858
Tel: (011) 4703 1546
Echeverría 2444
Tel: (011) 4788 4368
Two outlets run by the same owner. A delicious respite from Argentine beef, featuring fresh salads, soups, homemade wheat bread, brown rice, and stir-fried veggies, and various other meatless treats. **$**

MAR Y SIERRAS

Mar del Plata

There are literally hundreds of restaurants here. Most are acceptable, and seafood is likely to be fresh almost anywhere.

Tío Curzio
Blvd. Maritimo 2657 and Colón
Enjoy delicious seafood overlooking the beach. **$$$**

El Timón
In the center of the port, Loc. 16
Tel: (0223) 420 2674
Fresh seafood. **$$/$$$**

Taberna Baska
Martinez de Hoz, near 12 de Octubre
Fresh seafood. Spanish cuisine. **$$**

El Palacio del Bife
Córdoba 1857
Tel: (0223) 420 0209
Not just beef (*bife*) – they also do good chicken dishes and *parrillas*. **$$**

Popular Eateries

Some of the best-value-for-money restaurants in Buenos Aires are those that serve a mixture of local and international dishes, but which are most popular for the lively ambiance provided by their regular clientele.

Bárbaro
Tres Sargentos 415
Tel: (011) 4311 6856
Literally a BA landmark – a charming, old-world version of the hole-in-the-wall bar, a great place for a simple midday meal, or music, beer, and bar food in the evening. **$**

El Trapiche
Paraguay 5099
Tel: (011) 4772 7343
Typical neighborhood restaurant in Palermo, with cured hams, tins of olive oil, and bottles of wine decking the walls and ceiling. Great steaks, homemade pastas, and seafood. **$$**

La Casa de Esteban de Luca
Defensa and Carlos Calvo
In the heart of San Telmo, the restored colonial-era home of the Argentine "poet of the revolution"; popular Sunday lunch after the San Telmo fair. **$**

Pippo
Montevideo 345
No frills but great atmosphere and unbeatable prices. Try a *bife de chorizo* (T-bone steak), or a bowl of *vermicelli mixto* (pasta with pesto and bolognaise sauce). **$**

Restaurant Dora
L.N. Além 1016
Tel: (011) 4311 2891
An upscale version of a popular eatery, with rave reviews on the enormous steaks and simple seafood dishes; a downtown "don't miss". **$$**

Rodi Bar
Vicente Lopez 1900
Tel: (011) 4801 5230
Cozy, neighborhood restaurant nestled among the famous gourmets of the Recoleta, featuring simple homemade food. **$**

Ambos Mundos
Rivadavía 2644
Tel: (0223) 495 0450
Spanish and Argentine cooking. **$$**
Stella Maris
Corner of Alsina and Alberti, two
blocks from bus terminal
Outstanding *cazuela de mariscos*
and other fresh seafood. Highly
recommended. **$**

Villa Gesell
Cantina Caprese
Buenos Aires between Alameda
206 and 208
Good Italian cuisine. **$$/$$$**
La Cabaña
Paseo 119 and Av. 3
Good seafood and pasta. **$$**
La Jirafa Azul
Av. 3 between Buenos Aires and
Paseo 102
An informal restaurant and bar. **$**
Las Cortaderas
Calle 301 between Circunvalación
and 214
Excellent pastries and bakery
goods, as well as light meals. **$**

CENTRAL SIERRAS

Córdoba
There are many self-service
restaurants in the city center,
which cater to students and sell a
variety of dishes by weight, most
of which are good and cheap,
especially for the set lunch menu.
Otherwise, you could try the
following:
La Mamma
Figueroa Alcorta 270
Tel: (0351) 426 0610
Italian food, with good meat and
pasta. **$$**
Il Gatto
Rafael Nunez 3856 and
General Paz 120
Tel: (0351) 421 3619
Pasta, pizza and international
cooking, part of a national chain.
$$
Rancho Grande
Rafael Nunez 4142
International cooking, with lots of
beef. One of the oldest and most
traditional restaurants in Córdoba.
$$

Rías Bajas
Montevideo 271
Tel: (0351) 425 1845
Shellfish a specialty. **$$**
Betos
San Juan 494
Well-known for the serving the best
meat dishes in the city. **$$$**

Villa Carlos Paz
Il Gato
Libertad and Belgrano
Tel: (03541) 422 361
International cooking, pasta and
pizza. **$$**

Río Ceballos
Confitería Vienesa
On San Martín,the main street.
Delicious pastries. **$$**
Kupferhassel
Buonarotti s/n
Tel: (03543) 453 750
German-style restaurant, serving
fondues, tea, and cakes. **$$**

THE NORTHEAST

Rosario
There are a number of good
restaurants offering an attractive
view of the river. including the
following:
Club Náutico Rosario
Belgrano 1000
Tel: (0341) 440 9776
High-class meat and fish dishes. **$$$**
Rich
San Juan 1031
Tel: (0341) 440 8657
Upmarket, traditional restaurant. **$$$**
Señor Arenero
Costanera 2568
Tel: (0341) 454 2155
Another long-standing Rosario
restaurant. **$$**

THE NORTHWEST

Catamarca
Hotel Casino Catamarca
Pasaje Carmen
International menu, good service,
dinner shows. **$$$**
Sociedad Española
Virgen del Valle 725
Tel: (03833) 431 897

International, Spanish, and
Argentine cuisine, specializing in
parrillada and seafood. **$$**
Trattoria Montecarlo
República 548
Excellent pasta and meat dishes,
located on the plaza.
Recommended. **$/$$**
La Leña
Guemes 563
An inexpensive *parrilla* restaurant. **$**

Tucumán
Floreal
25 de Mayo 568
Good international cooking – a very
popular spot. **$$**
La Leñita
25 de Mayo 377
An attractive family-run restaurant,
specializing in *parrillada* meats.
$$/$$$
Carlos V
25 de Mayo 330
Located inside Carlos V Hotel.
International cooking, especially
Spanish and Italian. **$$**

Salta
Hotel Portezuelo
Av. Turística 1
Fairly standard Argentine beef and
pasta menu. Worth a visit for its
location on a hill with a beautiful
view of the city. **$$/$$$**
Santana
Mendoza 208
Good Argentine food, with regional
dishes. **$$**
La Estrella Orientál
San Juan 137
Arab cooking. **$$**
Los Gauchos de Guemes
Uruguay 750
Restaurant and folklore show.
Food is average and the show is
good but very touristy atmosphere.
$$/$$$
Boliche Balderrama
San Martín 1126
Traditional restaurant, with
regional dishes and folklore show.
$$/$$$

Jujuy
The two best restaurants are
located in the **Hotel Jujuy Palace**
(Belgrano 1060) and the **Hotel
Panorama** (Belgrano 1295); both

are moderate/expensive. **Hotel Alto La Viña**, a few kilometers out of town on Ruta 56, serves reasonable lunches, with spectacular views. The city center pedestrian street, **Belgrano**, has many bars and *confiterías*, all reasonable, and moderately priced.

El Exodo
El Exodo 190
Regional cooking, such as *locro* (stew), *empanadas* (savory pastries), and other local specialties. **$**

Madre Tierra
Otero and Belgrano
Vegetarian cooking. Inexpensive. **$**

Restaurant Prices

Categories are based on the cost of a meal for two people, with a bottle of house wine:

$$$	$40 or more
$$	$20–40
$	$20 or less

Cafayate
La Carreta de Olegario
Güemes 2 on the central plaza
Tel: (03868) 421 004
Regional cooking, including both meat dishes and *locro* and other local specialties. **$**

La Casona de Luis
Almagro 87
Tel: (03868) 421 249
Regional cooking in colonial building, also a hotel. **$$**

El Comedor Criollo
Guemes 254
Tel: (03868) 421 140
Local specialties, such as kid. **$/$$**

THE CUYO

Mendoza
Restaurante Sarmiento
Sarmiento 658
Tel: (0261) 438 0324
Traditional restaurant specializing in kid (*chivo*) and suckling pig (*lechón*). **$$$**

La Marchigiana
Patricias Mendocinas 1550
International cuisine, top-level service. **$$$**

La Nuova Pizza
Av. Sarmiento 785, Mendoza
Bright and lively pizza-parlor with air conditioning. **$$**

Trevi
Las Heras 70
Italian food, good home-made pastas and meat dishes. **$$**

Ferruccio Sopelsa
Paseo Sarmiento 35
Tasty ice-creams served in generous portions. Part of a chain with other branches around the city. **$$**

Class
Paseo Sarmiento and Av. San Martín, Mendoza
Good, inexpensive set meals and beer by the jug. Pleasant outside tables, or air conditioning inside. **$**

Dali
Espejo and 9 de Julio
Friendly restaurant serving good food of the standard variety – beef, *milanesas* (schnitzel) and pasta. Recommended. **$**

PATAGONIA

Bariloche
Kandahar
20 de Febrero 698
Tel: (03944) 424 702
Imaginative menu and delightful ambiance. **$$/$$$**

Cervecería Blest
Av. Bustillo, Km 11.6
Tel: (03944) 461 026
Out of town on the road to Llao Llao, attached to the area's only brewery, serving tasty snacks. **$$**

La Marmite
Mitre 329, Bariloche
Tel: (03944) 423 685
A popular coffee house and restaurant right in the heart of town. **$$**

El Boliche de Alberto
Villegas 347
Tel: (03944) 431 4338
Typically Argentine, this is the place for serious meat eating. **$$**

Casita Suiza
Quaglia 342, Bariloche
Tel: (03944) 423 775
Traditional Swiss-style restaurant, with wide range of dishes,

including raclette, fondue, and rosti. **$$$**

TIERRA DEL FUEGO

Rio Grande
Atlántida
Belgrano 582
Tel: (02964) 431 914
In the elegant Hotel Atlántida, with international cuisine and good seafood. **$$$**

El Comedor de May
Elcano 839
Tel: (02964) 430 868
The best eating place in town, in the hotel Posada de los Sauces, with tasty meat and seafood dishes, and a reliable wine list. **$$$**

Rotisería CAI
Av. Perito Moreno s/n
A popular local place, serving good meat dishes. **$**

Tolhuín
Tel-Amen
Cerro Jeujupen esq. Juan Villa
Tel: (02901) 492 152
Small bar and restaurant worth trying for its lunchtime snacks and sandwiches. **$$**

La Posada de los Ramirez
Av. Shelknam 411
Tel: (02901) 492 128
Friendly, small restaurant. **$$**

El Basco
Kooshten 324
Tel: (02901) 492 137
Specializes in *parrilla* meats. **$$**

Dulces Sueños
Cabecera Lago Fagnano
Tel (cellphone): 1556 6432
Huge place overlooking the lake. Reasonable food. **$$**

Restaurante Hostería Kaiken
Cabecera Lago Fagnano. Ruta 3
Tel: (02901) 492 208
Extremely nice restaurant belonging to the hostel 120 km (75 miles) south of Rio Grande. Good food, excellent views. **$$**

Ushuaia
Kaupé
Roca 470
Tel: (02901) 422 704
Small restaurant with excellent food and lovely view of bay. Friendly

atmosphere and highly recommended. The best in town so booking is advised. **$$$**

Tia Elvira
Maipu 349
Tel: (02901) 424 725
Excellent food – particularly good seafood and German-style dishes; very popular. **$$$**

Parrilla del Martial
Louis Martial 2135
Tel: (02901) 432 253
Excellent view of the mountains. Good atmosphere and tasty food. Grilled meats are the speciality. **$$$**

Opiparo
Maipú 1255
Tel: (02901) 434 022
Beautiful old house in front of the local Yacht Club. Specializes in pizza and pasta, which are excellent. **$$**

Club Naútico
Maipú y Belgrano
Tel: (02901) 424 028
Very nice restaurant in the Yacht Club on the seafront. Excellent views and good food. **$$**

Barcito Ideal
San Martín 393
Tel: (02901) 433 840
Beautiful old house in the town center. Good atmosphere and reasonable food. **$$**

El Turco
San Martín 1440
Tel: (02901) 424 711
The most popular place in town with the locals. Excellent food, friendly atmosphere and extremely cheap. Strongly reccomended. **$**

Restaurant Prices

Categories are based on the cost of a meal for two people, with a bottle of house wine:

$$$	$40 or more
$$	$20–40
$	$20 or less

Culture

Cultural Life

The Argentine people are extremely culture-oriented. European trends are watched carefully, but Argentines maintain their own traditions. Most cities, particularly those with a university, offer a lively round of cultural activities, centered around the local museums, galleries, theaters, bookstores, and libraries. Most museums around the country charge only a nominal entrance fee and many are free. Discounts for students are sometimes available, with a recognized international student card. Opening hours are generally the same throughout the country: open daily except Sundays and sometimes Mondays; and many places close for several hours in the middle of the day, then open again until mid-evening. Opening hours of specific museums, where known, are given in the relevant Places sections of this book.

Art Galleries

Art is greatly appreciated in this country, with a traditionally strong influence from France, where many artists go to study. Buenos Aires is the dominant force of the country's artistic output, but some provincial capitals, such as Resistencia in the northeast, are also important centers. Many art galleries can be found as you walk around Buenos Aires. Some well-known ones are:
British Arts Center, Suipacha 1333.
Centro Cultural Recoleta, Junín 1930. Tel: 4803 1041.
Galería Ruth Benzacar, Flórida 1000.
Galería Praxis, Arenales 1311.
Galería Palatina, Arroyo 821.

Colección Alvear de Zurbarán, Av. Alvear 1658. A small collection of modern art (mostly Argentine artists) which changes monthly.
If you have the time to browse, take the side streets and you might run into some exquisite old houses containing interesting exhibits.

Theaters

The **Teatro Colón** is Buenos Aires' opera house, probably the best-known theater in all Latin America. Tickets are available from the box office on Calle Libertad 621. Tel: 4382 0554. Information: 4374 8611. Most of the renowned performers of the world are acquainted with this magnificent theater. The building is Italian Renaissance style with French and Greek influence. It holds 3,500 people, with about 1,000 standing. The acoustics are considered to be nearly perfect. Opera is one of the favorite programs for the season. The Colón also has a magnificent museum, where all of the theater's history and its mementos are stored. For a guided tour, call 4378 7132 to make an appointment.
State-funded, innovative **Teatro San Martín**, Av. Corrientes 1550, tel: 4371 0111, offers a variety of plays and musicals. Check the local newspapers for performances.

Folk Festivals

To get a real feel for Argentine folkloric culture it is worth trying to attend one of the many folk festivals that take place in various towns around the country.
The National Tourist Office can provide information on the main events, such as the Annual Folk Festival in **Cosquín**, near Córdoba, which each January draws crowds from all over the country with a line-up of top artists from Argentina, as well as from other South American and European countries. Cosquín's festival starts in the second half of January and lasts for nine nights. Contact the Oficina de Turismo in Cosquín for more information (tel: 03541 450 500)

La Falda, a short distance to the north of Cosquín, also has a folk festival, at the beginning of February. Contact the Secretaria de Turismo in La Falda, tel: 03548 423 007.

Carnival season produces a spectacular procession in **Salta** (celebrated on Shrove Tuesday) with decorated floats and colorful and intricate displays of the northern folk dance, all accompanied by energetic traditional music.

The wine-growing region of **La Rioja** hosts a particularly interesting festival in the third week of February in the town of the same name.

The festival of **La Chaya**, despite being held during the carnival season, does not get its inspiration from the European custom that introduced carnival to the continent. Rather, it is steeped in pre-Columbian Diaguita legend.

Santiago del Estero in the central northern belt has a vibrant and rich folk culture. It is said to produce the country's best composers and musicians, in addition to being home to the Gato and Chacarera song. On July 24, locals pay homage to their patron saint San Francisco Solano with much drink, live music, and dance. Also in July, in neighboring **Catamarca**, the Poncho Festival gets underway, with four wild days of traditional celebrations.

Mendoza: Festival de la Vendimia. The grape harvest festival is held here, in the center of Argentina's wine country, every March. Three days of festivities culminate with an extravaganza of lights, music, and dancing, held in an amphitheater set in the Andean foothills.

Villa General Belgrano: This small village near Córdoba hosts at least two festivals a year: the Alpine Chocolate Festival in winter, and an Oktoberfest (Fiesta de la Cerveza).

San Antonio De Areco: In November this town, 115 km (70 miles) from Buenos Aires, celebrates Tradition Week, when *gauchos* show off their skills in rodeo events. The town also has a *gaucho* museum (R. Guiraldes) and, on weekends, the local artisans sell their wares around the town plaza.

Nightlife

Buenos Aires

The nightlife in Buenos Aires is more active than in most major cities of the world. People walk carefree in the late hours of the night. Crime, although rising, is still not a major concern.

The center of town, on Calle Flórida and Lavalle, at midnight can be as crowded as at midday.

Movie theaters are open past 11pm and some restaurants in the city never close.

The *cantinas* of La Boca have become a tourist attraction in their own right – loud and rowdy singalong floor shows in enormous, garishly decorated restaurants. Calle Necochea, between Brandsen and Olavarria has a whole string of *cantinas*, including: Spadavecchia, La Fragata, Il Piccolo Navio, Los Tres Amigos, Gennarino, and La Gaviota.

Discos, nightclubs, cabarets, and bars can be found in most of the city. Hear the latest hits from around the world and dance into the morning at **Cemento**, on Estados Unidos 700 – very young, and grungy and good.

There are a lot of sleazy nightspots. The more respectable places include:

El Codo, Guardia Vieja 4085. Tel: 4862 1381. Very cozy, thirtysomething creative crowd. Soul, funk music. Long-established.
El Dorado, Hipólito Yrigoyen 947. Tel: 4334 2155. For drinking, dining, and dancing.
El Living, M. T. de Alvear 1540. Tel: 4811 4730. Popular with the trendy set.
La Morocha, Dorrego 3307. Tel: 4773 3888. In an old railway station, beautifully done up. Jet-set

Rock as Protest

Far from merely assimilating rock music from the USA and Europe, Argentine rock is considered very much a homegrown product, with distinct roots in national affairs. León Gieco, Fito Páez, Charly García, Luis Alberto Spinetta, and bands such as Voxdei, Sui Generis, Serú Girán, and Soda Stereo are celebrated artists of *Rock Nacional Argentino* – National Argentine Rock.

They have built on the *nueva canción* (new song) movement of the 1960s, when artists such as Mercedes Sosa and Atahualpa Yupanqui used folk songs to denounce social injustice – to the great annoyance of the military regime and at great risk to themselves. Sosa, for example, was first arrested then exiled in the 1970s.

Carrying on the voice of protest, the most radical of today's Argentine National Rockers is Charly García, who has infuriated the establishment, and has been censured and threatened with imprisonment, not only during the years of severe repression but also in times of "peace".

García's provocative songs include *Survivors* and *Dinosaurs*, gibes at oppression in Argentina. He also voiced opposition to external aggressors – for instance during the Malvinas (Falklands) crisis with songs such as *Don't bomb Buenos Aires*. Not known for his subtlety, García closed a concert during the Malvinas war with a hail of simulated missiles.

In February 1999, before the authorities thwarted his plans, he dreamed up a dramatic finale for Buenos Aires' biggest annual concert. To remind the city of the errors of the past, he planned to drop hundreds of mannequins from helicopters into the River Plate, intended as a commemoration of those who fell victim to the "dirty wars."

The Battle of the Sexes in Traditional Dance

Argentina's music and dance traditions have been greatly influenced by colonization over the centuries. Most folk dances are based on the orchestrated couple dances of the Spanish courts and Parisian ballrooms. However, native influence in music is robustly present in the north of the country, which benefits from the Andean influences of Chile, Bolivia, and Peru. In the mountainous regions of Jujuy and Salta many ancient dances still exist in their most colorful, intricate, and bold forms. Archived in the choreography and arrangement of these ancient dances are the memories and rituals of highly sophisticated pre-Columbian civilizations.

The Zamacueca, originally from Peru, developed into two dances: the **Zamba**, which moves to a slowed melancholic rhythm, and the more light-hearted **Cueca** (or Chilena). The Cueca, the **Baile-citos**, and the **Carnavalitos** employ the use of indigenous instruments such as the *charango* (an Andean mandolin), small drums, and the shrill sound of the *zampoña* flutes. Clad in rich orange cloth and sporting black bowler-style hats, men and women perform the complex repertoire of group reels known as the Carnavalito. In short, scurrying steps spurred on by *bombo* drumbeats, panpipe bursts, and energetic *charango* chords, they follow the commands of a cane-wielding caller.

Most folk dances enact a form of role-play – the battle of the sexes. The female and male dancers play out a duel of evasion and seduction, flirtation and rebuttal, full of sudden dramatic movements and equally emotional responses.

The *gaucho* is a romantic figure in Argentine folklore, as wild and intractable as the landscape itself. Dances and music that are particular to *gaucho* culture are the **Chacarera**, the **Gato**, and the **Escondido**. Unlike the dances of the north, these forms descended from old colonial and modern European culture and are known as "Creole" dance. They reflect the harshness and joy of life on the open plains.

Both the Chacarera and the Gato resonate with the repetitive beat of large drums and employ guitar and accordion accompaniments and a soloist storyteller. The rhythm of both may often be uplifting and infectious; but the lyrical content of the Chacarera centers on themes of pain and misery – a favorite of the *gauchos* who were always keen to play heavily on melancholic moments – while the lyrics of the Gato celebrate the joys of life, dance, and drink.

The Escondido is a particularly entertaining dance to watch as man and woman act out a pantomime of hide and seek (the name of the dance means "the hidden or lost one"). The woman hides by crouching down on one knee, shielding her eyes, while the man-protector struts around in spurred boots, snapping his fingers in the air as he mimics a frantic search for her.

The arrival of salon dances such as the polka and waltz in the mid-19th century centered upon couples who embraced (some light relief from the preceding warfare). By the 1920s many of the older Creole dances were exiled to the northwest regions where they found new homes such as Santiago del Estero, which adopted the Chacarera and the Gato.

Salta is one of the best places in the country to hear folk music, with several restaurants and *peñas* (folk clubs) putting on live shows. Among the recommended places are: **Boliche Balderrama**, San Martín 1126; **Gauchos de Guemes**, Uruguay 750; and **Manolo**, San Martín 1296.

The city also hosts an annual festival in mid-June with folk music and *gaucho* parades.

crowd with lots of posing. Separate room for rock 'n' roll.
Ozono, Uruguay 142. Tel: 4373 2666. Nice mixed crowd. Quiet bar upstairs, dancing downstairs.

The Argentines, as a whole, enjoy staying up late. Restaurants in Buenos Aires open up as early as 8pm, but in the provinces many don't open until 9pm.

The big cities of the interior (Córdoba, Mendoza, Bariloche, Salta, etc) that attract many tourists, also have a lively nightlife. The theater shows are not as varied as in Buenos Aires, but a little bit of everything is available. A good tango show is always popular and can be found both in the provinces and in the cities.

Movies

Going to the movies is popular throughout Argentina. Recent national and international films are shown, usually in English with Spanish subtitles. Listings appear in all of the local papers. In central Buenos Aires, many cinemas can be found in Lavalle and Corrientes.

Tango Shows

Good tango shows can be found almost everywhere, but the best are in Buenos Aires.
Bar Sur, Estados Unidos 299. Tel: 4362 6086.
El Viejo Almacén, Balcarce/Av. Independencia 300. Tel: 4307 7388
Cano 14, Talcahuano 975. Tel: 4393 4626.
El Castillo, Pedro de Mendoza 1455. Tel: 4428 5270.
Michelangelo, Balcarce 433. Tel: 4331 8689. Mixed repertoire of tango and folk music and dance, in atmospheric former monastery.
La Ventana, Balcarce 425. Tel: 4331 0217. Small, atmospheric venue, with good food and excellent show, featuring both tango and folk music from around South America. Inclusive show and meal, with pick up and drop off from your hotel.

Shopping

The current economic situation means there are some great bargains to be had. In addition, the government has recently introduced a scheme in which every foreign tourist is entitled to a refund of tax (IVA) on any purchase over US$70. Goods must be Argentine-made and have been bought from an outlet with a "Global Refund" sticker in its window. You must obtain an invoice and appropriate form at the time of purchase, both of which need to be presented to customs on leaving the country. The amount will be credited to your credit card, or a check posted to your home address in dollars.

The two main shopping streets in Buenos Aires are **Florida** and **Sante Fe**. Flórida has many of the well-known names such as Benetton, Gucci, and Stefanel. On the corner of Flórida and Córdoba is **Galerías Pacífico**, a three-story mall of quality clothes shops and sports stores. **Vitamina, Chocolate,** and **Sol Porteño** have outlets here, offering fairly expensive but trendy clothes.

Patio Bullrich (Posadas 1245) in Recoleta, next to the Hyatt Hotel, offers an even smarter range of shops, while **Alto Palermo** (A.P. Shopping, Arenales 3360) falls between the two. A good local designer for women is **Jasmín Chezbar**, at República de la India and Libertador.

Galería Bond Street (Santa Fe 85) has a range of secondhand clothes. Here, young Argentine designers try their hand at selling their own ranges, and you will find some interesting garments on show.

The exclusive part of town is located in the Recoleta area along Av. Alvear, Quintana, Ayacucho, and down small side-streets.

For food, the main supermarkets are **Disco, Norte** ,and **Coto**.

A first-class travel bookshop, with a wide range of both Spanish and English books and maps, is **Patagonia & Tierra del Fuego Travel Shop**, at Viamonte 500, off Flórida.

For souvenirs, there are several stores clustered on Paraguay as it crosses Flórida. The main items are silver photo frames, *mate* holders (the traditional herb tea drunk through a silver pipe), ponchos, and leather goods.

Antiques

The best-known area of Buenos Aires for antiques is San Telmo. It's one of the most historic *barrios* (neighborhoods) of the city. Every Sunday the San Telmo Fair takes place. The plaza is surrounded by stalls which sell quite an array of objects, from new to old, ordinary to odd, and which can be very cheap or outrageously expensive. Only the trained eye can find the bargains. The rest just think they have found a unique piece, when in fact they have only purchased a copy.

Around the plaza, there are many reputable antique stores. Prices are high, but some beautiful pieces can still be found. Auction houses are very popular and good buys can be obtained. Some of these are:
Roldán y Cia, R. Peña 1673.
Naon y Cia, Guido 1785.
Banco de la Ciudad, Esmeralda 660.

Small antique shops can be found throughout the city. The prices are negotiable. There are quite a number of these shops along Avenida Rivadavia, around the 4000 block. As these stores are not known to many, the prices and the attention are good.

Also, along Avenida Libertador, toward Martínez and the San Isidro area, are a number of shops with some very worthwhile pieces; it just takes time and a little knowledge.

La Baulera, on Av. Monroe 2753, has quite a different assortment of collectibles, and the owners will try to help find that unique piece. Other listings of shops can be obtained either from your hotel or from your copy of the *Buenos Aires Herald*.

Jewelers

Koltai Joyeria, Esmeralda 616. Antique quality jewelry.
Ricciardi, Flórida 1001.
Antoniazzi-Chiappe, Av. Alvear 1895.
Stern Jewellers, Sheraton Hotel.
Lovasi Joyeria, Rodriguez Peña 419.

Leather Goods

Coalpe (handbags), México 3325.
Colicuer (handbags), Tte. Gral. Perón 1615, 1st floor.
Maximilian Klein (handbags), Humberto Primo 3435.
Viel (handbags and shoes), Viel 1550.
La Mia Scarpa (custom-made shoes), Thames 1617.
Belt Factory, Fco. Acuña de Figueroa 454.

Regional Handicrafts in Buenos Aires

Artesanías Argentina, Montevideo 1386.
Tuyunti, Flórida 971.
Cardon, Av. Santa Fe 1287 – a *talabartería* selling *gaucho* gear, leather, and silverware.

Artisan Fairs take place at the weekends in different parts of the city. Some of these are:
Plaza Francia – near the Recoleta area on Sunday

Plaza Manuel Belgrano – Juramento 2200 on Sunday
Plaza Mitre – San Isidro on Sunday
Tigre – Puerto de los Frutos every Saturday and Sunday

Artisan fairs also take place in other parts of the country – Mendoza, Bariloche, and El Bolson.

Kerquelen (custom-made and quick service), Santander 745/747.
Le Fauve (latest leather fashions and competitive prices with personal attention), Sarandí 1226.
Casa Bariloche, Uruguay 318.

"Shoppings"

American-style shopping malls, known simply as "shoppings", began appearing in Buenos Aires in the late 1980s. Shops are mostly chains, with some luxury outlets. Many of the larger malls have food courts, cinemas and other facilities.
Abasto, Corrientes Ave 3247, Balvanera. A shopping mall housed in an historic building, with restaurants, cinemas and ice-skating rink.
Galerías Pacífico, Florida 787, San Nicolas. Renovated mall that contains the Borges Cultural Center.
Patio Bullrich, Posadas 1245, Recoleta. Another mall in an historic building, with all facilities and games for children.

Outdoor Activities

Out and About

With its vast areas of sparsely populated countryside, and spectacular range of landscapes, from the multicolored rocky deserts of the northwest, to the mighty Iguazú Falls of the subtropical northeast, and down to the legendary steppes and Andean peaks of Patagonia, Argentina is a paradise for lovers of the great outdoors. The transport and tourism infrastructures are well-developed, with a wide range of activities available to suit all tastes and most budgets.

For the most energetic, the Argentine Andes offer some of the most challenging and exciting mountain-climbing, trekking, and skiing in the world. But if you just want to relax and be pampered in a tranquil setting, there are numerous *estancias*, working farms whose owners have opened their doors to guests, offering horseback riding or just lazing by the pool and waiting for the *asado* lunch to be served.

The following is a selection of outdoor highlights around the country, with details of specialist agencies for organized tours.

BUENOS AIRES

For a city of its size, Buenos Aires is surprisingly well-endowed with leafy *plazas*, sports grounds, and green spaces, where you can escape the traffic and the crowds.

In the city's northern neighborhoods, in particular, there are numerous parks, spread around the Parque 3 de Febrero in Palermo. Here you will also find the Botanical Gardens, Buenos Aires Zoo, horse-racing at the Hipódromo Argentino, as well as polo, pato, golf, and tennis clubs.

In the city center, behind the recently renovated Puerto Madero dockside area is the Parque Natural Costanera Sur, a large, open area of coastal meadows and lagoons. The park, which has been designated a protected ecological reserve, contains a wide range of water birds as well as other animals, which are protected against hunting. There is a network of pathways around the flat park, making it ideal for cyclists, walkers, and bird-watchers. The wildlife preservation organization, Fundación Vida Silvestre, which administers the park, offers guided tours, daily at 3.30pm. Overnight stay is not permitted, but there is a range of restaurants, fast-food stalls, and picnic sites (open daily from 8am–6pm, free admission.)

If you have more time in Buenos Aires, a weekend in the Pampas makes a relaxing excursion. Within a couple of hours' drive are many *estancias* that offer horseback riding, *asados* (barbecues), and displays of *gaucho* skills. Some also have rooms and offer inclusive packages *(see page 104)*.
Estancia La Bamba in San Antonio de Areco (115 km/71 miles from Buenos Aires) offers comfort and tranquility. Tel: (011) 4392 9707.
Estancia El Carmen de Sierra is an historical building in Arrecifes, 170 km (106 miles) from Buenos Aires, offering accommodations, horseback riding, and a swimming pool. Tel: (036646) 41 083.
Estancia Los Patricios, on Ruta 41 near San Antonio de Areco, is a beautiful ivy-covered *estancia* with horseback riding, golf, swimming pool, local music and folk dancing, barbecues in a barn, and overnight accommodations. Tel: (03326) 3823.

For a more relaxed environment, with horses wandering across the lawn as you savor your *asado*, try **Estancia Santa Clara**, 30 minutes in a *remise (see page 346)* from Buenos Aires. Tel: (011) 4274 1878.

MAR Y SIERRAS

Fishing is very popular along the Atlantic coast south of Buenos Aires, both in the sea and in the region's various lagoons and rivers.

Chascomús is a small city on the shore of the Laguna Chascomús, about 125 km (78 miles) south of Buenos Aires. It is accessible by car or train. The lagoon has brackish water, and the main catches are *pejerrey* (a type of catfish) and a very aggressive fish called the *tararira*. Equipment can be rented at the local fishing club, the Club de Pesca y Naútica, which has a boardwalk on the lagoon, at the end of Avenida Lastra. There are also a number of *estancias* near to Chascomús, which offer accommodations and *gaucho* shows, including **Estancia Santa Ana** (tel: 03241 436 236), and **Estancia La Euskera** (tel: 03241 430 915).

The chain of coastal resorts, from San Clemente del Tuyú south to Mar del Plata, Miramar, and Necochea are also popular for fishing, with most local clubs offering equipment for hire and sea-fishing trips. The following operators run regular excursions and have boats for hire:
• **Turimar**, Mar del Plata. Tel: (023) 484 1450. Boat excursions and fishing trips, daily in summer.
• **Daniel Rodriguez**, Mar del Tuyú. Tel: (0246) 421 508. Fishing trips by arrangement.
• **Casa de Pesca La Trucha**, corner of Calle 10 and 59, Necochea. Tel: (0262) 428 601. Fishing cruises, daily in summer.
• **El Pique**, Avenida Los Talas del Tuyú and Calle 72, San Clemente del Tuyú. Tel: (0252) 421 601. Fishing trips by arrangement.

The sierras around **Tandil** offer some excellent opportunities for outdoor activities. In Tandil there are various tour operators who organize the following activities:

• **Horseback riding tours**: to Sierra del Tigre, Cerro Centinela, La Cascada. Sr. Gabriel Barletta, Av. Avellaneda 673. Tel: (0293) 427 725
• **Mountain-bike hire**: Señor Rodriguez, Calle Uriburu 1488. Tel: 428669
• **Guided walks**: Calfucará, Calle Garibaldi 215. Tel: (0293) 424 450
• **Adventure sports**: canoeing, trekking, climbing, horseback riding, walking. Compartir, Calle Las Heras 346. Tel: (0293) 430 522.

THE CENTRAL SIERRAS

Birdwatching is one of the big outdoor attractions in the Sierras de Córdoba, with a wide range of species commonly seen, including condors, often spotted around the suitably named **El Cóndor**, to the south of Córdoba. The **Club Andino**, on Deán Funes 2100, in Córdoba, runs birdwatching and other safaris and trekking tours.

THE NORTHEAST

The main outdoor attractions of the northeast are the world-famous Iguazú Falls, bordering Brazil, and the Esteros del Iberá, a wetlands region formed around the old course of the Río Paraná. Both sites offer great opportunities for seeing a wealth of exotic animals, set in a lush, sub-tropical landscape.

Guided tours on bicycle or horseback through the forest trails around the Iguazú Falls can be arranged. Enquire at the Visitors' Center in the park.

The best way to see the wildlife in the Iberá wetlands is to stay at one of the lodges *(posadas)* in and around Carlos Pellegrini *(see page 350)*, or you can camp by the edge of the lagoon at the visitors' center outside the town.

Boat trips around the lagoon are also available from the visitors' center; enquire for times and prices. Staff at the center will

Eco-organization

The Fundación Vida Silvestre Argentina (Argentine Wildlife Foundation) manages some of the country's protected areas of special environmental importance. It is a useful source of information about these areas, and their facilities for visitors. Open Mon–Fri 10am–1pm and 2–6pm. Defensa 245, Buenos Aires. Tel: (011) 4331 3631.

take visitors on guided walks around the small wooded area opposite, where amazingly tame howler monkeys and timid deer may be seen.

THE NORTHWEST

Indisputably the most fashionable resort in the northwest is Termas de Rio Hondo, in the province of Santiago del Estero, 63 km (39 miles) north of the city of the same name. If you want something more strenuous than lounging in the thermal baths, the nearby Río Hondo Reservoir (Embalse) offers a wide range of watersports, organized by the Club Naútico, whose clubhouse is on the shore of the reservoir. There is also an ACA campsite here.

Calilegua National Park, to the east of Salta and El Rey National Park, to the north of Jujuy, contain some of the most impressive tropical *yungas* landscapes in the whole country. Neither park has any facilities for visitors, nor is there any public transport, which probably explains why their flora and fauna has been so well preserved to date. Camping is permitted however, and travel agencies in Jujuy and Salta run group tours, charging about $100 per person per day.
• **Puna Expediciones**, Braquiquitos 339, Salta. Tel: (087) 434 1875.
• **Ecoturismo**, Jujuy. Tel: Cintia Alvarado (0768) 425 216.

THE CUYO

The biggest attraction in this area is Mt. Aconcagua, South America's highest mountain. Many climbing expeditions are organized every year from Mendoza. Enquire at the **Club Andinista**, F.L. Beltran 357, Gillen. Tel: (061) 431 9870.

For an eight-day trip to the foot of Aconcaqua, contact Fernando Grajales, **Optar Tours**, Mendoza, Hostería Puente del Inca, Prov. Mendoza. Tel: (0361) 438 0480.

The Cuyo is also rapidly becoming one of the country's main adventure tourism centers, with a whole range of "white-knuckle" activities on offer, including white-water rafting, mountain biking, and snow-boarding. There are various travel agencies that specialize in these actiivities, including the following:

• **Betancourt Rafting**, Ruta Panamericana and Rio Cuevas, CP 5501, Godoy Cruz, Mendoza. Tel/fax: (061) 439 1949/439 0229
• **Exploring Turismo Aventura**, Av. H. Yrigoyen 423, San Rafael. Tel/fax: (0627) 436 439. E-mail: bessone-viajes@cpsarg.com
• **Ascensiones y Trekking**, Reconquista 702, Godoy Cruz. Tel/fax: (061) 424 4292. E-mail: ascensiones y trekking@arnet.com.ar

Transportation and a range of trekking expeditions are available to the Parque Provincial Talampaya, near to La Rioja in the north of the Cuyo. For information contact::
• **Sr. Carlos Declaro**, Delegacion de Turismo, Libertad, esq. Independencia, Chilecito. Tel: (0825) 422 688
• **Dirección Provincial de Turismo**, Avenida Pte. Perón 401, La Rioja. Tel: (0822) 428 839. Fax: (0822) 422 913/422648.
• **Adolfo Paez**, Guardaparque de Talampaya, Pagancillo. Tel: (0825) 47115.

PATAGONIA

This huge wedge of Argentinian territory has the lion's share of the country's most spectacular scenery, and a dazzling array of outdoor activities and wildlife safaris are on offer here.

Bariloche, on the shore of Lago Nahuel Huapi, in the heart of the Parque Nacional Nahuel Huapi, is one of Patagonia's most popular outdoor centers, with activities on offer ranging from bird-watching safaris to hang-gliding. There are many agencies in the town specializing in each of the activities, but one of the best places to visit first for advice is:

Club Andino Bariloche, 20 de Febrero, Bariloche. Tel: (0944) 424 531.

This region also has a number of *estancias* that are open to visitors. You can spend from half a day to a week riding under the open skies of the Andean foothills, near the town of Bariloche. Similar to dude ranching operations in the US, but more rugged, with camping beneath the stars. Contact: Carol Jones, **Estancia Nahuel Huapí**, (8401) Nahuel Huapí, Neuquen or Hans Schulz, **Polvani Tours**, Quaglia 268, (8400) Bariloche tel: (03944) 423 286, telex: 80772 POLVA AR.

The Península Valdés is probably Argentina's best-known wildlife center, particularly for its huge colonies of sea lions and penguins. The following agencies, most of them based in Puerto Pirámide, offer a range of wildlife safaris, including whale-watching boat trips:
• **Moby Dick**, tel: (0965) 495 014
• **Muelle Viejo**, tel: (0965) 451 954; (01) 4314 1537
• **Peke Sosa**, tel: (0965) 495 010
• **Pinino Orri**, tel: (0965) 495 015
• **Sur Turismo** Julio A. Roca, Puerto Madryn. Tel: (0965) 434 550. Fax: (0965) 421 292.

A short steam-train journey in Tierra del Fuego – evocatively named the Tren del Fin del Mundo ("The End of the World Train") makes a pleasant day-trip, particularly suitable for families. The train departs from the municipal camp-site outside Ushuaia, on a 2-hour round-trip journey to the entrance to the Parque Nacional de Tierra del Fuego. There are four daily departures throughout the summer season. Tel: (901) 431 600. Fax: (901) 437 696. E-mail: ush@trendelfindelmundo.com.ar

Ushuaia is also the main base for a number of boat trips around Tierra del Fuego's waterways, along the Straits of Magellan, and some longer cruises as far as Antarctica. The following are some local and international agencies and tour operators:
• Sergio Alejandro Rovira, Tolhuín Aventuras, Cerro Jeujepen 466, Tolhuín. Tel: (cellphone) 066 966 569.
Lake and river trips, mountain-biking, photo safaris.
• Rumbo Sur Excursiones Maritímas, San Martín 342, Ushuaia. Fax: (0901) 430 699. Catamaran trips to Isla de los Lobos, penguin colonies, and to Harberton.
• Tolkeyen Servicios Maritímos, Muelle Turístico del Puerto de Ushuaia. Tel: (0901) 433 080/430 532. Catamaran excursions to Isla de los Lobos, penguin colonies.
• Quark Expeditions Inc. 980 Post Road, Darien, CT 06820, USA. Tel: (203) 656 0499. Fax: (203) 655 6623. Toll Free (in US): 800 356 5699. E-mail: quarkexpeditions@compuserv.com
A wide range of fully inclusive cruises from Ushuaia to Antarctica and the South Atlantic Islands.

Falabella Horses

A visit to the Estancia El Peludo will provide an interesting side trip from Buenos Aires. Located 65 km (40 miles) from town, this ranch raises the unique and famous miniature Falabella horses (named for their breeder). Some of these horses are owned by such international figures as the Kennedy family, the Carters, and King Juan Carlos of Spain. Those interested in visiting the *estancia* (and perhaps buying a horse), can contact Sra Falabella at 444 5050/1404.

Sport

By far the most popular spectator sport in Argentina is soccer. The national team has won the World Cup twice (in 1978 and 1986), local teams attract a following of almost religious devotion, and rivalry between fans can be fierce. The country's top teams are in Buenos Aires, best-known of which are Boca Juniors and Rio Plate. Matches are usually played on Wednesdays and Sundays, but vary at different times of year. The season runs from April to September.
Boca Juniors, Brandsen 805. Tel: (01) 4362 2050.
River Plate, Avenida Figueroa Alcorta 7597.Tel: (01) 4785 1019.

Soccer is not the only sport to be seen around the country, however *(see page 128)*, and the following are also popular.

PATO

This uniquely Argentine sport is sometimes played for public audiences on the *estancias* around Buenos Aires. The **Club Campo Hípico y de Pato Barracas al Sur**, in Buenos Aires, has games, public exhibitions, and riding displays. Tel: (01) 4201 5196.

POLO

Argentine polo horses are prized around the world for their agility and speed. Many European teams come here to enhance their skills. The best place to see polo in Buenos Aires is at the centrally located Palermo field. The most important national championship is usually held here in November. Tickets can be purchased at the box office in the grounds, on Avenida del Libertador y Dorrego.

HORSE RACING

The two main tracks in Buenos Aires are the Jockey Club, on the corner of Avenidas Márquez and Centenario in San Isidro, and the Hipódromo Palermo, on Avenida del Libertador, between Dorrego and Olleros, in Palermo. Races are held about four times a week, in the afternoons and evenings. Smaller tracks are located in most of the major Argentine cities.

MOTOR RACING

Motor racing has been very popular for years and (now deceased) Juan Manuel Fangio, a five-time Formula One champion in the 1950s, is virtually a folk hero. It is of great sorrow to many Argentines that financial problems have prohibited holding a Formula One championship race here in recent years.

Argentina's trout fishing is considered to be among the best in the world. You can fish along the coast, in the streams up in the Andes, or in the countless lakes and rivers in between. Spend a secluded vacation fishing for trout in the clear lakes and streams of the Andes. Accommodations, equipment, and guides provided. Contact:
Caleufu River SRL, M. Moreno 1185, (8370) San Martín de Los Andes, Neuquén, Argentina, tel: (03944) 47199, telex: COSMA CALEUFU.
Cosmopolitan Travel, L. Além 986, 7th floor, Buenos Aires 1001, Argentina, tel: (011) 4311 7880/6695/2478/ 6684, telex: 9199 CASSA AR.

Skiing is very popular in Argentina, particular for visitors from the Northern Hemisphere, who can ski here during the season from May through October, with some variation between the resorts.

The main ski resorts in Argentina are the **Cerro Catedral Complex**, near Bariloche; **Valle de las Leñas**, in the south of Mendoza Province; and **Los Penitentes**, a small resort near the Cuyo provincial capital, Mendoza.

There are also a number of small centers located throughout the southern provinces, including one in Tierra del Fuego, and another near Esquel.

The nearest thing in Argentina now to grand-prix racing is the South American Formula Three series of which half a dozen races are held yearly in various parts of the country. Also very popular is stock-car racing of which there are several levels, all of which hold their own annual championship with races almost every weekend all over the country.

Yearly motor rally events are held every year as part of the world championship series, generally around August/September in the province of Córdoba.

RUGBY

Argentina is among the world's top-ten rugby nations, and during the season from April to November matches continue to attract large crowds. The Pumas national rugby team play in the Vélez Sársfield stadium, in the Liniers neighborhood of Buenos Aires (*see also page 131*).

Language

General

Of the many versions of Latin-American Spanish in South America, the Argentine version is amongst the most difficult to understand. However, it is much better to know a little Spanish when you arrive. English might be spoken at major hotels and by quite a few Argentines in Buenos Aires, but don't count on it outside of the capital.

Pronunciation & Grammar Tips

Argentines tend to use a local vocabulary with little resemblance to classical Spanish, while the local accent imposes a soft "j" sound on the "ll" and "y" and most people speak very rapidly without enunciating clearly. At the same time, when using the second person familiar, Argentines use the form "vos" instead of the more common "tu", while the verb form used with "vos" places the accent on the last, rather than the penultimate syllable (for example, "¿que hacÉs?" instead of "¿quÉ hAces?" – what are you doing?). Television newsreaders are the only exception, although here too the Italianate accent also prevails.

Language Schools

Argentina is not the ideal place to learn Spanish, because of its linguistic idiosyncracies explained above. (Best value for classes as well as best for understanding is probably Quito, Ecuador, if you are considering further travel in South America.)

Language schools, apart from advertized private tuition (see the Buenos Aires Herald, especially on Sunday), include the ILEE, CEDIC, and Del Sur, all of which also offer accommodations. These and other main private language schools, including Berlitz, offer tailor-made individual courses. The Berlitz also offers a cassette that is worthwhile for beginners. A couple of well-known language schools in Buenos Aires are:

Berlitz Language Centers
Avenida de Mayo 847
Tel: (011) 4342 0202.
CEDIC
Reconquista 715, 11th E
Tel: (011) 4312 1016
ILEE
Lavalle 1619, 7th C
Tel: (011) 4375 0730
Idioma Buenos Aires
M.T. de Alvear 852, 2nd B
Tel: (011) 4312 7774

It is not essential for foreign speakers to use the correct form of address, i.e. formal or informal, or even the correct masculine or feminine conjugations, as long as you can make yourself understood. Many travelers learn Spanish to the "present tense" stage and manage very well on this alone. However, in order to be well received in Argentina, there are a few things worth remembering. Upon meeting someone, whether they be a taxi driver or a long-lost uncle, you always use the greeting, "Good morning" or "Good afternoon/evening." It is then appropriate to wait for the response before continuing your conversation. A woman is addressed as Señora, a girl or young woman as Señorita, and a man as Señor.

Basics

Yes *Sí*
No *No*
Thank you *Gracias*
You're welcome *De nada/Por nada*
Okay *Está bien*
Please *Por favor*
Excuse me (to get attention)
¡Perdón!/¡Por favor!
Excuse me (to get through a crowd)
¡Permiso!

Excuse me (sorry)
Perdóneme
Wait a minute! *¡Un momento!*
Please help me (formal)
Por favor, ayúdame
Certainly
¡Claro!/¡Claro que sí!/¡Por cierto!
Can I help you? (formal)
¿Puedo ayudarle?
Can you show me...?
¿Puede mostrarme...?
I'm lost *Estoy perdido(a)*
I'm sorry *Lo siento*
I don't know *No sé*
I don't understand *No entiendo*
Do you speak English/French/ German? (formal) *¿Habla inglés/ francés/alemán?*
Could you speak more slowly, please? *¿Puede hablar más despacio, por favor?*
Could you repeat that, please?
¿Puede repetirlo, por favor?
here/there *aquí (place where), acá (motion to)/allí, allá, ahí (near you)*
What? *¿Qué?/¿Cómo?*
When? *¿Cuándo?*
Why? *¿Por qué?*
Where? *¿Dónde?*
Who? *¿Quién(es)?*
How? *¿Cómo?*
Which? *¿Cuál?*
How much/how many?
¿Cuánto?/¿Cuántos?
Do you have...? *¿Hay...?*
How long? *¿Cuanto tiempo?*
Big, bigger *Grande, más grande*
Small, smaller
Pequeño, mas pequeño
I want.../I would like.../I need...
Quiero.../Quisiera.../Necesito...
Where is the lavatory (men's/women's)?
¿Dónde se encuentra el baño (de caballeros/de damas)?
Which way is it to ...?
¿Como se va a ...?

Greetings

Hello! *¡Hola!*
Hello *Buenos días*
Good afternoon/night
Buenas tardes/noches
Good-bye *Ciao/¡Adios!/Hasta luego*
My name is... *Me llamo...*
What is your name? (formal)
¿Cómo se llama usted?

Mr/Miss/Mrs
Señor/Señorita/Señora
Pleased to meet you
¡Encantado(a)!/Mucho gusto
I am English/American/Canadian/
Irish/Scottish/Australian
Soy inglés(a)/norteamericano(a)/
canadiense/irlandés(a)/
escocés(a)/australiano(a)
Do you speak English? (formal)
¿Habla inglés?
How are you? (formal/informal)
¿Cómo está? ¿Qué tal?
Fine, thanks *Muy bien, gracias*
See you later *Hasta luego*
Take care (informal) *¡Cuídate!*

Telephone Calls

The area code *El código de área*
Where can I buy telephone cards?
¿Dónde puedo comprar tarjetas
telefónicas?
May I use your telephone to make
a local call? *¿Puedo usar su*
teléfono para hacer una llamada
local?
Of course you may *¡Claro!*
Hello (on the phone) *¡Aló!*
May I speak to...? *¿Puedo hablar*
con... (name), por favor?
Sorry, he/she isn't in
Lo siento, no se encuentra
Can he/she call you back?
¿Puede devolver la llamada?
Yes, he/she can reach me at... *Sí,*
él/ella puede llamarme en (number)
I'll try again later
Voy a intentar más tarde
Can I leave a message?
¿Puedo dejar un mensaje?
Please tell him/her I called
Favor avisarle que llamé
Hold on *Un momento, por favor*
Can you speak up, please?
¿Puede hablar más fuerte, por favor?

In the Hotel

Do you have a vacant room?
¿Tiene una habitación disponible?
I have a reservation
Tengo una reserva
I'd like... *Quisiera...*
a single/double (with double bed)/
a room with twin beds
una habitación individual
(sencilla)/una habitación
matrimonial/una habitación doble

for one night/two nights
por una noche/dos noches
ground floor/first floor/top
floor/with sea view *una habitación*
en la planta baja/en el primer piso/
en el último piso/con vista al mar
Does the room have a private
bathroom or shared bathroom?
¿Tiene la habitación baño privado o
baño compartido?
Does it have hot water?
¿Tiene agua caliente?
Could you show me another room,
please? *¿Puede mostrarme otra*
habitación, por favor?
Is it a quiet room?
¿Es una habitación tranquila?
What time do you close (lock) the
doors?
¿A qué hora se cierran las puertas?
I would like to change rooms
Quisiera cambiar la habitación
This room is too noisy/hot/cold/
small *Esta habitación es*
demasiado ruidosa/caliente/fría/
pequeña
How much is it?
¿Cuánto cuesta?/¿Cuánto sale?
Does the price include tax/
breakfast/meals/drinks?
¿El precio incluye el impuesto/
desayuno/comidas/ bebidas?
Do you accept credit cards/
travelers' checks/dollars?
¿Se aceptan tarjetas de crédito/
cheques de viajeros/dólares?
What time is breakfast/
lunch/dinner? *¿A qué hora está el*
desayuno/almuerzo/la cena?
Please wake me at...
Favor despertarme a...
Come in! *¡Pase!, ¡Adelante!*
I'd like to pay the bill now, please
Quisiera cancelar la cuenta ahora,
por favor

USEFUL WORDS

bath/bathroom *el baño*
dining room *el comedor*
elevator/lift *el asensor*
key *la llave*
Push/Pull *empuje/tire*
safety deposit box *la caja de*
seguridad
soap *el jabón*
shampoo *el champú*
shower *la ducha*

toilet paper *el papel higiénico*
towel *la toalla*

In the Restaurant

ice cream *helado*
sandwich *sandwich*
I'd like to book a table *Quisiera*
reservar una mesa, por favor
Do you have a table for...?
¿Tiene una mesa para...?
I have a reservation
Tengo una reserva
breakfast/lunch/dinner
desayuno/almuerzo/cena
I'm a vegetarian *Soy vegetariano(a)*
Is there a vegetarian dish?
¿Hay un plato vegetariano?
May we have the menu? *¿Puede*
traernos la carta (or el menú)?
wine list *la carta de vinos*
What would you recommend?
¿Qué recomienda?
home-made *casero(a)*
fixed-price menu *el menú fijo*
special of the day
plato del día/sugerencia del chef
The meal was very good
La comida fue muy buena
waiter *mozo*
main course *segundo/plato principal*
ice cream *helado*
sandwich *sandwich*
What would you like to drink?
¿Qué quiere tomar?
coffee... *un café*
with milk *con leche*
strong *fuerte*
small/large *pequeño/grande*
without sugar *sin azúcar*
tea... *té*
with lemon/milk *con limón/leche*
herbal tea *té de manzanilla*
hot chocolate *chocolate caliente*
fresh orange juice
jugo de naranja natural
orangeade *naranjada*
soft drink *gaseosa*
mineral water (still/carbonated)
agua mineral (sin gas/con gas)
with/without ice *con/sin hielo*
cover charge *entrada*
minimum consumption
consumo mínimo
a bottle/half a bottle
una botella/media botella
a glass of red/white/rosé wine
una copa de vino tinto/rosado/
blanco

beer *una cerveza*
Is service included?
¿Incluye el servicio?
I need a receipt, please
Necesito un recibo, por favor
Keep the change
Está bien/Quédese con el vuelto
Cheers! ¡Salud!

MENU DECODER

Entremeses/Primer Plato
(First Course)
sopa/crema *soup/cream soup*
sopa de ajo *garlic soup*
sopa de cebolla *onion soup*
ensalada mixta *mixed salad*
ensalada de palta con tomate
avocado and tomato salad
pan con ajo *garlic bread*

La Carne (Meat)
crudo *raw*
jugosa *rare*
término medio *medium rare*
a punto *medium*
bien cocida *well done*
a la brasa/a la parrilla
charcoal grilled
a la plancha *grilled*
ahumada *smoked*
alas *wings*
albóndigas *meat balls*
asado(a)/horneado(a) *roasted*
aves *(fowl)*
cerdo/chancho/puerco *pork*
chorizos *Spanish-style sausage*
chuleta *chop*
conejo *rabbit*
cordero *lamb*
costillas *ribs*
empanizado(a) *breaded*
frito(a) *fried*
guisado(a) *stewed*
hamburguesa *hamburger*
hígado de res *beef liver*
jamón *ham*
lengua *tongue*
lomito *tenderloin*
milanesa *breaded and fried thin cut*
of meat
muslo *thigh*
pato *duck*
pavo *turkey*
pechuga *breast*
pernil *leg of pork*
piernas *legs*
pollo *chicken*

rebosado(a) *batter fried*
riñones *kidneys*
salchichas/perros calientes
sausages or hot dogs
ternera *veal*
chicharrón de pollo *chicken cut up*
in small pieces and deep fried

Pescado/Mariscos
(Fish/Seafood)
almejas *clams*
anchoa *anchovy*
atún *tuna*
bacalao *cod*
calamares *squid*
camarones *shrimp*
cangrejo *crab*
centolla *king-crab*
langosta *lobster*
langostinos *prawns*
lenguado *sole or flounder*
mariscos *shellfish*
mejillones *mussels*
mero *grouper, sea bass*
ostras *oysters*
pulpo *octopus*
salmón *salmon*
sardinas *sardines*
trucha *trout*
vieras *scallops*

Vegetales (Vegetables)
ajo *garlic*
alcachofa *artichoke*
arvejas *peas*
batata *sweet potato*
berenjena *eggplant/aubergine*
brócoli *broccoli*
calabaza *pumpkin or yellow*
squash
cebolla *onion*
chauchas *green beans*
choclo *corn (on the cob)*
coliflor *cauliflower*
espárrago *asparagus*
espinaca *spinach*
hongos, champiñones *mushrooms*
lechuga *lettuce*
maíz, corn *(corn on the cob)*
pepino *cucumber*
pimentón *green (bell) pepper*
porotos *Lima beans*
puerro *leeks*
remolacha *beets/beetroot*
repollo *cabbage*
zanahorias *carrots*
zapallo *yellow squash*
zapallito *green squash*
zapallito largo *zucchini/courgette*

Frutas (fruit)
banana *banana*
palta *avocado*
plátano *green banana*
cereza *cherry*
ciruela *plum*
dátil *date*
durazno *peach*
frambuesa *raspberry*
frutilla *strawberry*
guayaba *guava*
higo *fig*
papaya *papaya*
lima *lime*
limón *lemon*
mandarina *tangerine*
manzana *apple*
melón *cantelope/melon*
mora *blackberry*
naranja *orange*
parchita *passion fruit*
sandía *watermelon*
pera *pear*
piña *pineapple*
pomelo *grapefruit*
uvas *grapes*

Miscellaneous
arróz *rice*
azúcar *sugar*
empanada *savory turnover*
fideos *spaghetti*
huevos (revueltos/fritos/hervidos)
eggs (scrambled/fried/boiled)
manteca *butter*
margarina *margarine*
mermelada *jam*
mostaza *mustard*
pan *bread*
pan integral *wholewheat bread*
pan tostado/tostadas *toast*
pimienta negra *black pepper*
queso *cheese*
sal *salt*
salsa de tomate *ketchup*
salsa picante *hot-spicy sauce*
panceta *bacon*
tortilla *omelette*

Tourist Attractions/ Terms

aguas termales *hot springs*
artesanía *handicrafts*
beer hall/pub *cervecería*
campamento *campsite*
capilla *chapel*
castillo/fuerte *fort*
catedral *cathedral*

cerro hill
cervecería beer hall/pub
club nocturno nightclub
comunidad indígena indian
(indigenous) community
convento convent
disco/discoteca discotheque
galería gallery
iglesia church
isla island
jardín botánico botanical garden
laguna lagoon
lago lake
mar sea
mercado market
mirador viewpoint
montaña mountain
monumento monument
nightclub club nocturno
Oceano Atlántico Atlantic Ocean
oficina de turismo tourist office
parque infantil playground
parque park
pico (mountain) peak
pileta swimming pool
playa beach
plaza town square
postál postcard
puente bridge
quebrada stream
río river
ruinas ruins
teleférico cable car
torre tower
ventisquero glacier
zona colonial colonial zone
zoológico zoo

Road Signs

autopista freeway
bajada/subida peligrosa
dangerous downgrade/incline
calle ciega dead-end street
calle flechada/de una sola mano
one-way street
carril derecho right lane
carril izquierdo left lane
carretera highway, road
gomería tire repair shop
cede el paso yield/give way
circunvalación by-pass road
conserve su derecha
keep to the right
conserve su carril
do not change lanes
cruce de ferrocarril (sin señal)
railway crossing (without signal)
despacio slow

desvío detour
distribuidor freeway interchange
doble vía two-way traffic
Enciende luces en el túnel
Turn on lights in the tunnel
encrucijada crossroads
entrada prohibida no entry
estacionamiento parking lot
fuera de servicio not in service
hundimiento sunken road
intercomunal interconnecting
freeway between two close towns
no estacione/prohibido estacionar
no parking
no gire en U no U-turn
no hay paso, vía cerrada
road blocked
sin salida no exit
no pare no stopping here
no toque la bocina no horn honking
¡ojo! watch out!
pare stop
paso de ganado cattle crossing
paso de peatones pedestrian crossing
peaje toll booth
peligro danger
pendiente fuerte, curva fuerte
steep hill, sharp curve
rotonda roundabout
**lomo de burro, reductor de
velocidad, obstáculos en la vía,
muros en la vía, policia acostada**
speed bump(s)
resbaladizo al humedecerce
slippery when wet
ruta highway
salida exit
semáforo traffic light
sólo tránsito local local traffic only
tome precauciones caution
un solo carril single lane
velocidad controlada
speed controlled or restricted
vía en reparación/en recuperación
road under repair
zona de construcción
construction zone
zona de derrumbes landslide zone
zona de niebla (neblina) fog zone
zona de remolque tow zone
zona escolar school zone
zona militar military zone

Traveling

airline línea aérea
airport aeropuerto
arrivals/departures
llegadas/salidas

bus stop
parada (de colectivo/micro)
**boat dock for small boats/large
boats** embarcadero/muelle
bus terminal terminal de pasajeros
bus colectivo (urban), micro
(long distance)
car coche, automóvil
car rental alquiler de coche
connection conexión
ferry ferry
first class/second class
primera clase/segunda clase, clase
de turista
flight vuelo
luggage, bag(s) equipaje, valija(s)
Next stop please (for buses)
En la próxima parada, por favor
one-way ticket boleto de ida
platform el andén
round-trip, return ticket
boleto de ida y vuelta
sailboat, yacht velero, yate
ship barco
subway Metro/subterráneo/
subte
taxi taxi

Terms for Directions

a la derecha on the right
a la izquierda on the left
al lado de beside
alrededor de around
arriba/abajo above/below
avenida (Av) avenue
calle/carrera street
cerca de near
cruce con/con
at the junction of (two streets)
**cruce hacia la izquierda/la
derecha** turn to the left/right
debajo de under
delante de in front of
derecho straight ahead
detrás de behind
edificio (Edif) building
en frente de/frente de/frente a
in front of
en in, on, at
en la parte de atrás
in the rear area (as behind a
building)
encima de on top of
entre between
esquina (Esq) corner
**PH – penthouse/PB – planta baja/
PA – planta alta/mezanina/sótano**
penthouse/ground floor/upper floor
(of 2)/mezzanine/basement

residencia (Res) *small pension*
torre *tower*
transversal(es) *crossroad(s)*
una cuadra *a block*

Airport or Travel Agency

customs and immigration
aduana y migraciones
travel/tour agency *agencia de viajes/de turismo*
ticket *boletos pasaje*
I would like to purchase a ticket for... *Quisiera comprar un boleto (pasaje) para...*
When is the next/last flight/ departure for ...? *¿Cuándo es el próximo/último vuelo/para ...?*
What time does the plane/bus/boat/ferry leave/return? *¿A qué hora sale/regresa el avión/el autobús/la lancha/el ferry?*
What time do I have to be at the airport? *¿A qué hora tengo que estar en el aeropuerto?*
Is the tax included? *¿Se incluye el impuesto?*
What is included in the price? *¿Qué está incluido en el precio?*
departure tax *el impuesto de salida*
I would like a seat in first class/ business class/tourist class *Quisiera un asiento en primera clase/ejecutivo/clase de turista*
lost luggage office *oficina de reclamos*

on time *a tiempo*
late *atrasado*
I need to change my ticket *Necesito cambiar mi boleto*
How long is the flight? *¿Cuánto tiempo dura el vuelo?*
Is this seat taken? *¿Está ocupado este asiento?*
Which is the stop closest to ...? *¿Cuál es la parada más cerca de ...?*
Could you please advise me when we reach/the stop for ...? *¿Por favor, puede avisarme cuando llegamos a/a la parada para ...?*
Is this the stop for ...? *¿Es ésta la parada para ...?*

Driving

Where can I rent a car? *¿Dónde puedo alquiler un coche?*
Is mileage included? *¿Está incluido el kilometraje?*
comprehensive insurance *seguros comprensivos*
spare tire/jack/emergency triangle *goma de repuesto/ gato/triángulo de emergencia*
Where is the registration document? *¿Dónde se encuentra el carnet de circulación?*
Does the car have an alarm? *¿El coche tiene alarma?*
a road map/a city map *un mapa vial/plano de la ciudad*
How do I get to ...? *¿Cómo se llega a ...?*
Turn right/left *Cruzar (or girar, doblar) hacia la derecha/izquierda*

at the next corner/street *en la próxima esquina/calle*
Go straight ahead *Siga derecho*
You are on the wrong road *No está en la vía correcta*
Please show me where am I on the map *Por favor, indíqueme dónde estoy en el mapa*
Where can I find...? *¿Dónde se encuentra...?*
Where is the nearest...? *¿Dónde se encuentra el/la ... más cerca?*
How long does it take to get there? *¿Cuánto tiempo lleva para llegar?*
driving license *licencia de conducir/manejar*
service station, gasoline station *estación de servicio*
My car won't start *Mi coche no arranca*
My car is overheating *Mi coche está recalentando*
My car has broken down *Mi coche se rompió/no anda*
tow truck *una grúa*
Where can I find a car repair shop? *¿Dónde se encuentra un taller mecánico?*
Can you check the...? *¿Puede revisar/chequear...?*
There's something wrong with the... *Hay un problema con...*
oil/water/air/brake fluid/light bulb *aceite/agua/aire/liga para frenos/bombita*
trunk/hood/door/window *maletín/capó/puerta/ventana*

Conversion Tables

LENGTH

Inches	Centimeters
1	2.54
2	5.08
3	7.62
6	15.24
9	22.86

Feet	Centimeters
1	30.48
2	60.96
3	91.44
6	182.88
9	274.32
12	365.76

WEIGHT

Pounds	Kilograms
1	0.45
2	0.90
3	1.36
4	1.81
5	2.27
6	2.72
7	3.18
8	3.63
9	4.08
10	4.53
20	9.07
50	22.68
100	45.36

VOLUME

Pints	Liters
1	0.47
2	0.95
3	1.42
4	1.89

Gallons	Liters
1	3.78
2	7.57
3	11.36
5	18.93
10	37.85
20	75.71
50	189.27

Emergencies

Help! ¡Socorro! ¡Auxilio!
Stop! ¡Parate!
Watch out! ¡Cuidado! ¡Ojo!
I've had an accident He tenido un accidente/Sufrí un accidente
Call a doctor Llame a un médico
Call an ambulance Llame una ambulancia
Call the... Llame a...
...police la policía (for minor accidents)
...transit police la policía de tránsito (for traffic accidents)
the fire brigade los bomberos
This is an emergency, where is a telephone? Es una emergencia. ¿Dónde se encuentra un teléfono?
Where is the nearest hospital? ¿Dónde se encuentra el hospital más cerca?
I want to report an assault/a robbery Quisiera reportar un asalto/un robo
Thank you very much for your help Muchísimas gracias por su ayuda

Health
shift duty pharmacy farmacía de turno
hospital/clinic hospital/clínica
I need a doctor/dentist Necesito un médico/dentista (odontólogo)
I don't feel well Me siento mal
I am sick Estoy enfermo(a)
It hurts here Duele aquí
I have a headache/stomach ache/cramps Tengo un dolor de cabeza/del estómago/de vientre
I feel dizzy Me siento mareado(a)
Do you have (something for)...? ¿Tiene (algo para)...?
a cold/flu gripe/virus
diarrhea diarrea
constipation estrenamiento
fever fiebre
aspirin aspirina
heartburn acidez
insect/mosquito bites picaduras de insectos/mosquitos

Shopping

antique shop antigüedades
bakery panadería
bank banco
barber shop peluquería para hombres
bookstore librería
butcher shop carnicería
cake shop pastelería
currency exchange bureau casa de cambio
delicatessen delicatessen
department store tienda por departamentos
florist florista
greengrocer's frutería
hairdressers?beauty salon peluquería, salón de belleza
hardware store ferretería
shopping center, centro comercial mall, shopping
jewelers joyería
laundromat lavadero
library biblioteca
liquor store licorería
market mercado
newsstand kiosco
post office correos
shoe repair shop/shoe store zapatería
small grocery store bodega, abasto
small shop tienda
supermarket supermercado, autoservicio
toy store juguetería

USEFUL PHRASES

What time do you open/close? ¿A qué hora abre/cierra?
Open/closed Abierto/cerrado
I'd like... Quisiera...
I'm just looking Sólo estoy mirando, gracias
How much does it cost? ¿Cuánto cuesta/sale?
It doesn't fit No queda bien
Do you have it in another color? ¿Tiene en otro color?
Do you have it in another size? ¿Tiene en otro talle/número (clothing), tamaño (objects)?
smaller/larger más pequeño/más grande
It's too expensive Es demasiado caro
Do you have something less expensive? ¿Tiene algo más económico?
Where do I pay for it? ¿Dónde está la caja?
Anything else? ¿Quiere algo más?
A little more/less Un poco más/menos
That's enough/no more Está bien/nada más

Colors

light/dark claro/oscuro
red rojo/colorado
yellow amarillo
blue azul
brown marrón
black negro
white blanco
cream color crema
beige beige
green verde
wine bordó
gray gris
orange color naranjo
pink rosada
purple púrpura
silver plateado
gold dorado

Numbers

1 uno
2 dos
3 tres
4 cuatro
5 cinco
6 seis
7 siete
8 ocho
9 nueve
10 diez
11 once
12 doce
13 trece
14 catorce
15 quince
16 dieciséis
17 diecisiete
18 dieciocho
19 diecinueve
20 veinte
21 veintiuno
25 veinticinco
30 treinta
40 cuarenta
50 cincuenta
60 sesenta
70 setenta
80 ochenta
90 noventa
100 cien
101 ciento uno
200 doscientos

300 *trescientos*
400 *cuatrocientos*
500 *quinientos*
600 *seiscientos*
700 *setecientos*
800 *ochocientos*
900 *novecientos*
1,000 *mi*
2,000 *dos mil*
10,000 *diez mil*
100,000 *cien mil*
1,000,000 *un millón*
1,000,000,000 *mil millones*

NOTE: In Spanish, in numbers, commas are used where decimal points are used in English and vice versa. For example, in English: $19.30 = in Spanish: $19,50; 1,000 m = 1.000 m; 9.5% = 9,5%.

Days and Dates

morning *la mañana*
afternoon *la tarde*
late afternoon, dusk *atardecer*
evening *la noche*
dawn *la madrugada*
sunrise *amanecer*
sunset *puesta del sol*
last night *anoche*
yesterday *ayer*
today *hoy*
tomorrow *mañana*
tomorrow morning *mañana por la mañana*
the day after tomorrow *pasado mañana*
now *ahora*
early *temprano*
late *tarde*
a minute *un minuto*
an hour *una hora*
half an hour *media hora*
a day *un día*
a week *una semana*
a year *un año*
weekday *día laboral*
weekend *fin de semana*
holiday *día feriado*

MONTHS

January *enero*
February *febrero*
March *marzo*
April *abril*
May *mayo*
June *junio*
July *julio*
August *agosto*
September *septiembre*
October *octubre*
November *noviembre*
December *diciembre*

DAYS OF THE WEEK

Monday *lunes*
Tuesday *martes*
Wednesday *miércoles*
Thursday *jueves*
Friday *viernes*
Saturday *sábado*
Sunday *domingo*

Seasons

spring *primavera*
summer *verano*
fall, autumn *otoño*
winter *invienrno*

Time

at nine o'clock *a las nueve*
at a quarter past ten *a las diez y cuarto*
at half past one/one thirty *a la una y media*
at a quarter to two *a las dos menos cuarto/quince*
at midday/noon *a mediodía*
at midnight *a medianoche*
it is five past three *son las tres y cinco*
it is twenty five past seven *son las siete y veinticinco/con veinticinco*
it is ten to eight *son las ocho menos diez/son diez para las ocho*
in five minutes *en cinco minutos*
does it take long? *¿tarda mucho?*

NOTE: Times are usually given by "morning – de la mañana" or "afternoon – de la tarde." Transport schedules are often given by the 24-hour clock.

Further Reading

History

Argentina: A City and a Nation by James R. Scoblie. New York: Oxford Univ. Press, 1971. The best general introduction to the country's history and geography.

The Battle for the Falklands by Max Hastings and Simon Jenkins. New York: W.W. Norton and Co., 1984. Well researched by reporter during Falklands campaign. Sobering but easy to read.

Gauchos and the Vanishing Frontier by Richard W. Slatta. Lincoln: Univ. of Nebraska Press, 1992. Fascinating account of the cowboys who roamed the pampas hundreds of years before the Wild West existed.

The Little School: Tales of Disappearance and Survival in Argentina by Alicia Partnoy. New York: Cleis Press, 1998. Chilling, true story of one of Argentina's 30,000 "disappeared" who was taken to a concentration camp and tortured.

The Invention of Argentins by Nicolas Shumway, Univ. of California Press, 1991. Cultural history from academic perspective.

The Voyage of the Beagle by Charles Darwin. Penguin, 1989. Shortened journal of Darwin's five-year voyage around the world, covering natural history and civil war in Argentina. A classic.

The Real Odessa: Smuggling the Nazis to Perón's Argentina by Uki Goni. Granta, 2002.

Literature

Labyrinths by Jorge Luis Borges. New Directions Pub., 1988. Short stories and other writings from one of the most original writers of modern literature.

On Heroes and Tombs by Ernesto Sabato. David R. Godine, 1981. Complex and sad tale of a tormented love affair.

Kiss of the Spider Woman by Manuel Puig. Vintage books, 1991.

Travel Literature

Far Away and Long Ago; Birds of La Plata; Idle Days in Patagonia by W.H. Hudson. London: Everyman's Library, 1984.

Tales of the Pampas by W.H. Hudson. Berkeley: Creative Arts Book Co., 1979. Early classic novel.

In Patagonia by Bruce Chatwin. Picador, 1998. A combination of fact and fiction, beautifully written by one of the greatest travel writers.

Tschiffely's Ride by A.A. Tschiffely. The Long Riders' Guild Press, 2001. Tale of author's equestrian journey from Southern Cross to the Pole Star in 1925.

Two Thousand Miles' Ride Through the Argentine Provinces by William MacCann. Ams Press. Reprint of 1853 historical account of the country and people.

The Uttermost Part of the Earth: Indians of Tierra Del Fuego by E. Lucas Bridges. Dover pubs, 1988. A true story – mix of biography and adventure.

Miscellaneous

Bad Times in Buenos Aires by Miranda France. Ecco, 1999. Personal and sometimes generalized overview of life in BA through a foreigner's eyes.

Santa Evita by Tomas Eloy Martinez. Vintage, 1997. A mix of fact and fiction about Argentina's most famous icon.

Wine Routes of Argentina by Alan Young. Augusta Foix, 1998. The first book written in English about Argentine wines. Follows an historical framework, illustrated with detailed maps.

Argentine Trout Fishing by William C. Leitch. Frank Amato Pubs, 1991. Detailed and entertaining, with color photographs.

Arts and Crafts

Arts and Crafts of Argentina by A. Bassetti de Roca. 2001

People

And Here the World Ends: The Life of an Argentinian Village by K.H. Ruggiero. Stanford Univ. Press, 1988.

Falkland People by Angela Wigglesworth. Paul and Co. Pub Consortium, 1992.

Evita: The Real Life of Eva Peron by N. Fraser. W.W. Norton and Co, 1996. Absorbing and definitive account of the mythical actress turned politician.

Food

Argentina Cooks! by Shirley Lomax Brooks. Hippocrene Books, 2001. One of the few books covering Argentine cuisine, with recipes from the nine regions.

Other Insight Guides

Among nearly 200 companion books to this one are several Insight Guides highlighting destinations in this region. Titles include *South America* (a general introduction to the continent covering 10 countries), *Buenos Aires, Brazil, Rio de Janeiro, Peru, Chile, Ecuador & the Galápagos,* and *Venezuela.*

Insight Guide: Amazon Wildlife vividly captures the flora and fauna of the world's greatest rainforest.

Films

Butch Cassidy and the Sundance Kid (Roy Hill 1969). Starring Robert Redford and Paul Newman.

Kiss of the Spider Woman (Hector Babenco 1985) with William Hurt.

The Mission (Roland Joffe 1986). Robert de Niro and Jeremy Irons are Jesuit priests in Argentina and Paraguay.

Evita (Alan Parker 1997) starring Madonna.

Feedback

We do our best to ensure the information in our books is as accurate and up-to-date as possible. The books are updated on a regular basis, using local contacts, who painstakingly add, amend and correct as required. However, some mistakes and omissions are inevitable and we are ultimately reliant on our readers to put us in the picture.

We would welcome your feedback on any details related to your experiences using the book "on the road". Maybe we recommended a hotel that you liked (or another that you didn't), as well as interesting new attractions, or facts and figures you have found out about the country itself. The more details you can give us (particularly with regard to addresses, e-mails and telephone numbers), the better.

We will acknowledge all contributions, and we'll offer an Insight Guide to the best letters received.

Please write to us at:
**Insight Guides
PO Box 7910
London SE1 1WE
United Kingdom**
Or send e-mail to:
insight@apaguide.co.uk

ART & PHOTO CREDITS

All photography by Eduardo Gil except for:

Fiora Bemporad 34/35, 36, 38, 39, 40, 41, 42/43, 44, 46, 47, 49, 50, 51, 53, 54, 55, 56, 57, 59, 60, 65, 79, 82, 98, 148, 162, 172, 269, 294
Fiora Bemporad/National Archives 58
Fiora Bemporad/Witcomb Collection 149T
Don Boroughs 14, 62, 83, 85, 128, 131, 154T, 155T, 228, 304, 322/323
Marcelo Brodsky/Focus back flap top, 156, 314
Roberto Bunge/PW 132/133, 199, 202T, 238, 255, 261, 267, 274, 276
Gustavo Calligaris/Focus 198T
Laurie Campbell/NHPA 281T, 297T, 300T
Marcelo Canevari 99
Maria Cassinelli/Focus 196, 299
Guillermo Cicchelli/Andes Press Agency 129
Roberto Cinti/PW back flap bottom, 8/9, 18, 19, 21, 22, 23, 115, 239, 242, 247, 250, 253, 254, 279T, 293, 296, 311L, 311R, 312, 316, 319, 327, 334
Chris Coe/Axiom 262
Pablo Rafael Cottescu 100, 120, 286/287, 305, 313
Keith Ellis 275T
Arturo Encinas/Focus 122
Abbie Enock/Travel Ink 97
Carlos Fadigati/Focus 84, 101, 257, 264/265
Sindo Fari 257, 264 121
Hugo Fernandez/Andes Press Agency 27
Glyn Genin 6/7
Carlos Goldin/Focus 310
Rae Goodall 324, 329, 330, 332
Thomas Goodall 325, 326, 331
Derek Hall 245, 251T, 279, 280
Huw Hennessy 150T, 171, 174, 175T, 177, 180T, 182, 182T, 184T, 191T, 192, 192T, 193, 229, 236T,

237T, 238T, 270T, 274T, 278T, 314T, 315T
Joseph Hooper 295
Dave G Houser 4/5, 91, 166, 178, 183, 270, 334T
Volkmar Janicke 33, 138, 173, 246, 248, 251, 252, 317
Marcus Joly/Focus back cover centre, front flap bottom,102, 103, 233, 263
Federico B Kirbus 111, 243
T Kitchin & V Hurst/NHPA 116
Walter Kvaternik/Naturpress 306
Eric Lawrie 298, 301
Eduardo Lerke/Focus 61, 125, 194/195, 204T
Luis Martin/Focus 32
G Miles 245T, 248T, 249, 254T, 257T, 258, 259T, 260
Quique Kierszenbaum/Getty Images 72
Kimball Morrison/South American Pictures 16/17, 273, 275, 277, 282
Tony Morrison/South American Pictures 45, 114, 117,189, 214T
Arlette Neyens front flap top, 30, 80, 113, 144/145, 146
Frank Nowikowski/South American Pictures 112, 269T
Alex Ocampo/PW back cover bottom, 37, 126/127, 149, 155, 158T, 163, 168, 188, 208/209, 210, 212, 222, 223
Carlos A Passera/PW 106/107, 108, 109, 110, 290, 308, 315, 333
Michael J Pettypool 231
Susan Pierres 234, 235
Rudolfo Rüst/Focus 118/119
Alfredo Sanchez/Focus 78, 226/227
Jorge Juan Schulte 24/25, 28, 31, 96, 185, 240/241
Eric Soder/NHPA 236
David Toase/Travel Ink 203
Topham Picturepoint 300, 309
Mireille Vautier 12/13, 20, 26, 48, 73, 161T, 164, 165T, 266,281, 281T, 283, 288/289, 291, 326T, 328, 335
David Welna front flap bottom, 161, 184
Martin Wendler/NHPA 237

Picture Spreads

Pages 104-105: *Top Row, left to right:* Mireille Vautier, Huw Hennessy, Abbie Enock/Travel Ink, Eduardo Gil; *Centre Row, clockwise from left:* Chris Coe/Axiom, Abbie Enock/Travel Ink; *Bottom Row, left to right:* Michael J Pettypool, Abbie Enock/Travel Ink, Eduardo Gil
Pages 186-187: *Top Row, left to right:* all Eduardo Gil; *Centre Row, left to right:* Eduardo Gil, Dave G Houser, Dave G Houser; *Bottom Row, left to right:* all Eduardo Gil
Pages 284-285: *Top Row, left to right:* Chris Coe/Axiom, Bowman/Axiom, Huw Hennessy, Chris Coe/Axiom; *Centre Row, left to right:* Huw Hennessy (both); *Bottom Row, left to right:* Huw Hennessy, Chris Coe/Axiom, Huw Hennessy
Pages 320-321: *Top Row, left to right:* Eduardo Gil, Frank Nowikowski/South American Pictures, Derek Hall, Frank Nowikowski/South American Pictures; *Centre Row, left to right:* Eduardo Gil, Eduardo Gil, Laurie Campbell/NHPA; *Bottom Row, left to right:* Frank Nowikowski/South American Pictures, Laurie Campbell/NHPA, Tony Morrison/South American Pictures, Eduardo Gil

Map Production
Colourmap Scanning Ltd

© 2005 Apa Publications GmbH & Co.
Verlag KG (Singapore branch)

Cartographic Editor
Zoë Goodwin
Art Director **Klaus Geisler**
Picture Research
Hilary Genin, Monica Allende

Index

Numbers in italics refer to photographs

m

A
B
C
D
E
G
H
I
J
a
b
c
d
f
g
h
i
j
k
l

INSIGHT GUIDES

The classic series that puts you in the picture

Alaska
Amazon Wildlife
American Southwest
Amsterdam
Argentina
Arizona & Grand Canyon
Asia's Best Hotels & Resorts
Asia, East
Asia, Southeast
Australia
Austria
Bahamas
Bali
Baltic States
Bangkok
Barbados
Barcelona
Beijing
Belgium
Belize
Berlin
Bermuda
Boston
Brazil
Brittany
Brussels
Buenos Aires
Burgundy
Burma (Myanmar)
Cairo
California
California, Southern
Canada
Caribbean
Caribbean Cruises
Channel Islands
Chicago
Chile
China
Colorado
Continental Europe
Corsica
Costa Rica
Crete
Croatia
Cuba
Cyprus
Czech & Slovak Republic
Delhi, Jaipur & Agra
Denmark

Dominican Rep. & Haiti
Dublin
East African Wildlife
Eastern Europe
Ecuador
Edinburgh
Egypt
England
Finland
Florence
Florida
France
France, Southwest
French Riviera
Gambia & Senegal
Germany
Glasgow
Gran Canaria
Great Britain
Great Gardens of Britain
 & Ireland
Great Railway Journeys
 of Europe
Greece
Greek Islands
Guatemala, Belize
 & Yucatán
Hawaii
Hong Kong
Hungary
Iceland
India
India, South
Indonesia
Ireland
Israel
Istanbul
Italy
Italy, Northern
Italy, Southern
Jamaica
Japan
Jerusalem
Jordan
Kenya
Korea
Laos & Cambodia
Las Vegas
Lisbon
London

Los Angeles
Madeira
Madrid
Malaysia
Mallorca & Ibiza
Malta
Mauritius Réunion
 & Seychelles
Mediterranean Cruises
Melbourne
Mexico
Miami
Montreal
Morocco
Moscow
Namibia
Nepal
Netherlands
New England
New Mexico
New Orleans
New York City
New York State
New Zealand
Nile
Normandy
North American &
 Alaskan Cruises
Norway
Oman & The UAE
Oxford
Pacific Northwest
Pakistan
Paris
Peru
Philadelphia
Philippines
Poland
Portugal
Prague
Provence
Puerto Rico
Rajasthan

Rio de Janeiro
Rome
Russia
St Petersburg
San Francisco
Sardinia
Scandinavia
Scotland
Seattle
Shanghai
Sicily
Singapore
South Africa
South America
Spain
Spain, Northern
Spain, Southern
Sri Lanka
Sweden
Switzerland
Sydney
Syria & Lebanon
Taiwan
Tanzania & Zanzibar
Tenerife
Texas
Thailand
Tokyo
Trinidad & Tobago
Tunisia
Turkey
Tuscany
Umbria
USA: The New South
USA: On The Road
USA: Western States
US National Parks: West
Venezuela
Venice
Vienna
Vietnam
Wales
Walt Disney World/Orlando

INSIGHT GUIDES

**The world's largest collection of
visual travel guides & maps**